THE BOOK
OF
DUARTE BARBOSA.

THE BOOK OF DUARTE BARBOSA.

AN ACCOUNT OF THE COUNTRIES BORDERING ON THE INDIAN OCEAN AND THEIR INHABITANTS, WRITTEN BY DUARTE BARBOSA, AND COMPLETED ABOUT THE YEAR 1518 A.D.

Translated from the Portuguese text, first published in 1812 A.D. by the Royal Academy of Sciences at Lisbon, in Vol. II of its Collection of Documents regarding the History and Geography of the Nations beyond the seas, and edited and annotated

By
MANSEL LONGWORTH DAMES,
INDIAN CIVIL SERVICE (RETIRED);
VICE-PRESIDENT ROYAL ASIATIC SOCIETY AND ROYAL ANTHROPOLOGICAL
INSTITUTE; F.R.N.S.; M.F.S.

VOL. II
INCLUDING THE COASTS OF MALABAR, EASTERN INDIA AS FURTHER INDIA, CHINA AND THE INDIAN ARCHIPELAGO

Published by

Gyan Publishing House
5, Ansari Road
Daryaganj, New Delhi-110002
Phone: 011-47034999, 9811692060
E-mail: books@gyanbooks.com

Distribution Network
gyanbooks.com
India, USA, Canada, UK, Australia, France

© **Publisher**

ISBN : 978-81-212-4499-2 (Set)
ISBN : 978-81-212-3757-4 (HB)
First Published, 1921

2nd Impression 2020

Printed at: Gyan Press, Delhi.

THE BOOK

OF

DUARTE BARBOSA.

AN ACCOUNT OF THE COUNTRIES
BORDERING ON THE INDIAN OCEAN AND THEIR
INHABITANTS, WRITTEN BY DUARTE BARBOSA,
AND COMPLETED ABOUT THE YEAR 1518 A.D.

Translated from the Portuguese text, first published in 1812 A.D.
*by the Royal Academy of Sciences at Lisbon, in Vol. II of its
Collection of Documents regarding the History and Geography of
the Nations beyond the seas, and edited and annotated*

BY

MANSEL LONGWORTH DAMES,

INDIAN CIVIL SERVICE (RETIRED);
VICE-PRESIDENT ROYAL ASIATIC SOCIETY AND ROYAL ANTHROPOLOGICAL
INSTITUTE; F.R.N.S.; M.F.S.

VOL. II.

INCLUDING THE COASTS OF MALABAR, EASTERN
INDIA, FURTHER INDIA, CHINA AND THE
INDIAN ARCHIPELAGO.

LONDON:
PRINTED FOR THE HAKLUYT SOCIETY.

MCMXXI.

MĀNAVIKRAMA RĀJA, ZAMORIN
of CALICUT from 1912 to 1915.

Reproduced and Printed for the Hakluyt Society by Donald Macbeth, 1921.

COUNCIL

OF

THE HAKLUYT SOCIETY.

CONTENTS OF VOLUME II.

BIBLIOGRAPHY.

SUPPLEMENTARY TO THAT IN VOL. I.

Title under
which quoted.   I. PORTUGUESE AND SPANISH WORKS.

ANONYMOUS. *Conquista do Reyno de Pegú.* Lisbon, 1569.
Published in vol. IV. of the *Peregrinação* of F. M. Pinto.
Lisbon, 1829.

DA CRUZ, FREY GASPAR. *Tractado da China.* Lisbon, 1569.
Published in vol. IV. of the *Peregrinação* of F. M. Pinto.
Lisbon, 1829.
Cronica dos Reys D'Ormuz. Lisbon, 1569. Published in
vol. IV. of the *Peregrinação* of F. M. Pinto. Lisbon, 1829.

DO COUTO, DIOGO. *O Soldado Pratico.* Lisbon, 1790.

EREDIA. *Declaração de Malaca* [1618]. By Godinho de Eredia.
First published at Bruxelles, 1882, accompanied by a French
translation (*Malaca et l'Inde Meridionale*) by L. Janssen.

FARIA Y SOUSA. *Asia Portuguesa.* 3 vols. Lisbon, 1666.

PINTO, FERNÃO MENDEZ. *Peregrinação.* Lisbon, 1614. 4 vols.
Reprint, Lisbon, 1829.

RIBEIRO, JOÃO. *Fatalidade Historica da Ilha de Ceilão* [1685].
First published in *Collecção de Noticias*, vol. V. Lisbon, 1836.

II. TRAVELS, HISTORY AND TOPOGRAPHY.

AIYENGAR, S. K. *Sources of Vyaganagar History.* Madras, 1919.

ANDERSON, J. *English Relations with Siam.* London, 1892.

BEVERIDGE, H. *The District of Bakarganj.* London, 1876.

BUCHANAN, F. *A Journey from Madras through Mysore, Canara
and Malabar.* 3 vols. London, 1807.

CAMPOS, J. J. A. *History of the Portuguese in Bengal.* Calcutta,
1919.

CLIFFORD, SIR H. *Farther India.* London, 1904.

CORDIER, M. H. *L'arrivee des Portugais en Chine.* (T'oung-Pao,
Leiden, vol. XII, 1911.)
Ser Marco Polo. London, 1920.

CRAWFURD, J. *History of the Indian Archipelago.* 3 vols.
Edinburgh, 1820.

DARMESTETER, J. *The Kandahar Inscriptions. Journal Asiatique.* 1899.

Title under
which quoted.

DELLON, C. *Relation d'un Voyage fait aux Indes.* Paris, 1699, and Cologne, 1711. *Relation de l'Inquisition de Goa.* Paris, 1688.

FERGUSON, D. *Letters from Portuguese Captives in Canton.* Reprint from *Ind. Antiquary.* Bombay, 1902. *The Portuguese in Ceylon.* *J.R.A.S., Ceylon Branch*, 1908.

FERRAND, M. GABRIEL. *Malaka, le Malǎyu et Malayur.* Reprint, *Journal Asiatique.* 1918. *Le K'ouen-Louen.* Reprint, *Journal Asiatique.* 1919.

FREDERICKE, CÆSAR. *Travels.* (In Hakluyt, vol. v., H.S. edition.)

GAZETTEERS—INDIAN.
  Eastern Bengal and Assam, 1909.
  Burma, 1908.
  District of Malabar, 1908 (Loftus Tottenham).
  District of Tinevelly, 1907.
  District of Cuttack, 1906.

GUJARAT, HISTORY OF.
  I. *Mirāt-i-Sikandari.* Trans. Fazlu'llah dutfullah. Bombay, N.D.
  II. *Brief History of the Gujarat Saltanat.* By M. S. Commissariat. (*Journal Bombay Branch, R. Asiatic Society,* 1920.)

HAMILTON, A. *New Account of the East Indies.* 2 vols. Edinburgh, 1727.

JOURNAL, ROYAL ASIATIC SOCIETY.
  I. G. Phillips. *Ma-Huan's Account of Bengal.* 1895.
  II. J. A. Beames. *Ma-Huan's Account of Bengal.* 1895.
  III. J. A. Beames. *Akbar's Subahs,* Bengal. 1896.
  IV. J. F. Fleet. *Tagara; Tēr.* 1901.

LOGAN. *Manual of Malabar.* Madras, 1884.

MARSDEN, W. *History of Sumatra.* London, 1780.

MARTINEAU, M. A. *Les Origines de Mahé.* Paris, 1917.

MASPERO, M. G. *Le Royaume de Champa.* (T'oung-Pao, Leiden, vols. XI–XIII, 1910–12.)

MORELAND, W. H. *India at the Death of Akbar.* London, 1920.

OVINGTON, J. *Voyage to Suratt.* London, 1696.

PHAYRE, SIR A. *History of Burma.* London, 1883.

PIERIS, P. E. *Ceylon and the Portuguese.* 1505–1658. Colombo, 1920.

PYRARD, F., OF LAVAL. *Voyage to the East Indies.* 2 vols. Ed. Sir A. Gray. (H.S.)

RAFFLES, SIR STAMFORD. *History of Java.* 2nd edition. 2 vols. London, 1830.

RHODES, PÈRE ALEXANDRE DE. *Voyages.* Paris, 1666.

Title under
which quoted.

ROCKHILL, W. W. *Notes on the Relations and Trade of China.*
(T'oung-Pao, Leiden, vols. XV, XVI, 1914–15.)

SWETTENHAM, SIR F. *British Malaya.* London, 1907.

THEVENOT, M. JEAN. *Travels.* London, 1687.

VALENTIJN, FRANS. *Oud en nieuw Oost-Indien.* 5 vols. Dordrecht, 1724–26. English translation of the Chapter on
Malacca : *Valentyn's description of Malacca. Journal,
Straits Branch R. Asiatic Soc.*, 1884. French translation of
the same : M. G. Ferrand's *Malaka*, pp. 68–81.

VARMARĀJA, K. RAMA.
A contribution to the History of Cochin. Trichur, 1914.

WALLACE, A. R. *The Malay Archipelago.* 2 vols. London, 1869.

WATTERS, T. *Yuan Chwang's Travels in India.* London, 1904.

III. ETHNOGRAPHY.

COCHIN CENSUS REPORT, 1901.

COCHIN TRIBES AND CASTES. (A. Krishna Iyer.) Cochin.

MADRAS CENSUS REPORTS. (Stuart.) 1891.
(Francis.) 1901.

MALABAR GAZETTEER. (Loftus Tottenham.) Madras, 1908.

PANIKKAR, K. M. *Some Aspects of Nāyar Life. (Journal
R. Anthropological Institute,* 1919.)

SKEAT, W. W. and BLAGDEN, C. O. *Pagan Races of the Malay
Peninsula.* 2 vols. London, 1906.

TRAVANCORE STATE MANUAL. 1906.

. IV. PHILOLOGY.

DALGADO, MONSENHOR SEBASTIÃO RODOLFO.
1. *Glossario Luso-Asiatico.* Coimbra, 1919.
2. *Contribuições para a Lexicologia Luso-Oriental.* Lisbon, 1916.
3. *Gonçalves Viana e a Lexicologia Portuguesa.* Lisbon, 1917.
4. *Influencia do Vocabulario Português em Linguas
Asiaticas.* Coimbra, 1913.

INTRODUCTION TO VOL. II.

HE second volume of the Book of Duarte Barbosa includes his account of the countries on the sea-board after passing the boundary of the Empire of Vijayanagar. It begins with the kingdoms of Malabar, the Maldive Islands and Ceylon. From these he follows the East Coast of the Indian Peninsula from Coromandel to Bengal, and here it will be noticed that his information was not nearly so full as that which he was able to give of the West Coast. This remark applies with still greater force to the sections which follow on the Countries of Further India until he arrives at Malacca which had recently been conquered by the Portuguese when he wrote. In Sumatra he shows some knowledge of the Northern and Eastern Coasts of the Island, but none whatever of the South-western coast. Beyond Sumatra, in dealing with the other islands of the Archipelago, he was dependent on the narratives of recent explorers, and in his account of Champa (Cochin-China), China and the Lequeos he had only the reports of merchants to guide him. Judging from the narratives themselves it may be considered as certain that his personal knowledge of the countries mentioned extended only to Malabar, the Maldives, Ceylon, some parts of Coromandel, Malacca and Northern Sumatra. Possibly Pegu may be added to the list, as his information of that country is much fuller than of any other part of Burma or Siam. The latest historical event alluded to which can be exactly dated is the foundation of a fort at Colombo in Ceylon by Lopo Soares D'Albergaria in September, 1518 (p. 109, n. 3). This may be compared to his mention of the attack on Berbera by Antonio de Saldanha earlier in the same year (Vol. I, p. xlv and p. 34, n. 2). As Barbosa sailed from Spain with Magalhães in September, 1519, it may be considered doubtful whether he could have remained in India as late as September, 1518, although it would not have been actually impossible for him to have made the journey to Lisbon in time to arrive at Seville by September, 1519. It may be noted that neither this passage nor that regarding Berbera is to be found in Ramusio or in the Spanish MS. translated by Lord Stanley.

Of all the countries dealt with by Barbosa, Malabar exceeds the rest in interest, as it was here that, owing to his long residence and his acquaintance with the language of the people, he was able to give a really full and accurate description of the inhabitants, their customs and their elaborate caste-system, such as is hardly to be found in the writings of any other early traveller. The structure of society in this corner of India continues almost unaltered at the present day, and it is possible therefore to test the accuracy of his observations on the caste-system by comparison with that still existing. Materials for making this comparison are abundant in recent publications, and I have been especially fortunate in obtaining the collaboration of Mr. J. A. Thorne, I.C.S., of Tellicherry, who has an intimate acquaintance with the people of Malabar, and has long been in charge of the estates of the late Zamorin of Calicut, the direct representative of the Zamorin or Çamodri of Barbosa's time. Mr. Thorne's full and abundant notes have enabled me to supplement the information derived from Mr. Thurston's valuable works and from the *Malabar Gazetteer* and other excellent ethnographical works issued by the Madras Government and by the States of Cochin and Travancore. Mr. Thorne's notes will be found in the following pages marked by the letter (T). He has also kindly furnished me with the photograph of the late Zamorin Mānavikrama Raja in mourning attire, which is reproduced as the frontispiece to this volume.

The valuable account which the Zamorin wrote of the ceremonies accompanying the installation of his predecessor as Zamorin, in which he himself took part as Erālpād or Heir Apparent (the " Prince " of Barbosa's narrative), with notes by Mr. Thorne is given in full in Appendix II (*a*) as is also a Note on the Funeral Ceremonies of the Zamorin (Appendix II (*b*)), and another in which Mr. Thorne explains the various titles borne by the rulers of Malabar (Appendix II (*c*)). The latter includes a new explanation of the much-discussed title Zamorin of which Mr. Thorne's derivation seems to me more satisfactory than any hitherto brought forward.

(With regard to the note on the procession of women (p. 20, n. 1), Mr. Thorne writes me that he now considers that this ceremony is connected not with the *puram* festival but with the *tirumasam* of which it forms an integral part. This correction was not received in time for incorporation with the note.)

It has been found possible to identify almost without exception the castes and tribes of Malabar mentioned by Barbosa, and his account of their system of marriage and matriarchal inheritance, and of the relative position of the castes with regard to one another, including distance-pollution and other remarkable customs, is proved to be of extraordinary accuracy. The places mentioned by him, mainly seaports, some of which are now obscure villages, can also in most cases be recognized owing to stability of conditions in this part of India which has to a great extent escaped the devastating floods of invasion, such as have swept over the northern and central parts of the country.

After rounding Cape Comorin the information at once becomes more scanty. The Portuguese never obtained the same influential position on the Coromandel Coast as they did on that of Malabar, and most of what they did obtain dates from a period later than that of Barbosa. This does not apply to Ceylon, and it seems clear from his accurate description of that island, and especially of the pilgrimage to Adam's Peak, that he must have visited it personally. On the east coast the most note-worthy points alluded to are the Legend of St. Thomas at Mailapur, a version of which was also given at Coulam (Quilon) on the Malabar coast, and the remarkable system of succession at Quilicare according to which each king was immolated by his successor with his own concurrence, after reigning for twelve years. The St. Thomas legends show signs of having incorporated local beliefs, possibly Buddhist in origin.

In Bengal Barbosa was dependent on reports received from merchants, as no Portuguese expedition had visited that country in his time. His account of that country is remarkable as giving one of the earliest instances of mention of the great city of Bengala which has been the subject of so much controversy. In attempting to elucidate this point I must acknowledge here the valuable assistance received from Mr. W. H. Moreland, C.S.I., C.I.E., who kindly placed at my disposal the result of his investigations on this subject made in connection with his recently issued work *India at the death of Akbar* (*vide* Appendix C. of that work). I have also received much assistance from Mr. H. Beveridge who has for many years studied this subject, and from the Hon. Mr. H. Hannen who has given special attention to the early maps. It must be recognized that the point to be dealt with is the identification of the Bengala of Barbosa and Varthema in the early part of the sixteenth century, and not the speculations of later writers long after Europeans had become more familiar with the country, when the name of Bengala for a city was no longer in use, and Chittagong and Satgāon were commonly known as Porto Grande and Porto Pequeno. I fear that my note on Bengala (pp. 135 to 145), may be of length out of proportion to its importance, but as Barbosa's allusion has been so frequently discussed, it seemed best to go into it as thoroughly as possible, and especially to bring out the information which can be derived from native writers and from numismatics.

Barbosa's account of Pegu is of great interest considering the period when it was written. It is impossible to decide whether he had visited Pegu personally. There is no evidence that he did so, but the accuracy of his observations seems to make it probable, and there would have been no great difficulty after the conquest of Malacca in his sailing there in one of the vessels trading between these two great emporiums or in one sailing across the Bay of Bengal from Pulicat on the Coromandel coast ; the trade from which place to Pegu is alluded to in § 100.

Siam, at the beginning of the sixteenth century, was in

possession of the coast of the Bay of Bengal from Martaban southwards, and at this point Barbosa brings in his account of the Kingdom of Anseam or Siam. His account of the ports on that coast is fairly full, but of Siam proper he has little to say. He alludes, however, to a heathen tribe on the borders of China and Siam, and from De Barros and other later writers we are able to identify it with the race known as the Gueos, who were often at war with Siam. The principal interest in Barbosa's account is his mention of the peculiar form of Cannibalism prevalent in this tribe ; a form, as far as I can ascertain, without any exact parallel elsewhere. It consisted in devouring deceased relatives evidently as a solemn ritual. The tribe seems undoubtedly, as Sir J. George Scott kindly informs me, to be identical with the Wa, the Lawa of the Burmese, who occupy the hills north of Chiengmai.

Sir J. George Scott considers that the cannibalism was a ritual or agricultural rite, but he adds " there seems no survival in the wild Wa country nowadays, and even head-hunting seems to be less active than it was." The later writers, De Barros and Linschoten, who mention the Gueos allude to the cannibalism but not to its peculiar form, and we have no account of it except that given by Barbosa.[1]

The remainder of Barbosa's work is concerned with Malacca, with the islands of the Eastern Archipelago, and with the coast of Indo-China and China. As regards Malacca his information is the earliest recorded by any

---

[1] See *infra* p. 167. Some information about these Wa is given in the *Burma Gazetteer* (1908), Vol. I, 182, and Vol. II, 334. They are said to be given to cutting off the heads of human victims " on a religious basis." Sir J. George Scott's information unfortunately reached me too late to be incorporated in the notes to the text.

Portuguese writer, and is of considerable value. For the Archipelago in general he was no doubt indebted to the reports brought back by D'Abreu's expedition, and for China and the Lequeos (Formosa) to the stories of merchants, and probably also to information from some of the earlier Portuguese adventurers before the voyage of Rafael Perestrello and the authorized expedition of Fernão Peres D'Andrade (*Infra*, p. 211, n. 1). Giovanni da Empoli's letter of November 15th, 1515, must, as I have been able to show, take precedence of that of Andrea Corsali (really dated January 6th, 1516, and not 1515 as wrongly given by Ramusio), as the first record of any such expeditions (p. 211, note), and Barbosa must have had access to the same sources of information as the Italian writers.

In my notes on the Islands of the Archipelago I owe much to the writings of the French scholars who have done so much to elucidate the early history of these regions, and especially to M. Gabriel Ferrand in his recent works *Malaka* and *K'iouen-Louen*. M. Ferrand has kindly assisted me with much valuable information.

I have also to acknowledge the extremely useful help I have received from Monsenhor S. R. Dalgado, Professor of Sanskrit in Lisbon University, who has not only assisted me in explaining many difficult words, but kindly gave me the opportunity of consulting proofs of Vol. II of his invaluable *Glossario Luso-Asiatico* previous to publication. Monsenhor Dalgado's work in the explanation of the interaction between Portuguese and various Asiatic languages fills a much-required part in philological enquiries and is a worthy successor to the work of Yule and Burnell. His *Glossario* has been preceded by several other works on similar subjects of which his *Influéncia do*

Vocabulário Português em Linguas Asiaticas and *Contribuições para a Lexicologia Luso-Oriental* may be specially
alluded to here. Many notes embodying information
received from Monsenhor Dalgado bearing on points
dealt with in Vol. I will be found in the additional Notes
and emendations given in the present volume (pp. 233–237)
In the same list will be found notes on several points
for which I have to thank Sir George A. Grierson, K.C.I.E.
I have also to thank Sir Richard Temple, Bart., for the
help derived from his Review of Vol. I in the *Journal
of the Royal Asiatic Society*, and also for the great
store of information in his recent · Hakluyt Society
Edition of the *Travels of Peter Mundy* and his
edition of Thomas Bowrey's *Countries round the Bay
of Bengal*.

In Appendix I, I have given translations or abstracts
of several passages from the *Decadas* of João de Barros.
which as far as I know have not hitherto been translated,
These passages relate to Malabar and Bengal. Translations
of the passages in the *Decadas* of De Barros and Do Couto
relating to Ceylon will be found in the *History of Ceylon*
by Mr. Donald Ferguson, and many passages relating
to Malacca and Sumatra are translated into French by
M. Gabriel Ferrand in his *Malaka* from various sixteenth-
century Portuguese writers. These include the *Commentaries of Afonso D'Alboquerque* (often differing from
Mr. De Gray Birch's translation), De Barros, the *Lendas
da India* of Gaspar Correa and the *Decadas* of Do Couto.
Most of the passages dealing with the first adventures of
the Portuguese in India and the Malay Archipelago are
therefore now accessible in English or French.

Another valuable work Godinho de Eredia's *Declaração
de Malaca* (A.D. 1618) was first published at Brussels in

1882, and is accompanied by a French translation by M. L. Janssen.

M. H. Cordier's work in re-editing Sir H. Yule's classical books *Marco Polo* and *Cathay* is too well known to need more than an allusion. M. Cordier has added to the value of the first by his recently issued volume *Ser Marco Polo*, and has made a valuable contribution to the history of the Portuguese in the East in his *L'arrivée des Portugais en Chine* published in *T'oung-Pao* (1911). This forms a chapter in his History of the relations between China and the Western World. All these works have proved invaluable for reference and for elucidating numerous obscure points in Barbosa's work. It is only necessary to allude to Yule's *Hobson-Jobson* and to Mr. W. Crooke's edition of it, which still remains an indispensable source of information to all students of Eastern Travel and Archæology.

In concluding this edition of the Book of Duarte Barbosa I have only to add that the value of his work becomes clearer on more intimate acquaintance. His careful and acute observations regarding the customs of the races of the East are, I believe, unrivalled among the writers of his period, and I may be allowed to hope that my endeavours to elucidate them may not be found unprofitable and may be useful to students of the sixteenth century.

M. LONGWORTH DAMES.

THE BOOK

OF

DUARTE BARBOSA.

§ 87. HERE BEGINNETH THE LAND OF MALABAR; AND THE ENTRY INTO THE KINGDOM OF CALECUT.

S THEN we leave this land and this Kingdom[1] and return to the seacoast the Land of Malabar[2] begins from the place called Cumbola, and in all from the Hill of Dely[3] and ending at the Cape of Comorin it is

---

[1] *I.e.*, Kingdom of Vijayanagar.

[2] *The country called Malabar.* Barbosa here commences his very full and accurate account of the country comprised under the name Malabar, which he begins at the point where the kingdom of Narsyngua or Vijayanagar came to an end, that is at Cambola on the Chandragiri River, described in Vol. I, § 82. This point on the coast is now included in the British District of S. Canara, and the District of Malabar begins rather further south at Kaváyu, a mile or two north of Mount Deli, according to a note furnished me by Mr. Thorne. But, as he says, the Malayālam language extends as far north as the Chandragiri, and Malabar may be reckoned as extending south from this point to Cape Comorin, about 350 miles. Taking the Portuguese league as four miles, Barbosa's 130 leagues is in excess of the actual distance, but on the other hand the seventy leagues of Ramusio and the Spanish version are short of the truth, which lies between the two. This country is now divided into the British District of Malabar, and the States of Travancore and Cochin. In the early sixteenth century it belonged to the Hindu States of Cananore, Calicut, Cochin and Coulam. Barbosa begins his account with the history of the country as preserved in local legends; he then proceeds to describe the people and their castes, and finishes with a list and description from north to south of the principal towns, most of which were on the coast.

[3] *Mount Dely.* The prominent foreland known to early European travellers as Mount Dely has been treated of by Yule in his *Marco Polo* (1st Ed., II, 321 ff.) and also jointly with Burnell in *Hobson-Jobson*. It was known to the Arab sailors as Ras Haili or Hili, and was

one hundred and thirty[1] leagues along the coast.   They

the first Indian land-fall made by Vasco de Gama in 1498. There has
been some difference of opinion as to the origin of the name. Burnell,
as a Dravidian scholar, was no doubt responsible for the note in
Hobson-Jobson (*s.v.* Mount Delly). He considered that the name
represented the Malayālam *Ēli Mala*, " High Mountain " and rejected
the common explanation that it was *Ēlu mala*, " Seven Hills " which
" arose from the compiler of the local Sanskrit *Mahātmya* or legend
who rendered the name *Sapta-saila* ' Seven Hills,' confounding *ēli*
with *ēlu* (or *ēzhu*) ' seven,' which has no application." He also
rejected Correa's explanation of Rat Hill, *ēli*, " a rat," being here
substituted for *ēli*. Yule's explanation in *Marco Polo* from *ēlam*,
" cardamom " (*l.c.* p. 321) is not supported in *Hobson-Jobson*. Mr.
Thorne in a note with which he has favoured me, says that these two
explanations are due to " ignorance of the value of the consonant *l*
in Dely. In Malayālam there are two *l*'s, and neither is found in the
vernacular original of Dely. The name is *Ēzhi mala* or *ēzhu mala*.
Zh is the accepted transliteration of this consonant, which it is impossible to reproduce accurately. In Tamil the sound is in common
speech *l* (cerebral *l*) hence *Ēli* and the Port of D'Eli. At the present day
the sound never has the value *l* in Mal. It is either *zh* or *y*, but it is
probable that the Tamil pronunciation was in vogue in Barbosa's
day. Thus Kōzhikkōd became Calicut. This cerebral *l* is quite
different from the *l* in *eli*—" rat," and *ēlam*, " cardamom," and *zh*
cannot be corrupted from the latter *l*. *Ēzhu* is *Mal.* for seven. Hence
it is possible that the name means " Seven Hills." Mount Dely is a
long narrow hill about 2½ miles long from north to south, and half
a mile broad, jutting out at the south-west corner into its highest peak
(851 feet). It would be easy to pick out seven peaks to support the
derivation. . . . But what is more striking is the abruptness of the
hill's rise from the flat alluvial country around, and its prominence by
contrast. This favours the derivation given by the lexicographer
Gundert. He derives *ēzhi* from the Dravidian stem *ēzhu*, meaning
height or prominence. (He also derives *ēzhu*, " seven," from the same
stem, and this is accepted by Caldwell, though the connection in
meaning is not very clear). I would hazard—with some diffidence—
another suggestion as to the origin of the European Dely. The country
round about Mount Deli is to this day called Rāman-tali, *i.e.*, the
temple of (Paraçu) Rāman. Is it not possible the Dely derives from
tali and that the attempt to derive it from the vernacular *ēzhi* came
when the origin of the word was obscured and confused ? The British
in the eighteenth century wrote of Rāmantali as Ramdilly."

This exhaustive note clearly sets out all the possible or probable
derivations, and any decisive opinion is impossible to one not a
Dravidian scholar, but one objection occurs to the last suggestion,
and that is that in the earliest recorded forms, those of Marco Polo,
Abulfeda and Ibn Batūta, the word begins not with a dental but
with the vowel *e* or with *h*—Eli, Hili or Haili. The use of the *h* alone
seems sufficient to show that it could not have begun with a *t* or *d*.

In a further note Mr. Thorne says that the old travellers' forms
Ely and Hili are no doubt forms of Ēli, the old pronunciation of Ezhi,
but that the forms Deli, Dilly, may have become established through
confusion with the *tali* in Rāmantali, as in the form Rāmdilly quoted
by Yule.

On the whole Burnell's opinion that it means High Mountain seems
preferable and Gundert's is not really inconsistent with it.

[1] Seventy leagues in the Spanish version and in Ramusio.

say that in ancient days there was a heathen King, whose name was Cirimay Pirençal,[1] a very mighty Lord : And after the Moors of Meca had discovered India they began to voyage towards it for the sake of the pepper, of which they first began to take cargoes at Coulam,[2] a city with a harbour, where the King ofttimes abides. " This will not be less than six hundred years ago, for the Indians of that period adopted the era by which those Moors are ruled." And continuing to sail to India for many years they began to spread out therein, and they had such discussions with the King himself and he with them, that in the end they converted him to the sect of the abominable Mafamede, wherefore he went in their company to the House of Meca, and there he died, or, as it seems probable, on the way thither ; for they say that the Malabarese never more heard any tidings of him.[3] Before he started,

---

[1] Spanish, Sernaperimal. The correct form is Chērumān Perumāl. De Barros has Sarama Pereimal (see Appendix I).

[2] There are two places known as Coulam in early Portuguese works ; the best known of these is the southern port shown in our maps as Quilon, now in Travancore, while the northern one is just north of Quilandi in British Malabar (T.). Either of these may be the Coulam of the text, and there is also another Cota coulam (given by De Barros as Cota, Coulam) in the extreme north just south of Cumbola (p. 65 and note). "The late account in the *Tuhfatu'l Mujāhidīn* is to the effect that the Perumāl of the legend after his conversion went by sea to the northern Kollam, thence to Dharmadam (just south of Tellicherry) whence he sailed for Arabia, and he asked the Arabs to sail only to one of these places or to the southern Kollam " (T.). It is evident therefore that there was an early confusion on this point. Both names, Mr. Thorne thinks, are abbreviated forms of Kovilagam, " a royal residence." At the northern Kollam the Zamorin still has a building called the Kovilagam, which probably occupies the site of the ancient palace which gave its name to the place. Barbosa's statement that Calicut was the site of Chērumān Perumāl's departure perhaps represents an earlier form of the legend.

[3] The account here given by Barbosa of the conversion to Islam of the King Chērumān Perumāl appears to be the first recorded mention of this tradition which has lasted to the present day. The story will be found in Buchanan (*Journey*, 1807, II, pp. 349 and 474), and in the *Gazetteer of Malabar* (1908), pp. 40, 41. Mr. Logan, in his *Manual of Malabar*, 1884, accepted the story on the authority of

this King divided his Kingdom [1] among his Kinsfolk into several portions as it yet is, for before that time all Malabar was one Kingdom. He went on making this partition in such a manner that when he had given a certain land to any person, he forthwith left it never to return thither. And at last, having given away all, and going to take ship from an uninhabited strand (where now is the town of Calecut), and accompanied by more Moors than Heathen, he took with him a

certain Mappilla manuscripts in which it is alleged that at Zaphar on the coast of Arabia (*i.e.*, Dhofār, see *supra*, § 38), the tomb of a Hindu King existed. He was stated to have been a convert to Islam, and to have borne the name of 'Abdu'r-rahmān Sāmiri. The dates of his arrival and of his death are given as 212 and 216 A.H. (827 and 831 A.D.). But there is no evidence that any such tomb actually exists, and the absence of any mention by Ibn Baṭūta, or any of the earlier Muhammadan writers, must be considered conclusive against the truth of the story. But there must have been some incident accompanying the great Arab settlements on the Malabar coast, some conversion probably, which gave rise to the legend. Possibly this may be found in Ibn Baṭūta's statement as to the towns of Jur-fatan and Deh-fatan and Budd-fatan, which are identified in Yule and Cordier's *Cathay* (IV, 76, 77) with Cananor, Tarmapatam, and Pudri-patam, the last of which is to " be identified with Puthupattanam (*i.e.*, new-town), the modern Puthupanam, on the north bank of the Kōtta river, not far from Badagara " (T.). Ibn Baṭūta says that the Kawīl or King of these places owned many ships trading to Arabia, and that a great Mosque had been built at Deh-fatan by one of his ancestors who had become a Musalman. His descendants reverted to idolatry (*Ibn Baṭūta*, IV, 83-87). Mr. Thorne suggests that some King may have been converted to Islam between 1450 A.D. and Barbosa's time, and may have been confused with the famous Perumāl of earlier times. In the *Keralolpatti*, a Malayālam history of Malabar, the convert is called Bāna Pĕrumāl, and not Chĕrumān.

This Kawīl is perhaps the Kolattiri of Cananor. The first mention of the Chĕrumān Perumāl story by a Muhammadan writer seems to be that in the *Tuḥfatu'l Mujāhidīn* in the beginning of the seventeenth century.

Barbosa gives the story very much in its present form. The sword alluded to by him figures in the modern legend, and is still preserved in the Zamorin's palace at Calicut (*Malabar Gaz.*, p. 41, note 2). Mr. Thorne says that there is no trace of the lamp, and adds " the sword still exists and I have seen it. It is preserved as a quasi-sacred relic by the Zamorins. It was brought out on a salver decked with the flower of *Chrysanthemum Ind.* used in temple worship. It is said to have been inscribed ' Die, slay and conquer,' or ' Stab, slay and conquer.' The sword is now rusted to pieces, and is enclosed in a copper sheath."

[1] *Division of the Kingdom.* The division between the Zamorin, the " King of Coulam," the " King of Cananor " and others, is a convenient explanation of the supersession of the Perumāls (who

nephew who served him as his page to whom he gave this piece of land, telling him to settle and inhabit it. He then gave him his sword, and a golden lamp which he carried with him as a matter of state, and left a charge to all the Kings and Lords to whom he had given lands that they should obey and honour him, save only the Kings of Cananor and Coulam whom he made independent. Thus he left in Malabar three Kings free one of another, but none was to coin money except his nephew, who was afterwards King of Calecut. This partition made, the old man took ship, and the nephew who stayed on that shore founded a city to which he gave the name of Calecut, and the Moors, in memory of the embarkation of the Indian King there on his way to become a Moor, began to take cargoes of pepper there before any other place, and so the trade of Calecut went on increasing, the city became great and noble, and the King made himself the greatest and most powerful of all in Malabar, and they called him Çamidre,[1]

---

came from the eastern districts) by the three dynasties of Calicut, Travancore and Cananor. All the chieftains among whom the Perumāl divided his kingdom are said in the text to be his kinsfolk, the Zamorin being his nephew. According to the Keralolpatti the Cananore king (Kōlattiri) was the son of a Kshatriya woman wrecked on the shore of Mount Dely, whom Chērumān Perumāl took to wife. There were two other women (S'ūdras) in the same boat, the descendants of whom by the Perumāl became minor chieftains in North Malabar. The Kōlattiri is even to this day closely connected with the Travancore dynasty, which takes wives from the northern family, and observes pollution in common with it. There is therefore some reason to believe that the Perumāl kingdom did split up into a number of kingdoms by the ordinary Malayālam modes of fissure, viz., (1) by inheritance through sisters as in the case of the Zamorin in the text, (2) by provision for sons as in the case of the Kōlattiri in the Keralolpatti story. But the Zamorin, and the Travancore dynasty also, were probably rulers some time before the extinction of the Perumāls. The Keralolpatti describes the partition in detail. Among the chiefs provided for were the Zamorin, the Kōlattiri, the Travancore Chief, the Cochin Chief, the Porlāttiri, Kurumbiattiri and Valluvanad Chiefs. All these families still survive, though only Cochin and Travancore are ruling chiefs.—(T.)

[1] Mr. Thorne's note on the titles of the Malabar kings is very full, and brings forward a new explanation of the word Zamorin and other

which is a distinction above the others. They are only three, to wit, the Çamidre whom they call Maly Conadary, and he of Coulam whom they call Benetady, and he of Cananor whom they call Cobertorim. Besides these, there are many great Lords in the Land who wish to be called Kings, which they are not, for they neither coin money, nor roof houses with tiles,[1] nor indeed in all Malabar can anyone roof them so, howsoever great a Lord he may be, for forthwith the Moors would rise against him, save only if it be a House of Prayer or a King's Palace. Afterwards, in the course of time the Kings of Cochim and Cananor struck money by force.

And in this Land of Malabar all men use one tongue only[2] which they call Maliama, the Kings are of one

---

titles. He rejects the accepted explanation of Zamorin (according to Gundert) as equivalent to Sāmūdri from Skr. Samudra (sea)=" Lord of the Sea." Mr. Thorne considers this improbable as the Zamorins never were Lords of the Sea, and finds the origin in *Swāmi*+'*sri*. The latter word, as in many other words, becomes *tiri*, and is found in other titles such as Kolāttiri and names of castes such as Nambūtiri. The argument is too long for insertion as a note, and too important to be omitted. It will be found in full in Appendix II(c).

[1] *Roofing of houses.* It was the prerogative of the Malabar rulers to forbid roofing with tiles instead of thatch without permission. Thus the English factors at Cananore had to get the Zamorin's permission to tile their factory. Even at the present day it is said that occasionally an important Nambūtiri or other powerful landlord makes trouble for some poor tenant who presumes to aspire to the cheap " mission " tile, but these stories may be malicious inventions.—(T.)

[2] The "one tongue only" is that now called Malayālam, of which Malayāzhma and Malayāyma are variants. It is still the official language of Travancore, Cochin and British Malabar, and is also in general use in the southern portion of the South Canara District (T.). (See Caldwell, *Grammar of Dravidian Languages*, 1875, p. 20.) For the origin of the name Malabar see *ib.*, pp. 27–29, also *Hobson-Jobson*, under the same name, and Yule and Cordier, *Cathay*, II, 132. The oldest form of the name is Male or Malai; this is found in Cosmas and in the Arab and Chinese authorities up to the eleventh or twelfth centuries. The Chinese traveller Yuan Chwang spoke of the Mo-lo-ya or Malaya Mountain and the T'ang-Shu puts the Mē-lai country in the extreme south of India (Watters, *Yuan Chwang*, II, pp. 228, 232). Afterwards the termination *bār* (Arabic or rather Persian) was added in the sense of land or territory.

caste, and custom, with little difference between them [1]
but that of the common folk varies much, for you must
know that in all Malabar there are eighteen castes of
Native Heathen, each separate from the rest, so much
so that they do not so much as touch one another under
pain of death or forfeiture of their property, so that all
have castes, customs, and idol-worship of their own, as
I shall relate as I go on.

The Kings of Malabar [2] are heathens and worshippers
of idols ; they are tawny men, almost white, but some
are blacker than others. They go naked, save that from
the waist down they are clad in white cotton or silk.
Sometimes they wear coats [3] open in front coming down
to the middle of the thigh, of cotton or silk, or very
fine scarlet cloth or brocade. They wear their hair tied

---

[1] *Kings of one caste with very little difference between them.* In this
Barbosa is accurate, as the customs of all these families, whether
Kshatriya or Sāmantan, are almost identical. There are, however,
some points of difference. Mr. Thorne notes the following :—

(1) Kshatriyas wear the sacred thread. Sāmantans do not.
(2) Kshatriya men can marry Kshatriya or Sāmantan women.
Sāmantan men cannot marry Kshatriya or " royal " Sāmantan
women, but women of subordinate Sāmantan or Nāyar families.
Kshatriya and Royal Sāmantan women may marry only Nambūtiris or Kshatriyas, while ordinary Sāmantan women in addition
may marry Sāmantans.
(3) Kshatriyas can as a rule eat with Brahmans, Sāmantans
cannot.—(T.)

[2] *The Kings of Malabar.* Only certain of the ruling families claim
to be Kshatriyas ; most of them call themselves Sāmantan. The
only ones which have a substantial claim to the title of Kshatriya
are the Raja of Kottayam (North Malabar) and the Rajas of Beypore
and Parappanād (South Malabar). The claims of the others are not
generally admitted. The Zamorin and the Valluvanād Raja do not
call themselves Kshatriyas, but Sāmantans. The Zamorin is considered to be an Erōde and the Valluvanād Raja a Vaḷḷōdi.
Much of Barbosa's description here is applicable to Nāyars and other
castes to whom the royal families approximate. It remains even to
the present day the best description by any foreigner of the customs
of the Rajas and chieftains of Malabar. It is clear that he made a
special study of the customs of the Zamorin.

[3] *Coats.* This is no longer so. The "rājas" or rather Tamburāns,
go simply clad in a cloth tied round the waist as do other decent
folk.

upon the top,[1] and sometimes they wear small hoods like Gallego caps, they shave their beards [2] with razors, leaving short moustaches after the manner of the Turks. Their ears are bored, and in them they wear very rich jewels of precious stones filled with great pearls and over their garments they are girt with belts of precious stones, well worked, and rich, three fingers broad. On their chests, shoulders and foreheads, are streaks of ashes in threes, which they put on, according to the manner of their caste,[3] to remind them that they must all become ashes, and they put these on mixed with sandalwood, saffron, rosewater, and aloes-wood, pounded together and made very fine.

They live in earthen houses, and seat themselves on high platforms made very smooth, and plastered daily

---

[1] *Mode of tying the hair*, that is in the distinctive *Kudumi* " knot " of the Malayali which does not hang down behind as with the Tamils, but lies on the top of the head or is drawn round to the left of the forehead. The small hoods like Gallego caps are not now worn. All Malayalis when in native dress go barefooted except when sandals are required to protect the feet.—(T.)

[2] *Shaving*. Malayalis including Tamburāns ordinarily shave the face and body all over, except during mourning periods. Barbosa, judged by present customs, was wrong in saying that Tamburāns wear moustaches " after the manner of the Turks," but old pictures show that this was once the fashion.

[3] Barbosa here makes the mistake often repeated in more modern works, of supposing these markings to denote caste. In reality they indicate the sect and not the caste of the wearer. Thus Vaishnavas are distinguished from S'aivas, etc. The ingredients of which the paste is composed frequently include sandalwood. The aloes-wood alluded to has nothing to do with the true aloes, for which see Vol. I, p. 61, n. 1. The aloes-wood, otherwise called eagle-wood, is the wood of the *Aquilaria Agallocha*, or of the *Aloexylon Agallochum*. The latter is the true aloes-wood, and is found mainly in Cochin China and Camboja. The former is a native of India and is probably what is here alluded to. In the table at the end of this volume, Barbosa mentions the true aloes-wood " *Lenho aloes verdadeiro*," as worth 1,000 *fanams* the *farazola*, while *Aguila* (*i.e.*, the common variety) was worth only 300 or 400. The name *aguila* derived from Mal. *akil*, has been turned into *Aquila* and mistranslated into eagle-wood (for details see *Hobson-Jobson, s.v.* Eagle-wood) and *Gloss. Luso-Asiatico, s.v.* Aguila, Aquila, also Garcia da Orta, *Coll.* 30. *Lenaloes* (*Orta*, p. 251 ff.). Cremation is the general method of disposal of the dead as with other Hindus, but burial is found among the lower castes.

with cowdung, on which they place a very white stool
four fingers in height and a coarse cloth of sheep's wool
dyed black,[1] as large as an Alemtejo cloak, folded in
three, and on this they sit, with some long and round
cotton pillows, and other rich cloths on which they
lean, and very fine carpets [2] on which also they sit, yet
they always keep that coarse woollen cloth with them,
or under them, it is a matter of ceremony, caste and
custom. And often they recline on couches with silk
rugs, and very thin white cloths. And if any visitors
come to see them, they bring him one of those woollen
cloths, and lay it by him, and when they go out a page
carries it folded in front of them as a ceremonial custom,
he also always carries a sword with them, and when
they change from one corner to another he always bears
it in his hand, [naked as they almost always carry them].

These Kings [3] do not marry, nor have they any marriage

---

[1] *Cloth of sheep's wool dyed black.* This is called *kavimpadam*
" dark cloth." This and the " white cloth," *vella,* are indispensable
for the state occasions of a Zamorin.—(T.)

[2] *Rich cloth, carpets, etc.* These luxuries are seldom seen now.
Most of the Tamburāns lead a simple life, and their *kovilagams* or
" palaces " are often unpretentious. Their incomes are not large, and
their expenses great, since much is frittered away in ceremonies and
feeding Brāhmans. Most of their treasures and jewels must have
been lost during the Mysorean invasions.—(T.)

[3] *Marriage of the " Kings " or Tamburāns.* Barbosa is right in
saying that Tamburāns do not marry in the European sense, *i.e.,*
their wives are not of the same rank as themselves, and the issue
of the connections are not received into the royal families. Practically every Tamburān takes a mate from among the Nāyars or
other Hindus of good caste. When the connection is lasting, as is
usually the case nowadays, he builds her a house as stated by Barbosa,
and maintains her. The children belong to the family of the mother,
and in theory should be maintained by her, but the custom is growing
of provision being made by the Tamburān for his children. Even so,
of course, the children are lower in the social scale than their fathers.
One of the sons of the late Zamorin was employed under him as a
rent-collector, and a son of the present Zamorin is employed on the
estate (which is now under the management of the Court of Wards)
as an inspector on Rs. 35 a month. This state of things—and indeed
the whole *maramakkathāyam* system of Malabar—at first appears
anomalous and unnatural to Europeans.—(T.)

For the marriage customs of the Kings of Malabar see p. 43,
note 1, *infra* on Nāyar marriage.

law. They keep as a concubine a woman of good family, of Nayre descent, and beautiful for their delight. These they keep in an inn near the palace, quite independently and very well supplied. They receive a certain sum by the month or year ; and when they are dissatisfied with one, they let her go and take another. Nevertheless many of them out of regard for the royal honour will not change or send away these women, and among them it is held a great honour for a maiden to become one of the King's women. The sons which the King has by them are not held to be his sons, nor do they inherit the Kingdom, nor anything that is the King's, they take only what comes to them from their mothers. As long as they are young the King treats them with great favour, like children of another whom he is bringing up, but not as his sons ; for when they are men they receive no more honour than comes to them from their mother's rank, yet the Kings ofttimes make them presents of money, so that they can live better than the other Nayres. The heirs of these Kings are their brothers, or their nephews, sons of their sisters. They consider that these are their true sons, for they know who is their mother,[1] and in this country for that the

---

[1] Under this system of descent through women there is also no marriage of women in the Western sense. The *Tamburāttis*, or ladies of the " royal " houses, take their mates from the Nambūtiri Brahmans, or sometimes from Kshatriya Tamburāns. They remain in their *kovilagams*, and are visited there by their mates, who, during their visits, are maintainable by the house visited. The children belong to the *kovilagams* in which they are born, and are heirs to the royal dignities. Their fathers are under no obligation whatever to maintain them, nor would it be considered at all proper for them to do so. These connections may be very fleeting, as is perhaps natural when the " husband " has no obligation, and is precluded from living with his " wife " and children even if he wished to do so. It is only in this sense that the Tamburāttis are " very free " ; they live a very secluded life, only moving from the *kovilagam* to bathe in the adjoining tank or worship in the adjoining temple, and their reputation and propriety are so jealously guarded that a scandal is practically unheard of.—(T.)

women are very free of their bodies, the true stock of the
Royal descent is through the women, and the first son born
to the King's eldest sister is heir to the throne, and thus
all the brothers inherit one after the other, and when there
are no brothers, the nephews, sons of the eldest sister
succeed.[1] If the sisters do not happen to have borne sons
there is no heir to the crown, and the King dies without
one ; then they meet in council and elect a relative as
King,[2] and if there is none, then any person who may be
suitable. For this reason the Kings of Malabar are always
old ;[3] their nieces and sisters from whom the heir to throne
is to proceed are well watched and served, and have their
own revenues on which they live, and when any of them
attains the age of twelve or fourteen, and is fit for intercourse with men, they send to summon some youth of
noble lineage from outside the Kingdom, appointed there
for that purpose, sending him money and gifts in order
that he may come and take the maidenhood of that girl.

---

[1] Barbosa's account of the system of succession is correct in the
main, but wrong in one particular—that is, in attributing special
rights to the eldest sister's descendants. A man's position is determined by his own age and not by that of his mother. The eldest
male in the line of descent succeeds, and an uncle may even have
to give way to a nephew who is older than himself. The case of a
younger Tamburātti's son going over the head of an elder Tamburātti's
son because he is the elder of the two is common.—(T.)

[2] *Election of a relative as King.* Without the device of adoption
the Malabar *kovilagams* could not have lasted as they have. The
Zamorin's family was kept alive by adoption from the Nilēsvaram
Kovilagam in South Kanara. In 1706 the only living members of
the family were two males. Three ladies with their children were
adopted ; the eldest of these became Zamorin in 1751 and was an
ally of the British in Tellicherry. It would evidently be useless to
adopt males only.—(T.)

[3] *Kings always old.* The fact Barbosa speaks of is a well-known
one, *cf.* Dellon (*Voyages*), Ed. 1711, p. 268, written in the
seventeenth century. " A young sovereign is the greatest rarity
that can be seen among the Malabares." Within the last century
there have been fifteen Zamorins, seven of them within the last twenty-
five years. The present Zamorin, who succeeded about five years
ago, is well over 70, and his heirs are very little younger than himself.
The disadvantages of the system are obvious. A Tamburān succeeds
when he is too old to administer his state or property well ; he holds
the title a year or two, and is then succeeded by another old man.—(T.)

When he has come, they do him great honour, with
feasts and ceremonies as if it were a wedding ; then he
ties round her neck a small golden jewel which she
wears for the rest of her life as a token that they have
performed that ceremony for her, and thereafter she
may dispose of herself according to her own desires,
which until then she may not do. The young man
remains with her some days, being very well served,
and then goes back to his own land. Thenceforward
she can choose any Bramene that pleases her and as
many as she likes, and bears them children.

And when one of these Kings of Malabar dies they
burn him in an open place with great store of sanders-
wood and aloes, and at the cremation all his nephews
and near kinsfolk gather together, as well as the great
men of the state and the attendants of the dead King,
and they allow three days to pass before they thus
dispose of the body awaiting the assembly of these
persons, and also to make it clear whether he died a
natural death or whether he was murdered, in which
enquiry they must take part as they are bound to do.[1]

And after these three days are past, they burn him
and mourn for him, and after his cremation, all shave
themselves from the crown of the head to the soles of
the feet saving only their eyelashes and eyebrows; this
they do from the prince to the least heir of the kingdom
of the heathen ; then they clean all the blackness caused
by the betel from their teeth, and no one may eat it
for the space of thirteen days. If during this time they
find that anyone eats it, they cut off his lips as a penalty.
And in these thirteen days the prince gives no order, he

---

[1] There is nothing here about taking vengeance in case of his having
died a violent death, as appears in the Spanish version and in Ramusio.
The latter says " *per vendicarlo, como sono obligati in caso di morte vio-
lenta,*" f. 304v.

does not rule nor is he raised to the throne until those days are past, waiting lest there should be someone to oppose him. When they are past, the assembly of the great men makes him swear to maintain all the laws established by the late King, and to pay the debts which he owed, and to strive to win what former Kings had lost ; and this is the manner in which they exact this oath ; they place a naked sword in his left hand, and his right hand they place on a lighted oil lamp with many wicks and in it is a gold ring which he touches with his fingers, so that he takes the oath on the lamp [1] and that gold to maintain everything with that sword. This done, they throw a little rice on his head, performing great ceremonies and worshipping with their faces to the sun.

Then forthwith certain nobles whom they call Cahimal,[2] together with him who is to be Prince, and with the other heirs take their oaths to the said King on the same lamp, to serve and help and to be loyal and true to him.

During the thirteen days, while they await this ceremony a Cahimal[3] governs the Kingdom, who is as it were the

---

[1] In describing this ceremony the Spanish version (p. 108) speaks of " a chain lit up with many oil wicks," an error which in this passage is not shared by Ramusio. The mistake was no doubt in the Spanish translation from the Portuguese, and arose from the similarity of the words *cadea*, " a chain," and *candea* (then usually written *cádea*), " a lamp." There is no such resemblance between the Spanish *cadena*, " a chain," and *candil*, " a lamp."

[2] *Cahimal*, see Thurston, *Castes aud Tribes of South India*, *s.v.* Kaimal. He states that it is a title used among Nayars, and is derived from the word *Kai*, " hand." For the use of the term in other early Portuguese writers, see *Hobson-Jobson*, *s.v.* Caimal. See also Thurston, *l.c.*, *s.v.* Nāyar, Vol. V, p. 296, and Kshatriya do., Vol. IV, and Dalgado, *Gloss. Luso-Asiatico*, *s.v.* Caimal, where many examples of the Portuguese use of the word are given. The *Malabar Glossary*, p. 114, says that some Sāmantans have the titles of Kartavu and Kaimal. The Sāmantans are an aristocracy above the ordinary Nāyars, but identical with them in their customs. See Art. " Sāmantan," Thurston, Vol. VI.

[3] *Mangāt Achan, the Cahimal of Barbosa*. There is at present no Mangāt Achan. The last holder of the title died last year. The

principal Secretary thereof, and this duty and honour are his by right. He is also Treasurer in Chief of the Kingdom, and the King cannot draw forth aught thence unless he is present, nor can he draw forth anything without great necessity, nor without the advice of this man, and others. And all the laws of the Kingdom also are in this man's possession.

During these thirteen days none may eat flesh or fish, nor may any boat go forth to fish under the penalty of death, and in this period much alms is distributed from the estate of the dead King to the fishers, and many poor

---

title passes by the ordinary rules of Marumakkathāyam in a Sāmantan Nambiyar family known as Chāthoth Idam. This house is situated in the Vattoli desam (hamlet) of the Kannavam amsam (Revenue-village) of Kottayam Taluk in North Malabar. The present head of the family is the Adhikāri (Village headman) of a neighbouring amsam (T.). In addition to his Adhikāri's post he holds the Sthānam of Vāzhunnavar (lit. ruler). This is a Sthānam conferred by the Kottayam Raja on the senior man of three Sāmantan Nambiyar families of the locality. When I asked him why he had not formally taken his title of Mangāt Achan (with sword and shield) from the hands of the Zamorin at Calicut, he told me that he thought his investiture would interfere with the duties as Adhikāri and Vāzhunnavar : but he assured me that the title would be assumed by one of his juniors, when old enough.

The Mangāt Achan now holds no property under the Zamorin. Large grants of land had been granted in the Zamorin's dominions, but these have all passed into other hands. The only perquisite is the yearly grant of 200 panams.

Nowadays the Mangāt Achan does not ordinarily live at the Zamorin's court, though this was customary till 20 or 30 years ago. As soon as a Zamorin dies, word is brought to the Achan, and he hastens to the Kovilagam and assumes the Regency. There is no doubt that he is the Cahimal (Kammal) to whom Barbosa refers. All the business of the Kovilagam is in his hands till the installation of the new Zamorin.

It is very curious to observe that the Mangāt Achan alone of all the dependants of the Zamorin comes from North Malabar. He belongs to territory over which the Zamorin never held sway, and which in historical times has been under the dominion of the Kottayam Rajas. How came it that the Zamorin's chief *Mantri* was chosen from outside his territories ? The traditional explanation is that the Mangāt Achan was given his sword and shield by Chērumān Perumāl who particularly attached him to the Zamorin when he divided up his realm. But this scarcely solves the difficulty.

The account Barbosa gives of the authority of the Kammal is fully borne out by popular tradition of the part many Mangāt Achans played as the *Mantris* of the Zamorin. He is the hero of many a ballad, and there is a couplet which says :—

" The coming of the Musalman and the pillage of Malabar are the fruit of the death of the gem-like Mangāt Achan."—(T.)

men and Bramenes are fed. When the thirteen days are accomplished and the King has been raised to the throne as above stated, they begin again to eat betel, flesh, and fish, saving only the new King himself, who continues his mourning for the late King for a whole year, and eats no flesh nor fish, nor betel, nor shaves his beard, nor cuts a single hair of his whole body, nor his nails. He prays at certain hours in the day, he may eat but once in the day, he must bathe before he eats, and after bathing he must see no one before he eats.[1]

The King of Calicut dwells always in the City in a palace[2] a little apart from it. And when the year from the late King's death is fulfilled, then comes he who is to be Prince,[3] and also the heirs, his brethren and nephews,

[1] The Spanish version has here " after washing he must not *drink anything* until he has eaten." Ramusio agrees with the Portuguese text.

[2] *Palace.* There is still a block of buildings in Calicut known as the Taḷi Kovilagam, which now houses the Zamorin's college. This was by way of being the headquarters of the Zamorin in comparatively recent times. But the palace of Barbosa was undoubtedly the old palace to the north of the Taḷi temple. The land is still called Kōtta paramba (Fort Garden) and traces of old buildings are visible there. It was here that Vasco de Gama visited the Zamorin, and it was here that when Haider invaded Malabar in 1766, the Zamorin was shut up ; he set fire to the place and perished in the flames. The Collector's office now stands in the precincts of Kōtta paramba. The fine Municipal tank in front of it was the Zamorin's bathing tank; it is known as Mānānchira, *i.e.*, Mānavikraman-chira (the tank of Mānavikraman, *i.e.*, of the Zamorin).

Between the Taḷi tank and Kōtta paramba buildings stand on sites still known as Ambāḍi Kovilagam, Puthiya Kovilagam, and Padinhara Kovilagam parambas. The Ambāḍi Kovilagam appears to have been the original (or parent) Kovilagam of the Zamorins. The Zamorin still speaks of the Valiya Tamburātti of the Ambāḍi Kovilagam (*i.e.*, the eldest lady of the family, as the Zamorin is the eldest man) as " Mother," though she may be younger than he is ; and every Zamorin speaks of his predecessor as " uncle," though the relationship is usually that of brother or cousin. The Ambāḍi Kovilagam no longer exists as a Kovilagam. The Puthiya Kovilagam has moved to Tiruvannūr, and the Padinhara Kovilagam to Mānkāvu.—(T.)

[3] The " prince " of Barbosa's narrative is the Erālpāḍ or next in succession.

Barbosa's extraordinary accuracy appears once more in this account of the manner of Erālpāḍ's approach to the Zamorin. I have been reading lately a contemporaneous narrative in Malayalam verse describing the Māmākam ceremony periodically held at Pirunnasayi,

all the other great Lords of the Kingdom, to assist in a ceremony [1] which he performs at the end of the year from the King's death by way of a funeral, in which much alms are given away, and much money spent in feeding many Bramenes and poor persons, and to all persons soever who come to see him, and to as many others as they bring with them. Here upwards of a hundred thousand men are gathered together. Then they confirm the prince as heir, and the others after him, each in their degrees. The offices are then taken away [2] from some of the Governors, and Officials of the late King's time, and some are confirmed in their offices. Then the Princes despatches everyone to his home, and the Prince himself departs [3] for the lands set apart for him, and he may come no more to Calicut as long as the King lives, all the others may come to visit him at the court, and walk

---

that curious ceremony at which numbers of Nāyars sacrificed their lives in a gallant but hopeless attempt to pierce the Zamorin's body-guard and cut him down. On the last day the Erālpād, attended by his minister, would come from his camp on the other side of the river, and, with great ceremony approach the Zamorin, who took his stand on a platform about half a mile from the temple. The manner of his approach—even to the number of the Erālpād's prostrations—is described precisely as in Barbosa's account.

The narrative referred to describes the Māmākam of 1691. For another description (of the ceremony of 1683) taken by Mr. Logan from original sources—*vide* Logan's *Manual*, p. 165 *et. sqq. Vide* especially foot of p. 167 and top of p. 168.—(T.)

[1] *Ceremony.* The Tirūmāsam. I remember on the Tirūmāsam day of the late Zamorin in 1916 seeing thousands of Brahmans thronging the road from the Mānkāvu Kovilagam to Calicut, after getting their meal and money-present. The ceremony cost the Zamorin thousands of Rupees. On that occasion the Court of Wards made the Zamorin a special grant of Rs. 8,000 to assist him to meet the expenditure.—(T.)

[2] *Offices are then taken away.* Even now the first act of a new Zamorin is to remove most of Kāriyastans (agents) of his predecessor, and put in his own men.—(T.)

[3] *Prince himself departs.* The headquarters of the Erālpād are at Karimpuzha in Valluvanād taluk. The new Erālpād goes in solemn procession to Karimpuzha from Koḍikkunnu in Ponnanitaluk. The journey (more than 20 miles) is done partly in a litter and partly on foot ; many shrines are visited on the way and many curious ceremonies performed. An interesting account of it was written by the late Zamorin.—(T.)

with him, saving the Prince only, who by law may not do so. When he is dismissed he takes his way to a certain bridge [1] where flows a river not far from the town; there he takes his bow and discharges an arrow towards the place where the King is, and then after offering up a prayer in an attitude of adoration, the Prince goes on his way.

And when he comes to visit (the King) or on the occasion of these funeral ceremonies, he comes accompanied by many great Lords who bring with them Nayres with numbers of drums, great and small, trumpets like the *anafils*,[2] flutes, cymbals, and tambourines [3] (and certain instruments like unto a sheath of brass), with which they make a great harmony. The Nayres go in front, and behind them come lancers, then bucklermen with bare swords in their hands, and the King cometh forth from the palace, and standeth on foot in a doorway, watching the coming of all these folk, and as each one arrives he does him reverence, as one who worships him and then withdraws himself apart ; and it occupies much time until all have passed, and the Prince appears at a bowshot's distance with a bare sword in his hand, which he brandishes as he comes with a lofty countenance, and his eyes fixed on the King, on seeing whom he adores him, casting himself flat on the ground, his arms spread out in front, and after lying thus for a while, he rises, and he goes on in the same fashion until he reaches the King, when he again casts himself down on the ground.[4] The

---

[1] *Certain Bridge.* That is, over the Kalláyi River, just to the south of Calicut.

[2] The Anafil (Ar. *an-nafil*) is the long trumpet used by the Moors of Morocco, which was well known to the Portuguese.

[3] For *cesto*, "a basket," read *sestro*, "a tambourine."

[4] Here the Spanish version adds "and at half-way he does the same thing again." Ramusio has the same, and as to the final prostration adds, "he again prostrates himself for the third time." Thus both these texts mention three prostrations, while the Portuguese text only mentions two.

B

King then comes two paces forward, takes him by the
hand, and raises him, and so they both go together into
the palace. There the King sets himself on his dais,
and the Prince with all the other heirs and lords stand
before him, holding their bare swords in their right hands,
and their left hands [1] in front of their mouths as a sign of
great politeness, and a little removed from the King, and
if he gives them permission to speak it must be very
softly so that he may not hear them, to such an extent
that if there are two thousand men in the same house
where the King is, they will not spit in his presence, nor
can anyone hear them speak.

The King of Calicut continually keeps a multitude of
writers [2] in his palace who sit in a corner far from him ;
they write upon a raised platform, everything connected
with the King's Exchequer and with the justice and
governance of the realm. They write [3] on long and stiff
palm leaves, with an iron style without ink ; they make
their letters in incised strokes, like ours, and the straight
lines as we do. Each of these men carries with him
whithersoever he goes a sheaf of these written leaves
under his arm, and the iron style in his hand, and by
this they may be recognised. And there are seven or
eight more, the King's private writers, men held in great
esteem, who stand always before the King with their
styles in their hands, and the bundle of leaves under
their arms. Each one of them has a number of these

---

[1] *Left Hands.* A person standing before the Zamorin must even
now stand with his left hand over his mouth and his right hand in
the left arm pit.—(T.)

[2] *Writers.* Those of the Zamorin's Nāyars who were engaged in
clerical capacities received the title Menon. The office was hereditary,
and a large proportion of Nāyars still call themselves Menons, their
ancestors having derived it from one or other of the Rajas.

[3] *They write.* This is precisely how writing on palm leaves (*ôlas*)
is still done. Paper has by no means altogether displaced the
ôla.—(T.)

leaves in blank, sealed by the King at the top. And when the King desires to give or to do anything as to which he has to provide he tells his wishes to each of these men and they write it down from the Royal seal to the bottom, and thus the order is given to whomsoever it concerns. These men are old and much respected, and trusted. When they rise in the morning and wish to write something, the first time they take a style in their hand they cut a little of the palm-leaf with a pen-knife which is kept in one of the cavities of the style, and on a corner of this same leaf, they write the names of their Gods, worshipping towards the sunrise with raised hands, then tearing up what they have written they throw it away, and this done, they begin to write (what they desire).

This King has a thousand women [1] who are constantly maintained by him, and attend at court as sweepers of his palace ; this is done for display, for to sweep it less than fifty would suffice. These are ladies of good caste, they sweep twice daily and each of them carries her broom and a brass basin containing cowdung mingled with water ; when they have swept everything they put on with the hand a very thin coating of this which dries at once. They do not all work at one time, but take turns ; and when the King goes from one house to another, or to a house of prayer, he goes on foot, and these women go before him with their brooms and basins in their hands, plastering the path where he is to tread. When a new King comes to the throne there are great rejoicings among these thousand women. When the year of his mourning and fasting is past, all of them, young and old

---

[1] *A thousand women.* Though the Zamorin's state is, of course, much reduced nowadays, he still employs numerous women servants. This office also is hereditary, and the women belong to the Menon families.—(T.)

alike, gather together in the King's palace gaily attired
with jewelled necklaces, golden beads of very fine work,
golden anklets on their legs, and great numbers of bracelets
and rings.   From the waist down they wear garments of
rich silk, above the waist they are naked,[1] as they ever
are, anointed with sandal-wood oil, and other scents,
and many flowers in their hair.   " On their heads they
wear nothing, but their hair, which is right black, is
very well dressed, and some of them tie it into a fine
knot."   Their ears are bored and in them they wear much
gold, they go barefoot as they use always.   And with
them come all the instruments of the Royal music,
firing of guns and fireworks of many kinds.

Many Nayres also assemble who accompany these
women and are their lovers, they are well attired and
gallant in their appearance, also seven or eight elephants
covered with silk draperies, numbers of hanging bells and
great iron chains thrown over their backs.   Thus they
bring an idol which they hold to be their patron, one of
whose priests holds it in his arms, and seats himself
with it on the greatest of those elephants, and thus they
go in procession, with much music, and fireworks, and
discharging of guns, and many jesters in front ; thus
they go on till they reach a certain temple, and there they
bring the idol down and place it with the others which
are already in that place, where they perform   many

---

[1] *Above the waist they are naked.*   Till quite recently (and I am not
sure whether the rule is yet repealed) no woman could enter temples
in Cochin State if clothed above the waist.

Though Barbosa describes this ceremony as occurring on the expiry
of the Zamorin's year of mourning, he is evidently writing of the
annual *pūram* festival as carried out in Calicut.   This takes place at
the end of March.   It is everywhere a festival in which women take
a peculiarly prominent part.   They go in procession, as described
by Barbosa, each girl carrying a brass plate (*tālam* or *taḷiga*) on
which rice is heaped, an earthern lamp being placed on the top of
the heap.   (The attentions of the Nāyar men described by Barbosa
would no longer be considered seemly.)—(T.)

ceremonies. Mighty crowds gather here to worship these idols, and pay their respect to their appearance. Each of the women holds her broad and flat brass basin full of rice, and on this oil lamps with many wicks and flowers all round. They continue these ceremonies[1] until night-fall, when they depart to go to the King's palace, where they must leave the idol ; they walk in front of it in ranks of eight each in good order, with their basins and their lamps lighted. They keep such good time that one does not take one step more than another. The men walk outside on each side of them, and keep putting betel into their mouths, which they are perpetually eating, and also carry their lamp-stands when they require it. The Nayres also who are in love with some of them, continue to speak to them of their proposals, and to wipe the sweat away from their faces, breasts and necks, fanning them with fans, as their hands are incumbered with their burdens. And they must discharge rockets, and explode bombs, and they also carry fire-trees which burn all the time so that this is one of the prettiest sights in the world, " at least during this night march."

And in front of the idol walk many Nayres with bare swords, slashing themselves wheresoever they can, and foaming at the mouth, and shouting so that they seem possessed of devils, and they say indeed that the gods enter into them and cause them to know it. With them come numbers of tumblers and jesters, also the rulers of

---

[1] At Calicut the festival is held at the Tali and Srivalayanād temples. These two temples are particularly revered by the Zamorins. The Srivalayanād deity (Bhagavati) is the family deity of the Zamorins, and the temple is regarded as the family chapel. Tali is also a temple of peculiar sanctity in the heart of Calicut. Srivalayanād is on a hill outside the town, about two miles from Tali. An ancient palace of the Zamorins adjoins the Tali temple, and now forms the premises of the Zamorin's College. At the *pūram* the idol is taken in procession from the Tali temple to the Srivalayanād temple (the " certain temple " of Barbosa's description), where the idol is temporarily housed, and then taken back to Tali.—(T.)

the state and men of high position ruling and regulating the procession ; and so they carry the image with complete order until they reach the King's palace where it breaks up.

One custom of this King of Calicut is that when he is seated, his private attendants stand by him and rub his arms [1] and legs and body, and a page waits on him constantly holding a towel slung over the shoulders full of betel leaves which he gives him to eat, sometimes in a small box, gilt or painted or ornamented in silver, or sometimes in a golden basin. From this the page takes it leaf by leaf, adding a little shell-fish salt (*i.e.*, lime) dissolved in rosewater as an ointment, which he keeps in a little golden box, and in this wise he gives him a leaf with areca-nut, " as I have already fully explained elsewhere, and the virtue of this betel is such that he continues chewing it night and day " (which is a small fruit cut into pieces, all mixed together, which thing makes his mouth red, and his spittle like blood ; and another page stands by holding a large cup, into which he spits out the juice of the leaves, so as not to swallow it, and frequently washes his mouth, so that he always continues chewing the leaf).

And the custom as to his eating [2] is this : no one must be

---

[1] *Rub his arms.* The duty of performing these offices for the Zamorin is hereditary and still attaches to certain Nāyar families. There are also families with the title of Panikkars whose duties (Vayarāttam) are kept shrouded in the greatest secrecy, the members of the family being sworn not to reveal them. It would be improper to violate this secrecy. But with regard to the privacy of the Zamorin's meals, as described by Barbosa, it may be mentioned that the deity at Srīvalayanād (*i.e.*, the family deity of the Zamorins) is a Sakti. Though the lurid description of Sakti-puja given in Dubois, *Hindu Manners, Customs and Ceremonies*, pp. 286 *sqq.*, is certainly untrue of modern Sakti worship in Malabar, it is the case that a feature of it is the taking of alcoholic liquor and other forbidden fare.—(T.)

[2] Barbosa's description of the Zamorin's ordinary rice meal is, excepting the appurtenances of state, an accurate description of any decent Malayali's mode of eating and drinking. The plate is, however, ordinarily a plantain leaf, round the edges of which are placed (not in saucers) the various condiments.—(T.)

present while he is eating, nor must see him eat, saving only four or five servants who wait on him. Before eating he bathes in a very clean and large tank inside the palace, where he performs his observances quite naked, worshipping thrice towards the east wind, walking round and dipping thrice under the water, then he attires himself in fresh garments, clean and washed, and he proceeds to seat himself in a house which is cleared for his meals, which is plastered, and a round board placed on the ground for his food, because they eat on the ground ; there they bring him a large silver dish without raised edges on which are little silver saucers, all empty, this is set out on another board on the ground, like that at which he sits, all the saucers being arranged in order round the edge of the dish ; then enters the cook, who is a Bramene, bringing in a pot of boiled rice, and places some of this with a spoon in the middle of the dish, and it comes in so whole and dry that you would say it had never been boiled ; and after the rice they bring in many other pots and dishes which they empty, each one into its own proper saucer. Thus he begins to eat with the right hand, filling his hand full of rice without a spoon, and in the same way he takes the other viands mixing them with the rice. He takes no food with his left hand. Then they place before him a silver ewer filled with water, and when he wishes to drink he takes this in his left hand, and raising it into the air lets the water flow from above into his mouth without its touching the ewer. All the food which he eats, whether of flesh or fish or vegetable, or other viands is flavoured with so much pepper that no man from our countries would be able to eat it. And when he cleans his hands he makes no use of a napkin or any other cloth, and when he finishes his meal, he washes himself. And if when he is about to eat there happen to be present any Bramenes of distinction, his private attendants, he commands them to eat on the ground a little way back from himself, and they place before them some leaves of the Indian fig (*i.e.*, the banana) which are always broad and stiff, on which he orders their food to be placed in the same way as it is set before himself. If they do not wish to eat, they go out, for no man must stay there while the King eats, those who stay must eat saving only two or three servitors, as I have already said. When his meal is finished, he returns to his dais where he again begins to chew betel.

When the King goes forth to amuse himself, or to perform his orisons before some idol, all the Nayres who are near by are summoned to accompany him, and the officers of state [1] and the Pagans ; and the King comes forth in his litter [2] borne by two men, which is lined with silken cushions. And the litter is of silk, and is slung on a bamboo pole covered with precious stones ; " it is as thick as the arm of a fat man, and they carry him with certain turns and steps to which they are trained from their birth." These two men raise the bamboo on their shoulders from which the aforesaid litter hangs.

[The King[3] carries an infinite number of golden crowns], " and precious stones, and on his right foot

---

[1] *Menistros* in the Portuguese text, probably *ministros* should be read. Stanley, however, translates " minstrels " ; and Ramusio, *sanatori*, " musicians." The plural of *menestrel,* " a minstrel," is *menestreis.* On the whole, the interpretation " Officers of State " seems preferable.

[2] *Litter.* There are two forms of litter in use in Malabar, (1) the *doly,* a sort of sedan chair, only used by notables: and (2) the *manjal,* a hammock slung on a pole. I take the *doly* to be a comparatively modern vehicle ; the word is from the Hindustani. Barbosa is certainly describing the *manjal.* The *manjal*-bearers hum and grunt in a curious antiphonic manner ; the weight of the pole is considerable, and the short jog-trot paces of the bearers are no doubt the result of training.—(T.)

[3] This passage is marked in the Portuguese text as borrowed from Ramusio, but cannot be found in the Italian text.

a very rich and heavy anklet. Many instruments of metal are played before him, and many Nayre archers with bows and arrows like those of the English, and others with long spears with heads an ell in length, and metal rings on their butt-ends." "They brandish them as they go, and other Nayre bucklermen also go with him with drawn swords in their hands, and they have other rings on the hilts thereof with which they make great disturbances, and as they go they shout one to the other in a loud voice in their own tongue, ' Go on ! ' ' Go on ! ' " Some of them fence with one another as they go in front of the King, and clear a space so that he may see them. They are very active, and great masters of the art of fencing, which art they hold in higher esteem than we hold that of horsemanship.

The king often halts to let them continue their play at his pleasure, praising and commending those who do best. In front of him the King takes a page [1] who carries his sword and shield, another who bears a golden sword of state, and yet another the sword which belonged to that King who ruled over the whole of Malabar and who became a Moor, [and departed to go and remain at Meca, which they keep as a relic]. And in his left hand he carries [a weapon which is like unto] a flower-de-luce. [2]

And on each side he has with him two men, one carrying a large round fan, and the other a fan made from the white tail [3] of an animal like a horse, which among them is much esteemed, fixed on a golden staff.

---

[1] In Ramusio and the Spanish version a Bramin.

[2] Probably this was a lotus-bud.

[3] This is the *chowrie* or " whisk," made of the tail of the yak, which is still much sought after in India. They have been in use from time immemorial, and may be found represented in early Buddhist sculptures from 150 B.C. (See *Hobson-Jobson, s.v. Chowry.*)

These men continue to fan him, two on one side, and two on the other ; and on his right hand walks a page bearing a golden ewer full of water, and on his left another with one of silver, and yet another with a towel, and when the King wishes to put his hand to his nose or eyes or mouth, they pour some water from the ewer on his fingers, and the other hands him the towel which he carries, to wipe himself. Other pages also accompany him, of whom one on his right side bears a golden cup, and one on his left side a silvern cup into which he spits . out the betel he is always chewing " which another page continues to hand to him."

" Behind him they bear two large round water-pots, one of silver on the left, and one of gold on the right, full of water. Further in front of him go four parasols [1] on their staves, that is to say, two of very fine white cloth, and two of worked and embroidered silk. Near him they carry an umbrella on a high support which keeps off the sun."

Behind the King walk his nephews and the Governors of the country and the Officers all on foot and all bearing drawn swords and bucklers, and thus they proceed in good order with extreme slowness, looking at the games and the jesters, tumblers, and musqueteers who entertain them. If the King goes forth by night he goes in the same manner, but he takes with him four large iron lamp-stands, with branches, like our cressets (*fogareos*) full of oil, with very thick wicks ; two go in front, and two behind, [and there are many torches of wood which burn a long time].

In the City of Calecut itself the King maintains a

---

[1] The word here used is *esparavel*, which apparently refers to a smaller and lighter umbrella than that mentioned just below, the *sombreiro de pee*, for which see Vol. I, p. 206, n. 1.

Governor who bears the name of Talixe,[1] a Nayre who holds jurisdiction over five thousand Nayres, to whom he pays the very large revenues assigned to him. He possesses the right of administering justice, but not to such an extent as to free him from rendering an account thereof to the King. And as there are many castes among the folk, so also do their rules vary, whereof I will speak further on ; and of those who belong to the Biabares at the bottom, for they say that they are the slaves of the King, and of the Nayres, and of the Lords. If any of these low persons commit any crime or theft, or if any person against who it is committed complain to the said Governor, he sends to arrest him, and if he confesses or is taken in *flagrante delicto*, if he is a heathen, they carry him to a spot where justice is executed, where are many high sharp stakes [2] and a small platform through which they pass the point of the stake. There they behead him with a sword, and then impale him on the stake between the shoulder blades, making it pass out through the belly, and project a cubit or more beyond it, and his head is put on another

---

[1] *Talixe.* This is the Kozhikkot Talachannavar, *i.e.*, the Calicut Talachan (*avar* is an honorific interpretation), mention of whom I have found in a ballad as being one of the Zamorin's ministers. The title also appears in the Keraḷolpatti as Talachaṇṇa Nāyar. According to Barbosa's description he was the Governor of Calicut.—(T.)
   This word is given by Ramusio as Talassen, and in the Spanish version as Talaxe.

[2] *Sharp stakes.* A description of impalement on the Kazhu, a recognised form of execution. Barbosa's account of the administration of justice agrees very closely with that in the report of the Joint Commissioners deputed to Malabar (1793). The rebel Pychy Raja employed the Kazhu as late as 1795 (*Mal. Gaz.*, p. 363). The ordeal of the boiling oil was common. In the diary of the Tellicherry factory for May 6th, 1728, there is an entry of an agreement with the Zamorin, "a grant that any Malabare having accounts with us must put his hand in oil to prove the verity thereof, given anno 1710 " (*Mal. Gaz.*, 363).
   To the modern mind the scales of justice in the ordeal seem to have been heavily weighted against the accused, however innocent.—(T.)

stake,[1] [and they tie ropes to his legs and arms, and
fasten them to four posts, so that the limbs are stretched
out, and the body on its back on the stand.—Spanish
version]. And if the evildoer is a Moor, they take him to a
wide open space and there slay him with sword cuts. The
stolen goods are kept with the Governor of the country,
the owner has no profit thereof, for the law having
done justice on the culprit the owner forfeits his goods.
But if the goods are found and the thief takes to flight,
the stolen property remains for certain days in the
Governor's hands, and if in that time they do not catch
the thief, they give back the goods to their owner. Yet
a fourth part of their value is kept by the Governor.
And if the thief denies his guilt and the goods are not
found on him, they take him to a lock-up like ours
and keep him there imprisoned for nine or ten days,
to see if he confesses, where he is badly fed, and very
evilly entreated. And if by the end of that period he
has not confessed then they call upon the accuser and
tell him that as the thief will not confess, he must say
whether he is to be sworn, or whether they shall release
him. And if he says that the thief is to be sworn they
bring him there in bonds, and tell him that he is to fast
and bathe well and commend himself to his god, and
that he must not chew betel, and must clean his teeth
of it in order to take the oath the next day. If he
does so, they bring him out of the prison next day, and
take him to a tank where he bathes well with many

---

[1] Ramusio's version differs somewhat from that in the text. He
says, " Gli tagliano la testa, ma se' l delitto e atroce e che meriti
maggior punitione, sopra un palo alto appuntato, gl' inspiedano il
corpo per mezzo le spalle, si che la punta gli esce fuori un braccio
dello stomaco, & a questo modo lo fanno morire "—that is to say,
death by beheading was the punishment for ordinary offences, and
death by impalement for the more atrocious crimes. The Spanish
version corresponds with the Portuguese.

ceremonies ; then they carry him to a house of prayer, and there he takes his oath on this wise :

If he is a heathen, they heat a copper pot full of oil until it boils (and that they may know when it is very hot they throw into it some leaves of a certain tree, and the oil makes them spring up) and when they see that it is so, two clerks take the evil-doer's right hand, and first looking to see if there is any wound on it or anything else, and the whole state of the said hand, they write it down and show it to him alone ; and this examination made, they order him to look upon his idol which is before him and to say three times, " I did not commit the theft of which this man accuses me, nor know I who committed it." Then they order him to put two fingers of the said hand into the boiling oil up to the knuckles, and he at once continues to say that he did not do it, and that he will not be burnt. "And when he puts in his hand and draws it out, the clerks standing by again look at it, and the Governor does the same, and after all these trials they attest the condition in which the hand is, and tie it up well in a cloth to know whether it is burnt or not. Then they take him back to prison, and thence bring him again after three days to the same place. Then clerks unbind the hand in the Governor's presence, and if they find it burnt he suffers in the manner aforesaid, and they inflict great tortures upon him to force him to confess where he is keeping the stolen goods or what he has done with them, and if he does not confess yet he is still punished. But if they find his hand whole they free him completely and either slay his accuser or make him pay a fine in money, or banish him. In the same manner they punish him who has slain another, or who has slain a cow, or laid violent hands on a Bramene or Nayre, or has had dealings with a Bramene's wife."

" To Moors they give the oath thus, they make them lick with the tongue a red-hot axe, and if it is burnt, they take him to an open space as I have said above, and there slay him with the edge of the sword."

" And if this Governor finds any youths or young men who are vagrant, and have no employ, nor father, nor mother, nor master with whom they dwell, these are forfeit to him, and he sells them as slaves to the Moors, or to any person whatsoever who is willing to purchase them, at a very low price from three to five cruzados each, whether men or women."

" And as to the Nayres who are privileged persons, as I shall relate below, justice is done to them on this wise : No Nayre may be imprisoned or fettered for anything he may do ; if a Nayre slays another, or steals, or kills a cow, or sleeps with a woman of low degree, or eats or drinks in the house of a low-caste man,[1] or sleeps with a Bramene's wife, or openly speaks ill of the King, and a complaint is made to the Governor against him who has committed such a crime, he sends to summon him, and if he does not come he summons three or four Nayres, stout men in their persons, and gives them a warrant (alvara)[2] signed with his own hand, in which he tells them to slay such and such a Nayre wheresoever they may find him, for such is his will. These then go in search of him and slay him wheresoever they find him with spear thrusts or arrows, for some of them are such that if they have warning, they will wound three or four before they are killed, and thus they slay him even if they light upon him in the city. When he is killed they lay him with his breast upwards, and upon it they place

---

[1] The word used in the text is *vilam* (villão in modern spelling) corresponding to the English *villain* in its ancient sense.

[2] *Alvara.* This word denotes a Royal Warrant or Commission from the Arabic *al-barât.* The Spanish form is *albala.*

the warrant, and there they leave him, and no man is so bold as to touch him, and the fowls of the air and the jackals [1] devour him. If they slay him within the city the dwellers in that street where he lies may not remove him thence unless they first ask for the King's order, and this order the King gives sometimes for money and sometimes by favour. But if such a Nayre has committed a great theft of property, belonging to the King, then they put him into a room very well closed and guarded, so that he may not escape, and then put him to the oath in the manner I have already described, save that in place of oil they heat butter and if they find him guilty they convey him to an open spot, and there slay him with sword cuts and spear thrusts."

"When the Governor summons the accused they summon at the same time the complainant, and when they are both there together they call on him to say all that he knows regarding the other. Then the complainant takes in his hand a small bunch of green grasses or a branch of a tree and says, ' So and so did such and such a thing.' Then the accused takés another like branch and says, ' I did not such and such a thing.' Then the Governor orders that two coins of base gold called fanams [2] shall be set before each of them, each of which is worth two and twenty *reis*, and when they have examined them the Governor tells them to return after eight days to establish clearly what each one has said. Then eight days past, they return to the Governor's house, and

---

[1] *Adibe.* This term for jackal was no doubt borrowed from the Moors of Morocco. The Arabic form is *dhib* or with the article *adh-dhib.* See Dalgado, *Gloss. Luso-Asiatico, s.v. Adibe, Adive,* for Portuguese use of the word. The above passage is the earliest in date. It is used in French in the form *adive* by Dellon (*Voyages,* Ed. 1711, pp. 222, 241).

[2] Fanões, pl. of *fanam* or *fanáo.*

thence they go to the temple to take the oath as I have told above." [1]

In this Kingdom of Calecut there is a Governor who resembles a Chief Justice, who is called *Contante Carnaxee* [2] who has his appointed deputies in every town. To him is allotted the execution of justice in all cases not liable to the penalty of death, for all other penalties are paid in money. To him they haste with every manner of plaints and wrongs, as to which he must give an account and explanation to the King, and he executes justice on the guilty in like manner to the Governor of Calecut. In this Kingdom no woman of what rank soever she may be suffers death by the law, but on evil-doers they inflict fines in money or banishment. If any woman who is a *Nayre* [3] by caste offends against the law of her caste, and the King knows thereof before it is known to her brethren and relations, he orders her to be taken and sold out of the Kingdom to the Moors or Christians, but if the brethren or kinsfolk know of it first they slay her

---

[1] In Ramusio's version a considerable part of the above narrative is missing, and at this point he makes the remark *qui mancano molte righe* " here many lines are missing." But the missing part is actually that marked here on p. 45. This is found in the Spanish version but is not so full as in the Portuguese text.

[2] *Contante Carnaxee.* As the Talachan was the Governor of Calicut, so the official here named had jurisdiction throughout the Zamorin's kingdom outside Calicut. The Spanish reading is *Coytoro tical Carnaver.* The last word is obviously Kārnavan. This nowadays ordinarily means the head (or any senior member) of a family. That it was formerly also used in the sense of Governor or Chieftain is clear from parallels in the Keralolpatti. The rest of the title cannot be reconstructed with certainty, but " coytoro " seems to be probably Kōyittara (*i.e.*, the dais—*tara*—of the palace—*kōyil*).—(T.)

[3] *Woman who is a Nayre.* The Zamorin still exercises caste authority by appointing tribunals to enquire into unorthodox conduct on the part of both Nambūdiris and Nāyars. For a description of this kind of tribunal (*smārta vichāram*) vide *Mal. Gaz.*, pp. 364, 365. There is an institution in North Malabar in which outcaste Nambūdiri women are received (T.). Dellon gives an instance of the sale of a Brahman woman to a Portuguese after her condemnation (*Voyages.* Ed. 1711, p. 261).

with swords and spears, for they hold that if they do not so, they suffer great dishonour, and the King does not act against them on this account as it is in accord with their caste and custom.

" There is also in this same Kingdom of Calecut a caste of people called *Bramenes*[1] who are priests among them (as are the clergy among us)[2] of whom I have spoken in another place."[3] These all speak the same tongue, nor can any be a Bramene except he be the son of a

---

[1] *The Brahmans* though strictly speaking the highest caste are here placed by Barbosa after the Kings or ruling families whom he no doubt considered to be entitled by their position to the first state, for to a European of that period it must have been unimaginable that a " King " should be of lower rank than a subject. The Brahmans alluded to are no doubt of the Nambūtiri section (called by *Mal. Gaz.*, Nambūdiri ; in *Cochin Tribes and Castes*, Nambuthiri ; by K. M. Panikkar, " Nampudiri " ; and by Buchanan, " Namburi ") who are very influential, and own a great extent of land. They are very exclusive, and all castes except the Nāyars pollute them without touch at varying distances, and even the Nāyars pollute them by touch. They have a privileged position with the ruling or so-called Kshatriya families as they are the favoured class among these and among all Nāyar women for the *sambandham* or actual marriage. It may be doubted whether the Nambūtiri men regard these connections as true marriage, but, as regards the majority it is the only form of marriage open to them. Only the eldest son in a Nambūtiri family marries within his own caste according to orthodox Hindu rites. All the rest are barred from such unions and have no other resource but to contract *sambandhams* with Nāyar women by whom they are gladly received, as they are subject to the rule of hypergamy and can only marry in their own or a higher caste while the men may find brides in a caste or section lower than their own. Any connection of a woman with a man of a lower status than her own is severely punished (Buchanan, II, 424 ff. ; Thurston, V, 152 ff. ; *Mal. Gaz.*, 104 ; *Cochin Tribes and Castes*, II, 169 ff.).

[2] *Bramenes, i.e.,* Nambūtiris (abbrev. Nambūri). The only other classes of Brahman proper in Malabar are those of the Pattars, immigrants from the Tamil country, settled mostly in the neighbourhood of Palghat, and the Embrāntiris, who have come in from the Tulu country. These Barbosa does not mention. The Nambūtiri is still a power in the land, owing partly to his spiritual ascendancy, and partly to his position as owner of much of the soil of Malabar. They are as a class orthodox and conservative, and wield a powerful conservative (or, as a reformer might say, reactionary) influence over the Tamburāns and high class Nāyars with whom they are associated. In most Tamburān families, the *tali-tier* is a Kshatriya Tamburān, *e.g.*, a member of the Beypore Raja's family. In some he is a Nambūtiri, but this is the exception rather than the rule. Barbosa (page 41) makes the *tali-tier* a Tamburān, and not a Nambūtiri.

[3] *E.G.* in *Gujarat*, Vol. I, p. 114.

C

Bramene. When they are seven years of age they put over their shoulder a strip [1] of two fingers in breadth of untanned skin with the hair on it of a certain wild beast which they call *Cryvamergam*, which resembles a wild ass. Then for seven years he must not eat betel for which time he continues to wear this strap. When he is fourteen years old [2] they make him a Bramene, and taking off the leather strap they invest him with the cord of three strands which he wears for the rest of his life as a token that he is a Bramene. And this they do with great ceremonial and rejoicings, as we do here for a cleric when he sings his first mass. Thereafter he may eat betel, but not flesh or fish. They have great honour among the Indians, and as I have already said, they suffer death for no cause whatsoever, their own headman gives them a mild chastisement. They marry once only in our manner, and only the eldest son marries,[3] he is

---

[1] *Strip.* This is the *Upanayanam*, or investiture with the thread as a sign of entering on the stage of life known as Brahmāchāryam. It is a peculiarity of the Nambūdiris that they invest boys, not with the ordinary thread, but with a strip of the skin of the black buck, as stated by Barbosa. For an account of the ceremony, *vide* Thurston, *Tribes and Castes*, Vol. V, p. 236. For *cryvamergam* we should probably read *crysnamergam*, i.e. *Krishnamrigam* or Krishna's antelope. The Brahmāchāryam of the South Malabar Nambūdiri is ordinarily spent at the Othummar matham (*i.e.*, hostel of the Veda-reciters) at Tirunnāvāya. This is maintained by the Zamorin for ten months in the year, and by the Vādhyān Nambūdiri for the remaining two months. The Vādhyān Nambūdiri is the instructor of the youths ; and there is an annual competition in proficiency in the Vedas between these young Nambūdiris (who belong to the Tirunnāvāya Yogam) and those of the Trichur Yogam who get their tuition at Trichur in Cochin state, where there is a similar institution.—(T.)

[2] *Fourteen years old, i.e.*, the *samāvarttanam*, which terminates the tuition period (Brahmāchāryam). The Nambudiri boy nowadays often continues his tuition period to the age of 16 or 18.

[3] *Only the eldest son marries.* This is correct. But the eldest son may, if he so desires, pass on the duty to a junior. Barbosa represents the married Nambūdiri as a monogamist. This is not nowadays the case. Polygamy is allowed ; and in fact many a Nambūdiri of poor family marries several Nambūdiri girls, in order to repair the family fortunes by the handsome dowries which Nambūdiri brides bring with them. I know of one case in which this laudable aim was

treated like the head of an entailed estate. The other
brothers remain single all their lives. These Bramenes
keep their wives well guarded, and greatly honoured, so
that no other men may sleep with them ; if any of them
die, they do not marry again, but if a woman wrongs
her husband she is slain by poison. The brothers who
remain bachelors sleep with the Nayre women,[1] they
hold it to be a great honour, and as they are Bramenes
no woman refuses herself to them, yet they may not
sleep with any woman older than themselves. They
dwell in their own houses and cities, and serve as clergy[2]
in the houses of worship, whither they go to pray at
certain hours of the day, performing their rituals and
idolatries. Their houses[3] have their principal doors

---

signally defeated. An indigent Nambūdiri married four Nambūdiri
girls, but his children by them were girls only—six or seven in number.
Thus his temporary gains by the dowries were more than discounted
by the necessity of providing *dots* for all his daughters if he wished
to marry them off.

Many a Nambūdiri, having done his duty by taking a Nambūdiri
spouse, finds it necessary for his pleasure to form sambandhams with
Nayar women. This conjugal laxity is not very favourably regarded
nowadays, and in fact there is a revolt on the part of advanced middle
class opinion against the whole system of hypergamy. There are
educated Nāyar girls who would rather remain single than form sambandhams with Nambūdiris whose lack of refinement they despise.—(T.)

[1] *Sleep with the Nāyar women.* The Spanish version " Sleep with the
wives of the nobles " is incorrect.

[2] *Clergy.* The highest offices in temples are filled by Nambūdiris,
The *Tāntri, i.e.,* supreme ecclesiastical authority of a temple, is always
a Nambūdiri. So are the *Sāntis,* at any rate in temples of repute.
though in minor temples they may be Embrāndiris (Tulu Brahmans)
or Pattars. There are also dignitaries, like the Azhuvānchēri Tambrākkal, the Tirunnavāya Vādhyān and the Cherumukku Vaidikan,
who wield spiritual authority over certain areas, and have particular
functions at the ceremonies in the families of Rajas.—(T.)

[3] The houses, *i.e.,* the " houses of prayer " or temples are here
described. The main gate is incorrectly said to face the west. Mr.
Thorne says that both houses and temples should face the east. The same
mistake is found in both the Spanish version and Ramusio. It would
seem probable therefore that the word *ponente,* " west," was employed
in the original MS. The passage from Ramusio is as follows : " Le dette
case hanno la porta principal verso ponente, and due altre, una per
banda, innanzi la principal di fuori vi è una pietra d'altezza d'un
huomo, &c." That is : " These said houses have the principal gate
to the west, and two others, one at the side ; and in front of the principal

facing the west, like ours, and every house has three doors in front of the principal door. Without the church is a stone of the height of a man,[1] with three steps round it, and facing it is a small chapel in the midst of the church, very dark inside, and in this is an idol of gold, silver, or metal where three oil lamps burn perpetually : there none may enter except its own minister who goes in thither with many flowers and sweet-smelling grasses and rosewater. This he takes out once in the morning, and again in the afternoon. He goes in after bathing, and brings it out on his head, facing backwards, and they accompany him with a great procession, playing many instruments of music. Some wives of Bramenes[2] walk in front with lighted lamps, and each time that they reach the principal door they place the lamp on that stone and worship it with many ceremonies ; then turning round three times towards the church, they return in the same order into the chapel. This house of worship is surrounded by a wall inside which they go in procession, and as they walk in it they carry to it a state umbrella.

---

gate outside is a stone as high as a man, etc." The words "one at the side" do not occur either in our text or in the Spanish version. They seem to be correct, as Mr. Thorne says that in addition to the main gate there is a smaller one at the back and an entrance also on the northern side. The Portuguese text should evidently be corrected by the transfer of the colon, and should read " every house has three doors : In front of the principal door without the church is a stone the height of a man, etc."

[1] *Stone of the height of a man.* This is the Mandapam, a stone platform with a tiled canopy, in front of the Sri-Kôvil but within the four walls of the temple enclosure. Only Brahmans may use the Mandapam, on which prayers are said by worshippers. The " small chapel " is the Sri-Kôvil, in which the idol is kept. The door is kept open so that the image is visible, but only the officiating Brahmans (Sāntis) can enter. They perform the toilet of the deity daily, washing, anointing and garlanding the image. Twice a day (as described by Barbosa) the deity—not the image itself, but a smaller idol called Tidambu—is taken in procession (*pradakshinam*) round the temple, preferably on the back of an elephant.—(T.)

[2] *Some wives of Bramenes.* This is known as Dīksha. Dīksha is also observed, both by Nambūdiris and lower castes, during periods of mourning.

This stone which stands by the door on which they place their offerings is washed thrice every day, and on it they feed the crows with boiled rice, as a ritual, twice a day. These Bramenes hold the number three in great reverence ; they hold that there is a God in three persons, who is not more than one ; their prayers are all ceremonials, they honour the Trinity and would as it were desire to depict it. The name which they give it is Bermabesma Maceru,[1] who are three persons and only one God, whom they confess to have been since the beginning of the world. They have no knowledge nor information concerning the life of our Lord Jesus Christ. They believe and respect many truths, yet do not tell them truly.

These men always put on their foreheads after bathing certain marks made with ashes, as a sign that of these they are made. They order their dead bodies to be burnt.

When the wives of these men are with child, and the husband knows it, he cleans his teeth and chews no more betel, nor trims his beard, and fasts until his wife is delivered. Some of these Bramenes serve the Kings in every manner except in arms. No man may prepare any food for the King except a Bramene or his own kin ; they also serve as couriers to other countries with letters, money or merchandise, passing wherever they wish to go in safety, and none does them any ill, even when the Kings are at war. These Bramenes are learned in their idolatry, and possess many books thereof. The Kings hold them in high esteem.

---

[1] These words represent the Sanskrit *Brahma Vishnu Mahêśvara*, the three gods who are combined into the Trimūrtti, or three-fold god of Hinduism, represented in sculpture by the three heads on one body. Mahêśvara is one of the names of Śiva. (See Vol. I, p. 115, n. 1.)

"I have already spoken many times of the Nayres,[1] and yet I have not hitherto told you what manner of men they are. You are to know then that " in this land of Malabar there is another caste of people called Nayres, and among them are noblemen who have no other duty than to serve in war,[2] and they always carry their arms whithersoever they go, some swords and shields, others bows and arrows, and yet others spears.

---

[1] The *Nayres* or *Náyars* have already been frequently mentioned, and Barbosa here begins a systematic account of this interesting caste and its customs, which form the principal feature in the peculiar caste system of Malabar. This system differs greatly from those prevalent elsewhere, and attempts to explain it have suffered much from efforts to fit it to the Procrustean bed of orthodox Hinduism as set forth in the so-called Code of Manu, which was never a real code, and never did, and does not now correspond to the facts in any part of India. As a result of this treatment the Náyars, the hereditary aristocracy and land-owning class of Malabar, are classed as Súdras, whereas their real analogy is with the Kshatriyas of ancient, and the Rájputs of modern, days. Some of the principal families have obtained a sort of grudging recognition that they are Kshatriyas, whereas they are in reality of the same class as the rest of the Náyars, and neither more nor less Kshatriyas than they. The status of the Náyars is in itself as good as that of any caste in India, and they gain nothing by attempting to identify themselves with long-lost tribes of Northern India with which they have nothing in common. The most interesting of the accounts of this caste or tribe which have appeared lately is that by Mr. K. M. Panikkar, himself a member of the caste (" Some Aspects of Náyar Life," *J. R. Anthropological Inst.*, 1918). The accuracy of Barbosa's description may be tested by reference to this account. His account of the *Kalaris* or Military Academies, which still exist, although shorn of their former importance, fully corroborates that on pp. 39, 40 of the text. Another close correspondence of Barbosa's observations with modern practice is shown by Mr. Panikkar's statement that " a Náyar young man or woman may not talk to relations of opposite sex in the same family if they are almost of the same age."

The origin of the name Náyar is doubtful. The explanation usually accepted identifies it with Náyak, or Naik, from the Skr. *Náyaka*, " a leader." Another derivation is from *Nága*, " a snake, or man of serpent descent," and some possibility is lent to this by the fact— vouched for by Mr. Panikkar—that every Náyar family still holds the serpent sacred. It is possible that the Naga was at one time the totem of the tribe. See Thurston, Vol. IV, 291ff. ; *Cochin Tribes and Castes*, Vol. II, 1 ; Panikkar, p. 290. None of these derivations can be accepted as satisfactory.

[2] *Serve in war*. The Náyar in the present war has shown that long disuse of martial practice has not emasculated the caste. Malabar has been the most fruitful recruiting-ground for the Indian army in the Madras Presidency during the war, and a great proportion of the recruits have been Náyars.—(T.)

They all live with the King, and the other great Lords ; nevertheless all receive stipends from the King or from the great Lords with who they dwell. None may become a Nayre, save only he who is of Nayre lineage. They are very free from stain in their nobility. They will not touch anyone of low caste, nor eat nor drink save in the house of a Nayre. They are bound to the service of the King or of their Lords, and guard them well, bearing their arms before them by day and night. They give little heed to what they eat and drink, but only to serve and to do their duty, thus ofttimes they will sleep on a bench without any covering, to protect him who gives them their food. They spend little money, and the most of them get no more than two hundred *reis* a month each, for himself and boy.

" The more part[1] of these Nayres when they are seven years of age are sent to schools[2] where they are taught many tricks of nimbleness and dexterity; there they teach them to dance and turn about and to twist on the ground, to take royal leaps, and other leaps, and this they learn twice a day as long as they are children, and they become so loose-jointed and supple that they make them turn their bodies contrary to nature ; and when they

---

[1] The passage from Johnston's Relations of the Most Famous Kingdom of the World (1611), quoted in Thurston, Vol. V, p. 285, would seem to have been borrowed from this part of Barbosa's account, no doubt from Ramusio's version of it (fol. 307 v.) (wrongly printed 308 in ed. 1563).

The passage which begins at this point up to p. 45, l. 2, is here missing in Ramusio. It is found in the Spanish version, though not so fully as here. The passage omitted does not end (as stated in p. 119, note 2, of the Spanish version) at the point marked on that page, but extends to p. 120, l. 14. Ramusio's note, " Here several lines are wanting," does not refer to this passage. See above (p. 32, n. 1).

Ramusio, however, brings in the same passage in a shortened form further on in the narrative. See p. 45, n. 2.

[2] *Schools*. The Kalaris. Unfortunately this indigenous system of physical training is now almost defunct. But many Pannikkar families still have the raised Kalaris in their compounds.— (T.)

are fully accomplished in this, they teach them to play with the weapon to which they are most inclined, some with bows and arrows, some with poles to become spearmen, but most with swords and bucklers, which is most used among them, and in this fencing they are ever practising. The masters who teach them are called Panicals,[1] and are much honoured and esteemed among them, especially by their pupils, great and small, who worship them ; and it is the law and custom to bow down before them wherever they meet them, even if the disciple is older than the master. And the Nayre are bound, howsoever old they may be, to go always in the winter (i e., in the rainy season) to take their fencing lessons until they die. Some of the Panicals dwell with the Kings and great Lords, and do not teach, but are captains in war, in which they have great repute. And in this science they take degrees as do learned men among us, and in this way they receive more victuals than those on which the other Nayres live."

These men are not married, their nephews (sisters' sons) are their heirs. The Nayre women of good birth are very independent, and dispose of themselves as they please with Bramenes, and Nayres, but they do not sleep with men of caste lower than their own under pain of death. When they reach the age of twelve years their mothers hold a great ceremony.[2] When a mother

---

[1] *Panical.* This word represents the title Panikkar (derived from *pani*, " work." They kept Kalaris or gymnastic and military schools (Thurston, V, p. 296, *s.v.* Nayar). See also ditto, III, p. 179, as to the Kalari Panikkan, who belonged to the Kaniyan caste.—(T.)

[2] *Great ceremony.* This is the Tāli-kettu Kalyānam (ceremony of *tāli*-tying). Barbosa seems to imply that it took place just after the girl attained puberty. Nowadays it is always performed before puberty. This ceremony is quite distinct from the real marriage and nowadays has no connection with marriage except that the *t li*-tier *may* be the man destined to be the husband of the girl when she is old enough. The origin and significance of this very peculiar custom are discussed

perceives that her daughter has attained that age,
she asks her kinsfolk and friends to make ready to
honour her daughter, then she asks of the kindred and
especially of one particular kinsman or great friend to
marry her daughter ; this he willingly promises, and
then he has a small jewel made, which would contain
a half ducat of gold, long like a ribbon, with a hole
through the middle which comes out on the other side,
strung on a thread of white silk.[1] The mother then
on a fixed day is present with her daughter gaily decked
with many rich jewels, making great rejoicings with
music and singing, and a great assembly of people.
Then the Kinsman or friend comes bringing that jewel,
and going through certain forms, throws it over the
girl's neck. She wears it as a token all the rest of her

at length in the Report of the Malabar Marriage Commission (1894).
From Barbosa's account it appears that the *tali*-tier, if not a kinsman,
actually had intercourse with the girl. This of course is never the
case now, but among some communities there is a mock consummation,
which may or may not denote that the former practice was as Barbosa
describes it.

However much the present-day Nāyar may dislike the fact, there
is ample authority for holding that polyandry, as described by Barbosa,
was once common among Nāyars. It is now extinct as a recognised
custom, except I believe among some Nāyars in Travancore. Among
certain lower castes it is still by no means uncommon for one woman
to be the common wife of several brothers.

At the present day matrimonial connections among Nāyars are
often as permanent as among any European community. The absolute
freedom of divorce by either party remains, however, in theory.
Not a few observers have considered the present-day Nāyar practice
to exhibit all the advantage of a sound monogamous system with
none of the disadvantages of the legal and social bonds which elsewhere bind together couples who would be happier apart. Perhaps
the chief flaw in the system is the conflict between the interests of a
man's Tarwād and those of his children.—(T.)

[1] Ramusio and the Spanish version both say that this ornament was
" a little shorter than the tag of a lace." The ornament alluded to is
the *tali* widely used to the present day as a marriage token in Southern
India. For its use in Nāyar weddings see Thurston, *l.c.* Vol. V.,
pp. 313–332. The *tali* is described here (p. 318) as " a small round
plate of gold about the size of a two-anna bit, with a hole at the
top." Probably Barbosa intended to compare it to a half-cruzado of
gold, a very small coin about the size of a two-anna piece. (See also
K. M. Panikkar, *I.R.A.I.*, 1919, p. 269 ff.)

life, and may then dispose of herself as she will. The man departs without sleeping with her inasmuch as he is her kinsman ; if he is not, he may sleep with her, but is not obliged to do so. Thenceforward the mother goes about searching and asking some young man to take her daughter's virginity ; they must be Nayres, and they regard it among themselves as a disgrace and a foul thing to take a woman's virginity. And when anyone has once slept with her, she is fit for association with men. Then the mother again goes about enquiring among other young Nayres if they wish to support her daughter, and take her as a Mistress so that three or four Nayres agree with her to keep her, and sleep with her, each paying her so much a day ; the more lovers she has the greater is her honour. Each one of them passes a day with her from midday on one day, till midday on the next day and so they continue living quietly without any disturbance nor quarrels among them. If any of them wishes to leave her, he leaves her, and takes another, and she also if she is weary [1] of a man, she tells him to go, and he does so, or makes terms with her. Any children they may have stay with the mother who has to bring them up, for they hold them not to be the children of any man, even if they bear his likeness, and they do not consider them their children, nor are they heirs to their estates, for as I have already stated their heirs are their nephews, sons of their sisters,[2] [which rule whosoever will consider inwardly in his mind will find that it was established with a greater and deeper meaning than the common folk think, for they say that] the Kings of the Nayres

---

[1] For *auorece* read *aborrece*.

[2] The text reads " *sobrinhos e das Mays*," which may be emended to " *sobrinhos filhos d'irmãs*."

instituted it in order that the Nayres[1] should not be

[1] The customs prevailing in Malabar as to marriage and the succession to property attracted the attention of travellers at an early date, and have been very fully dealt with in many works both ancient and modern by travellers, officials and anthropologists, both European and Indian. It is strange, however, that none of the Arab travellers in the Middle Ages who were familiar with Malabar through their trade, and had important settlements there, have left any notice of these remarkable customs. Nicolo de Conti, who travelled to India in the fifteenth century, returning to Venice in 1444, is probably the first traveller in point of time who has left any record of these customs. His account as given in *India in the Fifteenth Century* (II, p. 20), is as follows :— .

"In this district along (*i.e.*, Calicut) the women are allowed to take several husbands, so that some have ten or more. The husbands contribute among themselves to the maintenance of the wife, who lives apart from her husbands. When one visits her he leaves a mark at the door of the house, which being seen by another coming afterwards he goes away without entering. The children are allotted to the husbands at the will of the wife. The inheritance of the father does not descend to the children, but to the grandchildren."

Almost contemporary with him was 'Abdu 'r Razzāk, an envoy from Shāh-Rukh, the son of Timur, who was at Calicut in 1441 A.D. His account will be found also in *India in the Fifteenth Century* (I, p. 17). As to the succession to the throne of the *Sāmari* he says :—

"When he dies it is his sister's son who succeeds him, and his inheritance does not belong to his son, or his brother, or any other of his relations."

He says also :—

"Amongst them is a class of men with whom it is the practice for one woman to have a great number of husbands, each of whom undertakes a special duty, and fulfils it. The hours of the day and of the night are divided between them ; each of them for a certain period takes up his abode in the house, and while he remains there no other is allowed to enter. The *Sameri* belongs to this sect."

At the end of the fifteenth century the Genoese merchant, Hieronimo de Santo Stephano, made a journey to India which appears in Ramusio's Vol. I (1563), and was translated in *India in the Fifteenth Century*. Regarding the customs of Malabar he says :—

"It is lawful for every woman to take seven or eight husbands, according to her desires, nor do the men ever marry a woman who is a virgin ; but before the wedding, she being yet a maiden, they cause her to live for fifteen or twenty days with some man who takes her maidenhood."

João de Barros, in his first *Decade*, published in 1552 (see Book IX, Chapter 3, ff. 180 to 182 of the 1628 edition), gives a fairly full description of the Naires and their marriage customs, which in some respects corresponds with that of Barbosa, and is so close to it that it seems probable that he had seen a MS. of this book. The passages in question are given in full in Appendix I, i, as they have not hitherto been translated.

F. L. de Castanheda, the historian whose work (*Historia do descobrimento e conquista da India pelos Portuguezes*) was published in 1551–61, and who probably had personal knowledge on the subject, makes a statement very close to that of De Barros, beginning with the words, " By the laws of this country these Nayres may not marry."

Caesar Fredericke, whose evidence refers to the year 1563, speaks of the community of wives, and repeats the usual statement about the sword and shield of the visitor being left at the door. His account as given in Hakluyt's *Traffics and Discoveries* (Vol. II, p. 339, 1810 ed. ; Vol. V, p. 394, H.S. ed.) is as follows :—

" These Naires have their wives common among themselves, and when anyone goeth into the house of any of these women he leaveth his sword and target at the doore, and the time that he is there, there dare not any be so hardie as to come into that house. The King's children shall not inherit the Kingdom after their father, but of some other man, therefore they accept for their King one of the sonnes of the King's sisters or of some other woman of the blood roiall."

Barbosa is, however, the first observer who has given a complete account of these customs, and this account is not only fuller but more accurate than any other until modern times. Varthema, who visited the coast in 1510, alludes* indeed to the fact that the King of Calicut was succeeded not by his son but by a sister's son, owing to the " jus primae noctis " being exercised by the Brahmans with regard to the Queen, and also tells a tale about the exchange of wives among noblemen and merchants. He mentions the Nāyars merely as the second rank in the kingdom, and as being noblemen and warriors. He adds below the following, " And amongst other classes of pagans above mentioned (*i.e.*, given in Varthema, p. 141–42) one woman has five, six and seven husbands, and even eight. And one sleeps with her one night, and another another night. And when the woman has children she says it is the child of this husband, or of that husband, and thus the children go according to the word of the woman."

Linschoten (H.S. ed. I, 277 ff.) also gives an account very like that from De Barros but inferior in accuracy. He probably had access to the *Decadas*.

Pyrard de Laval, who was in Malabar in 1607, gives a fuller and more accurate account (H.S. ed., I, 384 ff). He says, however, that the " Nairs may have but one wife at the time," which is not correct, while a woman may have three husbands at once, " but a Nair woman of the Brameny race may have one only," which shows a certain confusion between the customs of the Nāyars and of the Nambūdiri Brahmans.

Mandelslo's notice of the custom is cursory and of no particular value (Eng. trans., ed. 1669, p. 88). His voyage to Malabar took place in 1639. Pietro della Valle, who was on the Malabar coast in 1623, mentions the Nāyars, but says nothing of their marriage customs, although he alludes to the succession in the family of the " Samori " going to the children of the King's sisters and not to his sons (Eng. trans., 1665, p. 184).

Thevenot, who was in India in 1666, does not seem to have visited Malabar. His account of the " Naires " must therefore have been derived from others (Eng. trans., ed. 1687, Pt. III, p. 88).

He says " The son inherits not after his father because it cannot be known who is the father of the child " born to any woman. " For succession the child of the sister is preferred." " The sisters (even of the Kings themselves) have liberty to chuse such Nairs or Gentlemen as they please." " When a Nair is in a ladies' chamber he leaves

---

* Italian Text in Ramusio, Vol. I, f. 160 b. and 161, Hak. Soc. Edition, pp. 144-146.

held back from their service by the burden and labour of rearing children.[1]

These men are called Nayres only from the time when they come forth for war, yet they enjoy full liberty in everything. "They receive no wages from the King, until they are armed as knights,[2] chiefly in the Kingdom

his stick or sword at the door that others should know that the place is taken up."

J. Ovington, a chaplain, who published his *Voyage to Suratt in the year* 1689, in 1696, alludes to the Malabar custom on pp. 80–81. After describing a similar custom near the mouth of the Congo, he continues :—

"And thus likewise upon the *Malabar Coast* the first lodging is allowed to the Bramin when the King marries any person ; and therefore the Sister's Sons, as in Africa, and not the King's, are heirs to the Crown, because the Blood Royal runs certainly in their Veins. And the King's Sisters are also indulged here the freedom of bestowing their Virginity on who they please."

Fryer, although he mentions the "Nayres," says nothing about their marriage customs.

More recent writers have written very fully on this subject. The most important in the seventeenth century is Dellon (*Voyages,* Ed. 1711, p. 272), and in the eighteenth century A. Hamilton (*A New Account of the East Indies,* 1727, Vol. I, p. 308). In the early nineteenth century the best account is that of Dr. F. Buchanan (*A Journey through Mysore, Canara and Malabar,* 1807). The latter is very valuable, and his account is probably the fullest and most accurate available, after Barbosa's, until the most recent ethnographical investigations. His account (Vol. II, pp. 346–350, and 411–412) of the history of the Nāyars, and of their marriage customs should be compared with that of our author.

In modern times the subject has been carefully investigated by enquiries on the spot, both British and Indian, and by anthropologists, who have used the history of Malabar customs to illustrate their theories on the early history of marriage. Of the former class, Mr. E. Thurston's exhaustive articles in his *Castes and Tribes of South India,* 1907, and his *Ethnographic Notes in Southern India,* are the most important. The full account in Chapter III of the *Malabar Gazetteer,* written by Mr. Loftus-Tottenham, is also excellent. Mr. Anantha Krishna Iyer's *Cochin Tribes and Castes* and *Cochin Census Report,* 1901, and Mr. V. Nagam Aiyar's *Travancore State Manual,* 1906, should also be referred to, as well as an excellent paper by Mr. K. M. Panikkar, himself a Nāyar ("Some Aspects of Nāyar Life," *Journal of the Royal Anthropological Institute,* 1919).

Of the anthropologists who deal with these customs as part of a larger subject it is sufficient to refer to J. F. Maclennan's *Primitive Marriage* (1876), pp. 147 ff. ; Mr. E. S. Hartland's *Primitive Paternity,* Vol. I, 266 ff., Vol. II, 41, n. ; Sir H. Risley's *People of India,* 2nd ed., 1915, p. 210 f.

[1] Spanish version "should not be covetous and should not abandon the King's service."

[2] Here Ramusio inserts the passage omitted above. (See p. 39, n. 1.) So also in the Spanish version.

of Cananor, where it is the custom that many are knighted by the King with his own hand. The youth who wishes to become a knight, calls together those of his kinsmen who are already knights, that they may come to do him honour, and thus many join them to him, and take him honourably to the palace, having had a time appointed[1] for this by the King. When he is come to the King's palace he commands him to enter with as many as are with him, whereupon he lays before the King on a leaf three small coins, which they call *fanões* (*fanams*) (whereof each one is worth two and twenty *reis*, as I have already said elsewhere). The King then asks him if he will maintain the customs and rules of the other Nayres, and he and his kinsmen respond ' Yes.' Then the King commands him to gird on his right side a sword with a red sheath, and when it is girt on he causes him to approach near to himself and lays his right hand on his head, saying therewith certain words which none may hear, seemingly a prayer, and then embraces him saying ' *Paje Gubramarca*,'[2] that is to say ' Protect cows and Bramenes ' ; " and when this ceremony is ended, a writer attends " who forthwith asks him in the King's presence in a high voice, so that all may hear, to declare his name and lineage, and they all repeat it that it may be yet more known. Then the scribe enters it thus in the pay-book, that he may draw thence his first stipend. His kinsmen then lead him with great respect to the house of the *Panical* who taught him, before whom, on perceiving him, he prostrates himself, and they go through many ceremonies.

---

[1] I take the word *prasme* in the Portuguese text to stand for *praso* or *prazo*, " a time fixed for appearing in a law court," etc.

[2] The word *Gubramarca* is evidently *Go-Brâhmana-cha* " Cows and Brahmans." Mr. Thorne suggests that for *Paje* we should read *Raje* which might stand for the Skr. *rakshaya*, " protect."

Then he springs to his feet. Then they conduct him to his house and give him a banquet in accordance with his quality; and thus he remains for a little while that he may be able to serve the King, go to the wars, or challenge any man at his pleasure. In the Kingdom of Calecut the *Panical* who instructed him, arms him as a Knight in the school with the consent of the King that he may be entitled to serve him and receive his salary. There with great formality they place a naked sword in one of his hands, and a buckler in the other, then they receive from him certain coins and repeat to him the same words as those given above; nevertheless they do not gird on his sword. From the school they conduct him to the King's palace, and then it is ordered that he be appointed on a salary, and at once they put into his hand two fanams as the beginning of the payment of his wages. This they consider a great honour, so much so that all must be armed as Knights before they can live with the King, or take arms to serve anyone soever. Yet the King of Calecut knights with his own hand certain noble persons in the same way as does he of Cananor in order to show them favour and distinction, however these are very few.

" These *Nayres* when they go to the wars fight very valiantly; they take the swords of any enemies whom they slay, and make great endeavours to accomplish this that they may earn great honour. They then take it to the King or Lord with whom they dwell, with great merry-making and rejoicing, accompanied by their kinsfolk and friends, carrying the sword he has taken, in the right hand, and his own in the left, and even if the King is far away from the field of battle they take it, and lay it before him with great joy. The King stands up, and stretching his hand towards the rising sun, he worships it ; then he accepts that sword showing great honour and favour to the Nayre who has brought it and forthwith causes one of his scribes to make an entry of it, and gives the Nayre a golden bracelet,[1] putting it on his arm as a token of honour. Then he receives his dismissal, and the sword they order to be placed in a magazine where are many other such, which are used no more save to serve as a memorial."

When these *Nayres* accept service with the King or with any other person by whom they are to be paid they bind themselves to die for him, and this rule is kept by most of them ; some do not fulfil it, but it is a general obligation. Thus if in any way their Lord is killed, and they are present, they do all they can even unto death ; and if they are 'not at that place, even if they come from their homes they go in search of the slayer or of the King who sent him forth to slay, and how many soever may be their enemies yet everyone of them does his utmost until they kill him (and when he is killed there comes another giving himself to the slaughter, and then yet another, so that sometimes ten or twelve *Nayres* will perish for their Lord). If any is in dread he takes one or two of these *Nayres*, or as many as are daring, to maintain ; to these he gives a certain small fee to protect him and for love of them none dares do him any hurt, for they and all their kindred will take vengeance for any injury done to such an one ;[2] and indeed, for this reason, the King

---

[1] *Golden bracelet.* Presents from Tamburans still ordinarily take this form. The bracelet is called " Vīrachangala."—(T.)

[2] These Guards are called *Sanguada* (Ramusio). This word is *Janguada* in the Spanish, p. 129. This word represents *Mal. changātham* tadbhava of Skr. *Sanghātham* (T.) A full account of the word *jangada* is given in Dalgado's *Glossario* and in his *Contribuições*, p. 138. The Mal. form is given as *changādam* from the Skr. *Sanghatta* union, junction or cohesion. The most usual Port. use of the word is in the sense of two boats lashed together, with a planking laid across

ofttimes refrains from slaying or chastising persons who have offended him who have a guard of *Nayres*, as he is unwilling to be the cause of their death, as, even if they were not present when such an injury was done they would die to avenge it.

These *Nayres* live by themselves outside the town, apart from all others in places girt about by very deep moats. Here they have their palm-groves and tanks : they have no dealings with any other folk, they eat only with *Nayres*. They drink no wine,[1] they do not sleep with women of low caste, all this is forbidden under pain of death.[2] When they walk along a street or road they shout to the low caste folk to get out of their way ; this they do, and if one will not, the Nayre may kill him without punishment ; even if he is a youth of good family but poor and worthless, and he

them, see quotation from Correa, IV, 273, in *Glossario;* also *Hobson-Jobson, s.v.* Jangar, where its identity with the *Sangara* of the *Periplus* is pointed out (Schoff's *Periplus*, p. 46 and note on p. 243, where the illustration shows a double canoe as now used on the Malabar Coast). The application of the word to the Nāyar guards is derived from the idea of the moral bond between the guard and his employer.

[1] This is no longer true. Indulgence in alcoholic liquors may not be respectable, but it is very common among Nāyars. Buchanan speaks of them as " excessively addicted to intoxicating liquors," but Buchanan was somewhat of a Puritan.—(T.)

[2] With this passage may be compared the account given of the present custom by Mr. Fawcett in the Bulletins of the Madras Museum (quoted in Thurston, V, p. 382). "The mere approach anywhere near his vicinity of a Cheruman, a Pulayan, or any inferior being, even a Tiyan, as he walks to his house from the temple, cleansed in body and mind, his marks newly set on his forehead with sandal-wood paste, is pollution, and he must turn and bathe again ere he can enter his house and eat. Buchanan tells us that in his time about a century ago, the man of inferior caste thus approaching a Nayre would be cut down instantly with a sword ; there would be no words. Now that the people of India are inconvenienced with an Arms Act which inhibits sword play of this kind, and with a law system under which high and low are rated alike, the Nāyar has to content himself with an imperious grunt-like shout for the way to be cleared for him as he stalks on unperturbed. His arrogance is not diminished, but he cannot now show it in quite the same way."

Buchanan's full account of the Nāyars of his day, alluded to in the above quotation, will be found in his Vol. II, pp. 408-412.

finds in his way a man of low caste who is rich and respected and in favour with the King, yet he makes him clear the way for him as if he were a King. The *Nayres* are great sticklers for this privilege, and their women do the same to other women. They say that they do this that their blood may not be tainted. If one of these low caste men, by accident or of his own will, touches one of these women her kinsmen slay him forthwith, as well as all his kinsfolk if they can lay their hands on them. If these *Nayres* order any work to be done by low caste men, or buy aught from them, the order is passed from one person to another ; they will not incur another punishment by touching them, for they could not enter their houses without first bathing and exchanging the clothes they wore for other clean clothes, and the women also behave thus. But these dealings must be outside and not in the houses, when they are once inside the towns to some extent, they touch the people more, yet the low caste men have to keep close to the walls and let them pass.

No Nayre woman may go into the towns [1] under pain of death, save once only in the year for which one special night is set apart, when they may walk with their *Nayres* wheresoever they will. On this night more than twenty thousand women, all *Nayres*, go in, for the most part in Calecut. In their honour the dwellers in the City set out many lamps in the streets, and the houses of the principal persons are hung with carpets and decorated with rich fabrics. The Nayre women visit the houses of

---

[1] Nāyar women no longer avoid the towns. The special night is the Tulā Vāvu, New Moon day in the month Tulām (October–November) when Nāyar couples visit the Varakkal Temple, just outside Calicut. Thousands gather there for this festival. This is, of course, the Dīpāvali season, which explains the "lamps in the streets." A brilliant show is still made at Dīpāvali by the illuminated shops of the foreign Hindu merchants.—(T.)

their friends, where they receive many presents and entertainments, they also offer them betel as a compliment, as is their custom (and sugared conserves which they hold it is a great honour to receive from the hands of friends). Some of them go veiled, and some with faces uncovered. The mothers, sisters, and nieces of the King also come to visit the towns, and walk about the whole night looking at them, and also visiting the houses of the chief merchants where they receive rich gifts and offerings because they take great care to sustain these merchants in the friendship and favour of the King.

These *Nayres* after they have been appointed to the King's service never lose their appointments, and even when they are of great age they hold them without diminution as long as they live, some indeed have their pay raised.

If some years pass during which these salaries are not paid four or five hundred of these injured men gather together before the palace gate and these send in a message to the King they are on their way to seek employment with some other Lord or King, because he gives them not the wherewithal to live, whereupon the King sends back to beg them to be patient, and they will soon be satisfied. If he does not forthwith pay them the third part of that which is due to them, promising at the same time to give them the rest soon, then they depart and go to some other King who they think is in need of them, and present themselves before him declaring who they are, and whence and wherefore they come. He entertains them and feeds them for three days without engaging them on salary, and during these days he pays them something every day, sufficient for their honourable maintenance. In this period he sends to enquire from the King whose service they have left, whether he is willing to pay them at once, and if they obtain not this remedy, then they take service with the other King ; this among Kings is a great disgrace and injury to his reputation.

When the Kings go to war they pay all the *Nayres* who serve therein, even though they be in the service of other Lords, their daily wages, that is to say, four *taras* each, every day (which contains five *reis*).[1]

And when they go to the wars they may touch any person soever, even though they be of low caste, and may eat and drink with them in their houses without bathing (as a purification). The King is obliged to maintain the mother and the nephews of *Nayres* who fall in battle,

---

[1] The *tara* is a small silver coin which was in use in the sixteenth century (and up to the beginning of the eighteenth century) on the Malabar coast. Sir Walter Elliot (*Coins of South India*, 1885, p. 57) says that specimens in his possession weighed 1·7 gr. each. Correa (I, 624) compares them to the scale of a sardine. Varthema (1510 H.S. Edition, p. 130) says that 16 cash go to a *tare* and 20 *tare* to a *pardao*, but in the Italian version in Ramusio, Vol. I (1563 Ed., f. 159b) the name tara is not given ; he there speaks of " a silver *fanon* (fanam) which is worth 16 *cas*, one *cas* being about an Italian *quattrino*."
'Abdu'r-razzāk however (1442), speaks of a silver coin called a *tar*, which is *one-sixth* of a *fanam*. In spite of this so many authorities state that it was one-sixteenth of a fanam, that we should probably here read " sixteenth" for "sixth." Correa, I, 624, says that for a *vintem* 20 silver coins called taras were received in exchange. The *vintem* being worth 20 reis, this makes the *tara* the equivalent of 1 real.
Varthema in the passage quoted above (in Ramusio's Italian text) goes on to say that 16 *cas* (each worth about an Italian quattrino) go to a silver *fanam*, and that this *fanam* is worth half of a silver *Marcello*. (The Marcello was a small silver coin struck in Venice named after the Doge Nicolo Marcello in 1473.) Later on in the seventeenth century we have the evidence of Pyrard de Laval (I, 344–412) who gives the value at 3 deniers, and says that 16 tarens go to a phanan or larin (1610), and towards the end of the same century that of Claude Dellon (*Voyages*, Ed. 1711, p. 233), who says : " Un Naher qui sert de garde dans une maison, gagne ordinairement quatre tares par jour, et s'il va en campagne il en gagne huit, alors ils recoivent double solde, . . . La tare est une monnoye d'argent, qui vaut à peu près deux liards; il en faut seize pour un fanon, qui est une petite piece d'or de la valeur de huit sols."
Pyrard too, in the passage alluded to above, gives 4 tarents as the daily wages of the Nair escort. This shows that 4 taras a day was still a customary rate of pay in the seventeenth century, as it had been in Barbosa's time. Fryer also gives the value of the *Tarr* at Cuttycony

and forthwith assigns them a pension. If they are wounded the King orders them to be well cured, as well as giving them their customary pay. Some of them possess also estates on which they live, and support their sisters for whom they have great regard,[1] especially for the eldest, and show much affection to them, but they never enter the same room with their younger sisters, nor even a house where they are alone, nor do they touch them, nor speak to them so as to give no occasion for sin by reason of their youth, which would be impossible as regards the elder sisters by reason of the respect they bear them. These *Nayre* women at their periods shut themselves up in a house apart for three days, touching no one, and preparing their food in separate pans and

---

near Mount Deli as 16 to the fanam (I, 149), though at Calicut he makes it 28 to the *fanam*. In 1673, 10 *tarrs* went to a fanam, at the same place, and it is hardly possible that 28 could have been correct.

The Portuguese text here is rather confused ; after the words " four taras each," these words follow : *e cada dia tem sinco rs*, " and every day they have five reis." I take this to imply that the value of the daily pay in Portuguese money of the period was five reis. Taking the *real* as ·28 of a penny (Vol. I, p. 101, n. 1) the *tara* according to this computation would be worth ·37*d*. The Spanish (p. 131) gives the same sense, using maravedis for reis, as is its usual practice. Ramusio however, puts it in another form " 40 cash daily, which are 40 maravedis." At the rate of 16 cash to the tara, which is usually given as the value, this would only give 2½ taras a day.

For quotations see under " Tare, tara," in *Hobson-Jobson* (Ed. 1903). The latest quotation is that from Logan's Malabar, III, 95 & 192, which shows that this coin was in use as late as 1884. He values it at 2 pies. See also Dalgado's *Glossario s.v.* Tara.

Buchanan (*Journey*, 1807, Vol. II, p. 562) speaks of " hired men or *Panicars*, who are *Nairs*, *Moplays* and *Tiars*," being paid " six to twelve silver Fanams (27½ to 55 pence) annually for oil and salt." These would seem to be the same coin as the tara, in which case its value must have risen to 4½*d*. by 1807. Possibly the coin alluded to is the 2-anna piece of Tippu, or of the restored Hindu dynasty of Mysore. Mysore coinage may have circulated in Malabar after Haidar's invasions.

In another place (*l.c.* p. 540) Buchanan speaks of a silver *fanam* being worth 10 paisas, but mentions also a copper " tarram, two of which are equal to one paisa," so that the tara was no longer a silver coin.

[1] This custom retains its full force at the present day. *Cf.* Panikkar, *l.c.*, p. 261, " A younger brother can talk to a sister considerably older than himself ; but under no conditions may he talk to a younger one."

dishes. When the three days are past they bathe themselves in hot water, and attire themselves in clean clothes,
then they go forth from the houses to a tank, wherein
they bathe a second time, and leaving those clean clothes
take yet others, and thus they may go to their houses
and speak with their mothers or sisters or other folk.
The house in which a woman has passed these three days
is plastered and swept, for in no otherwise would anyone
enter therein.[1] When they bear children these women are
thoroughly well washed in abundance of hot water for
the first three days, and many times afterwards, from
the crown of the head to the feet. These women do no
work except to prepare their own food, and to earn
their living with their bodies, for in addition to the
three or four lovers, whom every woman has, they never
refuse themselves to any *Bramene* or *Nayre* who gives
them money. These women are very clean, and fare
very well, and they consider it a matter of great honour
and gallantry and pride themselves greatly thereon, to
be able to give pleasure to men, and it is article of faith
with them that every woman who dies a virgin is damned.

"These *Nayres* show great respect to their kindred and
brethren ; the lesser of them comes into the presence of
the others with great courtesy, and keeps his hand on
his mouth as a sign of silence, answering only to questions,
showing also great respect to their masters, so much so
that the King himself stands up when his preceptor
enters, and both bow low one to the other, the preceptor
to him as King, and he to the preceptor as to his master.

"When the *Nayres* die, their bodies are sent to be
burned in their enclosures and gardens, and their mothers
and kinsfolk mourn for them, and cast their ashes into

---

[1] For the modern ceremonies on these occasions Panikkar, *l.c.*,
p. 272 f., is the best authority.

running water. The nephew, or whoever is the heir, wears mourning for a year (even as the prince does for the King), cooks his food with his own hand, or has it done by a *Bramene*, bathes before eating with great ceremony, changing the clothes he wears and donning others. He claps his hands before eating, whereupon numbers of crows quickly gather round him, and he feeds them and performs other idolatrous rites, and gives alms to the poor and to the Bramenes, according to his means. The year accomplished, he strips off his mourning garments and performs other rites of a funeral nature.

" All *Nayres* are mighty warriors, they believe in ghosts of many kinds ; they have among them lucky and unlucky days ; on the unlucky days they undertake nothing, and do nothing ; they believe also in omens, that if a cat crosses in front of any person who is about to do any business, he does it not ; or, if on coming forth from the house for any purpose they see a crow carrying a stick, they turn back ; or if in saying farewell to other persons with whom they have been, some one of them sneezes, he who was going, sits down again and does not leave so soon

" They worship the Sun, the Moon, the lamp and cows, and honour them greatly. They believe very easily ; if anyone is possessed they say that it is with God who has entered into him and that which the demon makes him utter, very terrible things, they believe it all ; and he makes them cut themselves with knives, and whatever they say to the King he does forthwith, and the demon, in order that they may believe in him works many devilish signs and wonders. They believe that with the proper signs a man who has died may be born again of another woman."

In this Kingdom of Malabar there is also another caste

of people whom they call *Biabares*,[1] Indian merchants,
natives of the land. They were there ere foreign nations
had sailed to India. They deal in goods of every kind
both in the seaports and inland, wheresoever their trade
is of most profit. They gather to themselves all the
pepper and ginger from the *Nayres* and husbandmen,
and ofttimes they buy the new crops beforehand in
exchange for cotton clothes and other goods which they
keep at the seaports. Afterwards they sell them again
and gain much money thereby. Their privileges are
such that the King of the country in which they dwell
cannot execute them by legal process. Should the King
know of any crime deserving of punishment committed
by one of them he tells the others and they gather in
council and themselves slay the culprit with spear and
sword, making known to the King the justice that they
have done. They are very wealthy, and have much
property in land inherited from of old. They marry
one wife in our manner, and their sons are their heirs;
when they die their bodies are burnt. Their wives follow
weeping to the fire, and coming thereto they· take from
their neck a little golden ornament which their husbands

---

[1] This name has been corrected in accordance with Ramusio's
reading from the form Brabares in the Portuguese text to *Biabares*,
as it represents the Mal. form *Vyābāri* or *Rāvari Nāyars*, a mercantile
class akin to the Taragans. The name is given by Thurston (VII,
412) in the form Vyapari, which shows its origin from the Skr. *Byāpāri*
found in North India, in the form *byopāri*, " a trader." *Rāvari* seems
to be a corruption of the same term. If Barbosa's account of their
marriage customs was correct they have been assimilated to some
extent to the ordinary Nāyar practice for although the men marry
only within the caste, the women may have *Sambandhams* with
Kiriyattil Nāyars. There seems to be a great resemblance between the
Vyābāri and two other classes of mercantile Nāyars, the Mūttāns,
and the Taragans (or Tarakans), and it is probable that Barbosa
included them all under the general title of Vyāpāri or traders. The
Mūttāns seem to be the closest of all to the caste described by him,
as *sambandham* is not allowed among them, and sons inherit their
fathers'· property (Thurston, V, 131 ; *Mal. Gaz.*, pp. 117, 118).
  " The Rāvari Nāyars are Marumakkathayam. They are numerous
round Quilandi and Nadapuram in Kurumbranad Taluk."—(T.)

give them when they first take them into their houses, and cast it into the fire, and so go back to their home. They do not marry again, even though they may be young girls. If they die, the husbands have them burnt, and afterwards may marry another wife. These men are of such established lineage that the *Nayres* may touch them.

There is in this land yet another caste of folk known as *Cuiavem*.[1] They do not differ from the *Nayres*, yet by reason of a fault which they committed, they remain separate from them. Their business is to make pottery and bricks for roofing the houses of the Kings and idols, which are roofed with bricks instead of tiles ;[2] only these, for as I have already said, other houses are thatched with branches. They have their own sort of idolatry, and their separate idols. [In their temples, which are called Pagodes,[3] they do many enchantments and witchcrafts. Those who are sprung from them may not adopt any other caste or occupation.]

As to their marriage, they have the same rule as the

---

[1] *Cuiavem or Cujavem.* This appears to be the potter caste called *Kusavan.* They are classed in the *Mal. Gaz.* (p. 120) among the " non-military classes ranking as Nāyars." Another name for them is Anduran. The Kusavan potters described in Thurston (IV, p. 188) appear to be found mainly in the Tamil country, and not in Malabar. In *Cochin Tribes and Castes* (p. 18), they are called Anduran Nāyars, and said to be makers of earthenware for use in temples. Dalgado in his *Glossario, s.v.* Cuiavem, gives the explanation " Casta de Oleiros do Malabar do Malayalam *Kuxavan*," i.e., " Potter caste of Malabar from the Mal. *Kushavan.*" Barbosa's spelling is probably intended to represent the sound *Kuzhavan.* " Kuswan is the correct form, but it is commonly corrupted into Kuyavan, which corresponds with Barbosa's spelling."—(T.)

[2] *Tijolo* instead of *telha* ; probably meaning that plain unglazed tiles were used instead of glazed or coloured tiles.

[3] *Called Pagodes.* " Pagoda " is supposed to be a corruption of " Bhagavathi " via Bhagothi. The shrines of lower deities in Malabar are called Kāvu as distinct from the temples (ambalam or Kshetram), and the " Bhagavathi kāvu " is the commonest kind.—(T.) This sentence is not in the Portuguese text but is found in Ramusio and the Spanish version. For a full account of the word Pagoda and its various meanings reference should be made to Dalgado's *Glossario, s.v.* Pagode, and to his *Contribuições.* He points out that in the sense of " temple " this word is used by Barbosa only as regards the temples of the *Cuiavens.*

Nayres, and the Nayres may sleep with their women on condition they cannot enter their own houses without bathing to cleanse themselves from such a sin, and changing their clothes.

There is another Heathen caste which they call *Mainatos*,[1] whose occupation is to wash clothes for the *Kings*, *Bramenes*, and *Nayres*. By this they live, and may not take up any other. They wash near to their own houses in great tanks and cisterns which they have for this purpose. They have much raiment as well of their own as of others ; for there are many *Nayres* who have no clothes of their own to wear but take shares with them, and give them so much every month to furnish them daily with well-washed garments ; and by this they gain their living.

The *Nayre* sends every day a youth who takes away some clothes and brings others, as is required by their rank. For other folk they wash for money, and for all they work with great cleanliness, and thus they live well enough. Those born of this class do not mix with others, nor others with them, save only that the *Nayres* may take their women as concubines if they bathe and change their clothes. These washermen have their own idolatry and separate temples. They have beliefs of various kinds. Their marriage custom is that of the *Nayres* ; their brothers and nephews are their heirs.

---

[1] *Mainatos*. The name Mainato is given by Ramusio as *Manantamar*, and in the Spanish as *Manatamar*, but no modern form closely corresponding to any of these has been found. There can be no doubt however, that the caste described is the Veluthēdan or Vannathān. They are members of the non-military Nāyar group, and are not subject to distance pollution. Their occupation is, as described by Barbosa, washing for the upper classes of Nāyars, and the clothes so washed carry no pollution. The name used by the Portuguese writer may therefore with some confidence be referred to Vannathān, the second title of the caste, strictly applicable only to one of its sections. The fullest account of this tribe will be found in Thurston, VII, p. 389; see also *Mal. Gaz.*, p. 121, and *Cochin Tribes and Castes*, II, p. 115.

There is another lower caste than these which they call *Caletis*,[1] who are weavers who have no other way of earning save by weaving of cotton and silk cloths, but they are low caste folk and have but little money, so that they clothe the lower races. They are apart by themselves and have their own idolatry. Their race is not mixed with any other, yet may the *Nayres* take their women as concubines, on the conditions given above. Many of them are sons of *Nayres*, and fine men in their appearance, like them they carry arms and go to the wars where they fight well. In their marriages they follow the *Nayre* custom, and their sons do not inherit from them. Their women are free with their persons doing whatsoever they please, but do not associate with any other caste than their own and the *Nayres*, under pain of death.

Besides the castes mentioned above, there are eleven others lower than they with whom the others do not associate, nor do they touch them under pain of death ; and there are great distinctions between one and another of them, preserving them from mixture with one another. The purest of all these low, simple folk they call *Tuias*.[2]

---

[1] *Caletis or Chaliens.* This caste of weavers is that known by the name of Chaliyan, who are found throughout Malabar. Barbosa describes them correctly as like the Nāyars in their marriage and inheritance customs, and also as being weavers of clothes for the lower castes. They are of low social status, yet are free from distance pollution, and are rightly included in the upper group by our author. They seem to be originally immigrants from the East coast. (Thurston, II, p. 11 ; *Mal. Gaz.*, p. 122 ; *Cochin Tribes and Castes*, II, p. 115. In the last mentioned there is a good illustration of a group of Chaliyans and their looms.)

[2] *Tuias*, called *Tiberi*, by Ramusio, and *Zivil Tiver* in the Spanish version. (*Zivil* is the Portuguese word *civil*, " rustic," turned into a Spanish form, and treated as a proper name.) The name Tuia represents the *Tiyan* (Thiyyan) of modern books, or the *Tiars* of earlier writers such as Buchanan. Although belonging to the so-called impure castes, and subject to " distance pollution," they yet occupy a respectable position, and hold themselves above the bulk of the low castes as Barbosa has correctly noted. They are in fact an aboriginal peasantry, tenders of palm-groves and drawers of toddy (" the wine

Their work is mainly that of tending the palm-groves, and gathering the fruit thereof, and carrying it away for wages on their backs, for there are no beasts of burden in the land. They are quarrymen as well, and earn their living by work of all kinds. Some learn the use of arms and fight well when they undertake it. They carry in their hands as tokens, sticks a fathom long. The more part of them are slaves bound to the lands of the Nayres to whom they are assigned by the King that they may live and support themselves by the labour of these men, and the Nayres protect and cherish them. They have their own idols,[1] in whom they put their faith. Their nephews are their heirs;[2] they are married but their sons do not inherit because their women openly earn their living with their bodies, and refuse themselves to no one save to foreigners; their husbands are privy to this and give them opportunity so to act. They make the wine of this land, and sell it, and no others may do this; they avoid strictly touching those of a caste lower than their own, and live apart from all other castes. Sometimes among them two brothers have one wife and sleep with her, and hold it nothing wonderful.

There is another caste still lower than these whom

---

of this land "). That polyandry existed among them, as stated by Barbosa and Buchanan (II, p. 416) admits of no doubt, and the custom still lingers on. " Two existing instances are recorded " according to Thurston (VII, p. 48) at the census of 1901. See also *Cochin Tribes and Castes*, I, p. 301. It is probably confined to the Tandan sub-caste. The Thiyyan caste is known in Cochin and Travancore by the name of Illuvan or Izhuvan. The name Thiyyan is prevalent north of Calicut in the country near Cananore, with which Barbosa was most familiar, and everywhere in Malabar except the part bordering on the Cochin State. (See also *Mal. Gaz.*, p. 124 f.)

[1] *They have their own idols.* This caste cannot of course worship in the caste temples. Nowadays they take to building temples of their own (*e.g.*, at Calicut and Tellicherry), wherefrom they exclude their inferiors just as they are excluded by the Nāyars.—(T.)

[2] *Their Nephews are their heirs.* This is only true of the North.—(T.)

they call *Manen* (Mancu in the printed text)[1] who
neither associate with others nor touch them, nor do
the others touch them. They are washermen for the
common people, and makers of sleeping mats, from
which occupations all but they are barred ; their sons
must perforce follow the same trade ; they have their
own separate idolatry. They wash clothes for the
Nayres when they are living apart according to their
custom, for these garments must be washed and wrung
by them and by no other. If this is not done the Nayres
are not freed from sin. They are slaves of the *King* and
of the *Nayres* as well.

There is another caste in this land still lower whom
they call *Canaquas*.[2] Their trade is making bucklers

---

[1] The *Manens* are omitted by Ramusio and the Spanish version. They
appear to be identical with the caste known as Vannan, and in Malabar as
Mannan or Bannan. (Thurston, VII, pp. 315, 318 ; also Thurston, VII,
p. 39 *s.v.* Tiyan.) Mr. Francis in the Madras Census Report, 1901,
describes them as " a low caste of Malabar washermen who wash only
for the polluting castes, and for the higher castes when they are under
pollution, following births, deaths, etc." This is a good instance of
the accuracy of Barbosa's observations. (*Mal. Gaz.* p. 170.)

[2] *Canaquas or Caniun.* In the name of this caste, Kaniyan, the
origin of the names Canaqua in the Portuguese text and Caniun in
Ramusio is apparent. The name Kaniyan becomes Kanisan in Malabar.
Kanakan rather relates to the profession than the caste, being the
Skr. *ganika*, an astrologer. The word used for umbrella in the Portuguese text is *sombreiro* (see Vol. I, p. 206, n. 1) and it should not here
be translated " hat," as in Lord Stanley's note on p. 139. The
umbrellas are made of palm leaves (Thurston, III, p. 194). This passage
from Barbosa is quoted on p. 187 of Thurston's work alluded to above,
where a full description of this caste will be found. Fraternal polyandry is
still prevalent in this caste (Thurston, III, pp. 195-6). Mr. Thorne adds,
" Barbosa's account is entirely apposite to the Kanisans of the present
day. Astrology and umbrella-making are both carried on by the ordinary
Kaniyans of British Malabar. There is no connection with the
Kanakkans who are a division of Cherumas much below the Kanisans."
Possibly however, the Skr. term may have been used occasionally
for the Kanisans, as they are known to be astrologers.

The greater part of this passage describing the manner in which the
Kings consult these astrologers is not found in Ramusio or the Spanish.
Mr. Logan's account of the Kanisans or Kaniyans in their capacity of
astrologers or casters of horoscopes is quoted in Thurston, III, p. 189, and
other accounts will be found in the *Mal. Gaz.*, p. 129, and *Cochin Tribes
and Castes*, p. 184 f, also in Pannikkar (*J.R.A.I.*, 1919), who describes
the Kaniyan as " a medicine man who has power to cast off spirits, to
, perform preventive magic, and keep general control over ghosts."

and umbrellas. They learn letters for purposes of astronomy, they are great astrologers, and foretell with great truth things that are to come ; there are some lords who maintain them for this cause. If the Kings would know what is to happen they summon these men, and going forth to their fruit gardens behind their palaces meet them there, and ask them whatsoever they desire to learn. They write it down and depart to their own houses to study it, and having done so they return to the same place (for owing to their low caste they may not enter the palace) " whither the King goes with some of his privy councillors, and having drawn near to him, they tell him what they have discovered regarding that matter for his information. They are also learned in their idolatry and soothsaying, so much so that no King or Lord will undertake any business, nor go forth from his house without asking them the day and the hour on which he shall do it. Some of the greater merchants also do the same for their voyages. Thus they make a livelihood for themselves and their wives and sons and also for the Lords whose subjects they are. No man departs from what they say. They always carry great sheaves of palm leaves inscribed with their deceptions. They may not enter the house of any person of good family, but take their seats in the street and there deliver their judgments and their tales." They know well the Signs (of the Zodiac) and the Planets, and have everything drawn out in plans as we do, and the months divided, save that they have months of nine and twenty days, of thirty, and of two and thirty, and thus there is but small difference from ours for certain months remain equal one to the other The first month of the year is April, for in this land in May, June, July, and August, and up to the middle of September, it is the

winter with great rains and storms.[1] From the middle
of September [2] on the other hand it is the summer with
many calms and little wind ; on the coast there are
always land winds, and light breezes. They sail only
in the summer, and beach their ships in the winter.

There is also another lower caste, also Heathens,
called *Ageres*.[3] They are masons, carpenters, smiths,
metal-workers, and some are goldsmiths, all of whom
are of a common descent, and a separate caste, and have
their idols apart from other folk. They marry, and their
sons inherit their property, and learn their fathers'
trades.

There is another caste still lower in this country called

---

[1] The rainy season is always called the winter by the early Portuguese writers. This practice was adopted by other Europeans and
lasted till the eighteenth century.

[2] In Ramusio and the Spanish version the rains are made to last till
the middle of October.

[3] The name *Ageres* undoubtedly represents the word *Asari*, an
artizan. The artizan classes are grouped together into a caste known
as Kammalan. There are five or six of these groups, each representing
a distinct craft. In *Cochin Tribes and Castes*, I, p. 342, the number
is given as six, named as follows :—

1. Marasāris ..	..	..	..	Carpenters.
2. Kallasāris ..	..	..	..	Stonemasons.
3. Kollans ..	..	..	..	Blacksmiths.
4. Musāris ..	..	..	..	Braziers.
5. Tattān ..	..	..	..	Goldsmiths.
6. Tolkollans ..	..	..	..	Leather-workers.

The *Mal. Gaz.*, p. 127, gives the list of five as follows :—

1. Tattān ..	..	..	..	Goldsmith.
2. Perinkollan	..	..	..	Blacksmith.
3. Musāri ..	..	..	..	Brazier.
4. Asāri ..	..	..	..	Carpenter.
5. Chemboti ..	..	..	..	Coppersmith.

The list given in Thurston, III, p. 126, on the authority of S. Appadorai Iyer agrees with the last except that the blacksmiths are called
Karumān. The leather-workers are included in the *Cochin* list only.
The *Mal. Gaz.*, p. 128, gives them as a separate caste. The carpenters
are frequently called simply Asāris, and are probably the most important
group in the caste. Barbosa probably found the word *Asāri* used for
artizans generally, and he employs it here to include masons, carpenters, smiths, metal-workers and goldsmiths. *Ajari* is the form
used in the Spanish version and *Aggeri* in Ramusio.

Mogeres,[1] they are almost the same as the *Tuias,* but they do not touch one another. They work as carriers of all things belonging to the Royal State when it moves from one place to another, but there are very few of them in this land ; they are a separate caste ; they have no marriage law ; the most of them gain their living on the sea, they are sailors, and some of them fishers ; they have no idols. They are as well slaves of the *Nayres.*

Some are very rich and own the ships in which they sail and trade with the Moors. Their nephews and not their sons are their heirs, because their women are very licentious, and give themselves to anyone they please. They are careful to refrain from touching others yet lower than themselves, and dwell in villages of their own. Their women are very comely and fair, they fare very well. They are descended from foreigners [whiter than the natives of the country, and the women go very well clad, with many gold ornaments].

There is another caste yet lower whom they call *Monquer,*[2] fishers who have no other work than fishing,

---

[1] *Mogeres. Moger* in Ramusio ; *Moguer* in the Spanish version. This is the *Moger* caste of fishermen, who are a Tulu-speaking race of South Kanara, but have spread into Malabar, north of Cananor, and are there known as *Mugavan* or *Mugayan (Mal. Gaz.,* p. 126). The *Mogers* are also porters and palanquin-bearers, as well as fishermen (Thurston, V, p. 65).

According to Buchanan they are very like the Mukkuvan (or Mucuar), but distinct from them in caste. According to *Cochin Tribes and Castes* (I, p. 266) the Malayālam *Mukkuvan* and the Canarese *Moger* are of common origin, both being derived from a root meaning " to dive." " The correct Malayālam is Mukavar or Mukayar. The pronunciation resembles ' Mogayar.' As Barbosa says, there are very few in Malabar ; they are confined to the extreme north of the district."—T.

[2] The *Monquer* (called *Muchoa* by Ramusio and *Mucoa* in the Spanish version) is the caste now known as *Mukkuvan,* the principal fishing caste throughout Malabar. Buchanan (II, p. 527) says, " The Mucua or, in the plural, Mucuar, are a tribe who live near the coast of Malayala, to the inland parts of which they seldom go." They are the principal sea-fishermen of Malabar, the fishing in the backwaters and inland lakes being mainly in the hands of other fishing tribes. In social standing they are below the Tiyans and the artizan classes. (Thurston, V, p. 106 ; *Cochin Tribes and Castes,* I, p. 266 ; *Mal. Gaz.,* p. 126.)

yet some sail in the Moors' ships and in those of other heathens, and they are very expert seamen. This race is very rude, they are shameless thieves ; they marry and their sons succeed them,[1] their women are of loose character, they sleep with anyone soever, and it is held no evil. They have their own idolatry, they pay no duty on fresh fish, but on some which they dry, they pay four per cent., thus fish is good cheap, and is the food most used among them, for they eat but little flesh meat, and in this land there is but little breeding of flocks and herds. Some of them are very rich and well off, and they have large houses and farms, of which the King takes possession whensoever he will, " they give great bribes to his governours that they may not take them."

In this land of Malabar there is another caste of Heathen even lower than these, whom they call *Betunes*.[2] Their business is salt-making, and rice growing, they have no other livelihood.

They dwell in houses standing by themselves in the fields away from the roads, whither the gentlefolk do not walk. They have their own idolatry. They are slaves of the *Kings* and *Nayres* and pass their lives in poverty. The *Nayres* make them walk far away from them and speak to them from afar off. They hold no intercourse with any other caste. They marry, and their sons inherit their possessions.

[1] *Their sons succeed them.* " *I.e.*, in the South. In N. Malabar they are Marumakathayam. Perhaps Barbosa confused these Northern Mukkuvans with his Mogeres."—(T.)

[2] *Betunes.* (Ramusio and the Spanish version, *Betua.*) This is the caste now called *Vettuvan*, " once salt-makers, and now masons, earth-workers and quarrymen " (*Mal. Gaz.*, p. 129). They are according to *Cochin Tribes and Castes* (I, p. 139), one of the four sections of the Kanakkan tribe ; but Mr. Thorne thinks that the Cochin caste was not alluded to by Barbosa, who was describing the castes around Calicut. At present they do many kinds of work, one of their principal employments being pumping water out of paddy fields.

There is another caste of Heathen, even lower and ruder, whom they call *Paneens*,[1] who are great sorcerers, and live by no other means.   They openly commune with demons who take possession of them, and cause them to utter astonishing things.   When any King is ill, he sends for these men and women, ten or twelve families of whom come, the best performers and the most approved of the devil, with their women and children.   At the palace gate they set up a tent of coloured cloths, where they establish themselves, and thence they go forth at the call of any other Lord who has need of them.   They paint their bodies in many colours, they make themselves paper crowns and other devices with many flowers and grasses.   They make great bonfires and light lamps, they bring kettle-drums, trumpets and cymbals, with which they make music.   Then they come forth from their tents two and two, with bare swords in their hands, yelling and making faces, running along the ground, leaping one after another.   Thus they continue awhile, giving each other sword strokes, putting themselves naked and bare-foot into the fire, until they are weary ;   then come forth other twos or threes, both men and boys singing, and they do something of a like kind ;   the women the while singing and shouting and brawling violently.   They go on with this two or three days, both by night and by day working one with another,

---

[1] *Paneens.*   This form is an amendment for Pancens, which appears in the printed text.   *Cf. infra, Pareens* for *Parcens.*   The misprint appears a natural one.   In neither case could the form with *c* possibly be correct.   This amendment is also adopted in Dalgado's *Glossario.*   The form in Ramusio is *Paneru,* in the Spanish version *Paneu.* It represents the modern Pānam.   They are correctly described as sorcerers by Barbosa ;   exorcism, magic and devil dancing are much practised among them ;   they are also umbrella makers, and barbers for most of the low castes, except the very lowest (*Mal. Gaz.*, p. 131 ; *Cochin Tribes and Castes,* I, p. 171 ; Thurston, VI, p. 29).   " Barbosa's account is excellent.   They are as he says Makkathayam," *i.e.,* their sons succeed.   " In N. Malabar they are called Malayans."—(T.)

and drawing circles on the ground with lines of ochre of a white clay. Within the circle they cast rice and red flowers, they place lamps round it and walk about inside it until the devil, in whose service they do this, enters into one of them, and makes them say what the King's sickness is, and in what manner he may be made whole ; they tell him, and he is fully contented therewith. He orders them to be given food, money, and raiment and does whatever they ask him. This race lives apart from all communication with those of high rank, they touch none of the other castes. They are as well great archers, hunters and mountaineers ; they kill many wild boars, deer, and other beasts of chase, also wild fowl on which they live. They marry and their sons succeed to their estates.

There is another caste lower and ruder than they, named *Revoleens*,[1] a very poor folk, who live by carrying firewood and grass to the towns, they may touch none, nor may any touch them under pain of death. They go naked, covering only their private parts with scant and filthy rags, the more part of them indeed with leaves of certain trees. [Their women wear many brass rings in their ears ; and on their necks, arms and legs necklaces and bracelets of beads.]

---

[1] *Revoleens.* (*Revoler* in Ramusio ; *Renoleni* in the Spanish version.) This name denotes the primitive jungle tribe known as Eravallen, or Eravallar, who live in the hilly tracts of Cochin, and in the Coimbatore District of the Madras Presidency. Their language is Tamil, though some speak Malayālam. They are often in a position of serfdom, and work for cultivators of higher caste, but occupy a higher position than the Pulayans or Cherumans, and the Pulayans (Thurston, II, p. 210 ; *Cochin Tribes and Castes,* I, p. 43). Mr. Thorne considers that the identification with Eravallars cannot be correct, because (1) Eravallars are a jungle tribe and no jungle men come near the towns, and (2) Eravallars are not found in British Malabar, which is the country Barbosa is describing, and suggests that this may be a caste which has died out in the 400 years since Barbosa wrote. The name, however, seems to be identical, and it may also be possible that the Eravallars once inhabited Malabar and have been forced to migrate.

And there is yet another caste of Heathen lower than these whom they call *Poleas*,[1] who among all the rest are held to be accursed and excommunicate ; they dwell in the fields and open campaigns in secret lurking places, whither folk of good caste never go save by mischance, and live in huts very strait and mean. They are tillers of rice with buffaloes and oxen. They never speak to the *Nayres* save from afar off, shouting so that they may hear them, and when they go along the roads they utter loud cries, that they may be let past, and whosoever hears them leaves the road, and stands in the wood till they have passed by ; and if anyone, whether man or woman, touches them his kinsfolk slay him forthwith, and in vengeance therefore they slay *Poleas* until they are weary without suffering any punishment. In certain months of the year they do their utmost to touch some *Nayre* woman by night as secretly as they can, and this only for the sake of doing evil. They go by in order to get into the houses of the *Nayres* to touch women, and during these months the women guard themselves carefully, and if they touch any woman, even though none have seen it, and there may be no witnesses, yet she

---

[1] *Poleas*. (*Puler* in Ramusio and the Spanish version.) This is the Pulayan caste, also known as Cheruman, one of the lowest in social position in Malabar. " They are akin to Cherumas, but there is a distinction ; *e.g.*, in N. Malabar Pulayas are numerous, but they are never called Cherumas " (T.). They were till recently slaves, and, although now legally free, yet in practice they still retain traces of servitude. The Nāyars were, and still to some extent are, their lords and owners. Some regard them as the aborigines of Malabar, and the name Cheruman is supposed to be connected with the ancient Kingdom of Chera. Certain districts in Malabar still bear the name *Cheranād*. The name *Pulayan* is supposed to be derived from Mal. *pula*, " pollution." This name is chiefly used in North Malabar and Travancore ; and Cheruman in South Malabar and Cochin. It was no crime to kill them till modern times. Barbosa's description of the trouble caused to these unfortunate people by " distance pollution " may be compared with the modern account by Mr. S. Appadorai Iyer (*Calcutta Review*, 1900). See also Thurston (*s.v.* Cheruman), II, p. 45 ff. ; *Mal. Gaz.*, p. 133 ; *Cochin Tribes and Castes*, I, p. 87 ff. The propensity of the Pulayans to revenge themselves by " touching " Nayar women no longer survives.

declares it at once, crying out, and she will stay no longer in her house that her caste may not be destroyed ; in general she flees to the house of some other low caste folk, and hides herself, that her kinsfolk may not slay her ; and that thence she may help herself and be sold to foreigners, which is ofttimes done. And the manner of touching is this, even though no words are exchanged, they throw something at her, a stone or a stick, and if it touches her she is touched and ruined. These people are also great sorcerers and thieves ; they are a very evil race.

Yet another caste there is even lower and baser called *Pareens*,[1] who dwell in the most desert places away from all other castes. They have no intercourse with any person nor anyone with them ; they are held to be worse than devils, and to be damned. Even

---

[1] *Pareens.* The spelling given is amended from the printed text form *Parcens.* * (See above, p. 66, under Paneens.) Ramusio has *Parea*, the Spanish version *Pareni*. The name is Parayan, a low-caste aboriginal tribe of basket-makers and agricultural labourers, who seem originally to have been included with others of the same character under the general name of Cheruman. (See *Mal. Gaz.*, p. 135, and Buchanan, II, p. 370.) The latter includes the "Parriar" with others under the head of *Churmar*. Mr. H. A. Stuart, in the *Madras Census Report* of 1891, says (speaking of the Paraiyans of the East Coast) that "in the eleventh century the word Pulayan was used to denote this section of the population as it is still in Malayālam to this day." It is clear, however, that the Pulayans and the Parayans were regarded as quite distinct in Barbosa's day, and there can be little doubt that they are connected only as being branches of the aboriginal Cheruman stock. Except the name there seems nothing to connect them with the better known *Paraiyans* of the East Coast, who as *Pariahs* have become a by-word throughout the world for the degraded outcast, although they are not actually the lowest. In Malabar they are not quite at the lowest end of the scale, as the *Nayadis* and the *Ulladans* are classed below them (*Mal. Gaz.*, p. 135 ; *Cochin Tribes and Castes*, II, p. 68). Mr. Thorne adds : "This caste now forms the important if humble community of scavangers in Malabar. Their powers of black magic in country parts of South Malabar are much dreaded. Their designs on pregnant women in order to obtain the fœtus for making potions are notorious, and more than one Parayan has been beaten to death in the belief that he has caused the death of such women."

---

* This emendation is supported by Mgr. Dalgado, who quotes this passage in his *Lexicologia Luso-Oriental* (Lisbon, 1916), p. 172.

to see them is to be unclean and out-caste. ˙They eat yams and other roots of wild plants.[1] They cover their middles with leaves ; they also eat the flesh of wild beasts.

With these end the distinctions between the castes of the Heathen, which are eighteen in all, each one separate and unable to touch others or marry with them; and besides these eighteen castes [2] of the Heathen who are natives of Malabar, which I have now related to you, there are others of outlandish folk, merchants and traders in the land, where they possess houses and estates, living like the natives, yet with customs of their own. These are the following. First of these races whom I call

---

[1] Here the Spanish version adds, "which is like the root of the maize which is found in the island of Antilla." (See Vol. I, p. 25, n. 2.) The true yam, *inhame*, is a native of Africa, and probably was introduced into India at a later date. The allusion is probably to some root of a wild plant of similar appearance. Roxburgh considers that no *Dioscorea* are wild in India (De Candolle, *Origin of Cultivated Plants*, London 1884, p. 77). Possibly the allusion is to the root of *Arum Colocasia*, often called *yams*.

[2] *The eighteen castes of Malabar.* The castes mentioned above by Barbosa amount actually to seventeen, but there is no doubt that he considers the Kings or Royal Sāmantans to be a separate caste, which is correct, as they were distinct from the Nāyars.

Including the Royal Caste and some Royal Sāmantans, among whom some are Kshatriyas, there are seven names in the first group, and eleven in the second, making a total of eighteen. Ramusio and the Spanish version both give the total as eighteen, but mention only seventeen ; one (Manen) being omitted by both.

The following table shows the castes mentioned by Barbosa in the order he assigns to them, with the variants of their names as given in Ramusio and the Spanish version. In accordance with his arrangement they are given in three groups, *i.e.*, the Upper Castes, the Lower Castes and the Foreigners. The modern forms of the names as far as they can be identified are given in the last column. There are slight variations from Barbosa's order of precedence in Ramusio and the Spanish version which correspond with each other. The list, though not exhaustive, includes nearly all the castes of importance which still exist in Malabar, which comprises not only the British District of Malabar, but the states of Travancore and Cochin. The correspondence is very close, not only in name, but in occupation and social precedence. In the first group, for instance, we have the Brāhmans and the Nayārs, and the Mercantile and Artizan sections of the latter, who approximate to Nāyars, and are not subject to the stigma of "distance pollution."

foreigners who dwell in Malabar is a caste called *Chatis*,[1] natives of the province of *Charamandel*, of which I shall speak further on. They are tawny men, almost white, and fat. The more part of them are great merchants,

CASTES.

GROUP I. HIGHER CASTES.

Barbosa.	Ramusio.	Spanish.	Modern Form.
1. Bramenes.	Bramini.	Bramenes.	Brāhman (Nambūtiri).
2. Nayres.	Nairi.	Nayrs.	Nāyar.
3. Biabares.	Biabari.	Brabares.	Vyāpāri or Rāvari Nāyar.
4. Cuiavem.	Cugianem.	Cujaven.	Kusavan.
5. Mainato.	Manantamar.	Manatamar.	Vannathamar.
6. Caletis.	Calian.	Chalien.	Chaliyan.

GROUP 2. LOWER CASTES.

Barbosa.	Ramusio.	Spanish.	Modern Form.
1. Tuia.	Tiberi.	Tiver.	Tiyan. Izhuvan.
2. Manen.	—	—	Mannan.
3. Canaqua.	Caniun.	Canion.	Kaniyān, Kanisan.
4. Ageres.	Aggeri.	Ajares.	Asārī.
5. Mogeres.	Moger (2).	Moguer (2).	Mukayar, Mukavar.
6. Monquer.	Muchoa (5).	Mucoa (5).	Mukkuvan.
7. Betunes.	Betua (6).	Betua.	Vettuvan.
8. Paneens.	Paneru.	Panek.	Pānan.
9. Revoleens.	Revoler.	Renoleni.	Eravallen (Cheruma ?).
10. Poleas.	Puler.	Puler.	Pulayan.
11. Pareens.	Parea.	Pareni.	Parayan.

GROUP 3. IMMIGRANT CASTES.

Barbosa.	Ramusio.	Spanish.	Modern Form.
1. Chatis.	Chelij.	Chetis.	Chetty.
2. Guzurates.	Guzzerati.	Guzurates.	Gujarāti Banyān.
3. Mapuleres.	Mapuleres.	Mapuleres.	Mappila or Mappilla (Moplah).
4. Pardesi.	Pardesi.	Pardesi.	Pardēsi or " foreign " Muḥammadan.

[1] *Chatis.* This is the widely spread commercial caste of South India generally known as Chettys, whose original home is on the East or Coromandel Coast, as Barbosa has correctly observed. They have not up to the present day become incorporated in the caste system of Malabar, and still remain Tamils and essentially foreigners. (See *Mal. Gaz.*, p. 138; Thurston, II, p. 91 ff.; *Hobson-Jobson, s.v.* Chetty.) The Malayālam form Cheṭṭi represents the Tamil Sheṭṭi, which is with much probability supposed to be derived from Skr. Shrēshtha, or Shreshṭhī, although some authorities dispute this. This derivation is supported by Dalgado, *Lexicologia Luso-Asiatica*, p. 119, and *Glossario, s.v.* Chatim. The usual Portuguese form is Chatim. J. de Barros gives this form as a nickname for a clever tradesman, and says that from this a verb *chatinar*, " to haggle," had been constructed. He uses the plural form Chatijs for the caste-name (*Dec. I*, ix, f. 182, Ed. 1628).

and they deal in precious stones, seed pearls and corals, and other valuable goods, such as gold and silver, either coined or to be coined. This is their principal trade, and they follow it because they can raise or lower the prices of such things many times ; they are rich and respected ; they lead a clean life, and have spacious houses in their own appointed streets ; they also have their own houses of worship, and idols different from those of the natives of the land. They go naked from the waist up, and below gather round them long garments[1] many yards in length, little turbans on their heads and long hair gathered under the turban. Their beards are shaven, and they wear finger marks of ashes mixed with sandal-wood and saffron on their breasts, foreheads and shoulders. They have wide holes in their ears,[2] into which an egg would fit, which are filled with gold with many precious stones, they wear many rings on their fingers, they are girt about with girdles of gold and jewellery and ever carry in their breasts great pouches in which they keep scales and weights of their gold and silver coins and precious stones. Their sons also begin to carry them as soon as they are ten years of age, they go about changing small coins. They are great clerks and accountants, and reckon all their sums on their fingers. They are given to usury, so much so that one brother will not lend to

---

[1] The complexities of the costume of Tamils and other Hindu foreigners are specially notable in Malabar, where the ordinary dress of Malayalis is just a cloth passed round the waist, the end being tucked in at the side, quite the simplest manner in which it is possible to wear a cloth. Malayalis wear no turbans, except where affected by alien custom or requirements. The long hair is the tuft hanging from the back of the head in Tamil fashion. The Mulayali gathers his hair in a knob on the top of his head, a far more pleasing fashion.—(T.)

[2] Compare the account of the Baneanes of Gujerat (Vol. I, p. 114, n. 3) where Barbosa uses a similar phrase as to the size of the holes in the ears. In the present instance Ramusio and Spanish have given the correct meaning of the Portuguese. Ramusio has converted the caste-name into Chelij.

another a *ceitil*,[1] without making a profit thereby. They are sober and orderly in eating and spending. They speak a tongue which differs from that of Malabar as it is with the Castilians and Portuguese.[2] They marry as with us, and their sons inherit their property. If her husband dies the wife never marries again, young as she may be ; if the wife dies the husband may marry again, and if she offends he may poison her without any punishment. They manage their own affairs, the Kings may not enquire into their crimes ; they do justice to one another with which the King is satisfied. When they die, their bodies are burnt ; they eat everything save the cow only.

In the Kingdom of Calecut there is another caste of Heathen merchants whom they call *Guzarates*[3] (but in Cambaya, of which they are natives, they are called *Baneanes*).[3] I have already under the head of Cambaia told of their customs, which they practise correctly in Malabar, for some dwell in Cochin, and some in Cananor, but the more part in Calecut, and trade in goods of every kind from many lands. The Kings delight in them because of the heavy dues they pay on their trade. They dwell in great houses and streets of their own, as the Jews are wont to dwell in our land. In the Idols they differ from the others. They have many bells both great and small, like ours.

---

[1] *Ceitil.* A very small Portuguese coin of copper which took the place of the *dinheiro* in the reign of D. Joao II (1481–95).

[2] The relation between Tamil and Malayalam is, in fact, very similar to that between Spanish and Portuguese.

[3] *Guzarates* (Buzaŕates in the printed text, Guzzerati in Ramusio). These are the Gujeráti *Banyáns* or *Baneanes* described under the Kingdom of Guzarate, Vol. I, p. 110. The copyist or printer has in the printed text turned the name into Banqueanes. They were and are a commercial race who trade extensively outside their own country. There is still a prosperous colony of Guzeratis in Calicut and other towns of Malabar.

And in this land of Malabar there are Moors in great
numbers who speak the same tongue as the Heathens
of the land, and go naked like the Nayres, but as a token
of distinction from the Heathen they wear little round
caps[1] on their heads, and long beards, "and they are
so many and so rooted[2] in the soil throughout Malabar
that " it seems to me they are a fifth part of its people
spread over all its kingdoms and provinces. They are
rich, and live well, they hold all the sea trade and
navigation in such sort that if the King of Portugal had
not discovered India, Malabar would already have been
in the hands of the Moors, and would have had a Moorish
King ; [for the Heathen if displeased at anything become
Moors, and the Moors show them great respect, and if it
is a woman, they take her in marriage]. " These follow
the Heathen custom in many ways ; their sons inherit[3]
half their property, and their nephews (sisters' sons) take
the other half. They belong to the sect of Mafamede,
their holy day is Friday. Throughout this land they
have a great number of mosques. They marry as many
wives as they can support and keep as well many

---

[1] *Little round caps and long beards.* The little round caps are still
worn. Mappilas are not, as a matter of fact, successful in growing long
beards. A Muḥammadan with a long beard is usually a foreign settler.
Most Mappilas either shave the face or cut the beard close to the skin.
—(T.)

[2] For " reiguados " in the Portuguese text read " arraigados."

[3] *Inheritance among Mappilas.* Barbosa's statement that among the
Mappilas " their sons inherit half their property, and their sisters'
sons the other half," is not true of the present custom. Mr. Thorne
says : " In Calicut and South Malabar Mappilas follow the ordinary
Muḥammadan (Shāfa'ī) law of inheritance. In North Malabar they
are most Marumakkathayam, and follow the rule of succession through
females, but even in this part there is a disposition to assimilate to
orthodox Muḥammadan law. An Act passed lately (Madras Act 1,
1918) provides that when a Māppila dies intestate his self-acquired
property, as distinct from the *tarwād* property, *i.e.*, the joint family
under the rule of descent through females, shall devolve according
to Muḥammadan law." It seems possible that Barbosa's account
relates to some similar compromise between orthodoxy and local
custom.

heathen concubines[1] of low caste. If they have sons or daughters by these they make them Moors, and ofttimes the mother as well, and thus this evil generation continues to increase in Malabar ; the people of the country call them Mapuleres.[2]

There are many other foreign Moors as well in the town

---

[1] *Heathen concubines.* It is no longer respectable to keep such concubines, but when a Hindu woman of low caste becomes compromised with a Mappila the result is often the conversion of the woman and her children, if any.—(T.)

[2] *Mapuleres.* This name denotes the greater part of the Muhammadan population of Malabar, who go under the name of Mappilla, which in English books usually appears under the form Moplah or Moplay. This name includes the great bulk of the Moslems who form fully 30 per cent. of the population. They are a mixed race, descended from the unions between Arab mercantile settlers and the women of the country, and from a considerable number of converts among some of the depressed castes and the fishermen. They are Sunni and Shī'a Muhammadans, and have the correct marriage system ; nevertheless in matters of inheritance most of them, especially in North Malabar, follow the Nāyar system of descent through females. The most probable explanation of their name seems to be that of Mr. Logan, that it is *Maha-pilla* or " child of a great man," and was originally an honorific title. Thus it would have some resemblance to such a form as *Khānzāda*, or *Amīr-zāda* in Persia and in North India, the latter of which, in its shortened form *Mirza*, has become a professional title in Persia. The same title Mappilla, is occasionally used for Syrian Christians, and Jews are also known as Juda Mappilla. The full name of the Muslims is Jonakan Mappillas ; the word Jonakan or Yonakan means Greek or simply foreigners, according to some. The derivation from Yavana, a Greek or Ionian, is commonly accepted, but cannot be considered as established. Having regard to the use of the name for Christians and Jews as well as for Muhammadans, Mr. Badger's derivation from the Ar. *Muflih*, " prosperous or victorious " (Varthema, p. 123, n. 1) does not seem probable. The influential position of these people at Cananor and Calicut owing to the long-standing proclivity of the rulers of Calicut towards Islam, to some extent accounts for the hostile attitude taken up by the Zamorin towards the Portuguese. His trade was clearly dependent on the Arabs and Moplahs, and the evident intention of the Portuguese to get it into their own hands was sufficient to ensure his enmity. João de Barros (I, ix, Ch. 3, f. 182) in speaking of these people uses the name *Naiteas*, applied also to the mixed Muhammadan population of the North and South Konkan (see Vol. I, § 59, p. 147, Note 1). He considers that they formed a fourth part of the population of Malabar, Barbosa gave it as one-fifth, while modern statistics raise it to 30 per cent (Thurston, IV, p. 455 ; *Mal. Gaz.*, p. 189-199 ; *Cochin Tribes and Castes*, II, p. 459 ff.). They are an energetic race, good sailors, and farmers ; and Buchanan (in 1807) spoke of them as the only people " who possess any spirit in agriculture " (II, p. 561). This spirit also has often shown itself in a tendency to risings and turbulence.

of Calecut, who are called *Pardesis*,[1] natives of divers lands, Arabs, Persians, Guzarates, Curasanes[2] and Daquanis, who are settled here. As the trade of this country is very large, they gathered here in great numbers with their wives and sons, and seem to have increased.

They sail everywhere with goods of many kinds and have in the town itself a Moorish Governor[3] of their own who rules and punishes them without interference from the King, save that the Governor gives an account of certain matters to the King. Before the Portuguese had discovered India, they were so many, and so powerful and independent in the city that the Heathen did not dare to enter it, on account of their pride. Afterwards, when they perceived the determination of the Portuguese they endeavoured to cast them out of India, which, when they could not do, little by little, they departed to their own lands abandoning India and its trade, so that but few of them have stayed there, unless in some way forced to do so.

In the days of their prosperity in trade and navigation they built in the city keeled ships of a thousand and a thousand and two hundred *bahares* burden. These ships were built without any nails, but the whole of the sheathing was sewn with thread, and all upper works differed much from the fashion of ours, they had no decks. Here they took on board goods for every place,

---

[1] Portuguese text *Pardetis* ; *Pardēsī*, the universal Indian term for a foreigner is no doubt intended. *Paradēsī* in Mal. There is a considerable Parsi colony in Calicut.

[2] For Curaanes in the Portuguese text read Curasanes, *i.e.*, Khorasānī.

[3] *Moorish Governor.* " In Calicut and elsewhere there are still Mappila ' Tangals ' and Kāzis whose authority is much respected. The Arab strain in them is easily recognisable "—(T.). Further information about these Tangals will be found in Thurston, IV, p. 46 ff., *s.v.* Mappilla. The Sunnīs and Shī'as each have their own Tangal. There can be no doubt that these are the modern representatives of the Moorish Governors.

and every monsoon ten or fifteen of these ships sailed
for the Red Sea, Aden and Meca, where they sold their
goods at a profit, some to the Merchants of Juda, who
took them on thence in small vessels to Toro, and from
Toro they would go to Cairo, and from Cairo to Alexandria,
and thence to Venice, whence they came to our regions.
These goods were pepper (great store), ginger, cinnamon,
cardamoms, myrobalans, tamarinds, canafistula, precious
stones of every kind, seed pearls, musk, ambergris,
rhubarb, aloes-wood, great store of cotton cloths,
porcelains, and some of them took on at Juda copper,
quicksilver, vermilion, coral, saffron, coloured velvets,
rosewater, knives, coloured camlets, gold, silver, and
many other things which they brought back for sale at
Calecut. They started in February, and returned from
the middle of August up to the middle of October of the
same year. In this trade they became extremely wealthy.
And on their return voyages they would bring with them
other foreign merchants who settled in the city, beginning
to build ships and to trade, on which the King received
heavy duties. As soon as any of these Merchants reached
the city, the King assigned him a *Nayre*, to protect and
serve him, and a *Chatim* clerk to keep his accounts and
look after his affairs, and a broker to arrange for him to
obtain such goods as he had need of, for which three
persons they paid good salaries every month. [They all
served him well, and when the merchant bought spices
the sellers gave him on every five and twenty pounds of
ginger, four pounds more for his three servants, and so on
with goods of other kinds.] "These men are white, well
bred and proper to behold ; they go well-clad and decked
in garments of silk, scarlet-in-grain,[1] camlets, cotton ;

---

[1] *Scarlet-in-grain*. I have here and elsewhere used this phrase to
translate the Portuguese *gram* or *grão*. This use has been criticised

turbans twisted round their heads. They had very fine houses and many servants. They were luxurious in eating, drinking and sleeping. Thus they continued to thrive until the Portuguese came to India. Now there are, it may almost be said, none, and those that there are do not live independently. Up to this point I have told very fully of all the castes and the divers customs of the people of Malabar, and also some specially of Calecut. I will now relate the position of each Kingdom separately and how the aforesaid land of Malabar is divided."[1]

by Sir Richard Temple in a review of Vol I in the *J R.A S.* for 1919, p. 413   He contends that " scarlet " in the sixteenth and seventeenth centuries was not a "colour" but a cloth, and that the exclusive use of the term for a colour came later   " One hears of scarlet of all colours in the earlier days "   In adopting the phrase I intended to give a translation of the Portuguese *grão*, which without doubt referred originally to the *kermes* or scarlet grain, and to cloth dyed with it. Owing to the lasting character of the dye its use in English in the seventeenth century extended to other fast dyes.   In its earliest use in English it was generally associated with the colour red, especially scarlet   Thus we have in Chaucer's *Tale of Sir Thopas*, " His rode is lyk scarlet in grain "   In *Manners and Household Expenses*, 1465 (quoted in New English Dict), " My maistyre delyverd of crymeson out of greyn ii yerdes."   Moryson's *Itinerary*, 1617, I–IV, p. 96 (ditto), " The Spaniards and Portugals brought graine for Scarlet Dye " North's *Plutarch* (1580), " This sail was not white but red, died in grain, and of the colour of Scarlet "   Holland, in his *Pliny* (1601) speaks of "scarlet grain which commeth of the Ilex," which may be compared with Barbosa's own remark (*infra*, § 106, p. 158, n 2) that the lac in its method of production resembles the "grain" produced in Europe from the Ilex or holm-oak   It is clear (1) that the " grain " produced a bright red or scarlet dye, and that the term was often transferred to the cloth dyed with it, and (2) that the use of the phrase (certainly in use in England in the fifteenth and sixteenth centuries) *scarlet-in-grain* may properly be used in a translation of a Portuguese book of the early sixteenth century   There is no doubt that scarlet was at a later time used for cloth independent of colour, but as a rule I think it implied the colour, as several cloths of other colours are mentioned while no other colour seems to be added to the name scarlet. It is impossible here to deal with this question fully.

[1] There is little to be added to Barbosa's full and picturesque description of the Muhammadan traders of various countries who resorted to the ports of Malabar, and grew wealthy and luxurious on the great profits they made there   The dependence of the rulers on this trade is well brought out, and it is easy to understand the consternation with which these people beheld the resolution of the Portuguese to divert this trade to a new route, and take it out of their hands   Hence the great combination between the Sultāns of Egypt and Gujarāt to drive the intruders out of India.

§ 88.   KINGDOM OF CANANOR.

YOU are to know then that following the coast southwards from *Cumbola* which pertains to the King of Narsingua, there is a place which they call *Cotecolam*[1] on the strand in a fortress where is posted a nephew of the King of Cananor, the Warden of the Marches.   Further on is a river named Miraporam[2] on which stands a seaport of Moors and Heathen, a place of much trade and navigation, where dwells another of his nephews who often rises against him, and the King again brings him under his power.   After passing this place further along the coast is the Mount D'Ely,[3] close to the sea, a mountain of great height and round, in the midst of low land whither all the ships of both Moors and Heathen steer, and from it they make their reckoning when they are about to sail. From this mountain flow many springs where the ships take in their water ; on it is much wood among which is abundance of wild cinnamon.   Close to its foot to the south is a place called *Maravel*,[4] an old town prosperous

---

[1] *Cotecolam.* The modern Kattakulam in South Kanara. De Barros commences his list of the places on the coast of Malabar (in *Dec. I*, ix, 1, f. 174 Res.) with this place, but divides Cóta from Coulão by a comma.   The Sommario in Ramusio (1563) gives it as Cote Coulam.

[2] *Mira-pura* in the Spanish version. This probably stands for Nileshwaram R. (see Yule and Cordier, *Cathay*, IV, 74, and *Mal. Gaz.*, p. 5).

[3] *Mount D'Ely.*   See former note, p. 1, n. 3.   As to the springs and the woods on this mountain Mr. Thorne says, "the country round is honeycombed with rivers.   The hill itself is on an island.   It has now been practically stripped of all timber except scrub jungle."

[4] *Maranel* in printed text, read *Maravel* (Spanish Marave).   This is the place now known as Madayi (also called Pazhayangadi, under which name it appears in the map in the *Mal. Gaz.*) (see also *ib.*, p. 397).   It is on the canal which connects Taliparamba R. with the creeks of Mount Deli R.   Under the name of Marāwī it was often spoken of by Muhammadan writers jointly with Hili, by which name they knew Eli or Mount D'Ely.   De Barros and Correa call it Marabia. Correa speaks of the Gulf of Marabia, close to the Monte Dely, which V. da Gama entered on his second voyage (Correa, I, 291).   De Barros (I, f. 174b) gives the following places from the commencement of Malabar southwards from the river Canherecora (Chandragiri), all

and well furnished with food, peopled by Moors, Heathen
and Jews, who speak the country language and have long
dwelt there.   In this place, and around the Mount D'Ely
there is a great fishery.   Near thereto, a short distance
along the coast is a river on which inside is a very fine
Moorish and Heathen town called *Balaerpartam*[1] in
which the King of Cananor constantly stays, where he
has a great and fair palace.   And on the strand there is
a hill on which stands a fortress.   Four or five leagues
inland from this town there is another town of both
Moors and Heathen which has great traffic with the
merchants of the Kingdom of Narsyngua.   It is called
Taliparam,[2] and much copper is used there.

On the coast passing *Balaherpatam* and going southwards there is a great city called *Cananor*,[3] inhabited

---

belonging to the Kingdom of Cananor, Cota, Coulão (*i.e.*, Cotacoulam),
Nilichilão (Nireshwara), Marabia, Bolepatan, Cananor, Tramapatan,
Chomba, Maim and Purepatan.

Maranel, Maravel.   " The derivation of Madayi from Mādā-Ēzhi
is probable, and is supported by the form here found.   It is still an
important Mappila centre containing an old mosque built by Malik
Ibn Dīnār, the early Arab apostle.   There are no Jews there now,
but a Jew's tank (Chūlā Kulam) exists on the hill near the Travellers'
Bungalow."—(T.)

[1] *Balaerpartam.* Tarmapatam in Ramusio, Balapatam in the Spanish
version.   It is doubtless the town of Vallarepattanam (or Baliapatam)
on the estuary of the river of the same name.

[2] *Taliparam* is an emendation of Faliparam in Portuguese text.   It
appears in the Spanish version under the form *eah paranco*, doubtless a
misprint.   No doubt Taliparam stands for the modern town of Taliparamba, a place of some importance.   A bathing shed was built
here in 1524, soon after Barbosa wrote (*Mal. Gaz.*, p. 399).   " There
is also an ancient temple at Taliparamba, which, however, is only
8 or 9 miles from Baliapatam."—(T.)

[3] *Cananor.*   The city of Cannanore, which plays such a large part
in the early history of the Portuguese in India and where Duarte
Barbosa spent so many years, was at that time the headquarters of one of
the principal States which resisted the hegemony of Calicut and welcomed
the Portuguese as their natural allies.   The Raja bore the title of Kollattiri
(see above, p. 4, n. 1 and Appendix II (*c*)).   It is also the seat of the
important Muhammadan family, the head of which was known as
the " Ali Raja," which still retains some of its old importance.   Here
was begun the first Portuguese fort on the mainland of India.   The
Viceroy, F. D'Almeida, having obtained the Raja's permission, began
to dig moats in 1505.   The fort, however, was not finished till 1507,
when the Viceroy, as Correa tells us, gave it the name of *Santdogil*,

by many Moors and Heathen ; they are great merchants and have many ships both great and small, and deal in goods of all sorts with the great Kingdom of Cambaya Ormus, Charamandel, Dabul, Chaul, Banda, Goa, Ceilam, and with the Isles of Maldiva. In this city the King our Lord possesses a fortress and a trading factory in perfect peace, love and safety, and around the fort is a town of Christians of this country, married men with their wives and children, who were converted to our Holy Faith after it was built and continue daily to be converted.

Leaving this city, and continuing along the coast southwards there is a town of Moors named *Craguate*.[1] They have ships on which they sail, and are natives of the land. Beyond this place is a river which divides

---

after the castle of Sant' Angelo at Rome (Correa, I, pp. 583 and 728). Meanwhile in 1506 another fort had been built at Cochin (Correa, I, 640). A fort had been built by Almeida on the Isle of Anchediva earlier in 1505 (De Barros, *I*, viii, Ch. 9, f. 165), but he ordered it to be dismantled soon after, in 1507 (Correa, I, pp. 726, 727). Linschoten describes the Cannanore fort as " the best fortress that the Portingalles have in all Malabar " (Linsch., I, 67).

Pyrard de Laval says (I, 445), " The Portuguese are at peace with him (*i.e.*, the Ali Raja), and by his permission hold a small fort in Cananor containing a Church and a Jesuits' College."

The fort now existing still bears the name of St. Angelo. The *Mal. Gaz.* (p. 394) says that the present fort is of later date. When it was rebuilt is not clear, but possibly the reconstruction is that carried out by Alboquerque, as we learn from the *Commentaries* (IV, 208) that " he rebuilt the fortress of Cananor with stone and mortar, but up to that time it was built with mud." The Dutch took this fort and that of Cochin from the Portuguese in 1663, about eighteen months after peace between the two countries had been signed, but Portugal was never able to obtain its return.

Buchanan (II, 553) gives an account of the town and fort in the beginning of the nineteenth century, and of an interview with the Bibi, the mother of the young Ali Raja, who at that time held the estates. (See also *Mal. Gaz.*, 393–396.)

Cannanor. " Mal. Kaṇṇūr, which is an abbreviation for Kaṇṇanūr (town of Krishna."—(T.)

[1] *Cragate*. (Crecate in Ramusio, Ciecate in the Spanish version.) I propose to read this *Eragate* and to identify it with Edakkād on the coast between Cananor and Dharmadam. It is now a station on the South Canara Railway.

Mr. Thorne thinks this is probably a correct emendation, and says the change of *d* to *r* is quite natural (*e.g.*) Madayi-

F

into two arms on which ships can sail, which surround
a great town of Moors, natives of the land, which they
call *Tremopatam*.[1] They are natives of the land, rich
merchants, owning many and great ships. This is the
last place which the King of Cananor holds against
Calecut, it has very fine mosques of the Moors, who are
so rich and powerful that they rise with the whole city
in rebellion for any injury they may receive so that the
King is ofttimes compelled to come and to threaten
them, or cajole them, " and had the Portuguese not
discovered India this city would by now have had a
Moorish King over it, and the whole of Malabar would
have been converted to the sect of Mafamede."

Higher up the same river at four leagues' distance
from this city there is another large and wealthy town
of the Moors, natives of the land, named *Quategatam*,[2]
the " inhabitants whereof carry on a very great trade

Maravel). He adds " It is however, possible that Ciecate is the
correct reading, in which case it would be Kakkād, a suburb of Cananore ;
but Kakkād is not actually on the sea." A further objection to this
reading is that in Spanish or Portuguese *C* before *i* could not have
the sound of *k*, and that Ramusio keeps the form with *r* after the *C*.
I think therefore that the reading Eragate may be adopted.

[1] *Tremopatam*. Tarmapatan in Ramusio and the Spanish version. This
place is undoubtedly the Deh-fatan of Ibn Baṭūta and the Darma-fatan
of the Tuḥfatu'l-mujāhidīn. Its modern form is Dharmadam, representing the older Dharmapattanam. It lies on an island formed by the
junction of the Tellicherry and Anjara-kandi rivers, just north of the
modern town of Tellicherry. It was a sacred place among Muslims,
and is still much honoured as the place whence according to the legend
(see above p. 3, note 2) Chērumān Perumāl sailed for Mecca (*Mal.
Gaz.*, p. 422 ; *Cathay*, IV, p. 76).
" It rises to a hill on which are the solid remains of a small fort
called by Malayalis Chērumān Kōtta (*i.e.*, the fort of Chērumān
Perumāl), and by Europeans ' Tippu's Fort.' There is no fine mosque
in the place now."—(T.)

[2] *Quategatam*. Capo gatto in Ramusio, Cotaogatto in the Spanish
version. This place is doubtless Kottayam in the same vicinity,
where are the palaces of the Raja of Kottayam (*Mal. Gaz.*, p. 423).
" The Spanish reading Cotaogatto puts the identification beyond
doubt. It is Kottayam. The oblique case of the word is Kottayakath,
hence Kottioth or Cotiote of the Tellicherry factors. It was and is
the seat of the Kottayam Rajas, the allies of the company. The
mercantile centre is now at the modern town of Kuthuparamba, a
mile away."—(T.)

with those of Narsyngua." Here, and throughout the Kingdom of Cananor right good pepper grows, but not in great abundance ; there is great store of ginger, cardamoms, myrobalans, canafistula, zerumba and zedoary.[1]

In this Kingdom in some of the great rivers are found also certain great *lizards*[2] which devour men, the breath thereof when they are alive, smells of civet, and in the land among the woods and thickets are found certain serpents which the Indians call *Murcas*[3] and we call them *cobras de capelo*, (hooded snakes) for they make a hood over their heads. They are very poisonous and any man bitten by them lasts no more than two hours [and sometimes two or three days]. Many jugglers carry these about alive in earthen vessels so charmed that they bite not, and they gain thereby much money, putting them round their necks and showing them. There is yet another kind of snake even more poisonous, which the natives call *Madalis*.[4] Such is their renown that they kill in the very act of biting, so that the person bitten cannot utter a single word, nor turn him round to die.

---

[1] See *Hobson-Jobson*, *s.v.* zedoary and zerumbet where this passage is quoted.

[2] *Lizards*. This refers to crocodiles which are abundant. Attacks on human beings are, however, rare. They are supposed to be most dangerous round Mount Dely.—(T.)

[3] *Murcas*. *Murcas* is an emendation from Nurcas of the Portuguese text, in accordance with the forms in the Spanish version and Ramusio. "It is the Malaya *Mŭrkhan* 'a cobra,' used in the term *Eṭṭaḍi mŭrkham* '8 paces cobra,' because a man dies within 8 paces of the spot where he is bitten. The usual name for a cobra is *sarpam*, 'snake,' or *nalla sarpam*, 'good snake.'"—(T.)

[4] *Madali* (Spanish version *Mandal*, Ramusio *Mandali*.) No doubt in the MS. this word was written Mādali, *i.e.*, Mandali, which is evidently the correct form. "It clearly means the *Maṇḍali*, varieties of which are regarded as very venomous. The *payydna maṇḍali* is—so I gather from descriptions—what we call Russell's viper. Malayalis do not consider it so instantaneously fatal as Barbosa represents it, but the bite is much dreaded as it usually tears the flesh 'like the bite of a dog.'"—(T.)

The Russell's viper (*Daboia Russellii*) is usually considered in Northern India to come next to the cobra in deadliness.

F 2

§ 89. THE KINGDOM OF CALECUT.

LEAVING this Kingdom of Cananor and going south-ward, on the further side of this same river of Tremo-patam is a town belonging to the Moors of the country which is called *Tiramuingate*,[1] where there are many ships and much traffic by sea. Beyond this place is a river on which lies a large Moorish town called *Manjaim*,[2] also a place of sea traffic, with many ships and much trade.

Beyond this is another place also of the Moors which they call *Chamobai*,[3] a place of much sea traffic. Inland

---

[1] *Tiramuingate.* The Portuguese text reads Firamuingate, but the initial letter is undoubtedly " T." (Teringate in Ramusio, Terivagaty in the Port. form represents the Mal. Tiruvan-gād. Identified with Tellichery in *Cathay*, IV, 76. The form Tellicherry seems to have been already in use when the East India Company occupied the place about 1683 (*Mal. Gaz.*, pp. 55 and 426.) The modern prosperity of the place dates from that time, and the decline of Dhar-mapattanam also, as political considerations prevented its occupation, although its site was better.
   " Tellicherry (Talassēri) is a modern name. Strictly speaking it applies only to the mercantile quarter which (as in Calicut) has arisen between the sea and the old town. The S.E. portion of the present municipality is *Tiruvangād*, still the Hindu residential quarter. It contains a famous and beautiful temple."—(T.)

[2] *Manjaim.* (Mazeire in Ramusio, Mazeri in the Spanish version. Maim in de Barros.) The form given by de Barros is closer to the modern form Mahé. Yet it would seem that this name was derived from Mahé de Labourdonnais who took it in 1725, and changed its original name of Mayyazhi to his own name Mahé (see *Mal. Gaz.*, pp. 57 and 435). It was several times occupied by the British but was restored to France in 1817, and still remains a French possession. Barbosa's form is close to the vernacular name. " The Spanish reading is nearest to the Mal. form " (T.). A full history of the French settlement is given in *Les Origines de Mahé de Malabar*, by Alfred Martineau, Paris, 1917.

[3] *Chamobai.* (Chemobay in Ramusio, and Combaa in his *Sommario de Regni*, f. 332b., Chemobay in the Spanish version.) The modern form is Chombāla (*Mal. Gaz., p.* 433).
   " Chombāla or Chombaya 3 miles south of Mahé. It is now negligible as a port. The Basel Mission has a station there.
   " Barbosa says that the country inland of Tellicherry, Mahé and Chombāla in his time was divided between two lords, whose status apparently was not that of kings. Undoubtedly this part of Malabar was exceptionally independent, being beyond the influence of the Zamorin to the south and having broken away from the Kolattiri to the north. Even to this day the land belongs largely to a number of Nāyar *janmis*, contrasting therein with the enormous estates of

from these three places the country is thickly peopled by *Nayres* who are very fine men and give obedience to no King, they are divided between two lords who rule them.

Passing by these places there is a river which they call *Pedirpatam*,[1] on which stands a Moorish town with much trade and navigation, and from this place begins the Kingdom of Calecut.

Passing thereby is another town on the coast called *Tircore*[2] and passing this there is another which they call *Pandanare*[3] beyond which there is yet another with

---

the ex-ruling families to north and south. Behind Tellicherry the chieftains were the Truvalinad Nambiyars (*i.e.*, Nāyars) one of whom was the Kurungoth Nāyar. Behind Mahé and Chombāla the Kadathanad dynasty, an offshoot of the Kolattiri, had not yet established its power."—(T.)

[1] In the printed Portuguese text *Hopedirpatam*, where the first syllable stands for the article *ho* or *o*. (Pudripatan in Ramusio and Pudepatana in his *Sommario*, Pudepatane in the Spanish version). It is the Bud-fatan of Ibn Batūta, and was known as far back as the time of Cosmas Indicopleustes as *Pudopatana* (*Cathay*, IV, p. 69). The note in *Cathay* (*l.c.*, p. 77) says " the name is not found in modern maps, but it must have been near the Waddakarre of Keith Johnston's."

Badagara or Vadakara is the form given in the *Mal. Gaz.*, p. 432. The town is still in the hands of Muhammadans (Mappillas).

" *Pedirpatam* stands for Puthupattanam ' new town,' now Puthupanam on the north bank of the Kotta River, near Badagara, a comparatively modern town. As Barbosa says, on crossing the river one comes into the kingdom of Calicut (the Zamorin's domain). To this day the Zamorin does not own an inch of land to the north of the Kotta River. His northernmost *Cherikkal* (rent-collecting centre) is at Kollam, included in which are lands running up to the river."—(T.)

[2] *Tircore*. (Tircori in Ramusio, but in his *Sommario* (*l.c.*) he makes it into two places, Tiri, Corci). The modern name is Tikkodi or Trikkodi (*Mal. Gaz.*, p. 433 and map). " There is now a fine lighthouse there."—(T.)

[3] *Padanare* (Pandarani in Ramusio and Poramdarani in his *Sommario*; Pandareni in the Spanish version). The modern form of the name is Pantalāyini or Pantalāyini Kollam. The latter form is close to that given from Ramusio's *Sommario* as quoted in *Cathay*, IV, p. 77 (Colam Pandarani), but this form does not appear in the 1563 Ed. of Ramusio, I, p. 332 b. Whether or not it is the *Patale* of Pliny is doubtful, but it is certainly the Fandaraina of Ibn Batūta and Idrisi, the Flandrina of Odoric (*Cathay*, II, p. 133) and the Fenderena of Fra Mauro and many others. (See *Hobson-Jobson*, *s.v.* Pandarani ; *Cathay*, IV, p.77 ; *Mal. Gaz.* p. 436). The modern town of Quilandi or Koilandi close by has now supplanted it. This is the Coulete of de Barros.

Mr. W. W. Rockhill in his *Notes on the Relations and Trade of China* in T'oung-Pao, Vol. xv (Leiden, 1914) p. 425, alludes to Chinese trade

a small river which they call *Capucate*.[1] This is a place of great trade and many ships, where on the strand are found many soft sapphires.

Two leagues beyond this place is the city of *Calecut*,[2]

---

with this coast in A.D. 1296, and mentions Panam and Fandaraina among the ports alluded to in the *Yüan Shih*. His quotation from Duarte Barbosa alludes to Panam or Pananie (Pananx on p. 153 of the Spanish version). Fandaraina or Pantalayini seems to be mentioned also in another Chinese authority of the same period (*ib.*, p. 435, note 1).

[1] *Capucate.* (Capucar in Ramusio and Capucad in the Spanish version.) This small port appears to be the Kappat or Kappata on the coast between Quilandi and Calicut, alluded to in *Mal. Gaz.*, p. 45, and shown in the map in the same volume. There can be no doubt that it is the Capua of the *Roteiro* (Ed. 1838, p. 50), which was the first town sighted in India by the Portuguese under Vasco da Gama. "And on this day (19th May, 1498) in the afternoon we anchored two leagues below this city of Calecut and this we did because it seemed to the pilot that a town which was there, called Capua, was Calecut, and below this town is another called Panderamy, and we anchored along the coast about a league and a half from the land." The writer of the passage in the *Mal. Gaz.* supposes that as the south-west monsoon was threatening "a few days later they moved to the shelter of the mud-bank off Pantalayini Kollam." But their return to this anchorage did not take place until after they had arrived at Calicut and had entered into communication with the King, by whose advice they made this move (*Hobson-Jobson*, s.v. Capucat ; *Mal. Gaz.*, p. 45).

There is now no trade worth mentioning, and apparently no soft sapphires are found there.

[2] *Calecut.* The important town of Calicut, once the capital of the ruler known to the Portuguese as the Zamorin or Çamidre, and now the headquarters of the British District of Malabar, although the Zamorins still maintain their state there, is famous as the first town in India reached by the Portuguese under Vasco da Gama. Yet in their subsequent history it is not as important as its neighbours Cochin and Cannanor. The Portuguese were not received with joy because the ruler was under the influence of the Muhammadan traders and feared to lose his profits. In addition to this the port was a bad one, and Cochin offered not only a more friendly reception but a safer haven. After many years of fighting and truces Alboquerque at length in 1513 succeeded in building a fort, but twelve years later the Portuguese lost it and their control was never effective. Yet their fort at Chaliyan on the Beypore river, only six miles away, gave them considerable power. The distance given from Capucate, two leagues, is correct. It is seven or eight miles.

"Barbosa does not refer to the popular explanation of this name, The Malayālam name is Kōzhi-Kōd, i.e., "Cock-fort" or "Cock-corner." The Keralolpatti story is that the Zamorin, who was over-looked in the partition of the Perumal's territory, had to be content with a piece of land so small that a cock's crow would be heard throughout it. This is too fanciful to be accepted as a serious explanation of the name. Kōzhi (which means fowl rather than cock) is curiously common in proper names in South Malabar, e.g., Kōzhisseri (fowl village), Kōzhiprath (a big *tarwad* near Calicut). Can it be that the fowl was some sort of totem ? Possibly a connection can

wherein more trade was carried on, and yet is, by foreigners
than by the natives of the land, where also the King our
Lord, with the full assent of the King thereof, holds a
very strong fortress. To the south of this city there is
a river on which lies another town called *Chiliate*,[1] where
dwell many Moors, natives of the land who are merchants,
and have many ships in which they sail ; and beyond
this town and river there is another city belonging to
the King of Calecut, called *Propriamguary*,[2] of both
Moors and Heathen, a place of trade. Passing this
there are two Moorish towns, five leagues apart one
from the other, one named *Parananor*,[3] and the other
Tanor,[3] and inland thence is a Lord who rules over them

be traced with the cock festival at Cranganore (Kodungallur) to
which pilgrims go, carrying fowls, from every part of Malabar."—(T.)

[1] *Chiliate* (*cf.* Vol. I, p. 53, note 1). Ibn Batūta gives the name
as Ash-Shāliyāt. Also see *Mal. Gaz.*, p. 51. The modern name is
Chāliyam, "oblique form Chāliyath " (T.), an island formed by the
Beypore and Kadalundi rivers, held by the Portuguese after they
left Calicut in 1525 ; they built a fort there in 1531, the foundations
of which have recently been excavated (*Mal. Gaz.*, pp. 382, 414).
"A mound where stood the Portuguese fort (destroyed by the
Zamorin in 1571) is still visible at the sea's edge. The merchant
town is now at Beypore on the N. bank of the river."—(T.)

[2] *Propriamguary*. Purparangari in Ramusio, Purpurangari in
Spanish. The modern form is Parappanangadi (*Mal. Gaz.*, 413, 419).
It was the centre of the dominions of the Parappanad Rajas, and
figures in their revolt against Tipu. " The Raja of Parappanad was
feudatory to the Zamorin."—(T.)

[3] *Parananor—Tanor*. "The latter is Tānūr, an important fishing
town. Parananor may be Paravannur, but not if Barbosa means
to imply that it is on the coast, for *Paravannur* is about eight miles
(as the crow flies) inland from Tānūr, to the south-east of it. From
the fact that Parananor is mentioned first it might be supposed that
it is a place north of Tānūr. In that case it might be identified with
Pazhanchanur—a village just north of Kadalundi. But the objection
to that is that Pazhanchanur is north of Parappanangadi already
mentioned. If " Parananor " is on the coast, south of Tānūr, it is
probably *Parapana* (*Paravana*), five or six miles south of Tānūr. In
any case " five leagues " seems to be too great a distance, for Parappanangadi is only about seven miles north of Tānūr, and Ponnani
only about fourteen miles south of it. The ' Lord who rules over
them ' is the Vettath Raja, an unruly feudatory of the Zamorin.
The family became extinct in 1793, when the secular estate was
escheated to Government and the religious endowments handed over
to the Zamorin, who still administers them."—(T.)

Parananor is Paravanor in the Spanish version (not in Ramusio).
Tanor is *Banor* in the printed text.

(and has many Nayres in his pay) and at times rebels against the King of Calecut, and does not obey him. These towns trade in goods of many kinds, and merchants of substance dwell therein.

Beyond these on the coast southward is a river, whereon stands a city of the Moors natives of the land, also some Heathen, which they call *Pananee*.[1] In it are many merchants who possess ships in great numbers, and from it the King of Calecut draws a great revenue in dues.

And advancing thence, there is another river which they call *Chatua*,[2] on which higher up, are a number of Heathen villages, and by this river comes out the greater part of the pepper [grown in the country].

And yet further along the coast is another river which forms the frontier with the Kingdom of Cochim, on the hither bank of which is a place called *Cranganor*,[3]

---

[1] *Pananee*. Pananie in Ramusio, Pananx in the Spanish version. This is the important modern port of Ponnani which lies south of the mouth of the Ponnani river, the largest river in Malabar. It is still a Moorish city, most of the inhabitants being Mappillas (Moplahs). It was attacked by Almeida in 1507 and by Menezes in 1525. The Portuguese fort begun in 1585 was, according to the writer in the *Mal. Gaz.*, never finished (*Mal. Gaz.*, pp. 454–6). It is the residence of the Makhdūm Tangal, the head of the Musalmans of Malabar.

[2] *Chatua*. Catua in Ramusio, Chatna in the Spanish version. This is the modern town of Chettuvayi, or Chetwai, on an island formed by the river of the same name, and the backwaters connected with it. The more important town of Chavakkad or Chowgat, which lies to the north of the estuary, is not named by Barbosa. Chetwai seems never to have been occupied by the Portuguese, although the Dutch and English held it intermittently in the seventeenth and eighteenth centuries (*Mal. Gaz.*, pp. 450, 451). It is the traditional landing place of St. Thomas.

[3] *Cran(g)anor*. Crangalor in Ramusio, Crongolor in the Spanish version This city (here spelt in the text Crananor) occurs further on in the more correct form Cranganor, the form still followed, representing the Malayālam Koḍangalur, a very correct representation of the sound, for here, as elsewhere, in the Dravidian languages a cerebral *ḍ* easily passes into *r*, and to European ears is often indistinguishable from *r*. It was called Muyiri-Khodu in an ancient copperplate inscription earlier than 1500 (see Burnell in *Indian Antiquary*, III, p. 334). It is undoubtedly the Muziris of Pliny and the Periplus. The *Periplus* (sec. 54) also states that it was in the Kingdom of Kerobothra, *i.e.*, Keralaputra. The outlet of the great backwater was then, and till much later, at this point. This is the river mentioned in the *Periplus*. The rise of Cochin and the decline of Cranganor was due to the water

where the King of Cochim[1] holds certain dues.   In these
places dwell many Moors, Christians and Heathen
Indians.   The Christians follow the doctrine of the Blessed
Saint Thomas, and they hold here a Church dedicated to
him, and another to Our Lady.   They are very devout
Christians, lacking nothing but true doctrine whereof I
will speak further on, for many of them dwell from here
as far as Charamandel, whom the Blessed Saint Thomas
left established here when he died in these regions.

" And after passing this town of *Cranganore* along
the shore of the sea, the land of the King of Cochim
begins in the inland region, and above Cochim, the
lands of Calecut extend,"[2] and this land, or rather the

---

of the lagoon finding its way into the sea near Cochin, and the conse-
quent drying up of the Cranganor channel from the beginning of the
fourteenth century (*Mal. Gaz.*, p. 402, 403).   It had gone down
considerably by the time of the arrival of the Portuguese, but still
retained some importance and was an *entrepot* of the pepper trade
according to the *Roteiro* (p. 108).   The ancient Christian population
of the Syrian Church attracted early attention, and was its principal
title to notice when Barbosa wrote.   There was also an early Jewish
settlement.   In earlier times Cranganor seems to have been known
to the Arab chroniclers under the name of Shinkali or other similar
names.   This name (as well as the Gingaleh of Benjamin of Tudela
and the Cyngilin of Fr. Odoric) appears to represent the second element
in the name Tiruvan-jiculam, one of the names of Kodangalur.   It
is now an unimportant village known chiefly for its local cock festival.
(For quotations see *Hobson-Jobson*, *s.v.* Cranganore and Shinkali.
Also *Mal. Gaz.*, pp. 9, 32, 148, 403 ; Schoff's *Periplus*, pp. 205, 208 ;
Vincent A. Smith, *Early History of India*, 2nd Ed., p. 401.)

[1] *Cochin* gradually superseded Cranganore and had become the first
harbour in India (South) at the time of the Portuguese arrival. (*Mal.
Gaz.*, p. 403.)

[2] Here Ramusio simply says, " After passing the town of Crangalor
the end of the Kingdom of Calicut towards the south, the Kingdom
of Cochin is situated."   And the Spanish version is to the same
effect.   What is intended by the statement in the Portuguese text
seems to be that Cochin territory extended along the coast and a short
distance inland, and that the Calicut territory lay still further inland,
being cut off from the sea by Cochin.
" When the Portuguese came to India the Zamorin was at the height
of his power.   He had extended his dominions on the south to the
borders of the present Cochin state and beyond.   The Portuguese
connection with Cochin effectually prevented him from further
encroachments in that direction, and eventually the Zamorin was
pushed back to the Chettuvayi river, which remains the southern
border of his estate."—(T.)

whole land of Malabar is covered along the strand with palm-trees as high as lofty cypresses, the trunk whereof is extremely clean and smooth, and on the top a crown of branches among which grows a great fruit which they call *cocos*,[1] it is a fruit of which they make great profit, and whereof they load many cargoes yearly. They bear their fruit every year without fail, never either more or less. All the folk of Malabar have these palms, and by their means they are free from any dearth, even though other food be lacking, for they produce ten or twelve things all very needful for the service of man, by which they help and profit themselves greatly, and everything is produced in every month of the year.

In the first place they produce these cocos, a very sweet and grateful fruit when green ; from them is drawn milk like that of almonds, and each one when green, has within it a pint [2] of a fresh and pleasant water, better than that from a spring. When they are dry this same water thickens within them into a white fruit as large as an apple which also is very sweet and dainty.[3]

---

[1] *Cocos.* Cocoanuts. Ramusio, " which they call ' tenga ' and we Cochi"; the Spanish version, " which they call tenga, by this they make great profit, and it is a great article of trade, for each year more than four hundred ships are laden with it for many parts. We call these fruits cocoas." " *Tenga* is correct as Mal. for cocoanut. The tree is *tĕnga* and the nut *tĕnga*."—(T.)

[2] *A pint.* The word *quartilho* here used is a measure denoting one quarter of a *canada*. As the *canada* is about three pints, the *quartilho* strictly speaking is about three-quarters of a pint.

[3] The description here given of the various uses of the cocoanut palm and its products may be compared with that given in *Mal. Gaz.*, pp. 223-4. " Products of the cocoanut—cocoanut oil, copra, coir yarn, rope and poonac, to mention the most important—accounted for about half the total exports from Malabar in 1903-04, valued at close upon 500 lakhs of rupees. But apart from these products every part of the tree is of value. It is tapped for toddy, and from the toddy jaggery is prepared and arrack is distilled. Its leaves are used for thatching, their stems and the hard shells of the kernels for fuel, the ripe nut or *elanīr* is full of the most refreshing liquid, and in the last resort the tree is cut down and its trunk utilized for building." Almost all these uses can be found in Barbosa's account. Perhaps the *poonac* or refuse which is made into oilcake is the only one to which he does

The coco itself after being dried is eaten, and from it they get much oil by pressing it, as we do. And from the shell which they have close to the kernel is made charcoal for the goldsmiths who work with no other kind. And from the outer husk which throws out certain threads, they make all the cord [1] which they use, a great article of trade in many parts. And from the sap of the tree itself they extract a *must*, from which they make wine, or properly speaking a strong water, and that in such abundance that many ships are laden with it, for export. From this same *must* they make very good vinegar, and also a sugar of extreme sweetness [2] which is much sought after in India. From the leaf of the tree they make many things, in accordance with the size of the branch. They thatch the houses with them, for as I have said above, no house is roofed with tiles save the temples or the palaces ; all others are thatched with palm-leaves. From the same tree they get timber for their houses and firewood as well, and all this in such abundance that ships take in cargoes thereof for export.

Other palm-trees there are of a lower kind whence they get the leaves on which the Heathen write ; it serves as paper.[3] There are other very slender palms the trunks

not refer. The oil and thread are referred to as far back as the *Periplus*. The word *copra*, which is of Indian origin and has now spread all over the world, is not used by Barbosa. *Cayro* or coir, is not named here, although he used the word in an earlier mention (Vol. I, p. 27, note 1 ; and p. 197, note 3). See also *Hobson-Jobson, s.v.* Coco, etc. For early use of palm-oil and coir, see Schoff's *Periplus*, pp. 29, 36, 99, 154.

[1] The cord known as *Cairo* or Coir. (See Vol. I, p. 27, note 1.) "The correct Mal. form is kåyar not kåyar."—(T.)

[2] Here both Ramusio and the Spanish version add " as yellow as honey." The allusion is to the coarse sugar known on the west coast of India as *Jaggery*, called above by Barbosa *jagara* (Vol. I, p. 185, note 1).

[3] The palm alluded to is the Palmyra or fan-palm (*Borrassus flabelliformis*). *Hobson-Jobson, s.v.* Palmyra.

of which are of extreme height and smoothness ; these bear a fruit as large as walnuts which they call Areca,[1] which they eat with betel. Among them it is held in high esteem. It is very ugly and disagreeable in taste. It is so abundant that ships take many cargoes of it for Cambaia and Daquem and many other countries, whither they take it preserved and dried.

---

§ 90. THE KINGDOM OF COCHIN.

FURTHER in advance along the coast is the Kingdom of *Cochin*, in which there is much pepper which grows throughout the land on trees like unto ivy, and it climbs on other trees and on palms, also on trellises to a great extent. The pepper grows on these trees in bunches. Here also grows very much fine belide[2] ginger, cardamoms, myrobalans, canafistula,[3] zerumba, zedoary[4]

---

[1] For the betel palm (*Areca Catechu*) see Vol. I, p. 168, note 1.   Mal. *adakka*, applied only to the nut.   The tree is called *kazhungu*.

[2] *Belide*.   The comma after the word ginger in the Port. text is omitted in Ramusio.   Dalgado in quoting this passage (*Glossario, s.v. gengibre*) also reads "gengibre belide."   The comma is undoubtedly wrong.   I have adopted this reading in the translation.   The Ar-*baladī* means "belonging to the country."   Stanley translates "ginger of the country," and has the note "Beledy: Arabic word no longer in use."   The remainder of the list of products is identical with that on p. 83, which is headed by ginger without the addition of *belide*. Stanley's explanation is the correct one.   The word was still in use in trade in the seventeenth century.

[3] *Canafistula* should probably be read here and elsewhere as *Cassia fistula* (Vol. I, p. 188, note 3).   Myrobalans are alluded to in the same note.

Garcia da Orta has a colloquy on this tree, and its uses (Garcia, p. 133).   The name *Cana*, was no doubt derived from the resemblance of the long stiff pod (sometimes two feet in length) to a stick.   The pulp with which it is filled is still much used as a purgative in Indian medicine (Brandis, *Forest Flora of N.W. India*, p. 164).

[4] For *Zedoary* and *Zerumbet* see *Hobson-Jobson, s.v.* Zedoary, where the passage in the text is quoted.   There is no difference in meaning between the two words.   The Persian *zurumbād* is merely another name for the Arabic *jadwar* or *zeduward*.   Shakespear calls it "China root," which is correct, as it is a native both of Bengal and China. The plant is *Curcuma Zedoaria*, sold in India either as *zurumbād* or *jangli haldi*, and employed as a stomachic (Murray, *Plants and Drugs of Sind*, p. 21).

wild cinnamon.[1] This Kingdom possesses a very large and excellent river,[2] which here comes forth to the sea by which come in great ships of Moors and Christians, who trade with this Kingdom. On the banks of this river is a city of the Moors natives of the land, wherein also dwell Heathen Chatims, and great merchants. They have many ships and trade with Charamandel, the great Kingdom of Cambaia, Dabul, and Chaul, in *areca* (great store), cocos, pepper, *jagara*, and palm sugar. At the mouth of the river the King our Lord possesses a very fine fortress, which is a large settlement of Portuguese and Christians, natives of the land, who became Christians after the establishment of our fortress. And every day also other Christian Indians who have remained from the teaching of the Blessed Saint Thomas come there also from Coilam[3] and other places. In this fort and settlement of Cochim[4] the King our Lord carries out the repairs of his ships, and other new ships are built, both galleys and caravels in as great perfection as on the Lisbon strand. Great store of pepper is here taken on board, also many other kinds of spices, and drugs which come from Malacca, and are taken hence every year to

---

[1] *Canela Brava* or Wild Cinnamon. This, no doubt, was the wild plant of Malabar which is inferior to the fine cinnamon of Ceylon. See Garcia's *Colloquy*, No. 15, p. 127. They are both from the same plant, *Cinnamomum Zeylanicum*. Vide *infra*, p. 112, note 1.

[2] The river here alluded to (known as the Cochin River) is "hardly a river at all," as the *Mal. Gaz.*, p. 6, remarks. It is the only outlet of the great system of lagoons and backwaters which extends along this part of the coast.

[3] *Coilam, i.e.,* the Southern Kollam or Quilon often spelt Coulam see § 91.

[4] *The Fortress of Cochin.* This fortress was founded by the two Alboquerques, Afonso and Francisco, who arrived in 1503 with instructions from the King to build a fort there. They were just in time to rescue the few Portuguese left there by Cabral and V. da Gama, who were besieged by the invading King of Calicut. It became the headquarters of the Portuguese in India until Goa took its place. It was again besieged by the Calicut forces in 1504, but bravely and successfully defended by Duarte Pacheco.

Portugal. . The King of Cochim has a very small country
and was not a King before the Portuguese discovered
India, for all the Kings who had of late reigned in Calecut
had held it for their practice and rule to invade Cochim
and drive the King out of his estate, taking themselves
possession thereof,[1] thereafter, according as their pleasure

---

[1] The Raja of Cochin found in the Portuguese powerful allies against
his ancient enemy of Calicut, and Barbosa is probably right in stating
that his state would soon have been annexed to Calicut had not the
Portuguese interfered. They were glad to be on friendly terms with
Cochin, for the harbour there was the best on the Malabar coast, far
superior to that of Calicut, and the King was willing to allow of the
construction of a fort. In 1510 a dispute as to the succession to the
throne took place, which involves a question of the peculiar rights of
succession in Malabar which have been so fully and correctly related
by Barbosa. The story is told in the *Commentaries of A. D'Alboquerque,*
Vol. II, pp. 36–38 ; as it is told it is hardly intelligible, but it would
appear from a work lately published (*A Contribution to the History of
Cochin,* by K. Rama Varmaraja, Trichur, 1914) that the claimant to
the vacant throne in 1510 was in reality not the legitimate heir, and
that his recognition by the Portuguese was therefore contrary to the
recognised rule of succession according to which a sister's son should
have succeeded. Mr. Rama Varmaraja states the case as follows
(*ib.*. p. 13 ff) :—

(1) The land Kocchi (Cochin and vicinity) belonged to Idapilli, but
early in the fifteenth century the Raja of Idapilli made a present of it
to the King of Cochin, who happened to be his son. This is explained
thus.

(2) Early in the fifteenth century a prince of the royal house of
Perumpadappu, who happened to be the son of the Raja of Idapilli,
received the N. part of the Karapuram tract as a gift from his
father, and founded the *small* kingdom of Cochin as distinguished
from the large state of the north (Perumpadappu Nād). This prince,
it is suggested was not the head of his royal house, but a junior member,
perhaps second in the line of succession (*Elaya Tavazhi*). As he got
his title from his father as well as from his (own) maternal house, he
was doubly royal, and as a junior prince was addressed as *Kocchu
Thampuran,* the kingdom also took the name *Kocchi-rajyam.*

(3) When he (the junior Raja) became the senior he was to move to
the royal residence in the Perumpadappu village and leave the junior
throne to the next in rank.

(4) But when Goda Varma, the friend of the Portuguese, died in 1510,
they abolished the custom, and restricted succession to the Cochin
throne to the branch of the deceased king, which was henceforth
known as the Elaya Tavazhi, having permanently retained therein
the titles, estates and sovereign authority attached to the second
rank.

(5) But if *this* ruler happened to be senior member of the whole joint
house and at the same time refused to give up the *junior* throne of
Cochin, the next in the line would object. Hence family feuds
followed.

(6) On account of his violation of the customary rule of succession he
was denied the rank and privileges of the Perumpadappu Chief, and

was, they would give it back to him or not. The King of
Cochim gave him every year a certain number of elephants,
but he might not strike coins, nor roof his palace with
tiles under pain of losing his land. Now that the King
our Lord has discovered India he has made the King
independent and powerful in his own land, so that none
can interfere with it, and he strikes whatsoever money he
will.

§ 91. THE KINGDOM OF COILAM.

GOING yet further along the coast southwards, and passing
by the Kingdom of *Cochim* we enter forthwith the
Kingdom of *Coilam*[1] and midway between it and the
Kingdom of Cochim is a small town which they call
Porqua[2] under its own Lord, where dwell many Heathen

the temple of the family patron deity at Pazhayannur was shut against
him for ever. Hence he ever after carried on his worship in private
shrines in his own palace. *Perhaps* he may have taken an oath never
to enter the temple unless he recovered the crown worn at the last
capital. In any case there was a *taboo* of some sort. The chieftainship
of Perumpadappu was ultimately recovered. (See also Whiteway's
Rise of Portuguese Power, pp. 107–8.)

Cochin remained as one of the important centres of
Portuguese power for a century and a half. Vasco da Gama died there
soon after taking over the Government as Viceroy in 1524. In 1634
an English factory was established there with the consent of the
Portuguese Government. In 1663 Cochin fell into the hands of the
Dutch, and the Portuguese power in Malabar was at an end. The
English factory received no toleration from the Dutch company, and
was removed to Ponnani. Cochin passed into British possession in
1795 (see *Mal. Gaz.*, p. 402 ff). In 1806 the fort which the Dutch had
maintained (although in a reduced form) and the Cathedral were blown
up by order of the E.I. Company, who it is said, feared that the place
was to be given back to the Dutch (*Mal. Gaz.*, p. 505).

[1] *The Kingdom of Coilam or Coulam* (spelt both ways in the text)
corresponds very closely with the modern State of Travancore, which
obtained its old name from the City of Kollam or Coulào, now generally
known as Quilon (see below).

[2] The two towns mentioned as lying between Cochim and Coilam
are given here in the order of their actual position on the coast. *Porqua*
or *Porca* represents the modern small town of *Porkad*, which appears
to have been at the time one of the pirate ports which preyed upon
the trade of the Malabar coast. The Portuguese afterwards had a
small station here, and were succeeded by the Dutch in the seventeenth
century. Its position in the debateable land between Cochim and

fishers whose livelihood in the winter season is nought but fishery, and in the summer they live by robbery of all they can find, and everything they can take on the sea. They make use of small rowing vessels like a *bargatim.*[1] They are great oarsmen and a multitude of them gather together all armed with bows and arrows in plenty, and thus they surround any vessel they find becalmed, with flights of arrows until they take and rob it. Those who are taken therein they put ashore. Thus with these boats of theirs which they call *catures,*[2] they take much spoil, part whereof they give to the lord of that land.

Passing this place we come at once to another, the first in this kingdom of *Coilam,* which they call *Cale Coilam,*[3] whither come numbers of Moors, Heathens and

---

Coulam no doubt encouraged the maritime population to take to piracy. It may with great probability be identified with the Bakare of the Periplus (Barkare of Ptolemy), one of the principal pepper ports in early days (Schoff's *Periplus*, p. 211). In the present day its trade has passed to Alleppey a little to the north.

[1] *Bargatim,* probably to be read *bargātim.* These vessels had no resemblance to the modern brigantine, but were light rowing boats of some size, drawing little water and suitable for coast work. These were familiar to the Portuguese, and were much used in the Mediterranean.

[2] *Catur.* The *catur* as used on the coast of India was something of the same kind as the bargantim, although according to Castanheda it was smaller. Cotgrave says it was smaller than a foist, but larger than a " fregat." The suggestion made by Yule in *Hobson-Jobson, s.v. Catur,* and by Burton in his *Commentary on Camões,* IV, 391, that this name is the origin of the English " cutter," is not supported by the *New English Dictionary.* Mgr. Dalgado (*Glossario, s.v. Catur*), however, considers it probable. He thinks that the origin of the term is to be found in the Malayālam *Kattiri,* which comes from the Skr. *kartari,* "scissors " or " cutter." The first instance of its use in English is in 1745, and as the word *catur* must have by that time become familiar to the English in India its adoption in English as *cutter* seems by no means inadmissible.

[3] *Cale Coilam* (called in the Spanish version Caymcolan) is evidently the modern Kayankullam, a port on the backwater. It was a centre of the Syrian Christians from an early period, a church having been built there in A.D. 829. The form Cale Coilam appears to be an Arab form of the Malayālam name, *Cale* being clearly the Arab *Kal'a,* " a fort."

Christians of the doctrine of the Blessed Saint Thomas and many of them also dwell in the inland country. Here there is great store of pepper, of which many ships take cargoes ; sometimes also our own ships do likewise.

Passing *Cale Coilam* there is on the coast immediately to the south of it a very great city with a right good haven which they call *Coilam*.[1] Hither come Moors, Heathen and Christians in great numbers. The Moors and Heathen are great traders and possess many ships dealing in goods of divers kinds, in which they sail in all directions, to *Charamandel* and *Ceilam*, to the *Isles*, to *Benguala*, *Malaca*, *Çamatra* and *Peeguu*, but they trade not with *Cambaya*. Here there is great store of pepper, and there is a great river.

In this Kingdom reigns a Heathen King,[2] a great Lord over many lands and treasures and armed men, the more part of whom are skilful archers and very trustworthy. At a certain point where the land projects into the sea

---

[1] *Coilam* or *Coulam*, the modern port known as Quilon in the Travancore State, represents the Malayàlam Kollam, which the Arabs knew as Kaulam or Kaulam-Male. It was well known to the Chinese, who prior to the Yüan dynasty called it Ku-lin, but from the time of the Mongol Emperor Kubilai Kaan gave it the name of Hsiao Ko-la-n or Little Quilon. It is described in some detail in works dealing with that period. Ibn Batūta (IV, 99, 103) states that Chinese merchants were settled at Kaulam, and that envoys from the King of China arrived there during his visit (W. W. Rockhill, *Notes on the Relations and Trade of China*, T'oung-Pao, Vol. XVI, 1915, pp. 445–449). Marco Polo a short time before visited the Kingdom of " Coilum " and found both Christians and Jews there. Fr. Jordanus and Marignolli call it Columbum. (*Marco Polo*, Bk. III, Ch. 22, ed. 1871, p. 312.) Odoric turns it into Polumbum (see *Hobson-Jobson*, *s.v.* Quilon).

Portuguese dealings with Coulam began in 1503 when A. D'Albo-querque obtained permission to open a factory there for trade. He was well received, as the southern kingdom was jealous of Calicut, with which the Portuguese were at war (De Barros, *I*, vii, 3, f. 130 ; Castanheda, Bk. I, Ch. 62, Vol. I, p. 175). The Portuguese were paramount here until the capture of Quilon by the Dutch in 1661. A. Hamilton (*East Indies*, I, 331) calls it Coiloan, and mentions the small Dutch fort. The trade was much decayed in his time.

[2] *Heathen King*. The descendant of this king (if the term may be used of a Marumakkathayan dynasty) is the present Maharaja of Travancore.—(T.)

G

is a very great church, miraculously built by the Apostle
Our Lord Saint Thomas [1] before he died (as the Christians
of Saint Thomas asserted to me that they had found this
written in their book which they preserve with extreme
reverence). It was in this manner. He arrived at the
City of Coilam (all there being Heathen) in poor attire,
and thenceforward he began to convert some poor
folk to our holy faith. He took with him some companions who were natives of the land. One day as he
was going about in the city at daybreak a great log of
wood from the sea was seen in the harbour and grounded
on the strand. Tidings of this were forthwith brought
to the King, who sent many men and elephants to draw
it to the land, but they could not move it, and when the
King ordered that they should do everything in their
power to draw it forth, yet they had no power to do so.

---

[1] *Christians of St. Thomas.* This story of the miraculous foundation
of the church at Coulam by St. Thomas is told also by Marignolli,
who, however, ascribes it to Mirapolis, that is Mailapur in Ma'bar
or Coromandel and not to Columbum or Coulam. His account differs
to some extent from the version given by Barbosa, for Marignolli's
legend states that the log was cut down by two slaves of St. Thomas
on "Adam's Mount in Seyllan" and drawn to the seaside by the
Saint's girdle, and then by his orders floated to the haven of Mirapolis.
He also adds that the Saint was murdered afterwards while engaged
in the task of building churches (*Cathay*, Yule and Cordier, III, 249–251).
Marco Polo relates the story of the martyrdom also under his account
of Ma'bar, but says nothing about the log (*Marco Polo*, II, Ch. 18).
Under his account of Malabar (*ib.*, Ch. 25) he says nothing about
St. Thomas.
   Friar John of Monte Corvino also visited Ma'bar, "the country
of India wherein stands the church of St. Thomas the Apostle," and
there spent thirteen months. His companion, Friar Nicholas, died
there and was buried in the church. Yule, in his *Marco Polo* (ed. II,
p. 293, 1st ed.), says that this was about the time of Polo's homeward
journey. It is probable, therefore, that at the end of the thirteenth
century this legend was not in circulation.
   It is not easy to say when the legendary connection of St. Thomas
with South India began. The early forms of the legend connect
him with Gondophernes who, in the first century A.D., was reigning
over an extensive kingdom in North-west India and Afghanistan,
including Taxila, Sind, Kābul, Kandahār and Sistān (see *Ind. Antiquary*, 1903, pp. 1, 145). There can be little doubt that the story
was brought to India by the Christian immigrants in the fifth and
following centuries (see Milne Rae, *The Syrian Church in India*,
1892).

The Blessed Saint Thomas then perceiving that they had no hope of moving it, went to the King and said to him that he would draw forth the log to the land on condition that the King would give him a piece of land whereon he might build a church in honour of the Lord who had sent him thither. Whereat the King laughed and said that if he with all his might could not make it stir how could the Saint be bold enough to drag it out. Saint Thomas replied that he would draw it out by God's power, which was very great. The King then ordered that all the land of which he had need should be given to him, and this being done and the grant made out, he went there where the log lay and bound it to a rope with which, by divine grace, he began to draw it to the land without help from any person, and this same log came behind him to the spot where he would build his church. The King having witnessed this notable miracle then ordered that he should do whatever he would with the wood and the land which he had given him (treating him) with all honour and favour, and holding him to be a saint. Many men of that land became Christians, but the King would not. The Apostle then, whom they called *Matoma*, ordered that all the carpenters and sawyers in the land should be called together, and began to fashion the wood, which was of such a size that it sufficed to build the church, and so it was done. It is the custom among the Moors and Indians that when the workmen come to begin any work they give them a certain quantity of rice to eat, and when they depart at night they give them a *fanam* each. The Blessed Saint Thomas at midday took the measure wherewith the rice was to be measured and to every man he gave it full of sand, and it was turned into good rice and when they departed at night he gave every man a chip of wood,

and it became a *fanam*.   Thus the work was accomplished
and all the workmen were well pleased.   Beholding these
miracles and many others, which Our Lord daily worked
through him, many became Christians from Cochim to
the great Kingdom of Coilam, which extends to the coast
facing towards Ceilam, in which there may be well twelve
thousand households [1] of Christians scattered among the
Heathen, and there also some churches in the inland
country.   The more part of these lack both doctrine
and baptism, having only the name of Christians, for
St. Thomas in his time baptised all who desired baptism,
and as the King of *Coilam* perceived that so many people
were receiving his doctrine he took heed of it, saying
that they would take possession of the land.   So he
began to shun them, and on this Saint Thomas departed
thence, persecuted by them and by the Heathen, towards
the land of *Charamandel* and came to a great town named
Mailapur, where he received martyrdom and where he
lies buried, of which I will speak more fully in its place
further on. [2]   Thus from that time the Christians remained
in this Kingdom of *Coilam* with that church, and levied
duties on pepper, of which it possesses somewhat, and also
other duties.   These Christians, thus continuing without
instructions and with no priest to baptise them, were for
long Christians in nothing but name only.   Then they
gathered together and took counsel one with another, and
determined to send forth some from among them into the
world where the Sacrament of Baptism was known.   With
this intent five men set forth into the world at great
cost, and came to stay in the land of *Armenia* where they
found many Christians and a Patriarch who ruled them,
who, understanding their object, sent with them a

---

[1] The Spanish version has 2,000 and Ramusio 7,000.

[2] *Infra*, p. 126.

Bishop and five or six clerks to baptise them and say mass and instruct them, which Bishop tarried with them for five or six years, and when he went back there came another, who stayed with them for as many years. Thus for a long time they continued to improve.[1]

These Armenians are white men,[2] they speak Arabic and Chaldee. They have the church law and recite their prayers perpetually. Yet I know not whether they recite the whole office as do our Friars. They wear their tonsures reversed, hair in the place of the tonsure and the head around it shaven. They wear white shirts, and turbans on their heads, they go barefoot, and wear long beards. They are extreme devout and say mass at the altar as we do here, with a cross facing them. He who says it walks between two men, who help him, one on each side. They communicate with salted bread instead of the host, and consecrate thereof sufficient for all who are present in the church, they distribute the whole of this as if it were blessed bread, and every man comes to the foot of the altar to receive it from the priest's hand. And the wine is in this wise, as at that time there was no wine in India they take raisins brought from Meca and Ormuz, and leave them for the night to soak ; the next day when they go to say mass they press out the juice, and say the mass with that. " These men baptised for money, and when they returned from Malabar to their country they had great riches, and thus for lack of money many went unbaptised."

---

[1] After " improve " Ramusio adds : " And the said priests having remained there for a time return to their house in Armenia, taking with them great riches, for they demand money from everyone who would be baptised, which is very ill done, for some having no money cannot receive baptism." (This passage in Portuguese is at the end of the paragraph.)

[2] After " White men," Ramusio adds: " they speak Arabic and have the Holy Scripture in the Chaldee tongue." Do. in the Spanish version.

" Passing southwards from this City of Coulam, there is on the coast a village of Moors and Heathen which they call *Tiramgoto*,[1] where there is some sea traffic also. It pertains to a Lord who is of the King of Coulam's kindred. The land is rich and produces supplies of rice and flesh in great plenty."

§ 92. CAPE OF CUMERI.

[Further in advance on the said coast is the Cape of Cumeri, where ends the Land of Malabar, yet, as for the said Kingdom of Coulam, it extends another ninety miles as far as a city named Cael.[2]]

[At this Cape Comory there is an ancient Church of Christians which was founded by the Armenians, who

---

[1] *Tiramgoto*. This name stands for Tiruvankodu, a small town, now nearly deserted, but with the ruins of an ancient fort. It was originally the capital of a small state, as described by Barbosa, but this state has developed in later days into the state of Travancore, which has taken its name from this now obscure place which long ago lost its importance. The present capital of the state is Trivandrum, which is not mentioned by Barbosa or other early Portuguese writers. De Barros gives the name of the state and town of Travancore in the form of Travancor; while that given by Barbosa is closer to the Malayālam form. The passage from De Barros in his topographical chapter (*I*, ix,. 1) is as follows :—

" From Porca to Travancor is the Kingdom of Coulão, of which the coast may be about twenty leagues ; the towns of which are Cale Coulão, where we hold a fortress, Rotora, Berinjan, and other towns and ports but little known. And at the town of Travancor, at which the Kingdom of Coulão ends, begins another taking its name from the said Travancor, whom our people call the Great King, for that he is greater in land and dignity than those which we have passed in Malabar, and he is subordinate to the King of Narsinga."

The port of Berinjan mentioned by De Barros is probably Vizhingani, on the south coast of Trivandrum, which was sacked by the Portuguese in 1505, and was a place of some importance under the Dutch (*Trav. State Manual*, III, p. 602).

" Berinjan might very well (etymologically speaking) be from Vizhingani. The letter *zh* does in fact sound something like *r* to inexperienced European ears."—(T.) .

[2] This paragraph is not found in the Portuguese version nor in the Spanish, and is quoted in the Portuguese text and in Lord Stanley's translation from Ramusio. The distance from Cape Comorin to Cael is given in Ramusio (ed. 1563, f. 313) as ninety miles, which the Portuguese editors give as eighty, and Lord Stanley as thirty leagues.

still direct it, and perform in it the Divine Service of Christians, and have crosses on the altars. All mariners pay it a tribute and the Portuguese celebrate mass there when they pass. There are there many tombs, amongst which there is one which has written on it a Latin epitaph : " Hic jacet Catuldus Gulli filius qui obiit anno ——."[1]]

§ 93. THE ISLES OF MALDIO.

Across the sea facing the greater part of this Land of Malabar at forty leagues distance lies an archipelago of islands,[2] whereof the Moors report that they number twelve thousand. They begin in the sea of Mount Dely where are the shallows of Padua,[3] and extend towards

[1] As this passage appears, according to Lord Stanley's note, neither in the Barcelona MS. nor in the Munich MS. No. 570, and is not found in the Portuguese text nor in Ramusio, it depends only on the Munich MS. No. 571. It would seem, therefore, to be a rather late interpolation.

[2] Cf. De Barros, III, iii, 7, f. 726. " This line (of the Maldiva Is.) runs like a band stretched in front of the coast of India ; it begins at those shoals to which we give the name of Padua in the roads of Mount Dely, and continues till near to the land of Java and the coast of Sunda." It will be noticed that Barbosa's mistake as to the eastward extension of the Maldives was shared by De Barros as late as 1563. The whole passage is translated in Sir A. Gray's edition of Pyrard, II, 479 ff., para. 22.

[3] The shallows of Padua (os baixos de Padua) will be found denoted in Ribero's map of 1529 [in pocket, Vol. I] immediately to the north of the northern group which appears to bear the name Mahldio, although the reading is uncertain. This group is now designated separately as the Laccadive Is. They are also shown, as Sir A, Gray has already noted, in Vaz Dourado's map of 1570 (Pyrard, II, 477, n. 3).

The bank appears (unnamed) in Rennell's map of 1782, but is still to be found in modern maps as the Bank of Padua or Munyal Par, extending between 12' and 14' N. Lat. (see " India " in Keith Johnston's Royal Atlas, 1873, and others).

It is referred to in the Commentaries of Alboquerque (III, 55). In February, 1511, Alboquerque was prevented from passing this bank owing to the lateness of the season, i.e., the breaking of the monsoon, and was therefore unable at that time to carry out his intention of attacking Aden. Correa (II, 179) attributes the failure to bad weather, but does not mention the shoals of Padua. De Barros, however, corroborates the statement in the Commentaries : he says, " He turned back to Goa before passing the Baixos de Padua " (II, f. 127). Alboquerque himself alludes to this occurrence in a letter to Duarte Galvão

Malaca. The first are four little isles, extremely flat, which are called Maldio ; they are inhabited by Malabar Moors,[1] and they say that they belong to the King of Cananor ; nothing else grows here save palm groves, by which they live, as also on rice which goes thither from Malabar on ships which go to take in cargoes of *cairo* cord.

§ 94. THE ISLES OF PALANDURA.

[In front of Pananie, Cochin, and Coulan are other islands, ten or twelve whereof are inhabited by tawny Moors of short stature, who speak a tongue of their own.

The King is a Moor, and dwells in an island called Mahaldiu, and to all these said isles they give the name of Palandura. The men of these isles have no weapons whatsoever ; they are a feeble folk yet right cunning, and above all things they are mighty magicians. The King of these Isles is chosen by certain Moors, merchants from Cananor, and they change him whenever it pleases them. To them he pays a yearly tribute in ship's shrouds

(without date) in which he explains how he was prevented from prosecuting his journey to the Red Sea, and undertook the Malacca expedition instead. He says, " For the space of eight days, turning hither and thither, I could never double the shoals of Padua, and as the season was a little late the wind did not allow me to pursue my way, therefore having sent Diego Fernandez of the wardrobe with three ships in advance to destroy the fort of Çamatra and to wait for me up till an appointed time there, our Lord, in whose hands is all the Indian business, as you, Sir, say, turned our journey and our voyage to the taking of Malaca " (*Cartas de A. de Alboquerque,* Vol. I, p. 396).

[1] *Malabar Moors.* Barbosa is right in saying that the inhabitants of these islands (now called the Laccadives) are Mappilas. In Barbosa's days these islands were under the nominal suzerainty of the Kolattiri. Some time in the sixteenth century he made them over to the Ali Raja of Cannanore, who also obtained later the island of Minicoy (the northernmost island of the Maldive group). On account of the Ali Raja's maladministration they passed to the British Government. The Laccadive islands and Minicoy are fully dealt with in *Mal. Gaz.,* ch. xvi.—(T.)

and *cairo* cordage, and other things produced in the land, and ofttimes these Moors go thither to lade certain ships taking no money with them, and then either by love or by force they must receive whatsoever they ask.[1]]

There is in these isles great store of dried fish, and they carry hence as well certain small shells (*buzios*), which are much sought after[2] in the Kingdom of Cambaia and in Bengal, where they pass current as small change, for they hold it to be cleaner and better than copper.[3]

---

[1] See Sir A. Gray's note in *Pyrard*, ii, 477, as to this passage here inserted from Ramusio. Sir A. Gray's opinion is that " this is a paraphrase of the preceding paragraph by the Spanish translator whose text Ramusio used. Unfortunately this has not been noted in the Hakluyt Society's translation of this work, and the author is thus made to describe two separate groups in strangely similar language ; whereas it is tolerably clear, if we omit this passage in brackets, that he regards the Laccadives and Maldives as one group, some of the more northerly islands of which were occupied by Malabars. With these he seems to include Male (*Mahal-diu*) probably on account of the close commercial relations of that island with Cananor. It will be seen that De Barros follows Barbosa in all his mistakes. *Palandura* (or, as Lord Stanley reads, *Palandiva*) is unintelligible." There can be no doubt that Sir A. Gray was right in this opinion, and that a better idea of what Barbosa really wrote can be obtained by omitting this passage altogether. *Palandiva* or *Palandura* still remains unidentified, and is evidently a corruption of some name ending in *diva, i.e., dvipa,* " an island."

[2] Ramusio calls them large and small snails (*caracoli*), imitating the Spanish (*caracoles*), or little pigs (*porcellette*). The last epithet evidently refers to the pig-like shape of the cowrie.

[3] The Maldive Islands have long been known as the principal source of the supply of cowries, and a full list of ancient authorities on the subject is given by Sir A. Gray in his notes to *Pyrard*, Vol. ii, pp. 429, 432, 444, &c., &c. The earlier Portuguese travellers called them *buzios.* The first contemporary record of the use of the word *cowry* or *caury* is probably that in an entry in the Torre do Tombo of 1520 (quoted on p. 242 of Mgr. S. R. Dalgado's *Glossario*). That in Correa's *Lendas* (of which a full translation will be found in *Pyrard, l.c.* II, 473) although relating to the events of 1503, cannot be placed earlier than the date of the work (1563). Other early instances will be found in the *Livro de Pesos e Medidas* (*Subsidios* I, pp. 35, 37), which dates from 1554. The best modern account of Maldive coinage, including the cowry and the larin, is that by Mr. J. Allan, of the British Museum (*Num. Chron.*, 1912, p. 313 ff).

Castanheda's mention, quoted in *Hobson-Jobson, s.v.* Cowry, and in the *Glossario*, is dated 1552. After that its use became common among Europeans. In Arab writers the usual form was *al-wada'.* but the Indian word *kauri* or a slightly altered form *kaudha* or *kauda* are occasionally found from the time of Alberūni (1020) onward. Examples of this use will be found in *Hobson-Jobson, l.c.*

" In these islands they make very rich cloths of cotton and silk and gold, which are worth great sums of money among the Moors for their garments and turbans. The men of these isles wear very fine and thin kerchiefs round their caps,[1] so finely wrought and perfect that our workmen would not be able to make them, and having no difference between right and wrong sides (*lit.* unless he has both right and wrong side). They find in these islands shells of tortoises which they call *alquama*,[2] these they divide into little pieces, very thin, which also is a great article of trade in the Kingdom of Gujarate."

Here too ambergris[3] is found in large lumps, some

---

[1] The turban itself appears to be intended by the word *lenço*, while *touqua* designates the cap or *kulla* round which the turban is wound among many classes of Muhammadans.

[2] *Alquama.* Mal. for tortoise is āma, which is obviously the second part of the word. The first part is unrecognisable. In the Maldives they speak Mahl (not Malayālam). In Logan, Vol. II, p. 114, I find " Kāmpuphai " as the Mahl word for tortoise-shell. Malayalis distinguish between Vellāma (white turtle) and Kārāma (black turtle). —(T.)

[3] *Ambergris.* Here and elsewhere among the Portuguese writers of this period the word *ambre* means " ambergris " and not " amber." The fullest account is that given by Garcia da Orta (*Coll.*, 3, pp. 20 ff, of Sir C. Markham's translation). The word " amber " is, however, used throughout in this translation, which is misleading. The translator in a note on p. 23 says that Averroes, who is quoted, " here obviously refers to ambergris," but he omits to note that the whole colloquy refers to nothing else, and could have no possible meaning as applied to amber. Orta describes the white, grey and black ambergris much in the same way as Barbosa, and alludes to the Maldive Islands as one of the principal spots where it was found. Linschoten, II, 92, also mentions the Maldive Islands as one of the find-spots. Here, as elsewhere, he draws freely on Garcia da Orta, without acknowledgment (*Cf.* Vol. I, p. 226, Note 2, as to diamonds). *Pyrard* alludes to ambergris, when washed up on the shore in the Maldives, being one of the King's rights, as in the " flotsam " of old English law (H.S., Ed. I, 229) where Sir A. Gray in a note gives an exhaustive account of the actual nature of ambergris and of the various notions which have been prevalent regarding it.
Here, Barbosa calls the white ambergris *Ponambar* and the black *Minambar:* the name for the grey apparently was omitted by the transcribers of the MS., but the Spanish version gives the three names as *Ponabar, Puambar* and *Minabar.* Ramusio (f. 313) gives the three names as *Porabat, Puabar* and *Minabar.* It may be taken therefore on comparison of these texts that the forms intended by the author

white, some grey, and some black. I have ofttimes asked these Moors what thing this ambergris was, and whence it sprang. Among themselves they hold it to be the dung of birds, and they say that in this Archipelago among the uninhabited islands there are certain great fowls which alight on the cliffs and rocks of the sea, and there drop this ambergris, where it is tanned and softened by the wind, the sun, and the rain, and pieces both great and small are torn by storms and tempests and fall into the sea until they are found or washed up on the strands or swallowed by whales. And those which they find white, called *Ponambar*, they say have been in the sea but a short time, and these they value most ; the grey has been long in the sea and thus obtains that hue ; this too they hold to be good, but not so good as the white. The other which is found black and crushed they say was swallowed by whales and thus turned black, and it has such strength that the whale cannot bear it but vomits it up altogether. This they call *Minambar ;* it is worth less than the others. (It is heavier and lacks scent.)

And in these Maldio Islands they build many great ships[1] of palm trunks, sewn together with thread, for

---

were *Ponambar, Puambar* and *Minambar,* in all of which the last element is the Ar, *'ambar,* and the first element the local word for the colour. " The names still used in Malabar are Ponnambar and Minambar. This is explained as follows : Ponnambar is the slightly yellow ambergris (*pon* means golden in Malayālam). The native theory still is that this is the dung of birds. The Minambar (which is dark) is so called because it is got from the stomachs of big fishes (*min* = fish in Malayālam). This is precisely what Barbosa was told. My informant is an educated Nāyar. I believe that the prefixes *pon* and *min* are, as this account implies, the Malayālam terms. According to Logan (II, p. 111), in Mahl black is *khalu* and white *dōm*. The term Puambar is unknown in Malabar. Such a word is, however, etymologically possible, *pū* meaning flower in Malayālam."—(T.)

[1] As to these vessels large and small Barbosa is a good witness, as he had a practical experience in shipbuilding, having been commissioned by Alboquerque to build ships for his Hurmuz expedition. (See Introduction, Vol. I, p. xliv.)

they have no other timber, and in these they sail to the main they have keels and are of great burden. They also build smaller boats for rowing, like *bargantins* or *fustas ;* these are the most graceful in the world, right well built and extremely light. In these they voyage from one island to the others, and also cross in them to Malabar.

Many ships of Moors which pass from China, Maluco, Peegu, Malaca, Çamatra, Benguala and Ceilam towards the Red Sea touch at these islands to water and take in supplies and other things needful for their voyages. At times they arrive here so battered that they discharge their cargoes and let them go to the bottom. And among these isles many and rich vessels of Moors are cast away,[1] which, crossing the sea, dare not through dread of our ships finish their voyage to Malabar " and from these the natives obtain much valuable merchandize, which they sell to the Malabares who come hither to take in *cairo*, as I have already said."[2]

---

[1] An interesting parallel to the many rich vessels the Moors cast away for fear of the Portuguese is furnished by the victims of the " Emden " in the late war. The " Emden " destroyed a number of vessels in the neighbourhood of the islands. The island boats brought to Cannanore immense quantities of scrap iron, which was part of the wreckage, and some ingots of bronze. These were claimed on behalf of Government by the Receiver of Wrecks, and fetched very handsome prices when sold.—(T.)

[2] *The Chinese in the Maldives.* The late Mr. W. W. Rockhill in his *Notes on the Relations and Trade of China*, published in T'oung-Pao in 1914–15, has given an interesting version of what he believes to be the first reference to the Maldive Islands in Chinese literature (T'oung-Pao, 1915, p. 387). This is from the *Tao i Chih lio*, a work dating from A.D. 1349 (*ib.* pp. 61, 62). The author calls the northern Maldives *Pei Liu*, and his description may be compared with that of Ibn Baṭūṭa of a slightly earlier date. The trade in cowries (p. 388), ambergris (p. 388) and coir (p. 388) is alluded to. Further details about ambergris are given in a later Chinese work, the *Hsi yang chao kung tien lu*, of 1520 (*ib.*, p. 392, Note). It says : " Their boats are not clamped with iron, but bound with cocoanut fibre. They are caulked with melted ambergris. Great is the quantity of ambergris that they get at the Lia Islands. There are numbers of coiled up dragons among the rocks of these islands. In the spring they vomit spittle which flocks of birds collect and schools of fish suck it up. The

§ 95. THE ISLAND OF CEILAM.

LEAVING these Maldio isles and proceeding further
[where the Cape Comorim is turned] we come to the
great island *Ceilam* [1] [which Moors, Arabs, Persians and
Syrians call by that name, but by the Indians it is called
Tenarisim, the meaning whereof is Land of Delight],[2]
" where the King our Lord possesses a fortress for trade,
newly built, which was established by Lopo Soares [3]

---

yellow kind is like fish glue, the black like *wu-ling* (?), the white like
medicine (?). When heated its odour is rank. It is also procured
from the bellies of fishes in balls as big as a bushell measure. It is
sold by the ounce weight, an ounce bringing twelve gold coins." It
will be seen that the Chinese writer mentions three colours, yellow
taking the place of Barbosa's grey.

[1] *The name Ceilam or Ceylon.* J. de Barros, in his account of
Ceylon, *Dec. III*, ii, f. 25, rev., says that the ancient name of the
island was " Ilanare or Tranate as others say." The old Tamil name
was Ilam, which Burnell (*Hobson-Jobson, s.v. Ceylon*) says represents
Silān, the Pāli form of Siṅhāla-dwipa, Tamil having no proper sibilant.
Cf. the Sielidiba of Cosmas, p. 363. D. Ferguson (*Hist. of Ceylon*, p. 30),
in a note on this passage of De Barros with regard to the name Ilanare,
says that all these varieties of spelling represent the Tamil name
Ilan-nādu, " the country of Ilan, viz., Ceylon." Ilam represents the
form Silam by omission of the sibilant, and Sīlam = the Pāli form
Sīhalam for Skr. Siṅhāla-dwipa. The Tenarisim of Ramusio is evidently a clerical error for some such form as Ylinarim as found in
the Spanish version. The Tranate given by De Barros as an alternative
name is probably also due to a similar blunder. Castanheda's Hibenaro
may be referred to the same origin. The changes in the forms of the
name of Ceylon are faithfully reproduced by the Chinese travellers
who visited the island from time to time. In the fourteenth century
it still is given its ancient title of Siṅhāla (*Seng-kia-la*), while in works
of the fifteenth century the modern form Silān (*Hsi-lan*) has been
adopted. In each case the forms reported belong to a considerably
earlier date than that borne by the compilations in which they are
recorded (W. W. Rockhill, *Notes on the Relations and Trade of China*,
T'oung-Pao, Vol. XVI, pp. 375, 377, 381).

[2] This passage from Ramusio occurs also in the Spanish version,
with the exception that *Tenarisim* is turned into *Ylinarim*.

[3] *Lopo Soares D'Albergaria*, who succeeded Alboquerque as Governor,
made an expedition to Ceylon and founded a fort (see De Barros,
III, ii, ch. 2 ; Correa, II, p. 539, ff., where a view of the fort is given)
at Colombo in September, 1518, having come to terms with the King
of Candy. The fort was to be for the protection of a trading factory.
The first Portuguese expedition to Ceylon was that in 1506 under
Lourenço D'Almeida, son of the Viceroy Francisco D'Almeida. The
mention of the foundation of this fort by Barbosa shows a knowledge
of the events of 1518, and is one of the passages to be considered in
fixing the probable date of his departure from India (see *infra*, § 126,

when he was Governor of India." The people of this
island are Heathen, yet in its seaports dwell many Moors
in large towns, who are subject to the King of the land.
The natives of this island, as well Moors as Heathen, are
great merchants. They are stout and well-liking, tawny
almost white in hue, the more part of them are
big-bellied ; they are extreme luxurious and pay no
attention to matters of weapons, nor do they possess
them. All are merchants and given to good living.
They go naked from the waist up, and below they are
clad in silk and cotton garments ; they wear small
turbans on their heads ; their ears are bored, and in
them they wear much gold[1] [and precious stones in

p. 211, note 1). The passages relating to the first Portuguese expedition
under Lourenço D'Almeida in 1506, and the second in 1518 under
Lopo Soares D'Albergaria, from De Barros and Do Couto, have been
carefully translated and annotated by Mr. Donald Ferguson in his
Hist. of Ceylon. The account of Lourenço D'Almeida's voyage is on
pp. 20-25 of this work. Mr. Ferguson, in his *Discovery of Ceylon
by the Portuguese* (*Journal, Ceylon Branch, R.A.S.*, Vol. XIX, 1907),
fixes the time as September, 1506.

[1] This passage, descriptive of the products of the country, is taken
from Ramusio and occurs in a much-abbreviated form in the Spanish
version. "The sweet and beautiful oranges which are larger than
Adam's apple," seem to be some kind of citrus fruit according to
Yule (*Hobson-Jobson*, s.v. Adam's apple), but the large size of the
fruit makes it at least possible that the Jack-fruit is alluded to ;
this always attracted the attention of newcomers by its size. Garcia
da Orta (*Coll.*, 28) says "they are the size of very large melons, and
some larger," and in more modern times Sir E. Tennent (*Ceylon*,
1860, Vol. I, p. 119) speaks of "the ubiquitous Jak, with its huge
fruits weighing from 5 to 50 lbs., the largest eatable fruit in the world."
The Adam's apples seem to have been plantains or bananas in early
usage, though some writers considered them to be some kind of *citrus*
(Yule, *Marco Polo*, ed. 1, I, p. 93). Marignolli (Yule and Cordier,
Cathay, III, p. 236) distinctly makes it the plantain. But in Barbosa's
time the Portuguese universally called the plantain the Indian fig.
Garcia da Orta alludes to it simply as the fig (*Coll.*, 22). It is therefore
improbable that Barbosa could have alluded to this fruit as Adam's
apple. The fruit was evidently of the orange family, and its large
size makes it probable that it may have been the shaddock or pommelo.
This fruit, though not indigenous in Ceylon, is believed to have been
introduced from Java, and possibly may have been established in
this congenial climate when Barbosa (or the author of Ramusio's
additions) wrote. The Adam's apple with which it is compared for
size, if not the Jack-fruit, must have been some large fruit of the
citron family.

such quantity and so great that their ears touch their shoulders ; on their fingers they wear many rings set with the finest gems, and they gird themselves with golden belts set with stones. Their language is drawn partly from Malabar and partly from Coromendel.[1] Many Malabar Moors come to settle in this island by reason of the great liberty which they there enjoy, and also because it is not only well furnished with all the comforts and delights of the world, but is also a country with a very moderate climate, where men live in good health longer than in any other part of India, and very few become ill. Here grow many and excellent fruits, the hillsides are covered with sweet and bitter[2] oranges with three or four distinct flavours, and of some the rind is sweeter than the juice, and they are even larger than Adam's apple ; lemons of a sweet bitterness, some large and some very small and sweet, also many other kinds of fruit not found in our lands, and the trees are continually laden with them throughout the year, so that flowers and fruits ripe and unripe are seen perpetually. There is also very great plenty of flesh of divers kinds of animals, and of fowls of the air, all delicate food, of fish as well great store, which are taken close to the island. Of rice there is but little, they bring the more part of it hither from Coromendel,[3] and this is their

---

[1] This is Ramusio's spelling. The Spanish form here and elsewhere is Cholmendel. In the Portuguese text the spelling Charamandel is always used. The Tamil language is identical with that of the Coromandel Coast, but the Sinhalese has no connection with the language of Malabar, Malayālam being an Aryan-language.

[2] *Sweet and bitter oranges.* The word for *bitter* used by Ramusio is *garbi*, which belongs to the Venetian dialect. As to the abundance of fruits of the *citrus* family we may compare what Robert Knox said (1681). " Rare sweet oranges and sower ones, Limes but no Lemons, such as ours are ; Pautaurings in tast all one with a Lemon, but much bigger than a man's two fists, right Citrons, and a small sort of sweet Oranges " (ed. 1911, p. 23).

[3] Ceylon still depends for its supplies of rice mainly on imports from the Indian mainland.

principal diet.   There is also great plenty of good honey,
and of sugar which is brought from Bengala.   Butter in
abundance is found on the island.]
   In this island is found the true and good Cinnamon.[1]

---

   [1] *Cinnamon.*   The principal object which the Portuguese had in
view in their first expeditions to Ceylon was to obtain the control of
the supply of the cinnamon grown there, which was considered far
superior to that of Malabar and fetched a much higher price.   Yet
in more ancient times Ceylon was unknown as a source from which
good cinnamon came.   The eastern horn of Africa got the credit
of supplying it in the first century A.D. (*Periplus*, sections 10, 12
and 13, and the note in Schoff's ed., p. 82), and in the present day
the best cinnamon comes from China.   Whether the quality found
in Ceylon owed its superiority to better conditions of soil and climate
than those of Malabar, or whether it was another species, is doubtful.
The Dutch are said to have improved the cultivation in Ceylon as
late as 1770 A.D.   Garcia da Orta gives a full account of what was
known of Ceylon cinnamon in the middle of the sixteenth century
in his fifteenth *Coll.*   He says that one *quintal* of Ceylon cinnamon
cost 10 *cruzados*, while in Malabar four *quintals* could be bought for
1 *cruzado*.   The earliest mention of the cinnamon trade with Ceylon
is believed by Yule to be that in a letter of Friar Menentillus, dated
1292.   He says, " The cinnamon tree is of a medium bulk, not very
high, and in trunk, bark and foliage is like the laurel " (*i.e.*, the bay
tree) ; " indeed altogether it resembleth the laurel greatly in appearance.
Great store of it is carried forth of the island which is hard by Maabar "
(Yule and Cordier, *Cathay*, III, p. 62).   Marignolli, who travelled between
1338 and 1353, and describes many of the wonders and fruits of Ceylon,
does not mention cinnamon.   Ibn Baṭūṭa, at the same period, certainly mentions the cinnamon tree, but says nothing of the use of
its bark as a spice.   He mentions only its use as firewood (Ibn
Baṭuṭa, IV, p. 99), and in his account of Ceylon (IV, p. 166) he speaks
of the logs of cinnamon wood being piled up on the strand as they were
washed down by the torrents, and adds that the people of Ma'bar
and Malībār were allowed to carry them away for nothing on condition of making a present to the king.   It is not the case therefore
as Sir E. Tennent supposed (*Ceylon*, II, p. 6, note 2) that Malabar was
supplied with cinnamon from Ceylon, according to Ibn Baṭuṭa's
account.   It may be noted that according to Knox in the seventeenth
century the cinnamon tree was freely cut down for use as timber
(*l.c.*, p. 26).   Niccolò Conti, whose journey to the East ended in 1444,
gave a good account of the cinnamon tree in Ceylon, and of the use
of the bark, but says nothing of the trade (*India in Fifteenth Century*,
Conti, pp. 7–8).   Hieronimo di Santo Stefano, in the latter part of the
fifteenth century, visited Ceylon and mentions the growth of the
cinnamon tree, but he too says nothing about the trade.   It seems
probable that the Arab merchants who brought it to the Indian ports
kept the place of its origin secret, and it was not till the Portuguese
found their way to the west coast of India that they discovered that
the good cinnamon did not grow in Malabar, but was brought from
Ceylon.   In 1500 A.D. the author of the *Navegação de Pedro Alvares
Cabral* (Ch. XV) mentions *canella* among the articles brought
for sale to the emporium of Cambaya, but says nothing about its
place of origin ;   while in 1502 Thomé Lopes (*Navegaçāo as Indias
Orientaes*, Ch. XIX) says, " The people of Cochim relate that a

It grows on the hillsides in bushes like bay trees. The King has it cut into fine branches and the bark is stripped and dried during certain months of the year. With his own hand he makes it over to those merchants who come to buy it, for no dweller in this country, save the King only, may gather it.

And in this island are reared many wild elephants which the King has caught and tamed. These he sells to the merchants of Charamandel, of Narsingua, Malabar, Daquem and Cambaia, who come hither to seek them. And the manner in which they take them is this[1] : They

---

hundred and fifty leagues thence is the Island of Ceylon, a wealthy island 300 leagues long, where there are lofty mountains ; and it produces *canella* in greater abundance than any other place, and also of the finest quality." It is evident therefore that the fact that the best cinnamon was to be got in Ceylon became known to the Portuguese very soon after their arrival in India, and that it is not correct to give Barbosa the credit of being the first to proclaim its superiority as Sir E. Tennent did (*Ceylon*, II, p. 6, note 2). The fact of the despatch of the expedition under Lourenço D'Almeida in 1506 is alone sufficient to prove this, for De Barros tells us that one of the Viceroy's reasons for sending the expedition was to get possession of this trade. " When the Viceroy learnt of this new route that they " (*i.e.*, the Moorish merchants) " were taking, and also of the Island of Ceilam, where they loaded cinnamon, because all that was to be found in those parts was there . . . ." (D. Ferguson, *Hist. of Ceylon* (J., Ceylon Branch, R.A.S., 1908) p. 22, quoting De Barros, *Dec. I*, x, p. 15). Further on De Barros (*II*, iii, p. 1) tells us that in 1508 Nuno Vaz Pereira failed to obtain any cinnamon because the king was ill and the Moors had incited the Heathen of Ceylon against the Portuguese.

[1] The fame of Ceylon for elephants is of ancient date. Strabo (II, i, p. 14) mentions ivory as one of the exports of Taprobane. The *Periplus* does not mention elephants in its notice of the island. Aelian, in the third century A.D., mentions the trade in elephants between Ceylon and the mainland ; and Cosmas, in the sixth century, describes the purchase of elephants by the King of Sielediba at a price in proportion to their height, varying from 50 to 100 nomismata, that is, according to Yule (Yule and Cordier, *Cathay*, I, p. 230, n. 3), from £32 to £65. Barbosa's prices, nearly a thousand years later, are also in gold, 1,500 to 400 or 500 cruzados, that is, about £750 to £200 or £250. In Vijayanagar the prices varied from £731 to £975 (Vol. I, p. 210, n. 1). ·Ibn Baṭūṭa (IV, p. 171, ff.), after leaving the port of Salāwāt (*i.e.*, Chilāw), crossed a rough country full of wild elephants. Further on he speaks of Kunār the Sultān of Kunakār, who possessed a white elephant, the only one the traveller had ever seen. (See also Yule and Cordier, *Cathay*, pp. 32, 33.) Odoric (Yule and Cordier, *Cathay*, II, p. 171) had also spoken of the abundance of wild elephants. The system of taking elephants described by Barbosa is of great antiquity, and was practised long after his time. That described by Robert Knox

H

place a female elephant as a decoy on the hill where they are wont to graze, which is fastened by the foot to a tree with strong chains. Around it they dig three or four very deep pits covered with very fine branches spread over the ground as cunningly as they can. The wild elephants, seeing the female, fall into these pits where they keep them seven or eight days without food, and many men watch them night and day and speak to them so as not to suffer them to sleep, until they become tame, and then feed them from their hands. When they are tame and broken-in they surround them very softly with thick chains, and in order to draw them forth from the pit they throw in so many branches that the elephant gradually rises until he can come out. They then tie him to a tree where they keep him several days more, men with fires always watching by night, coaxing him and speaking to him constantly, and giving him food in small quantities until they have him at their disposal. In this way they take both male and female, great and small. Sometimes two fall into one pit. These elephants are a valuable merchandize among them, they are worth

---

in the latter part of the seventeenth century was almost identical, the use of a tame female elephant as a decoy being a principal feature in it (Knox's *Ceylon*, ed. 1911, p. 34) ; and Wolf (quoted in Tennent's *Ceylon*, II, 334, n. 1) mentions a similar method as followed as late as 1750. The corral system was introduced by the Portuguese ; the use of the Portuguese word *corral* is alone enough evidence of this.

Ribeiro, in his *Fatalidade Historica* (1685), says that the revenues of the King Paria Pandar—Perea Pandar in Couto, see Ferguson, p. 410 ; properly Dharmapāla, *ibid.*, p. 102—(who made the King of Portugal his heir in 1597) consisted mainly in the income derived from cinnamon and elephants, and that he sold about twenty to thirty elephants every year to the " Mogor," *i.e.*, the Mughal Emperor of Delhi, at a very high price (*Collecção de Noticias*, Vol. V, p. 27). Further on (*ib.*, p. 50) he says that the price varied from eight to twelve or fifteen thousand *pardaos*. His account of the method of taming newly-caught elephants resembles that in the text. He says, " The best means of taming them is not to let them sleep one instant for the first three days and nights, and if they are inclined to sleep to keep them from it by blows. After this they encourage them by speaking kindly to them, and in the time we have mentioned they are tamed "

much, and are greatly esteemed by the Kings of India, who keep them for war and to labour on various tasks. Some are very tame and have as much sense and understanding as men. The best and most thoroughly trained are worth a thousand or a thousand five hundred *cruzados*, others four or five hundred according to their training, this in Malabar and Charamandel. In this island their price is small. No one save the King may take them [who pays those who catch them].

In this island also are found precious stones[1] in plenty

---

[1] The precious stones of Ceylon, though not now considered to be of the highest quality, were far-famed in ancient days, and its pearl fisheries were also believed to be the most productive in the world. The *Periplus* (§ 61) says that the island of Palaesimoundou produces pearls and transparent stones. Ptolemy and Pliny both mention precious stones and pearls as produced in Taprobane, but their information appears to be derived mainly from Megasthenes, and is not therefore contemporary. It is of value as showing that in the third century B.C. Ceylon had the reputation of producing gems (McCrindle's *Ancient India*, Ptolemy, pp. 247 and 251 ; Pliny's *Natural History*, Bostock and Riley's trans., Bohn 1855, pp. 51, 52). Ptolemy also mentions beryls and hyacinths among its products. Fah-Hian, the Buddhist pilgrim from China, found that the country produced precious stones and pearls, and also that the sacred gem of Buddhism, the Mani, was found in one district (Beal's *Fah-Hian*, p. 148.) His journey supplies a link between the period of the Periplus and that of Cosmas in the sixth century. Cosmas found that the hyacinth or jacinth was one of its principal products, and that the great hyacinth, an object of reverence, was on a high peak (Cosmas, pp. 364–5). This gem may undoubtedly be identified with the Buddhist " Mani " alluded to by Fah-Hian. Moses of Chorene, in the fifth century, also alludes to the gems of Ceylon. Yuan Chwang, in the seventh century, gives an account very similar to that of Fah-Hian as to the great gem, but says nothing as to gems in general. It is, however, probable, according to Mr. Watters, that he did not visit Ceylon in person, but relied on tales and books (Watters, *Yuan Chwang*, II, pp. 235–6).

After the rise and spread of Islam we are dependant for many centuries on the reports which found their way into the Arabic chronicles. Albērūnī (I, p. 211) alludes to the pearl fishery which he says had died out, the pearls having migrated to the east coast of Africa. Rashīd-u'd-din reports that rubies and other precious stones were found in Ceylon (Sarandīp) (Elliot and Dowson, I, p. 70).

In the thirteenth and fourteenth centuries the Chinese chronicles report the despatch of embassies to Ceylon to collect gems and drugs (Tennent, I, p. 621). Ibn Baṭūta, here as elsewhere, supplies valuable information, for in the early part of the fourteenth century (IV, p. 173) Kunakăr, according to him, was the centre of production, some, especially rubies or carbuncles, being found in the waters of the gulf and others in the earth. Some were red, some yellow, and some of various kinds, and also many lapidaries, who are skilled to such an extent, that if one should bring one of them a handful of earth in which precious stones were mixed he would say at once " There are rubies in this hand or sapphires in that." And in the same manner when they see the ruby or other stones they say " This must be kept for so many hours in the fire," and it will turn out very clear and good. The King sometimes ventures to place a ruby in a very fierce charcoal fire for the time the lapidary tells him ; and if any ruby endures it without peril of destruction it remains much more perfect in colour. When this King finds any precious stone he keeps it for himself and places it in his Treasury.

[Nigh to this Island there is in the sea a shoal covered by a depth of ten or twelve fathoms of water whereon are found pearls both great and small in extreme abundance. Of these some are shaped like a pear. The Moors and Heathen of a city named Cael, pertaining to the King of Coulam, use to come hither twice in every year to fish for them. They find them in oysters smaller and smoother than ours. Men dive and find them at the bottom of the water, where they can stay for many hours. The little pearls belong to the pearl-

---

bluc. The king had a right to all gems worth 100 fanams, while all of lower value belonged to the finder. 100 fanams, he says, were equivalent to six gold dinārs. He also speaks of the great abundance of gems worn by the women.

Friar Odoric, at about the same time, speaks of the collection of gems by the poor in the water of a certain leech-infested swamp, but says that the king allowed them to keep all they could find (Yule and Cordier, *Cathay*, II, p. 171), and also speaks of the finding of rubies and diamonds, although, as Yule remarks, there are no diamonds in Ceylon. Marignolli also speaks of gems being found in the waters of a pool near Adam's Peak, and mentions with disapproval the legend that they were formed from Adam's tears ! (Yule and Cordier, *Cathay*, III, p. 235). Hieronimo de Santo Stefano, at the end of the fifteenth century, speaks of garnets, cat's-eyes and jacinths in Ceylon, and adds that the finest were found in the mountains (*India in Fifteenth Century*, IV, p. 5).

gatherer and the great ones to the King, who keeps his factor there. They pay him as well certain fees to obtain his permission to fish.

The King of Ceilam resides in a city called Calmucho,[1] which stands on a river with a good port whither sail every year ships from divers lands to take cargoes of cinnamon and elephants and bringing gold, silver, very fine Cambaya cotton cloths and goods of many other kinds such as saffron, coral, quicksilver, cinnabar, yet is their greatest profit in gold and silver for they are worth more here than elsewhere. Likewise many ships come from Bengala and Coromandel, and some from Malacca to buy elephants, cinnamon and jewels. There are also four or five other ports in this island, populous towns, where great trade is carried on, which are under the rule of other Lords, nephews of the King of Ceilam, to whom they owe allegiance ; yet at times they rise up against him.]

In the midst of this Island there is a lofty range of mountains among which is a very high stony peak,[2] on

---

[1] *Columbo* in the Spanish version. Calmucho appears to be a clerical or transcriber's error for Columbo, as there is no such place, and Columbo was the capital of the part of Ceylon best known to the Portuguese at this period. The passage is not found in the Portuguese MS.

[2] The incidents attending the pilgrimages to Adam's Peak have been narrated by many travellers. Ibn Batūta's account corresponds in many points with that of our author. Especially the tales of the attacks on the pilgrims by "flying leeches" and the ascent of the peak by means of chains fastened to the rock may be noted (*l.c.*, IV, pp. 178–181). The print of Buddha's foot was accepted by Ibn Batūta with complete faith as that of Adam. The chains still exist, and travellers to the peak are still attacked by land-leeches, as described by Tennent (II, pp. 137–9). The Cave of Khidhr described by Ibn Batūta is also evidently of Buddhist origin. It is not described in any modern work, and Captain Suckling, in his *Ceylon* (1876), says (II, p. 19) that the "seven caves and the ridge of Alexander cannot now be identified, unless he meant the deep ravines and the great mass of granite near Deabatine."

The chains do not seem to have been mentioned by any traveller before Marco Polo, who gave a good description of the mountain, and was able to discriminate between the Buddhist and Muhammadan

the summit whereof is a tank of water deep enough to swim in[1] and a very great footprint of a man in a rock, well shaped. This the Moors say is the footprint of our father Adam, whom they call Adombaba, and from all the Moorish regions and realms they come thither on pilgrimage declaring that from that spot Adam ascended to Heaven. They travel in pilgrims' weeds girt about with great iron chains, and clad in the hides of leopards, lions and other wild beasts of the field, on their right arms they have great blisters[2] caused by fire which they perpetually expose on the way that they may always bear open wounds with them, saying that they do so for the love of God and of Mafamede and of Adam. Many of them carry money secretly, and are very wealthy, intending therewith to purchase precious stones, which they do. Before they reach that lofty mount where is the footprint they call Adam's they pass through flooded lands and valleys and

---

versions of its legends, for which see Ch. XV of *Marco Polo* (Yule and Cordier). Friar Odoric at the same period speaks of the leeches infesting the passage, and like his contemporary Ibn Baṭūṭa alludes to the pilgrims' practice of squeezing lemon juice over their bodies as a protection. He, however, says that this prevented the leeches from attacking them, while Ibn Baṭūṭa says it made the leeches drop off after biting them. So also Ibn Baṭūṭa says that the bitten men used a wooden knife to scrape the place where they had been bitten, while Barbosa simply says that they used knives to get rid of the leeches. Barbosa probably heard the phrase Adam Bābā used of Buddha by Muhammadans. I have myself heard the God S'iva called Bābā Adam in Northern India, and the identification of one of the leading gods with Adam may have come down from the Buddhist period.

[1] Here Ramusio has "a pool of clear water which flows perpetually," and the Spanish version, "a pool of spring water." Neither of these keeps the meaning of the Portuguese *nadivel*, "which can be swum in.".

[2] Ramusio here says, "On their arms and legs they have certain buttons (*bottoni*) with sharp points with which they continue to hit themselves as they go, causing wounds from which blood flows "; and the Spanish version, "On their arms and legs they inflict wounds continually along the road to keep up open sores." Both seem to have missed the idiomatic meaning of *botões de fogo, i.e.*, blisters caused by burns.

rivers, and must always go for five or six leagues up to their waists in water, and they all carry knives in their hands in order therewith to rid themselves of the leeches, which are so many that they would kill them if they did not so. When they reach the mountain[1] they go up, but they cannot ascend the peak by reason of its steepness save by the ladders of very thick iron chains which are placed there with which it is surrounded. At the top they bathe in the water of that tank, and recite their prayers, and therewith they hold that they are saved and freed from all their sins.

This Island of Ceilam is very near to the main land and between them there are two shoals[2] in the midst of which is a channel called by the Moors and Heathen Chilam[3] whereby pass all the *zambucos* of Malabar on their way to Charamandel. Many of these are lost on the shoals every year, for the channel is very narrow. In the year when the Admiral came the second time to settle the affairs of India so many of these ships and *zambucos* of Malabar were lost, that it is reckoned twelve thousand men were drowned, who came thither

---

[1] Reading *serra* for *terra*, which seems to be the writer's intention. Ramusio and the Spanish version both have " mountain."

[2] The shoals of Chilam are alluded to by De Barros in his general description of Ceylon as very dangerous to navigation (*Dec. III*, ii, p. 1, of which a translation will be found in D. Ferguson's *Hist. of Ceylon*, p. 31). The name is evidently derived from the port of Chilãw. De Barros fancied that the name Ceilam was derived from that of these shoals, which it is needless to say was a mistaken derivation. The name, however, seems to have been applied to the whole Gulf of Manaar by the Tamils engaged in the pearl fishery. According to Sir E. Tennent (*l.c.*, I, p. 440) they called both town and gulf *Salãbham*, " the sea of gain." Mr. Ferguson, however (*l.c.*, p. 31, n. 5), says there is little doubt that Chilãw represents the Tamil *salãpam*, " diving," and this seems the most probable origin for a name connected with the pearl fishery.

[3] *Chillá* in Ramusio and *Chylam* in the Spanish version. Ceilam in the Portuguese text is undoubtedly a scribe's error for Chilam

determined to drive away the Portuguese fleet from India without allowing it to obtain cargoes.[1]

---

§ 96. QUILICARE.

LEAVING this island of Ceylon I return to the mainland, and after the Cape of Comorim has been passed there is hard by a land belonging to.the King of Coulam and to other lords who are subject to him which is called Quilicare[2] wherein are many and great towns of the

---

[1] It is not clear whether Barbosa means to say that all these vessels were lost in the shallows near Ceylon. It may be that ships from Malabar were engaged in the pearl fishery or in trade with Ceylon, and were summoned thence to take part in the attack on the Admiral (Vasco da Gama) organised by the Zamorin. This was during his second voyage to India, in the year 1502.

[2] *Quilicare.* This is the small seaport now known as Kilakarai situated in the Rāmnād estate, Madura district, about 10 miles south of the town of Rāmnād. It is a decaying place, and what trade there is is in the hands of the Muhammadans known as Labbāis, who occupy a similar position on the Coromandel Coast to that of the Māppilas in Malabar. They are a Tamil-speaking Hindu race converted to Islam, with some admixture of Arab blood. They are described as "industrious and enterprising, plucky mariners and expert traders." Some are divers in the pearl and chank fisheries of the Gulf of Manaar, and others are weavers of sedge mats. A good deal of the trade is carried on with Penang and Singapore, and among the imports from those regions is the Malay blow-gun which Dr. N. Annandale found in use at Kilakarai for shooting pigeons. There are also among them many fishers for *dugong,* and growers of betel. There can be little doubt that these enterprising folk are the descendants of the Moorish traders mentioned by Barbosa. They must be classed as a mixed race springing from the union of Arab traders with women of the country, and their position is thus similar to that of the Nivāyats of the Konkan (Vol. I, p. 147, n. 1, and p. 187, n. 1) and the Māppilas of of Malabar (*supra*, p. 74). (See Thurston, *s.v.* Labbai; *Madras Gazetteer, s.v.* Kilakarai.)
Lassen and H. H. Wilson identified Kilakarai with the Colchos of the *Periplus*, but this identification has been generally abandoned in favour of Korkai (*Tinnevelly Gazetteer, s.v.* Korkai, p. 430).
Allusions to Kilakarai in older writers are lacking, but Yule thought that the great port of Fattan (or Patan) mentioned by Ibn Baṭūṭa and Rashīdu'd-din was probably the port of the city of Madura "and therefore should be looked for in the vicinity of Rāmnād, as at Devipatam or Killikarai, which have both been ports of some consideration" (Yule and Cordier, *Cathay*, IV, p. 35, n. 1). This Fattan was also he thinks the city of Maabar of John of Montecorvino and Marco Polo (*ibid.*, III, pp. 65 and 67). It may be considered not improbable

Heathen and many others with havens on the sea where dwell many Moors, natives of the land. Its navigation is carried on in certain small craft which they call *champanes*[1] in which the Moors come to trade there, and carry thither the goods of Cambaya. Here certain horses are of great value, and they take cargoes of rice and cloth and carry them to Malabar. In this Province of Quilicare there is a great Heathen House of Worship wherein is an Idol which they hold in great honour. Every twelve years [2] they celebrate for it a right great festival whither come all the Heathen with indulgences, considering that thereby they obtain salvation as at a jubilee. This temple possesses many estates producing great revenues, and it is so great that it has its own

---

that this celebrated " Fattan " or port was Kilakarai, as no other place seems to fit the position so well.

It is remarkable that Barbosa, or his copyist, has reversed the correct order of Quilicare and Cael. The latter is nearer to Cape Comorin and would be first approached after rounding the cape. Possibly, however, the more usual route from Ceylon was by Quilicare, and the writer mentions that town as first approached after leaving Ceylon.

[1] *Champanes.* The small boats now known as sampans. The term is Malay, and apparently ultimately Chinese. (See *Gloss. Luso-Asiatico, s.v.* Champana ; *Hobson-Jobson, s.v.* Sampan.)

[2] *The death of the priest-king.* This is a remarkable example of the widely-spread early custom of—

" The priest who slew the slayer,
And shall himself be slain,"

which forms the starting-point of Sir J. Frazer's *Golden Bough.* It is clear that the successor to the priest, who was also a king, if he did not actually slay him with his own hands, was obliged to be present and assenting to his death ; also that although the departing king began to mutilate himself, he was not allowed to administer the final stroke. The period of twelve years is remarkable.

In Ramusio and the Spanish version, however, the dying king himself gives the blow. Ramusio says, " He himself cuts his wind-pipe (*canna della golla*) and makes himself a sacrifice to the idol." A. Hamilton relates a custom similar to that here described, but applies it to the Zamorin in his account of Malabar (*New Account of the East Indies*, Ed. 1727, I. 306). The period for which the Zamorin could reign is stated, as here, to be twelve years. It is most unlikely that such a custom, had it really existed, could have escaped Barbosa's attention, considering his minute acquaintance with Malabar, and it is probable that the account given to Hamilton was based on a distorted version of Barbosa's narrative.

King, who cannot reign more than twelve years from one jubilee to another should he live so long. In this manner when the twelve years are accomplished on the day when the festival is held a great crowd of people is here assembled, and much money is spent in feeding a multitude of Bramenes. The King has a platform (*andaimo*) made, which is hung with silken draperies, and on the appointed day he goes to bathe in a tank with music and much ritual. Thence he proceeds to offer his orisons to the Idol, and this done he goes up into this wooden stand, and there in the sight of all he takes certain very sharp knives, and therewith he proceeds to cut off his nostrils, then his ears and lips, and what members soever he is able to cut off himself, and casts them away quickly until he has lost so much blood that he begins to faint, when they cut his throat with a sword and thus accomplish his slaying. Thus they offer him up to their Idol. And whosoever would reign in the lordship of this Church for another twelve years must take part in that martyrdom, for the love of the Idol, and must himself behold it. And there straightway they make him King.

§ 97. THE CITY OF CAEL.

ADVANCING further along the coast there is a city which they call *Cael*,[1] also pertaining to the King of Coulam

---

[1] *Cael.* The identification of the great port of Cael described by Marco Polo was first made known in Yule's *Marco Polo* in 1871 from notes furnished him by the late Bishop Caldwell, the great Dravidian scholar. It is now accepted that Cael is represented by the deserted site among the lagoons of the delta of the Tāmbraparni river now known as Palayakāyal or Old Kāyal. Yule had been at first inclined to identify it with the still existing port of Kāyalpattanam or Kāyal-town further south along the coast, but at once admitted the correctness of Caldwell's opinion. The ancient port of Colchoi, as mentioned in § 59 of the *Periplus* and also by Ptolemy, has been shown to be the spot now known as Korkai (formerly Kolkai) in the same delta. The successive abandonment of Colchoi and Cael was due to

inhabited by Moors and Heathen merchants of importance. It has a very good haven whither every year sail
many ships from Malabar and others from Charamandel
and Benguala, so that here there is traffic in goods of
many kinds coming from divers regions. The *Chatis* of
this land are men of high standing dealing in abundance
of precious stones and of seed-pearls also, for the right
of fishing for these belongs to the King.[1] A wealthy and

the accumulation of silt and the advance of the shore at the mouth
of the river. For a fuller account reference should be made to Yule's
Marco Polo (ed. Cordier, where there is a fuller map than in the
1870 ed.) ; also to the article " Korkai " in the *Tinnevelly Gazetteer*
(1917), p. 429 ff., and Schoff's *Periplus*, p. 237.
    The histories represent this country of Chola as under the rule of
Vijayanagar at this period, but it is clear that from the middle of
the fifteenth century the King of Coulam successfully disputed the
authority of the Vijayanagar kings, and throughout the Tinnevelly
district inscriptions of these rulers have been found from 1439 to
1532 (*Tinnevelly Gazetteer*, p. 58). After the latter date Vijayanagar
was again supreme. Barbosa's statement about the residence of the
King of Coulam at or near Cael, and his successful resistance to
" Narsyngua," is therefore correct. Varthema also at the same period
states that he made his way from " Colon " to " Chayl " belonging to
the same king (*Varthema*, p. 184). Kāil was one of the ports visited
by the Chinese in the early fifteenth century. It is alluded to in the
travels of the eunuch Chêng-Ho under the name of Kia-i-lê (Rockhill, *l.c.*, *T'oung Pao*, Vol. XVI, p. 83).
    [1] The pearl fishery on this coast had been important from the
earliest times. It has generally been in the hands of a fisher caste
known as Paravans, who have their headquarters at Tuticorin, which
has long since supplanted Kāyal as the principal port on this coast.
The Muhammadans, accustomed to the pearl fishing of the Persian
Gulf, had, however, established their supremacy at this period, and
the Paravans did not recover their independence until the Portuguese
took their part in 1532. Most of them adopted Christianity at this
time, and to the present day most of them are Roman Catholics, and
many bear Portuguese names (*Tinnevelly Gazetteer*, p. 231 ; Thurston,
Vol. VI, p. 143 ff.). In Barbosa's time the " Moors " were still in
possession and he well describes the strong and independent position
of their chief. It may be presumed that the King of Coulam supported
him and received a share of his profits. The report of the Dutch
Commandant and Senior Merchant in 1669 (quoted in Thurston, *l.c.*)
gives an account of the state of things in the early part of the sixteenth
century, which shows that the Raja and the Moors combined to exact
all they could from the fishermen. Mr. Hornell's report, also quoted
(*l.c.*), states that these " Moors " were Labbais, and that their chief
settlement was at Kāyal. It is possible that the Friday impost in
favour of the owner of the boat was imposed by the Muhammadans,
as Friday is their sacred day. They were no doubt owners of the
boats. The King of Coulam's corps of female archers does not appear
to be mentioned elsewhere.
    The trade in pearls with Vijayanagar has been alluded to already
(Vol. I, p. 203).

distinguished Moor has long held the farm of the duties levied on seed-pearls. He is so rich and powerful that all the people of the land honour him as much as the King. He executes judgment and justice on the Moors without interference from the King.

The fishers for seed-pearl fish all the week for themselves save on the Friday when they work for the owner of the boat, and at the end of the season they fish for a whole week for this Moor, whereby he possesses great abundance of seed-pearl. The King of Coulam is always near to this city, who by reason of his title thereto is a right noble, wealthy and mighty lord, and master of many armed men. In his land are found the best archers in the whole world, and he ever carries with him three or four hundred woman archers who march in his escort and has them instructed from their youth. They wear very tight bands on their heads of silk and cotton ; they are very active. This King is often at war with the King of Narsyngua (who is very powerful as I have said above), and defends himself well from him.[1]

---

§ 98. CHARAMANDEL.

YET further along the coast the land turns northwards and bears the name of Charamandel,[2] which land may

---

[1] The practice of duelling was according to Ramusio's version of *Marco Polo* practised at Cael in his time under royal auspices. Yule, in his *Marco Polo*, in a note quoted Barbosa's passage under Batecala, where a similar practice is recorded, and added, " This is the only passage in Ramusio's version as far as I know that suggests the possibility of interpolation from a recent author." In my note on this passage (Vol. I, p. 190, n. 2) I considered that this remark referred to Barbosa's text and was not justified, but on reading it again I have come to the conclusion that the reference is to Marco Polo's text and not to Barbosa's, which also is quoted from Ramusio and not from the Portuguese text.

[2] *Charamandel.* This spelling is followed throughout in the printed Portuguese text, but probably Barbosa himself wrote Choramandel,

have seventy or eighty leagues of coast. Here are many cities, towns and villages wherein dwell great numbers of Heathen folk. This land is under the King of Narsyngua, it is very fruitful and abounds in rice, flesh-meat, wheat and all vegetables of other kinds are found there ; it is a land of open plains. Numbers of ships from Malabar sail hither every year, most of them to take cargoes of rice by which they make great profits : and they bring hither abundance of goods from Cambaya, copper, quicksilver, vermilion, pepper and goods of other kinds. In this Province of Charamandel are also found many sorts of spices and drugs which come from the kingdoms of Malaca, China[1] and Benguala in Moorish ships for they dare not pass by Malabar through fear of our fleets. This is the best supplied of all the lands in this part of India, saving only Cambaya, yet in some years it so happens that no rain falls, and then there is such a dearth among them that many die of hunger, and for this reason they sell their children for four or five *fanams* each. At such seasons the Malabares bring them great store of rice and coco-nuts and take away ship-loads of slaves.

The more part or all of the Heathen merchants or

---

that is, Chola-mandalam or Chora-mandalam, the Country of the Cholas. Barbosa does not attempt to fix the name to any special city, as some early writers did, but understood it in its proper sense, viz., the country extending from the point where the coast turned northwards, *i.e.*, from Point Calimere, at which point the coast, which runs in a north-easterly direction from Cape Comorin, takes a due north and south line extending to the delta of the Krishna River. The only towns he mentions on this coast, which in his time formed part of the kingdom of Vijayanagar, are Mailapur and Paleacate (see Vol. I, p. 227, n.). Madras, which is a creation of the East India Company's rule, was an unknown name in his time.

[1] That there was some Chinese trade with the Coromandel coast cannot be doubted. It was visited by Cheng-Ho in 1408 and 1412, and is alluded to under the names of So-li (Chūla) and Hsi-yang So-li (Southern Chūla) (Rockhill, *l.c.* T'oung-Pao, Vol. XVI, p. 83). It did not, however, occupy the same prominent position as Malabar, and no special ports are named with the exception of Kāil.

Chatis who live throughout India are natives of this country, and are very cunning in every kind of traffic in goods. At the seaports also are many Moors, natives of the land ; who are great merchants and own many ships.

§ 99. MAILAPUR.

GOING yet further and leaving behind Charamandel and its lands there is on the sea strand a city, which is right ancient and almost deserted, called Mailapur,[1] which erewhile was very great and fair, pertaining to the King of Narsyngua.

Here lies buried the body of the Blessed Saint Thomas [2]

[1] Mailapur is now practically a suburb of Madras, but there is no doubt as to its antiquity. The name is sometimes given as Maliapur, and is by Marignolli turned into Mirapolis. It is mentioned by Thomas Bowrey (*l.c.*, pp. 38, 45) as Mylapore, and by A. Hamilton (*l.c.*, I, p. 356) as Malliapore. The Portuguese maintained an establishment there, but lost it in 1662, the Dutch assisting the Muhammadan Governor in the attack. Towards the end of Aurangzeb's reign it became a mint of the Mughal Emperors (Whitehead, *Cat. of Coins in Lahore Museum*, Vol. II, cxii).

[2] The legend of St. Thomas as here related must be read in connection with what has been told above in the account of Coulam (§ 88). It seems probable that this legend was of local origin, and was influenced by an earlier story of Buddhist or Hindu origin. This is suggested not only by the form of the story, but by the prominent part taken by the peacock. The incident of the assembly of the peacocks on a flat rock may be compared to the similar assembly of peacocks and other birds in the Nacca Jātaka or Haṅsa Jātaka, which is represented among the sculptures of the Barāhat Stūpa (Cunningham, *The Stupa of Bharhut*, Pl. XXVII).

It is remarkable that Barbosa's is the only version of the story which represents the saint as assuming the appearance of a peacock, and, after being pierced by the hunter's arrow, rising into the air and then turning into human form and falling to the ground. The earliest form in which we have it is that of Marco Polo (Yule, *Marco Polo*, pp. 278, 290, 291). He simply says that the saint was shot accidentally by a " Govi " who was shooting peacocks. Odoric, Montecorvino and Conti only mention the fact of the saint's burial at Mailapur. Marignolli, however (Yule and Cordier, *Cathay*, III, p. 250), says that the saint wore a mantle of peacocks' feathers and retired at night to a place where there were many peacocks, and was there shot. There is, as Yule noted, an evident hiatus here, and it is possible that some such incident as is related by Barbosa may have been intentionally omitted by the pious chronicler. Marignolli makes this the conclusion of his narrative of the log of wood, localised by him at Mirapolis or Mailāpur.

in a little church near the sea.   The Xtians of Coulam
say that when Saint Thomas departed thence, being

J. de Barros, who probably had access to Barbosa's narrative
among others, tells first the legend about the log of wood at " Māliapor."
After the saint's success an envious Brahman killed his own son and
accused him of the murder.   The saint confounded his accuser by
causing the dead boy to speak and declare that his father was his
murderer.   The Brahmans afterwards attacked the saint and stoned
him, and while he was lying at the point of death he was pierced with
a spear and killed.   There is here no mention of peacocks (*Dec. III*,
vii, ch. 11, ff. 204–206, wrongly printed 304–306 in ed. of 1563).   He
says that the first investigations here by the Portuguese were made in
1525–6 by Duarte de Meneses.   He appointed Antonio Gil as overseer
of some works of repair to the church, who in excavating for a new
foundation under a pinnacle which was in danger of collapsing found
a tomb he believed to be that of Saint Thomas, and among the bones
an iron spearhead and parts of an iron-shod shaft.   This find, taken
in connection with the whiteness of the bones as compared with other
bones found near by, was considered as establishing the fact that
these were the saint's bones.   Afterwards, when Nuno da Cunha
was Governor, in 1533, he founded a Portuguese town near Paleacate
(Pulicat) which he called San Thomé.
A version of the story is given in the seventeenth century by
Mandelslo (English edition, 1669, p. 93).   He follows De Barros, and
had no doubt read his account.   The town of Saint Thomas, he says,
was situated 13° 32' north of the line, which would make it correspond
very closely with Pulicat but not with Mailapur.
See, for a more modern consideration of the subject, M. Cordier's
note in *Cathay* (Yule and Cordier, II, pp. 141–2), in which Yule's note
in *Marco Polo* (ed. 1871) is embodied.   It should be noted, however,
that the date of 1522 there assigned as that of the Commission sent
by D. Duarte de Meneses to search for the saint's body is not correct.
De Barros (*Dec. III*, p. 204) and Correa (II, p. 722) both agree that the
first information on this point reached the Portuguese in 1517, being
brought by Diogo Fernandez and Bastião Fernandez, who had been
guided from Paleacate by an Armenian.   They had visited the
church, which it may be noted they found in charge of a very old
blind pagan, and very much ruined.   This heathen, among other
stories, told them that some twelve or fifteen years before an English
duke named George had visited this shrine and had died there and
was buried with other pilgrims.   This incident is mentioned by
Correa only.   Was this an echo of some rumour that George, Duke of
Clarence, had not in reality been made away with by Richard Crook-
back, but had escaped and spent the remainder of his life in pilgrimages
to holy places ?   The dates would correspond, and there was no other
English duke named George.
These events were reported to the Governor, D. Lopes de Sequeira,
who made the matter over to his successor as Governor (not Viceroy),
Duarte de Meneses (who succeeded in the beginning of 1522) according
to Correa, who is on this point a witness of the highest value, as he
took part in the expedition.   His narrative is given below (p. 129, n. 1),
and the date of the visit to the church was Corpus Christi Day, 1521.
It would seem, therefore, that the orders must have been given by
Sequeira before the arrival of Meneses as Governor.
Barbosa had evidently heard only of the first discovery, that made
in 1517, and his description (including that of the old man who acted

persecuted by the Heathen, he came with certain of
his fellows to the city of Mailapur which in those days
was a city ten or twelve leagues in length, and far
removed from the sea[1] which afterward ate away the
land and advanced well into the city. At first Saint
Thomas began to preach the faith of Christ, and converted certain men thereto, wherefore the others went
about to slay him, and he for this reason dwelt apart
from the people, wandering ofttimes in the wilderness.
On a certain day a hunter while walking through the
hills, bow in hand, saw a great number of peacocks
near to the ground, and in the midst of them one
exceeding great and fair which had alighted on a flat
rock. The hunter shot at this and pierced it through
the middle with an arrow ; both it and the others rose,
and flying through the air it turned into the body of a
man. The hunter on beholding this stood astonished
until he saw it fall, whereupon he went straightway to
the city to declare so great a miracle and in what wise
it had taken place. The Governour of the city with
other great men went then to see the place which the
hunter shewed to them, and they found that it was
the body of the Blessed Saint Thomas. They went also
to see the spot where he had wounded it, and on the
flat rock they found two clearly impressed footprints
which he had made as he rose when wounded. When
they perceived how great a miracle had been wrought
they said " Of a truth this man was a saint, and we

---

as custodian of the church) was certainly derived from the first
explorers, for he must have left India at the latest in 1518. Many
writers speak of the church as at or near Paleacate, and it is probable
that this was the nearest seaport from which it was accessible. Correa
calls the distance seven leagues, or about 28 miles, which corresponds
very closely with the actual distance from Pulicat to Mailapur.

[1] Ramusio : " was about six miles distant from the sea." Spanish
version : " was twelve leagues distant from the sea."

believed him not," and thereupon they carried the body to the town and came to bury it in the aforesaid church wherein it lies to this day. They also brought the stone with the footprints and placed it beside the grave, but they could never bury the right arm nor put it into the grave ; if they placed it inside, when they came on the following day it was outside, and thus they let it stay, and thus it remained for a long time. The Heathen of the land held it to be a saint's body, and did it much reverence. Folk from many lands came hither on pilgrimages, and the Chinese when they came wished to cut off the arm and convey it as a relic to their own land, but when they would strike it with a sword the Blessed Saint Thomas drew it back into the grave, and they never again struck it. Thus he lies very modestly in the church which his disciples and fellows built for him. The Moors and Heathen used to burn lights on it, each one claiming it as his own. The church is arranged in our fashion with crosses on the altar and on the summit of the vault, and a wooden grating, and peacocks as devices, but it is now very ruinous, and all around it covered with brushwood, and a poor Moor holds charge of it and begs alms for it, from which a lamp is kept burning at night, and on what is left they live. Some Indian Christians go there on pilgrimage and carry away many relics, little earthen balls from the same tomb of the Blessed Saint Thomas, " and also give alms to the aforesaid Moor, telling him to repair the said house."

§ 100. THE CITY OF PALEACATE.[1]

PROCEEDING yet further and leaving the town of Mailapur there is on the coast another City belonging to the King

[1] The town of Paleacate, now called Pulicat, is situated on the south end of an island which separates the lake or lagoon of Pulicat

I

of Narsyngua, inhabited by both Moors and Heathen, great traders. It has a very fair sea-haven whither resort ships of the Moors in great numbers conveying goods of divers kinds. By land also from the Narsyngua kingdom come many traders to buy goods of many kinds, for

---

from the sea (lat. 13° 25′ N., about 25 miles N. of Madras). When the Portuguese first made its acquaintance it formed part of the territories of Vijayanagar, being comprised in the province of Telingāna, called Telingu by Barbosa (Vol. I, p. 183). This province extended to the Orissa boundary, and wars between the kingdoms of Vijayanagar and Orissa were frequent. The allusion to the mountains called Odirgualemado (Diguirmale in the Spanish version ; Udirgimale in Ramusio) is to Udayagiri south of the Krishna River, to which point the forces of Orissa had advanced in the early part of the sixteenth century, and Barbosa's account was evidently written before Krishna Dēva had recovered his lost provinces south of the Krishna. As to these wars, see the note under § 101, p. 133, n. 1.

The first mention of Paleacate or Pulicat by a European traveller appears to be that of Varthema (l.c., p. 194). He arrived there after leaving Ceylon, and alludes to its subjection to the King of Narsinga, and also to its trade with Ceylon and Pegu, especially in jewels. He speaks of its wars with Tarnassari, by which he probably meant Orissa, as there is no probability of any actual war having taken place with Tenassarim or any place on the eastern side of the Bay of Bengal.

Mr. Badger's note on p. 195 of his edition of *Varthema* alludes to Faria y Souza's statement that the Portuguese " established a colony at Pulicat as early as 1522 A.D. " ; and he adds that " the name does not appear in the list of their *forts* on the Coromandel coast." It may be added that no mention of any such post can be traced in any of the earlier chronicles. Gaspar Correa, who was himself on the Coromandel coast at this period, and alludes to the appointment of Manuel de Frias as *feitor* on this coast in 1522 (II, p. 721), does not mention it, although he alludes to Paleacate and its trade under the events of 1519 (II, 567). In 1521 he records that he himself was present at the investigation made regarding the relics of Saint Thomas and this passage deserves translation. It is as follows (*ib.*, p. 725) : " I, Gaspar Correa, who write this story, went in the company of Pero Lopes de Sampayo to visit this holy house. And the Captain Pero Lopes left the ship at Paleacate, and twelve or fifteen men landed with him on a pilgrimage to the holy house which is seven leagues away (*i.e.*, at Mailapur), all on foot, singing and rejoicing, with plenty of food and drink. On coming in sight of the holy house we were all overcome by a devout sadness so that we sang no more nor spoke one to the other with a new devotion in our hearts, remembering our sins. Each man recited his prayers with so great a trembling that his legs and arms weakened and shook, for we seemed to be planting our feet on holy ground. And outside the door of the holy house we fell on our knees, and shed so many tears that I know not whence they came. There we all confessed and the Father said mass (having brought with him all that was needful therefor), and we all took the holy sacrament. And this was the first mass that was said in the holy house, being the day of Corpus Christi of the year 1521." Then he goes on to describe the repairs done to the church, and the discovery

which reason they bring hither from Peeguu, of which I will speak below, great store of rubies and spinels, and abundance of musk [which precious stones are good cheap here, for him who knows how to buy and to choose them].

---

of some of the bones of the king who had been converted by Saint Thomas, who was reported by the country-folk to have been called Tanimudolyar, interpreted as " Thomas, servant of God."

Mandelslo's apparent identification of the town of St. Thomas with Pulicat (judging by the latitude given, see § 99, p. 126, n. 2) may be due to the fact that Pulicat was the best port available for pilgrims to the shrine. He also remarks on this point (ib., p. 94), " The south and south-west Winds reign here from April to September, during which time the Road is very good ; but all the rest of the year, small Barks are constrained to get into the river *Palacatte* (*sic*), and greater Vessels into the Haven of *Negupatam*." He also alludes to the Dutch fort of *Geldria* at *Paleacatte*.

Although the Portuguese never made any settlement on the east coast of India north of Mailapur, the Dutch turned their attention to this neglected coast at an early period. The fort called Geldria was built by them in 1609. This fort at Pettipolee or Nizampatam was, according to Mandelslo (*l.c.*) founded in 1606, and an English factory followed in 1621. Madras was not founded till 1639. The Dutch retained Pulicat till 1781, when it was surrendered to the English. British authority was finally admitted in 1825.

A full note on Pulicat, including Schouten's description of its condition in 1662, is given in Sir R. Temple's H.S. edition of Bowrey's *Countries Round the Bay of Bengal*, pp. 51, 52. Bowrey compares Pulicat favourably with Fort St. George (Madras) as a port, although the bar was an obstacle to all vessels over 40 tons, and he adds, " all this coast indeed wanting nothing but some good harbours for shipping." This lack of harbours is the clue to the neglect of the Coromandel coast by the Portuguese, although during the south-west monsoon its roadsteads afforded safer anchorage than the Malabar coast. The best of these roadsteads was the port generally known as Masulipatam, which was famous for its trade in the seventeenth and eighteenth centuries and up to modern times. It has been identified with the Maisola of Ptolemy and the Masalia of the Periplus. But during the sixteenth century it does not seem to have been well known, and its absence from Barbosa's list of ports is remarkable. In the seventeenth century it seems to have been the principal outlet for the trade of the Central Deccan. The accounts of Bowrey (*l.c.*), Fryer (I, p. 78 f.), Tavernier (*l.c.* Part II, p. 70) and A. Hamilton (*l.c.* I, 369) give full information for this period. For the sixteenth century there seems to be nothing earlier than Fitch's account of the port and of his journey thence via " Servidore " to Balapur and Burhānpur (Fitch, *l.c.* p. 94). Whatever may be the modern name of " Servidore," it is clear that Fitch was following the old trade route leading from the east coast to Western India, which, as J. F. Fleet has shown in his paper identifying the ancient Tagara with the modern Tēr (*J.R.A.S.*, 1901, pp. 537–552), led from Masulipatam and Vinukōnda through Golconda or Haidarabad, Tēr and Paithan to Daulatabad and thence to Broach, and evidently to Burhānpur as well. In the same paper the author shows that the merchandise brought to Tagara and

In this city the King of Narsyngua maintains a
Governour under his orders, and collectors of his duties.
Here are made great abundance of printed cotton cloths
which are worth much money in Malacca, Peeguu,
Çamatra and in the kingdom of Guzerate and Malabar
for clothing. Here also copper, quicksilver and vermilion
as well as other Cambaya wares, dyes in grain [Meca
velvets and especially], rosewater. Beyond this town of
Paleacate the coast continues towards the north in the
direction of Bengala, on which coast are many towns
belonging to the King of Narsyngua as far as a range of
mountains called Odirgualemado, where his kingdom
comes to an end.

---

§ 101. KINGDOM OF OTISA.

THUS going forward and leaving behind this boundary
of the great kingdom of Narsyngua there lies on the coast
the kingdom of Otisa,[1] which is held by Heathen, very

Paithana, according to the Periplus, "from districts bordering on the
sea," was derived from the east and not the west coast. At the time
when the Periplus was written, the first century A.D., the Andhra
kingdom extended right across the Deccan from east to west. Its
capital lay between the lower courses of the Krishna and Godávari
Rivers, not far from Masulipatam, and Paithan and Tagara were
in its western parts, so there was evidently strong ground for the
development of such a trade route. Possibly in Barbosa's day the
great power of Bijapur and Vijayanagar led rather to the use of the
more southern route westwards starting from Pulicat. In Lord
Stanley's version from the Spanish the following passage (which is
not found either in the Portuguese text or Ramusio) is given at the
commencement of § 101 : " Further on, after passing Marepata, along
the coast which trends to north-east by east, the kingdom of Orissa
commences." It would seem that this must be a later interpolation,
for Barbosa had already given Udayagiri quite correctly as the
boundary between Vijayanagar and Orissa in his time. When this
passage was written the boundary must have been further to the
north-east, although I am unable to identify Marepata. The "Mountain of Diguirmale " is indeed mentioned in the Spanish version
(p. 177) in the heading of a section, but not in the text, which is
evidence that some alteration had been made.

[1] Orissa has already been alluded to by the author in § 85 among
the border countries at war with Vijayanagar, and he adds little
here to the scanty information given there. It is doubtful whether

good fighting men, and its King who has a mighty army of foot soldiers and is ofttimes at war with him of Narsyngua.[1] This kingdom extends far inland and has but few seaports and little trade. It extends along the coast northwards where there is a river called Ganges [2]

---

any Portuguese had visited Orissa, and certain that no expedition had been made to any part of its coast. What is told was doubtless derived by reports which came through Vijayanagar. The form Otisa represents the vernacular Odĩsā or Orisā. The coast may be roughly said to extend from the Chilka Lake (south-west) to the Subarnarēkha River (north-east).

[1] *Narsyngua.* Barbosa is correct in asserting that Orissa was often at war with Vijayanagar. There had been wars in the fourteenth century when the Gajapatis of Orissa were defeated by Sangama II, but in the fifteenth century, when the power of Vijayanagar had declined, the King of Orissa was able to extend his borders southwards as far as Udayagiri, south of the Krishna River. This conquest was carried out by Kapilēndra Dēva, founder of the Solar dynasty, who also waged war successfully against the Bahmanis and Bengal. His successor, Purusōttama Dēva, was also successful in his war against Vijayanagar, but his son Pratāparudra Dēva, in the early part of the sixteenth century, was defeated by Krishna Dēva, the Vijayanagar King of Barbosa's time, and lost all the conquests south of the Krishna ; and shortly after the district between the Krishna and Godāvari was lost to Kuli Kuṭb Shāh, the founder of the Kuṭbshāhi dynasty of Golconda. At one time, in the latter half of the fifteenth century, the conquests of Orissa had extended over the whole of the northern half of what is now the presidency of Madras. At its furthest it reached Kānchī (Conjeeveram), and for a long time the Pennār River was its southern boundary. When Barbosa wrote, as noted under Paleacate p. 129, n. 1, Udayagiri marked the border line, and the final delivery of Northern Telingāna by Krishna Dēva must have taken place at a later date.

A lately published volume (*Sources of Vijayanagar History,* by S. Krishnaswami Aiyengar, Madras University Press, 1919) gives a good deal of information on these wars contained in Telugu poems and prose records. One of these poems (p. 132) claims to be by Krishna Dēva himself and records his advance across the Krishna and the Godāvari Delta, and the erection of a pillar of victory at Potnūru, and adds that the Gajapati had even to flee from his own capital (at Cuttack).

[2] The river Ganges stated to form the boundary between Orissa and Bengal cannot be the great river universally known by that name. It is also mentioned as the boundary in the following paragraph on Bengal. The similarity of name led to its being confounded with the true Ganges, the sacred river. The name Gangā, originally meaning "river," is applied to many streams in India, generally as an appendix to some qualifying term, such as Rāmgangā and Pain-gangā.

In Lavanha's map of Bengal (reproduced facing p. 135) a river named Ganga is shown as falling into the estuary of the Hugli from the south, while the actual Ganges is given its classical name and is not called Ganga.

(but they call it Guorigua), and on the further bank of
this river begins the kingdom of Bengal where also the
King of Otisa is somtimes at war.

To this river of Ganges go all the Heathen on pilgrimages, and bathe therein, saying that thereby they
obtain salvation, for that this river issues forth from the
fount of the Terrestrial Paradise. This river is very
great and fair on both banks and well peopled with
fair and wealthy Heathen cities. Between this river and
Eufrates lies the First India [and the Second], a country
very fruitful and healthy, and with a very temperate
climate, and hence onward towards Malaca lies the
Third (India) as the Moors say " who have known it
longer than we. And between these aforesaid rivers
there are fertile and well-furnished lands, in the interior
as well as on the strand of the sea. The people thereof
is very polished and wealthy. The more part of them
are very stingy and spend little. It is a land of very
good air, many trees and evil smelling streets ; all live with
but little toil, there is here neither great heat nor extreme
cold, but rather it is well tempered."

This Ganga is shown as a branch of another river falling into the
sea further south near Cape Cegogara (now called Point Palmyras).
This is the broad estuary now known as the Dhamra River, which is
the outlet for the joint stream of the Brāhmani and Baitarani Rivers
and even for some of the northern branches of the Mahānadi Delta
(*Cuttack District Gazetteer*, Calcutta, 1906, pp. 4–6). The Baitarani is
a sacred river. Mr. O'Malley, in the *Cuttack Gazetteer*, says " it is
the Styx of Hindu mythology, and legend relates that Rām, when
marching to Ceylon to rescue his wife Sitā from the ten-headed demon
Rāvana, halted on its banks on the borders of Keonjhar ; in com-
memoration of this, large numbers of people visit the river every
January." The Brāhmani flows from the mountainous regions of the
Gāngpur state, and there the confluence of the Sānkh and the South
Koel, which form the Brāhmani, is also a sacred spot (*Bengal Gazetteer*,
1909, I, p. 236). It is possible that the name Gangā was applied to
this holy stream, and that it may be connected with the name Gāngpur.
In this case the joint stream of the two holy rivers with the Dhamra—
the best harbour on that part of the coast, " a noble estuary " (*Cuttack
Gazetteer*, pp. 6, 8–9)—would be well known to navigators, and confusion with the great Ganges was inevitable.

In Rennell's map of 1782 the Brāhmani River is given the name

Map of Bengal. From Lavanha's map in Vol. IV of the *Decadas* of J. de Barros, Madrid, 1615, p. 555.

§ 102. THE KINGDOM OF BENGALA.

FURTHER on, leaving this River Ganges[1] and following the coast in a northerly direction, comes the Kingdom of Bengala wherein are many towns, as well inland as on the coast, the inhabitants whereof are Heathen. Those who dwell inland are independent but under the over-lordship of the King of Narsyngua.[2] The Moors dwell in the seaports where there is great traffic in goods of many kinds and sailing of ships both great and small[3] to many countries ; for this sea is a *Gulf* which runneth in between two lands, and going well into it there is to the north a right great city of the Moors, which they call Bengala,[4]

of Gunjoory or Gawitry. · These names suggest Barbosa's alternative name Guorigua, which is not found in Ramusio or in the Spanish version. It may, however, be a misreading for Ganga, written Guangua. Ramusio calls it Guenga.

It is evident that Lavanha's Ganga is intended for the Subarnarēkha, the actual boundary between Bengal and Orissa, and also that it was considered to be a branch of the Brahmini River. This is confirmed by the following passage from *Dec. IV* of De Barros as edited and emended by Lavanha :—

" These same mountains further towards the south divide Bengal from the kingdom of Orixa, the plains of Bengal lying between the mountains and the stream of the Ganges. Another river, which falls into the Ganges below Satigam, runs through Orixa, and has its springs on the mountain slopes (called by the Indians Gate in the parts near Chaul), and as it is a great river and flows through many lands the natives, in imitation of the Ganges into which it flows, call it also Ganga and hold its waters to be as sacred as those of the Ganges " (*Dec. IV*, ix, 1, ed. 1615, p. 556).

The remainder of Barbosa's description refers to the Ganges proper, which in accordance with the prevailing ideas he believed to be one of the four rivers flowing from the Earthly Paradise.

Linschoten (I, p. 92) repeats Barbosa in stating that the Ganges was the boundary of Orissa and Bengal, and also in his allusion to the Earthly Paradise.

[1] For the River Ganges here alluded to see p. 133, n. 2 under Orissa.

[2] The overlordship of the kingdom of Narsyngua is a mistake due apparently to some confusion with Orissa. There is no record of any war between Bengal and Vijayanagar and the two countries were not conterminous.

[3] In original " naos " and " navios."

[4] *The City of Bengala.* The mention by Barbosa, and at a slightly earlier date by Varthema, of a great city of Bengala (Banghella in the latter) has given rise to a controversy as to the identity of the city so called in which Sir H. Yule in *Hobson-Jobson* and *Cathay* (and M. Cordier in the second edition of the latter), Mr. G. Badger in his edition

a very excellent sea-haven ; it has its own independent

of *Varthema* (H.S., 1863), Mr. H. Beveridge in *The District of Bakarganj* (1876) and others have taken part. Various theories have been advocated, the cities whose claims have been discussed being Chittagong, Sunārgaon (or another port near it, Srīpur), Satgāon, and lastly Gaur, the ancient capital of Bengal. Varthema simply states that it was a great town which he arrived at by sea from Tenassarim. Barbosa is more definite, and no doubt expresses accurately the accounts he had been able to collect from merchants and sailors as well as traders travelling by land. He says it was a seaport, at the head of a gulf or estuary running northwards with land on each side. It was a Muhammadan city and the residence of the King, and situated in an extensive and fertile region where cotton and sugar were grown ; it was also known for its fine cotton fabrics. The claims of the cities mentioned may be considered *seriatim*.

(1) *Chittagong.* This port lies entirely outside the Ganges Delta, on the eastern coast of the Bay of Bengal, not far from its most northern point. It is situated on the estuary of the small river Karnaphuli. Chittagong had long formed part of the Kingdom of Arakan, but was occasionally occupied by the Bengal Kings and sometimes by those of Tipara. Coins were struck at Chittagong by Jalālud-dīn, of Bengal, who died in 1430. In the same year a Bengal army restored the King of Arakan to Chittagong from which he had been expelled by the Burmese (*Phayre*, p. 78), and Arakan was for a short time tributary to Bengal, but this did not last long, and Chittagong was recovered by Arakan in 1459. Husain Shāh of Bengal seems to have occupied it for a time in 1512, but it was again recovered by Arakan, and held until its absorption in the Mughal Empire in Akbar's time. (*The Gazetteer of Eastern Bengal and Assam*, 1909, p. 395, strangely speaks of the temporary annexation of Chittagong by the *Mughal* Empire in the thirteenth century !) It is clear then that Chittagong only occasionally for short periods came under the power of Bengal, and that it was never the capital of a Muhammadan King. It does not in fact answer in any way to Barbosa's description.

Sir H. Yule considered that Varthema's account was fictitious both as regards Tenassarim and "Banghella," and therefore negligible. He held Chittagong to be Bengâla mainly on the ground that it was the Porto Grande of the Portuguese at a later period, but this cannot be considered as affecting the use of the word at the beginning of the sixteenth century. The port of Chittagong was undoubtedly much used from the first days, and the principal reason for this was that it was an open port *outside* the power of the Sultans of Bengal, and easily approached and dominated by Portuguese ships in comparison with the ports of the Ganges Delta, which were dominated by those rulers and approached by channels difficult to navigate and exposed to attack.

This is illustrated by the history of the first Portuguese expeditions in the year 1516–17, of which evidently no information had reached Barbosa when he wrote his account of Bengal. Fernão Perez D'Andrade was sent out by the Governor Lopo Soares D'Albergaria on a voyage of exploration to China and Bengal. He started for China, but was delayed by the burning of his best ship at Pacem, in Sumatra, and determined to go to Bengal instead. As a forerunner he sent off a certain João Coelho in a ship belonging to a Moor named Gromalle (Ghulām 'Ali) who was related to the Governor of Chittagong (apparently a representative of Husain Shāh of Bengal, who had occupied Chittagong in 1512). Fernão Perez D'Andrade afterwards resumed his journeys to China, making another start in August, 1516, and again

Moorish King. The inhabitants thereof are white men,

in June, 1517. The last expedition was successful, but he never resumed his journey to Bengal. He did not return to India till the end of 1518. Exactly when J. Coelho was despatched is not clear, but he was in Chittagong when a second expedition under João da Silveira arrived there. He had been sent first by the Governor (Lopo Soares) to the Maldives, where strange to say he captured a ship on which was Gromalle, apparently the same man who conveyed J. Coelho. After this the Governor, evidently knowing nothing of the Coelho episode, sent him to Bengal. On his way up the coast he touched at the Aracan River (near by modern Akyab) and was there asked by the Aracanese to help them in their war against Bengal ; he refused to do this, but on arriving at Chittagong he was regarded as a pirate and pretender, as J. Coelho had arrived with a message from the King of Portugal sent by Fernão Perez D'Andrade. This led to complications and conflicts. He was detained in the river all through the Monsoon , and never succeeded in getting into communication with the King of Bengal, and it is doubtful how far the " Governor " was under the latter's authority. (See De Barros, *Dec. III*, ii, 3, and *III*, ii, 6.) Correa gives no account of this expedition, but says that Fernão Perez D'Andrade on his return from China was informed at Malacca by D. Aleixo Meneses that the Governor had entrusted the Bengal adventure to his brother-in-law D. João da Silveira, and that he (Fernão Perez) was to return to India (Correa, II, p. 530).

This account shows clearly how far Chittagong was from being a principal port of Bengal or an outlet for its abundant products. It was only a step on the way to the real Bengal, and to any place which could be called Bengala. Similarly the next Portuguese expedition, that of Martim Affonso de Mello, in 1528, came to grief at Chacuria, on the coast south-east of Chittagong and ended in the imprisonment of de Mello and his companions by Codovascam (Khudā Bakhsh Khān), a local chief. The whole romantic story is told in *Dec. IV*, Bk. ii, pp. 90–91, where an omission in De Barros's narrative is supplied by quotations from do Couto and Castanheda. M. Affonso de Mello was sent on another expendition in 1534. He went again to Chittagong and succeeded in sending a messenger with presents to the King Mahmūd Shāh at Gaur, but in reply Mahmūd Shāh sent orders that the ambassador and his companions were to be imprisoned. Many of them were killed and the remainder taken to Gaur as prisoners. In revenge the Governor Nuno Da Cunha sent an expedition against Chittagong under Antonio da Silva Meneses, which attacked and burnt Chittagong. (For the whole story see *Dec. IV*, Bk. ix, Ch. 3, and a good version of it in *The Portuguese in Bengal*. pp. 31 to 37.)

Just at this period Bengal was attacked by Shĕr Khān Sūr (the Xercansor of some Portuguese writers), afterwards better known as Shĕr Shāh, and Mahmūd Shāh finding himself in danger thought of obtaining Portuguese help. At the same time Diogo Rebello, captain of the pearl-fishery of Callecarè or Quilicare (§ 96), who had been despatched by Nuno da Cunha with a small flotilla to find out what could be done for the release of the captives, made his way up the western or Hūgli branch of the Ganges to the port of Satigam (Satgāon) with two *fustas* and an *atalaya*, causing some dismay there, as they knew what Meneses had done at Chittagong. This is the first Portuguese expedition which we know to have visited Satgāon. This led to the despatch of ambassadors, and, as Castanheda tells us (Bk. 8, Ch. 187), to the sending of a fleet from Goa to help Mahmūd Shāh. Most of the prisoners were released, and Martim Affonso de Mello and the

well-built ; and there dwell there as well strangers from

others who remained took some part in fighting against Shēr Khān, and were at last released just before his final conquest of Maḥmūd Shāh and the latter's flight to take refuge with Humāyūn.

The object of the Governor to obtain sanction for the erection of a fort at Chittagong was never attained ; Maḥmūd Shāh made many promises, which were all futile, as he lost his crown and his life in 1538. Shēr Shāh paid little attention to Eastern Bengal, which was long in a state of anarchy. For some reason the Portuguese took no steps to secure their position at Chittagong or at Satgāon, as Castanheda (Bk. 8, Ch. 198) thought they could have done without difficulty. Their trade settlements continued on a precarious footing, and for some time flourished exceedingly, but no place in Bengal was ever under Portuguese rule.

Chittagong had been often made use of by travellers as a convenient point from which to enter the Meghna and attain the port of Sunārgāon, and thence to ascend the eastern branch of the Ganges to Gaur. This was probably the course followed by Ibn Baṭūṭa and afterwards by the Chinese traveller Ma-Huan in the early part of the fifteenth century. (See Ma-huan's account of the kingdom of Bengala by G. Phillips, *J.R.A.S.*, 1895, p. 523 f.) Ibn Baṭūṭa after leaving Chittagong went northwards to the mountains of Kāmrū (Kāmrūp) to visit a celebrated saint. Apparently he went by a mountain route, as he took a month on the way, but he returned by river and landed at Sunārgāon. For this journey, and the identification of the city of Habank and of the country visited (Sylhet) Sir H. Yule's Note E (in Yule and Cordier, *Cathay*, iv, p. 151) should be consulted. On his return Ibn Baṭūṭa came back by the Surma River (in Yule's opinion). In any case whether he came by this river or the main stream of the Brahmaputra he would have passed Sunārgāon.

The Chinese traveller made no such divagations but went straight to Sunārgāon in small boats. He then travelled in a south-westerly direction for thirty-five stages to the Kingdom of Bengala. Mr. Phillips commenting on this passage says " the probability is great that the city of Bengala (if such a city ever existed) was situated still further to the southward of Dacca than Sona-urh-kong." Mr. J. Beames in a letter in the same volume of the *J.R.A.S.* (p. 898) pointed out that thirty-five stages or 105 miles south-west from Sunārgāon would bring the traveller to " the boundary of the Sarkār or fiscal division of Satgāon, and forty miles further in the same line is the site of the famous ancient city of Satgāon, which if not precisely the capital of Bengal was the residence of one of the provincial Governors, and the largest and most important commercial town and trading port in the country. Satgāon is I think beyond doubt the place meant by Mahuan."

In the *J.R.A.S.* for 1896, p. 203, Mr. Phillips continues his notes on the journey of Ma-huan, and shows that the capital of the country of Bengal was Pan-tu-wa, a large walled city, although Ma-huan does not name it himself, and that there can be little doubt that this was Panduā, actually at that time the temporary capital of Bengal. The name of the capital is given as *Pan-tu-wa* in a Chinese encyclopædia, and it was only for a short period the capital. See also Mr. W. W. Rockhill's notes on the Pêng-ka-la or Pang-ko-la of the Chinese travellers in *Toung-Pao*, Vol. XVI, pp. 435–44. In a paper in the same volume of the *J.R.A.S* (*Notes on Akbar's Subahs—Bengal*) Mr. Beames gives a map based on the Ain-i-Akbari. In this there are two places named Panduā, one in the present Maldah district, north of the ruins of Gaur, and one in

many lands, such as Arabs, Persians, Abexis and Indians.

the present Hugli district between Satgāon and Bardwān. This Panduā was in the Sarkār of Sulaimānābad in the Aīn-i-Akbari (*ib.*, p. 99), but the northern Panduā near Gaur is not mentioned under the Sarkār of Lakhnauti. There can be little doubt that that Sulaimānābad, distinguished for its ruins (now in the Hugli district and a station on the Calcutta and Bardwān Railway), is the ancient capital. (Yule and Cordier, *Cathay*, IV, p. 85, although another note on p. 83 of the same volume identifies it with the Panduā in the Māldah district.) Its neighbourhood to Satgāon provided it with a good port.

Ibn Baṭūṭa speaks of Lakhnauti as separate from Bengal ; he says, according to Defrémery and Sanguinetti : " Les Bengalis ont sur la fleuve (Gange) de nombreux navires avec lesquels ils combattent les habitants du pays de Lacnaouty " ; and the same passage in *Cathay*, IV, p. 83, reads : " The people of Bengal maintain a number of vessels on the river with which they engage in war against the inhabitants of Lakhnaotī." But a reference to the Arabic text shows that there is no mention of the " people of Bengal " or the " Bengalis." The allusion is evidently to the war waged by Fakhru'ddin (when he made Sunārgāon his capital and called himself King of Bengal) against 'Ali Shāh (alias 'Ali Mubārak). Fakhru'ddin's coins in the India Museum were struck at Sunārgāon in the years A.H. 745-749, and those in the British Museum in 743-750 (*Catalogue of Coins in India Museum*, Vol. II, p. 149 ; *British Museum, Catalogue of Coins of Muḥammadan States*, p. 13.) The division of Bengal was therefore temporary. The coins show that Fakhru'ddin was living as late as A.H. 750 (which commenced March 22, 1349).

The three provinces which made up Bengal are given by Firishta (lithographed text, p. 137) as متارکانو ,لکهنوتي (read سنارگانو) and سنگام (read متگام), that is Lakhnauti, Sunārgānw and Satgānw (not Chittagong as Briggs has it in his translation). (See also the note on this point in *Cathay*, IV, p. 83.) Barnī also gives these three names in his Tārikh-i Fēroz Shāhī (in Elliot and Dowson, III, pp. 242-3) in a passage to which attention has already been drawn by E. Thomas in his *Chronicles of the Pathān Kings of Delhi*, p. 262, note 2.

Firishta probably drew his information from Barnī. It is clear therefore that Fakhru'ddin, who practically began the series of independent Kings of Bengal was not concerned with Chittagong, but mainly with Sunārgāon, and that Satgāon and Lakhnauti or Gaur were also in his possession.

In later days the Portuguese continued to make Chittagong their principal port principally because there was no strong government there to fight against, and until Akbar's conquest it was not in the power of the Bengal Kings. It was called Porto Grande and Satgāon Porto Pequeno, as may be seen in the quotation from Fitch given below, and other quotations in *Hobson-Jobson* under Porto Pequeno and Porto Grande.

The later name of Porto Grande given to Chittagong seems to have influenced the cartographers of the second half of the sixteenth and the early part of the seventeenth century to place the city of Bengala in its neighbourhood. Thus it appears in the Portolano of Diego Homem of 1568 (reproduced in *Kartographische Denkmäler*, Leipzig, 1903) and in Hondius's great map of 1608, now in the Royal Geographical Society's map room. This is repeated in Blaeuw's great atlas of 1663. The latter shows Bengala to the south of the river (the Karnaphuli) to the north-west of which Chittagong stands. It is from such sources that Ovington, writing of the year 1689, obtained

And this by reason that this land is large, fruitful and

the information alluded to in the following paragraph on the Kingdom of Aracan (*A Voyage to Suratt*, London, 1896, p. 553). " It (viz., Aracan) is bounded on the north-west by the Kingdom of Bengala, some authors making *Chatigam* to be its first frontier city, but *Teixeira* and generally the Portuguese writers reckon that as a city of *Bengala*, and not only so, but place the city of Bengala itself on the same coast, more south than *Chatigam*. Though I confess that a late French geographer has put Bengala into his catalogue of imaginary cities."

Chittagong, in spite of its nominal conquest (with Bengal) in Akbar's time, remained practically independent. (See the remarks on this point of Mr. Beames in *J.R.A.S.*, 1896, p. 135.) It was finally conquered and renamed Islāmābad by Aurangzēb in A.H. 1075 (A.D. 1665), when it became a mint of the Mughal Empire. The earliest known Mughal coin struck there is dated A.H. 1106. When Peter Mundy wrote (1628–34) Chittagong was under Aracan (*Peter Mundy*, II, p. 152).

With regard to the location of Bengala on the coast south of Chitta-gong the suggestion first made by Mr. Badger in his edition of *Varthema*, identifying it with Bacola seems deserving of consideration. The island of Bacola as shown in Lavanha's map (and mentioned by De Barros in the text of his description of Bengal) corresponds very closely with that assigned by Hondius to Bengala. The resemblance of the names is sufficiently close to render some confusion probable. Bacola was visited by Fitch after he left Chittagong.

Sunārgāon and Satgāon. These two places were situated near the mouths of the two principal branches of the Ganges and were both ports of great importance till the early part of the sixteenth century. Sunārgaon seems to have been replaced by another place lower down the Meghna River, Srīpur, and no doubt the change was due to altera-tions in the river bed.

In the same way Satgāon was given up by the Portuguese in favour of Hūgli (Hooghly) owing to the drying up of the channel on which it stood (the Saraswatī). The process of transition was in progress at both places at the time of Fitch's journey (1586). Both Hūgli and Satgāon on the western and Srīpur and Sunārgaon on the eastern branch were important places. The coast in the Ganges delta has advanced a great deal since that period, and all these ports were much nearer to the open sea than they are now. Abu'l Fazl in the Aīn says that "the Ganges after dividing into a thousand channels joins the sea at Satgāon"; Satgāon was adopted by the Portuguese as one of their principal marts as soon as they were allowed to settle in peace, and on the diversion of the channel of the Saraswatī, Hūgli, a few miles off, took its place.

Satgāon was a mint in the time of Muḥammad Tughlak and coins were struck there by the independent Kings of Bengal in the fourteenth and fifteenth centuries. After A.H. 821 (A.D. 1418) apparently the mint fell into disuse, but was revived by Shēr Shāh after his conquest of Bengal and continued by his son Islām Shāh. It was never a mint after the conquest of Akbar.

Sunārgāon is not found among the mints of Muḥammad Tughlak but occurs frequently under the independent Kings of Bengal in the fourteenth century, nor was it revived by Shēr Shāh. Its importance was to some extent due to its having been the capital of the first independent King Fakḥru'ddin.

Both Srīpur and Sunārgāon as well as Satgāon are mentioned by Fitch, and his notice deserves quotation (Ralph Fitch, Ed. 1899, p. 110 f.). He begins by describing how he came down the Ganges to

healthy.   All of these are great merchants and they

Tānda in the land of Gouren (Gaur).   Thence he made a detour to
" Couche " (Kuch Bihār).   He continues : " From thence I returned
to Hugeli " (apparently he came back to Tānda and thence down-
stream to Hugli) " which is the place where the Portugals keep in the
country of Bengala which standeth in 23 degrees of northerly latitude,
and standeth a league from Satagan : they call it Porto Piqueno "
. . . . . " Not far from Porto Piqueno, south-westward, standeth
an haven which is called Angeli in the country of Orixa " (*i.e.*, Hijilī
in the Midnapur district ; called Angelin by W. Clavell, see *Countries
on the Bay of Bengal*, pp. xxxvii 162, n. 2, 166, n. 2).   " Orixa standeth 6
daies journey from Satagan south-westward " . . . . " Satagan
is a fair citie for a citie of the Moors, and very plentiful of all things."
. . . . . " From Satagan I travelled by the country of the King
of Tippara or Porto Grande, with whom the Mogores or Mogen" (*i.e.*,
the Maghs of Aracan, *not* the Mughals) " have almost continual warres.
The Mogen which be of the Kingdome of Recon " (Aracan) " and
Rame " (apparently the Chittagong country, see Phayre's *History of
Burma*, p. 170) " be stronger than the King of Tippara so that Chatigan
or Porto Grande is oftentimes under the King of Recon." . . . .
" From Chatigan in Bengala I came to Bacola, ... from Bacola
I went to Serrepore which standeth upon the river of Ganges ; the king
is called Choudery.   They be all hereabouts rebels against their King
Zebaldim Echebar : for here are so many rivers and Islands that they
flee from one to another whereby his horsemen cannot prevaile against
tham. . . . . Sinnergan is a towne sixe leagues from Serrepore
where there is the best and finest cloth made of cotton that is in all
India. . . . . Great store of Cotton cloth goeth from hence and
much Rice, wherewith they serve all India, Ceilon, Pegu, Malacca,
Sumatra and many other places."
    (P. 153).   " I went from Serrepore the 28th of November, 1586, for
Pegu in a small ship or foist of one Albert Caravallos, and so passing
down Ganges, and passing by the Island of Sundiva, Porto Grande,
or the countrie of Tippara, the Kingdom of Recon and Mogen, leaving
them on our left side with a faire wind at northwest, our course was
south and by east, which brought us to the barre of Negrais in Pegu."
    Gaur.   From the above it is clear that the real entry to Bengal was
either by the port of Sunārgāon (and later by " Serrepore " or Srīpur
lower down stream) on the Meghna or by Satgāon (and later by Hugli)
on the western branch of the Ganges.   These two ports were the centres
of trade and by both these routes the capital, Gaur (Lakhnauti, Tānda),
could be reached.
    Gauḍa or Gaur was the ancient name of Bengal and its capital seems
from an early date to have been situated near the diverging point of
the Eastern and Western branches of the Ganges.   The town took its
name from the country.   For a time it was called Lakhnauti after a
Hindu King, but the name Gaur came into use again, although the
country had ceased to be called Gaur.   The more modern name of
Bangāla seems in its turn to have passed in common usage from the
country to the capital (E. Thomas, *Chronicles of the Pathan Kings of Delhi*,
p. 107, n. 1 ; Yule and Cordier, *Cathay*, IV, p. 83, n. 1).   From the date
of the Catalan map, about 1375 (see Yule and Cordier, *Cathay*, Vol. I,
pp. 300 and 309) the existence of a city of Bengāla had become known
to travellers, and at the beginning of the sixteenth century, as the notices
of Barbosa and Varthema show, it was well known by name.   That it
was known by this name not only to sailors or travellers approaching
by sea is clear from various indications.   Mr. H. Beveridge has pointed

possess great ships after the fashion of Meca ; others

out to me its occurrence in an inscription in a cave at Ḳandahār, in which the various cities forming part of Bābur's empire are detailed. There are as a matter of fact three inscriptions and the third dated 1002 H. (1594) in Abkar's time is that containing the detailed list. The earliest copy of this inscription is that made by Mohan Lāl in 1831, and published in the first edition of his travels in 1834 at Calcutta. The Persian text given here was not reproduced in the London edition of 1846. Another copy made more recently is given by M. James Darmesteter in his article " La Grande Inscription de Qandahâr " in *Journal Asiatique* (Tome XV, 1890. Fév.—Mars., pp. 195, 230), but Mr. Beveridge considers that Mohan Lāl's version, made by a competent Persian scholar when the inscriptions were more perfect than they are now, is more to be relied on. In this inscription (Mohan Lāl's version, p. 281) the boundaries of Bābur's empire are thus described : " Its length is from the bounds of Sarandīp and Udīsah (Orissa) and Bandar Gorā Kāt (Ghorāghāt) and Gaur Bangāla to Thaṭha and Bandar Lahorī and Hurmuz, which is nearly a two years' journey, and its width from Kābul and Kashmīr to the bounds of the Dakan (and Berār) about a year and a half's journey " The word given as Berār has been misread by Mohan Lāl and is inserted from Darmesteter, and *yak-nim* (1½) is misprinted *yak-rim*. Darmesteter, however, mistranslates this as " half-a-year " instead of " a year and a half." The important point of difference is that Gaur Bangāla in Mohan Lāl's version becomes Gor wa Bangāla in Darmesteter's. The latter reading is apparently wrong, as no names of countries, only those of towns, are given in the list. I think, therefore, that the correct reading is Gaur Bengāla, the two names for the town being given, as we find sometimes on coins (such as Shāhābād-Ḳanauj). This is confirmed by the fact that in the list of mints for gold given by Abu'Fazl in the Ayin-i-Akbari the name Bangāla is given as one of the four mints for gold in Akbar's reign. No gold coins of this mint have yet been discovered, but on the other hand several rupees bearing Bangāla as the mint town have been found bearing dates from A.H. 1002 to 1010 (1593 to 1602). (Whitehead, *Punjab Museum Cat.*, Vol. II, pp. lvii, 39 ; *J.A.S.B.*, " Numismatic Suppt." XI (1909), p. 319 ; *Numismatic Chron.* 1902, *Some Coins of the Mughal Emperors*, No. 16.) A still further piece of evidence is found in the statement in the Memoirs of Bāyazid Biyāt, of which an abstract was published by Mr. H. Beveridge in the *J.A.S.B.*, 1898, pp. 296-316. P. 315 gives an account of Munīm Khān's removing his headquarters from Tānda to Gaur, and the pestilence which broke out there in 1575. He uses the words Gaur-Bangāla just as the contemporary Ḳandahar inscription does. There is thus good evidence for the use of the word Bangāla for the capital of Bengal in Akbar's reign and it may be considered probable that this practice did not originate then.

It remains to consider Yule's opinion that this use of Bengala was derived from an " Arab custom of giving an important foreign city or seaport the name of the country in which it lay " (*Hobson-Jobson, s.v.* Bengal). This has been widely accepted on Yule's authority, which is undoubtedly great, but I am not aware of any sufficient evidence that there was any such custom. The only example adduced by Yule in the article in question is the city of Solmandala (under Coromandel). This instance of its use, however, is not from an Arab source but from the seventeenth century Dutchman Valentijn, who speaks of the foundation by the Portuguese of a town on the site of " the old Gentoo City of Chiormandalem." The Editor here remarks :

" It is not absolutely clear what place was so called, probably by the Arabs in their fashion of calling a chief town by the name of the country." This seems an example of argument in a circle. The Arabs in fact called the Coromandel coast Ma'bar and no other name, as Yule often pointed out. Another instance is given in *Cathay*, III, p. 67, where John of Monte Corvino speaks of Maabar as a " city in the province of Sitia in Upper India." This proves nothing as to any Arab usage. Mahāchīn as used for Canton is alluded to in *Cathay*, II, p. 180. Odoric's Censcalan is supposed to be from Sin-Kalān, a translation of the Indian form into Persian, but M. Cordier in the same note derives it from Sin-Kyālan ; the Muhammadan name for Canton (صين كيالن).

The Arabs occasionally used the reverse custom of calling a country by the name of its chief town, as when they called Gujarāt the kingdom of Kambāyat, but I believe there is no instance of their using the name of a country for its chief town or port.

We have to consider which of these places was that alluded to by Barbosa, and this should be recognised as entirely a different question from that of the use of the terms Porto Grande and Porto Pequeno at a later date. It must, I think, be considered as most probable that the capital of Bengal under its independent Kings was the place intended. Barbosa derived his information not only from sailors and merchants approaching Bengal from the sea but also from Indian sources, especially Vijayanagar and the Muhammadan kingdoms of the Deccan, and in their mouths it could only have meant Gaur. The only objection to this solution is that Gaur was not a seaport in the strict sense of the word. It was on a great navigable river, and on the two branches of this river were the ports of Satgāon and Sunārgāon. It seems probable that one or both of these ports may have been included with the capital as the entries by which it was approached, for, as Mr. Moreland has pointed out, the word " Porto " was undoubtedly often employed to comprehend not only any actual point of embarkation, but all the various landing places on a gulf or inlet. Thus Bengala may be held to denote the capital and its ports either Satgāon or Sunārgāon. It is impossible to be more definite than this, but it is, I think, probable that Barbosa, following his usual custom, alluded to the first branch of the Ganges which would be reached by ships following the coast line from the south after passing Pulicat and Orissa, and that his allusion was therefore to the Hūgli branch of the Ganges up to and including Gaur, the capital of the Muhammadan Kings of Bengal. This corresponds more closely than the eastern branch with Barbosa's description of a gulf or inlet (*enseada*) running northwards between two lands and leading (" going well into it ") to a great Muhammadan city under its independent King (*Rey Mouro sobre sy*).

Reference should be made to Mr. W. H. Moreland's *India at the Death of Akbar* (1920), pp. 211, 212 and Appendix C ; *The Seaports of Bengal*, p. 307, as regards the use of the word Porto, and the names Porto Grande and Porto Pequeno, as well as Sunārgāon, Srīpur and Satgāon. I must here acknowledge my indebtedness to Mr. Moreland for much information on the subject which has been utilised in this note.

In the *Sommario de Regni, Città et Popoli Orientali* appended by Ramusio to his version of Barbosa (translated by him from a Portuguese original) the following passage regarding the city of Bengala occurs on f. 333 Rev. of the 3rd Ed. of 1563, Vol. I :

" Of the ports of the kingdom the principal is at the city of Bengala, from which the kingdom has taken its name. It is two days' journey from the mouth of the river Ganges to the city, and in the greatest ebb of the tide there is a depth of three fathoms (*braccia*) of water. The city contains forty thousand hearths (*fuochi*), where the King has his residence constantly. This alone is roofed with tiles and built of good brick masonry. The river Ganges is the greatest river in India, and the inhabitants say that it flows from Paradise."

According to Ramusio's " *Discorso*," or preface to Barbosa's book, this *Sommario* was written " by a Portuguese gentleman who had sailed all through the East, and having read Barbosa's book desired to write on the same matters in his own manner according to the information he had obtained." Further on Ramusio adds that he had obtained a copy from Lisbon with great difficulty and that he regretted that it was imperfect, as was also the case with the copy of Barbosa's book he had obtained at Seville.

This seems to be an important piece of evidence that Bengala was a city some distance up a branch of the Ganges and that it was the capital of Bengal. The information would probably date from some period before Ramusio's first edition, which was in 1553, and might refer to the time of the kings of the Sūr dynasty. The actual site of the capital may have at that time been at Tānda, not far from the site of Gaur.

I have been favoured by the Hon. H. Hannen with his notes on the subject of the identification of Bengala, made some years ago. These unfortunately reached me too late to be incorporated in my note.

Mr. Hannen has compiled a list of all the maps bearing on the question at issue in addition to those mentioned by Sir H. Yule and Mr. Badger. For reasons already stated I am of opinion that the later maps, certainly those published after the end of the sixteenth century, are of no value, and from the earlier ones I have here selected only those which distinctly show Bengala as a city. Mr. Hannen considers that Bengala is represented under various spellings, *i.e.*, Baracura, Baratulla, Batacouta, Bagdala, Bagnela, Bōgla (" probably misprint for Bāgla or Bāngla ") Bangella, and adds " If Bacola was the same place we must add Vacalia, presumably for Bacalia, Balkhada, and, according to Phayre, Batecala or Bakla." He suggests that " Batecala and Bengala were one and the same place, that it was a place of considerable importance at one time, and that the confusion arose from the similarity of name."

The following maps from his list seem to be those of most importance :—

Ptolemæus-Romæ, 1490 (11th map of Asia).—To S.E. of Ganges Delta between two rivers " Baracura Emporium."

Waldseemüller's World-map, 1507.—" baratula " or " boratula " to E. of Ganges Delta between two short rivers.

Waldseemüller's Carta Marina, 1516.—" bagdala " as a city about where Chittagong should be. " Bagnela Regnum " stretching from N.E. of Ganges Delta far down the coast of Burma. In centre of it on the coast a town called " Bagnela Regalis."

Orontius Finnæus, 1531.—" bōgla " at head of bay to E. of Ganges.

Mercator's double cordiform map, 1538.—" Bagal," inland to E. of Ganges.

O. Finnæus-Cordiform map, 1566.—" Bongla," well to E. of Ganges, and, close to W. of Bongla, Magdala, (?) Bagdala.

Parcacchi. I isole piu famose, 1572 (in the map of the Moluccas, p. 98).—Bengala, on an island in centre of Ganges Delta.

Mercator, 1587.—Bengala as a city between the two mouths of the Ganges.

Cornelius.—(De Judæis Ant. 1593).—Bēgala as a kingdom, and Bangalo as a city on an island in the middle of Ganges Delta.

After carefully considering the maps in this list I am unable to find any sufficient reasons for altering the conclusions arrived at in my

there are from China, which they call "*juncos*,"[1] which are of great size and carry great cargoes. With these they sail to Charamandel, Malaca, Çamatra, Peeguu, Cambaya and Ceilam,[2] and deal in goods of many sorts with this country and many others. In this city are many cotton-fields, patches of sugar-cane, of ginger and long pepper ; in it are woven many kinds of very fine and coloured clothes for their own attire and other white sorts for sale in various countries. They are very precious, also some which they call *estravantes*,[3] a certain

---

note to the effect that Gaur taken together with its subsidiary ports was the place known as Bengala in the early part of the sixteenth century.

[1] *Juncos*. This is an early instance of the use of the word junks. The Spanish version has it in the form *jungos* (now in use in Portugal), and Ramusio as *giunchi*. This is the first case in which Barbosa employs it. See also § 115 for its use in Java. In Portuguese early instances are also to be found in the documents of the Torre do Tombo and in Alboquerque's letters (*Glossario Luso-Asiatico, s.v.* Junco). Instances of its use by Ibn Baṭūṭa, Odoric and Marignolli will be found in *Cathay*, IV, p.103, ii, p. 131, and iii, p. 230. Sir H. Yule, in a note to the last-named, considers it " perhaps the oldest item in the Franco-Indian vocabulary." In his introductory essay to *Cathay* (IV, p. 25) he considers it to be derived from the Malay *jong* or *ajong*, a " great ship." For details also see *Hobson-Jobson, s.v.* Junk.

[2] *List of ports with which trade was carried on.* Ramusio omits Pegu and adds Tarnasseri and Malabar. The Spanish version adds these two without omitting Pegu.

[3] *Estravantes.* See Vol. I, p. 93, n. 1. Mgr. Dalgado, in his *Glossario Luso-Asiatico*, p. 383, suggests that this word (which only occurs in the present passage and in the versions of the passage in Vol. I. given by the Spanish version and Ramusio) is identical with " seerband " which appears in an old list of exports from British India. He adds, " probably from the Hindustani *sirband*, band or fillet for the hair." This is probably correct, and the meaning corresponds with Barbosa's explanation. The word is no doubt Persian in origin and should be written *sar-band*, which is explained by Shakespeare as " a wreath or fillet for fastening the ladies' head-dress." It does not seem impossible that the word turban is in some way connected with *sar-band*. See quotation from A. Hamilton, *s.v.* Turban in *Hobson-Jobson.* From the variations in the form in the text the original may be either *saravantes* or *taravantes*. See the same note for the other fabrics mentioned in this passage.

In Ma-huan's Account of the Kingdom of Bengal, translated by Mr. G. Phillips (*J.R.A.S.*, 1895, p. 523 f.) this Chinese traveller in the early part of the fifteenth century gives in Chinese characters the names of several of the fabrics produced in Bengal. See also Mr. W. W. Rockhill's remarks on these Chinese names in *T'oung Pao*, Vol. XVI, pp. 439–40. These are Pi-chi (or Bit-ti) for which Mr. Phillips suggests

K

sort, a very thin kind of cloth much esteemed among us for ladies' head-dresses, and by the Moors, Arabs and Persians for turbans. Of these great store is woven, so much so that many ships take cargoes thereof for abroad ; others they make called *mamonas*, others *duguazas*, others *chautares*, others *sinabafas*, which latter are the best of all, and the Moors hold them the best for shirts. All these sorts of cloth are in pieces, each one whereof contains about three-and-twenty or four-and-twenty Portuguese yards. Here they are sold good cheap, they are spun on wheels by men, and woven by them. Much good white *sugar* is also made here from canes ; but they know not how to compress it and make it into loaves ; so they wrap it as a powder in parcels of untanned leather, well sewn. Great store of this is taken in cargoes and carried for sale to many lands, for it is a principal article of trade. When these merchants were wont to go freely and fearlessly to Malabar and Cambaya with their ships, a *quintal* of sugar would bring in one

---

Betteela as the origin, Sha-na-kieh, Hin-pei-tung-tali, Sha-ta-urh (most probably *Chautar*), Mo-hei-mo-leh and Man-chê-ti. Of these Mo-hei-mo-leh may be the *mahmūdis* alluded to by Barbosa under the name of *mamonas*, or possibly *malmal*, " muslin." Mr. J. Beames's letter on Mr. Phillips's paper (in the same Vol. of the *J.R.A.S.*, p. 898) gives some notes on these identifications. He remarks that *beatilha* was introduced by the Portuguese, and could not be the origin of Pi-chi at such an early date (see also Vol. I, p. 161, n. 1). He suggests the Bengāli and Hindustāni *buti* (or *butidār*), " embroidered muslin," as a possible origin. He also suggests the Persian *ṭaḥn*, the *sanes* of the sixteenth century, as the original form of *sha-na-kieh.* Possibly *sina-bāfta* or *shanbaff*, Barbosa's *synbafo*, may be intended.

The Spanish version gives the length of each piece as about 20 cubits, and Ramusio as 25 Venetian *braccia* : the *cantaro* (or *quintal*) of sugar was worth, he says, 2½ ducats in Malabar : a piece of *beatilha* 300 *maravedis* (so also in the Spanish version), a piece of *Cautar* (*i.e., Chautar*) 600 maravedis, of *sinabafo* 2 ducats (the last only in the Spanish version). *Maravedis* and *ducats* stand for *reis* and *cruzados*, and 1,300 *reis* becomes 2½ *ducats*.

Mr. Moreland has noted that the abundance of these fine fabrics shows that the port of Bengala was situated in Bengal proper, always famous for such manufactures, for which Chittagong never was a centre. This is one among other reasons for holding that Chittagong was not Bengala.

thousand three hundred *reis* in Malabar, a *chautar* of the best kind six hundred *reis*, a *sinabafa* two *cruzados*, and a piece of the best *beatilha* three hundred *reis*; and thus those who carried them thither made great profits by selling them. And in this city they make as well great store of ginger conserve, also of oranges, lemons and other fruits which grow in this land. And there are here horses, cows and sheep in great numbers, herds of many other kinds in plenty, and barndoor fowl great abundance.

The Moorish merchants of this city ofttimes travel up country to buy Heathen boys [1] from their parents or from other persons who steal them and castrate them, so that they are left quite flat. Many die from this; those who live they train well and sell them. They value them much as guardians of their women and estates and for other low objects. "These eunuchs they hold in high esteem as men of upright character, and some of them become their lords' factors, and some Governours and Captains of the Moorish Kings, so that they become very rich and have great estates."

The respectable Moors walk about clad in white cotton smocks, very thin, which come down to their ankles, and beneath these they have girdles of cloth, and over them silk scarves, they carry in their girdles daggers garnished with silver and gold, according to the rank of the person who carries them; on their fingers many rings set with rich jewels, and cotton turbans on their heads. They are luxurious, eat well and spend freely, and have many other extravagancies as well. They bathe often in great tanks which they have in their houses. Every one has three or four wives or as many

---

[1] The trade in eunuchs from Bengal was of ancient date. The slave trade alluded to by Ibn Baṭūta (Yule and Cordier, *Cathay*, IV, p. 82) and Marco Polo (ed. 1871, II, pp. 78, 79; ed. Yule and Cordier, II, p. 115) alludes to the traffic in eunuchs and slaves.

as he can maintain. They keep them carefully shut up, and treat them very well, giving them great store of gold, silver and apparel of fine silk. They never go forth from the house save at night to visit one another, at which time they have great festivities and rejoicings, and superfluity of wines, of which they make many kinds, for the most part from palm-sugar, much whereof is consumed among these women. They are cunning performers on musical instruments of divers kinds. The lower castes of this town wear short white shifts, which come half way down their thighs, and on their heads little twisted turbans of three or four folds ; they are all well shod, some wear shoes and some sandals, well wrought and gilded. The King is a great and rich Lord over wide and thickly-peopled lands. The Heathen of these parts daily become Moors to gain the favour of their rulers.[1] On issuing forth from this city of Bengala and going further on there are many other towns likewise inhabited by Moors and Heathen both up country and on the coast, subject to this King. In these he keeps his Governours and Receivers of the customs and revenues which he possesses.

In this Gulf all the cities lie along the seacoast, and the coast begins to turn again towards the south.

§ 103. KINGDOM OF BERMA.

GOING past the Kingdom of Bengala and following the coast towards the south there is another Heathen Kingdom called that of Berma,[2] and the King thereof is called

[1] The large Muhammadan population in Eastern Bengal is of almost unmixed Hindu origin, and there is no doubt that conversion proceeded rapidly at the period in question.

[2] It is evident that very little information about Burma properly so-called had reached the Portuguese at this period. It was in fact

the same. There are no Moors therein inasmuch as it has no seaport which they can use for their traffic. The inhabitants are black men; they go naked from the waist up, and are clad in cotton garments below. They have their own indulgences (or idolatry) and houses of prayer. They are ofttimes at war with the King of Peeguu.

As to this Kingdom there is no further information for the reason that there is no means of sailing thither, save that on one side it is bounded by Bengala and on the other by Peeguu. [And it has a gulf in the middle which enters the country in a direction north-east by east forty leagues and is fourteen leagues wide at the mouth and twenty leagues wide further in, and in the middle of it is a large island which is thirty-six leagues long and from four to ten leagues broad.[1]]

---

an inland Kingdom, as Barbosa says, and inaccessible to maritime traffic. It is also alluded to in the next section under the name of Daba, which should be read D'Aba or " of Ava." In Ramusio and the Spanish version it is called Ava. This city had been founded in 1364 as the capital of the Burmese Kingdom, which had been struggling for existence against its enemies the Shans of the north and the Talaings of Pegu on the south. The Talaings were also in power at Martaban to the south, and supported by Siam had conquered Pegu. The Burmese, however, who had once ruled Pegu, still endeavoured from time to time to assert their authority, and wars were frequent. During the fifteenth century the Shans became very powerful at Ava, and the pure Burmese tended to make Taungū the centre of their power, and at the time when the Portuguese first began to make acquaintance with this region there were distinct Kingdoms of Ava and Taungū. The state which had its capital at Taungū is evidently the Kingdom of Burma of our text. North of it lay the Kingdom of Ava, and south of it that of Pegu. Aracan lay to the west and cut it off from the Bay of Bengal. A full account of the tangled history of this period is given in Sir A. Phayre's *History of Burma*, Ch. X ; see also the *Burma Gazetteer*, Vol. I, p. 18. Barbosa recognises the separate Kingdoms then existing, viz., Burma with its capital at Taungū, Ava (§ 107), Aracan (§ 104), Pegu (§ 105) and Martaban (§ 106). The statement that Burma is bounded on one side by Bengal can only be explained by the supposition that Aracan, which was occasionally under the power of the Kings of Bengal, was considered as a part of that Kingdom, but this cannot be reconciled with the account of Aracan in § 104.

[1] The concluding paragraph is given only in the Spanish version and does not appear in Ramusio. The great gulf alluded to is

§ 104. KINGDOM OF ARACANGIL.

IN the immediate interior of this Kingdom of Berma there is another Kingdom, also of the Heathen, which possesses no port on the sea bounded on one side by Bengal and on the other by the country of Daba (*i.e.*, of Ava) which they call Aracangil.[1] The King thereof is a Heathen also, and a great Lord.[2] They say that he

undoubtedly the Gulf of Martaban, which is described by De Barros in his geographical chapter on the Bay of Bengal (*Dec. I*, ix, Ch. 1, see Appendix). It had nothing to do with the Burma Kingdom as it existed in Barbosa's day. De Barros's description leaves no doubt that its shores and islands were a deltaic region resembling the Ganges Delta, and there is no other gulf which answers to this description. De Barros is mistaken, however, in placing this gulf on the further side of Tavoy. There seems to have been some confusion with the islands of the Mergui Archipelago, which lie south of Tavoy.

[1] Aracan was certainly almost perpetually at war with its neighbours Bengal and Tippera to the north, Burma and Pegu to the south, but none of these Kingdoms were subordinate or tributary to it. On the contrary, it was with difficulty it maintained its independence, and it was at times itself tributary to Bengal and Burma (see Phayre, *Hist. of Burma*, Ch. IX ; *Burma Gazetteer*, I, p. 174).

[2] There are very few notices of Aracan in the early travellers to the East. The earliest probably is that of Conti (*India in Fifteenth Century*, p. 10), who arrived at the River Rachan, and sailing up it for six days arrived at a large city of the same name. Thence he travelled across the mountains (*i.e.*, the Aracan Yoma) to Ava. His form of the name (*Rachani fluvii* in the Latin) may be compared with Fitch's Recon, and no doubt represents the form Rakhaing, the native name of the country (*Hobson-Jobson, s.v.* Arakan, Aracan). Mendez Pinto also has the form Racão (*Peregrinação*, ed. 1839, II, Ch. CXLVI, p. 269, and Ch. CXLVII, wrongly printed CLXVII in *Hobson-Jobson*, p. 275). How the name was changed into Arracão or Aracan is not clear, but it seems possible that some such form as Al-Rakān (pronounced Ar-Rakān) with the Arabic article may have been used by Arab sailors and passed into common circulation.

It is probable that the syllable *guy* or *gil* stands for the Burmese *gyi*, " great," which Dr. Anderson considers explains the last syllable of Mergui. He thinks that the " European form Mergui was a corruption of Marit with the addition of the Burmese word *gyi*, meaning *gyi*, meaning great, an affix that frequently occurs in Burmese names of places." It may evidently have been used in the same way as an affix to Recan or Aracan. In § 107 the name is given in the form Racanguy. In the Spanish version in this section the name is given as Ere Can Guy, and in § 107 as Daran Canguy. Ramusio has Aracan and Aracam.

The first recorded visit of a Portuguese fleet to Aracan was that of João da Silveira, who put into the Arakan River on his way to Chittagong (see above under Bengala, p. 137), and was asked to join the Arakanese in their war against Bengal.

possesses towns and cities in great numbers, he has also many horses, and elephants to boot, which come from the Kingdom of Peeguu. His folk are tawny and go bare, save that from the waist down they are girt with raiment of cotton.[1] They are given to the use of bows[2] of gold and precious stones. They worship Idols and have great houses of prayer. The King is ofttimes at war with the Kings his neighbours, of whom some do him obeisance and some pay him tribute.

He lives luxuriously in very good houses, and wherever he may be sojourning he has many tanks of water and right pleasant gardens, for the more part in twelve chief cities of the Kingdom, in each he has a very fine palace and a governour in charge thereof, and each one of these takes every year from his own city twelve maidens born in that year, daughters of the noblest and the fairest women that can be found. These he has brought up at the cost of the said King. There is great luxury in those palaces, and these maidens are bathed every day until they are twelve years of age, they give them also the best food with scents and flowers in plenty. They go bravely attired and are taught to dance and sing. Thus each governour has in his palace one hundred and twenty maidens great and small, and every year they take to the king twelve who have reached the age of twelve years, wheresoever he may be, all are sent well washed

---

Another visit was that of Martim Afonso, who was sent to Bengal by Lopo Vaz de Sampayo in 1528, and was wrecked on the island of Negamale close to the town of Sodoé (see above note under Bengala). Sodoé is undoubtedly the town now known as Sandoway, and it may be conjectured that Negamale was the island called Cheduba on modern maps (*Burma Gazetteer*, I, p. 225). The siege of Sandoway in 1545 by the King of Burma is alluded to by Mendez Pinto, who calls it Savady (*Peregrinaçdo*, Ch. CLXX, *Phayre*, p. 100).

[1] Ramusio and the Spanish version add " and of silk."

[2] For *arquos*, " bows," Ramusio reads *concieri* ; the Spanish version has " ornaments."

and clean with very thin garments, in a white robe, on the edge of which the name of each is written. Early in the morning they are sent to an open space and there seated in the sun, and must stay there fasting till noon in the full force of the sun, whereby they sweat so much that the garments they wear are completely wet. The King then orders them to be brought to a room where he is himself and to have their wet clothing removed and other clothes given them to wear. The wet clothes they carry there where the King is with many of his kinsmen and Governors of his Realm with other Lords and Gentlemen, and he smells them one by one[1] and those that have (not) a good smell he gives to those who are with him making them a present of the maidens whose they were, as each one bears a name ; so by this distinction everyone take his own maiden : the King keeps for himself those that smell well [for thus they say they know those who are healthy and of a good constitution]. Thus every year they bring to him a hundred and twenty[2] maidens of twelve years old, from whom he selects for himself and deals out to his followers ; thus they have no marriage law. He is very wealthy in money and Lord of much people. He has many pleasures as well in hunting, riding, dancing and music, and many other recreations which they make for him.

§ 105.   KINGDOM OF PEEGUU.

THUS following the seacoast and leaving the Kingdom of Berma there is to the south another Heathen Realm of great fertility and with much trade by sea in many

---

[1] The curious custom here described of selecting women by scent does not appear to be mentioned elsewhere.

[2] In the Spanish version and Ramusio, one hundred and forty-four, the correct number.

kinds of goods. They call it Peeguu[1]; it possesses three or four havens where there are rich merchants and great towns inhabited as well by Moors as by the Heathen who possess it. The city of Peeguu is situate inland seven or eight leagues from the sea on a small river which is a branch of another river, very great, which flows through this Kingdom coming down from certain mountains. During some months of the year it brings down so much water that it overflows its natural course and inundates widespread lands on which grows and is harvested great store of rice with which the city is right well supplied, as well as with flesh and other foods which are laden at its ports. There are in that place great ships of three or four masts, which they call *Juncos*,[2] which sail to Malaca [and Samatra] and many other places. They carry from this Kingdom of Peeguu great store of white cane sugar in loaves.[3] Hither come every year many Moorish ships to trade and bring abundance of printed Cambaya [and Paleacate] cloths, both cotton and silk, which they call *patolas*.[4]

---

[1] Pegu being a port with a lucrative trade and the capital of a powerful kingdom was better known to the outer world when the Portuguese first began to explore the coasts of the Bay of Bengal than the other regions which make up modern Burma, and this is clearly shown in this account, which is much fuller and more accurate than the passages relating to Berma, Aracangil and Ava. The situation of the city of Pegu from which the country took its name, is correctly described. The Pegu River is not indeed a branch of the Irrawaddy, but it flows into the Hlaing or Rangoon River, which is itself a part of the Irrawaddy Delta, so the mistake was a natural one.

[2] *Juncos.* See above, p. 145, n. 1.

[3] *Cane Sugar in loaves.* This is worth noting, as in Bengal our author says that making sugar into loaves was not understood, but it was a powder made up into packets wrapped in palm leaves, in fact the fine powdery sugar made in India up to the present day as distinguished from the globes of crystallised sugar known as *khand*, crystallised in unbaked clay bowls which are broken away, leaving the globe of sugar.

[4] *Patola.* From Canarese and Malayālam *paṭṭuda*, a silk cloth. *Hobson-Jobson. s.v.*

These are coloured with great skill, and are here worth much money ; they also bring opium, copper, great store of scarlet-in-grain cloth, coral threaded, round [and in branches and well set], vermilion, quicksilver, rosewater and many other Cambaya drugs, and they take here cargoes of very fine lac which is produced in the country, and mace, cloves and many other goods from China brought hither from Malaca, and with the rest of their money they buy abundance of musk [and rubies], which comes from an inland city called Ava, whereof I will speak below. The Heathen of this Kingdom are much given to Idol-worship, they go bare covering only their middles ; they are not good fighting-men.

They are very luxurious in their habits.[1] They wear on their members certain hawk-bells, round, closed and very large which are joined and fixed inside between the skin and the flesh so as to make it very large. Of these they wear as many as five, some of gold, some of silver or other metal according to those who carry them, and when they walk they give out a loud sound which they hold to be a distinction and to be admired, and the more of them the more honourable. The women delight in this and do not like men who have them not. I say no more of this on account of its indecency.

This King of Peeguu is called the King of the White Elephant,[2] there are in this Kingdom great mountains

---

[1] The extraordinary custom here alluded to (if it was based on fact and not a mere figment of the imagination such as sailors picked up from the loose talk of seaports) seems to exist no longer. The story attracted the attention of a number of travellers, but some doubt may be raised by the fact that Conti (*India in the Fifteenth Century*, p. 11) tells it about Ava, while Linschoten and Mandelslo (who copied him) follow Barbosa in putting it down to Pegu. (See Linschoten, 1, pp. 99, 100, and n. 1, Mandelslo, 1669 ed., p. 97 ; also Yule's note in *Mission to Ava*, 1858, p. 208.)

[2] *King of the White Elephant.* The Royal White Elephant is alluded to by Conti (*India in the Fifteenth Century*, p. 13) under the

where many wild elephants breed, and it is their rule to take one every day which are sent to be trained, and thus they ever have a great number which they sell in many

---

Kingdom of *Macinus* which had its capital at Ava. Yule (*l.c.*) on p. 208, says that Conti was probably " the first traveller who mentioned the white elephant and the name of Ava, which had not then existed a century." Sir H. Clifford (*Further India*, p. 83) says " he is the first traveller to speak of the famous white elephant, the dust-coloured beast with pink eyes and unsightly skewbald patches, which is in reality such an unsightly object when seen in the flesh." With this may be compared the description in C. Bock's *Exploration in Upper Siam*, 1881, p. 25, where the " white elephant is said to be of a pale reddish brown colour with a few real white hairs on the back." This is supported by the illustration in colours (*ib.*, p. 30) taken from a drawing made by the author from the King of Siam's white elephant. The association of the white elephant with the Kings of Further India has been noted by many travellers. In addition to Conti already quoted,· Linschoten (I, p. 98) says " the Portingalles that traffique there affirme that the King of Pegu hath a white elephant which he prayeth unto and holdeth it to bee holy." Fitch (*l.c.*, p. 158) says " (The King) among the rest hath foure white elephants, which are very strange and rare : for there is none other which hath them but he : if any other King hath one hee will send unto him for it. . . . . The King in his title is called the King of the white elephants. If any other King have one and will not send it to him, he will make warre with him for it."

The King of Pegu at this period was one of the most powerful and successful of the Talaing Kings previous to their conquest by the Burmese of Taungū, Binya Ran, who reigned from 1491 to 1526. In his reign various European travellers found their way to Pegu. The earliest of these was Hieronimo di Santo Stefano, who visited Pegu about 1496. He describes the King as a great lord, who possesses more than ten thousand elephants, and every year he breeds five hundred of them. Varthema who seems to have visited Pegu about 1505 describes the King as so kind and gentle that a child might speak to him (Ramusio, I, f. p. 165, Rev.). In the same year Correa (I, p. 611) speaks of a ship bringing a cargo of lac, benzoin and musk from Pegu. When Barbosa wrote a few years later it is evident that Portuguese traders must have acquired a good knowledge of the city, although no Royal expedition was sent there.

The Portuguese in Pegu. Portuguese trade with the kingdom of Pegu was opened up in 1519 (see *infra*, p. 157, n. 2) and flourished exceedingly both under the Talaing Kings and their Burmese successors. In the various wars between Burma, Pegu, Aracan and Siam bodies of Portuguese took part, sometimes fighting on both sides. They were purely mercenaries and were highly paid, but their activities were of no real value to the Portuguese position and influence in Burma and Siam. In the wars which followed the death of Bureng Naung, the conqueror of Ava and restorer of the Burmese Kingdom, the whole edifice built up by him and his predecessor, Tabeng Shwehti, fell to pieces, and Burma as Phayre says " was left to be parcelled out by petty local chiefs and European adventurers." Pegu itself was destroyed by the Aracanese in 1599. It was in the following year, 1600, that a Portuguese flotilla under Salvador Ribeyra de Souza entered the Pegu River and combined with Filipe de Brito, who had

lands but most of them in the Kingdoms of Narsyngua, Malabar and Cambaya. They have also in this land many very proper nags, great walkers, whereof they make

---

been for many years in the service of the King of Aracan, to establish Portuguese power in the country. The Aracanese King gave de Brito permission to form a factory at Siriam, on the further side of the river from the modern Rangoon. De Souza immediately began to build a fort, when the King of Aracan, repenting of what he had done, sent a fleet to attack it. This attack was defeated and the fort was completed. After many other attacks he established himself in power, and ultimately actually attained the position of a " King " or no doubt in reality a subordinate prince, under the title, according to the Portuguese Chronicler, of King Massinga of Pegu. De Brito, who had been absent from Siriam while these events were in progress, appears to have obtained credit for them with the King of Portugal and the Viceroy, and was appointed Captain in Chief of the fort. De Souza unwillingly obeyed the order, and made over charge to De Brito. This is the account given in the anonymous work the *Conquista do Regno de Pegu* (Lisbon 1829). Faria y Sousa tells the story in a manner more favourable to De Brito. In any case de Brito maintained himself for several years and his son married a daughter of the King of Martaban. His rule lasted till 1613, when Siriam was attacked by the Burmese King and after a long resistance De Brito was taken and impaled. This ended the only attempt at a permanent Portuguese establishment in Burma ; De Brito, though an adventurer, seems to have been recognised by the Portuguese authorities, and had he been supported the result would probably have been different.

The first English traveller who is known to have visited Pegu was Raph Fitch, who sailed from Srīpur in Bengal in November, 1586. He entered the Bassein River (the western branch of the Irrawaddy), crossing " the Barre of Negrais," and went up the river for three days to Cosmin, a port often mentioned by early travellers. It seems to have corresponded to the modern town of Bassein (not to be confounded, as Sir R. Temple has remarked, with the Indian Bassein on the west coast). Bassein is 75 miles from the mouth of the river, and is still accessible to ocean going steamers (*Burma Gazetteer*, 1908, Vol. I, p. 165), and even if not absolutely identical with Cosmin, there cannot be much doubt that it was in the same neighbourhood. It is mentioned also by Cæsar Frederick and Gaspar Balbi, as well as by the author of the *Conquista de Pegu* (p. 5), who gives a list of the principal ports of Pegu, viz. : Negrains, *i.e.*, the entrance to the Bassein River, Cosmi, Siriam, Sartão (probably Sitlang), Martaban. Fitch gives in order after Cosmin the following ports : Medon ("passing up the rivers"), Dela (with " a faire port unto the sea "), Cirion (also " a faire port unto the sea "), Macao and Pegu. Dela may be identified with Dāla, on the Dāla branch of the Irrawaddy, and Cirion with Syriam. The Dāla branch and town of Dāla are shown in Keith Johnston's Atlas of 1873, but not in the map accompanying the *Gazetteer* of 1908. The *Gazetteer*, however, alludes to the Dāla branch in Vol. I, p. 346. Dāla was an ancient town and is recorded to have been taken by Benya Keng and made the seat of a government in A.D. 1420). [Phayre, pp. 81, 82.] Medon may be Yandoon (Burmese, Nyaungdon), in the Ma-ubin District, situated on the Irrawaddy at the apex of the delta (*Gazetteer*, *l.c.*, p. 345). Macao was evidently on the Pegu River, somewhere between Rangoon and Pegu. Fitch's editor suggests (Meh-Kay ?), but I have been unable to trace this place.

use perpetually and many horses also which they ride
on high-pommelled saddles.[1] With these and their
elephants they go to war as well as with a multitude of
foot-soldiers. They have also great store of sheep and
swine bred indoors and wild as well. These Heathen
are mighty riders and hunters.

§ 106. MARTABAM.[2]

LEAVING this city of Peeguu and sailing towards Malaca
there are three or four sea-havens which belong to the
Kingdom of Peeguu, whereof I know not the names.

---

[1] Cf. Vol. I, p. 180, n. 1.

[2] *Martaban.* The city of Martaban, situated on the north-west
bank of the estuary of the Salwīn, facing the more modern Moulmein,
is of great antiquity and was formerly a capital and port of great
importance, but is now a small place. It seems to have been long the
capital of the Eastern section of the Talaings, sometimes under the
suzerainty of the Burmese Kings of Pagan, and sometimes under
Siam. At the time when the Portuguese became acquainted with it
it was under the Talaing King of Pegu, Binya Ran, and Portuguese
trade was encouraged. In 1519, shortly after Barbosa wrote, a treaty
was conclued with the Viceroy of Martaban by Antonio Correa. The
historian Gaspar Correa under the events of this year says (II, pp. 566-7) :
" The Governor gave Antonio Correa, Captain of Cochym, the command
of three ships with orders that after visiting Malaca, and leaving it
safe, he should sail to China. But Simão d'Andrade presented to him
a royal order giving *him* the China voyage, to see his brother Fernão
Peres (d'Andrade), so the Governor detained him (*i.e.*, Antonio Correa)
and gave him a ship (sending Garcia de Sá with him as far as Malaca,
in order to help Malaca), and after settling Malaca he was to go and
make treaties of peace in Pegu and Martabão, and to endeavour to
get cargoes of as much *lac* as possible." A considerable trade was
soon developed between the Coromandel coast from the ports of
Pulicat and another place which Correa calls Canhuneyra (which his
editor identifies with the Canhameira of De Barros (*I*, ix, p, 1, f. 175 Rev.).
De Barros says that at Canhameira is a remarkable cape 10° N., which
bears the same name. This is evidently Calimere Point. The trade
was carried on with Pegu and Martaban, and Martaban continued to
be a centre of Portuguese trade until after the conquest of Pegu by
Tabeng Shwehti, the Burmese King of Taungū. The Talaing Viceroy
of Martaban long resisted him, and was assisted by the Portuguese
with ships and munitions. There was also a considerable body of
Portuguese mercenaries in the Burmese army. In 1540 the city of
Martaban was taken after a long siege, and was sacked and thoroughly
destroyed. Fernão Mendez Pinto has given a detailed description
of the siege and sack. He arrived in the port while the siege was
proceeding ; after the fall of the city he fell into the hands of

Between these is one called Martabam [1] whither come
many ships from divers regions to trade and obtain
cargoes of food and many other goods, for the most part
of lac [2] which is produced in that land and is better by
far than that of Narsyngua. This the Indians and
Persians call *laquar Martabam*, " Martaban lac." As to
this lac some say it is the gum of a tree and others that
it grows on the fine branches of the trees as in our own
land the grain grows on the holm-oak, [3] and this argument
appears more in accordance with nature as it grows on
trees and fine twigs, which for that reason cannot yield
so much gum. At this town are made also many great
porcelain jars [4] very big, strong and fair to see; there are

the conqueror, and after surprising adventures finally got away in
1545 (*Peregrinação de F. Mendez Pinto*, Lisbon, 1829, Ch. 147 to
153 ; Phayre, *History of Burma*, pp. 96–98 ; Yule, *Mission to the Court
of Ava*, 1858, p. 209). Martaban seems never to have recovered
from its destruction in 1540, and in later times its place has been taken
by Moulmein on the south-eastern bank of the Salwin estuary.

[1] *Martaban*. Origin of the name. Dr. Anderson in *English Intercourse with Siam*, p. 15, points out that the Malay name for Martaban
is Maritanau, and that this name is formed from the two names Marit
(the Siamese name for Mergui), and Tānao (the old Siamese name for
Tenasserim). At present the Siamese call it Motama and the Talaings
Mutaman. The Malay name no doubt became the Martabān of the
Arabs.

[2] *Lac.* Pegu and Martaban were both much resorted to for *lac*
(see above under Pegu and the quotation above from Correa, p. 157,
n. 2). The allusion to the holm-oak or *quercus ilex* is no doubt to the
production of the kermes dye on that tree by the puncture of the
coccus ilicis, a near relation of the *coccus lacca*, which produces the
Indian *lac*. This is a good instance of Barbosa's powers of observation
and comparison.

[3] The name of the tree used for comparison is omitted by both the
Spanish version and Ramusio.

[4] *Martaban jars.* These tall glazed earthenware jars had long
been known to the Arab traders from whom the Portuguese doubtless
learnt the name. Ibn Baṭūta in the early part of the sixteenth
century found Martabans (مرطبانات) in use at the port of Kailūkarī
in Tawālasī (probably Tonkin) for holding preserved ginger, pepper,
lemons and mangoes. (IV, p. 253). In the sixteenth century after our
author's time these jars became well known to Europeans. Linschoten
(I, p. 101) speaks of " Nype " (a drink made from *Nipa fructicans*) being
transported " in great pottes of Martavan," also mentioned by him,
I, p. 30. Thomas Bowrey in his diary (p. 81) speaks of a man intoxicated
with *bhang* running his head " into a great Mortavan Jarre," and
Tavernier speaks of " a great earthen pot, well glazed within, which

some of them which will hold a pipe of water. They are glazed in black and greatly esteemed and highly prized among the Moors, who take them from this place with great store of benzoin in loaves.

----

§ 107. THE CITY AND KINGDOM OF AVA.

In the inland country of this Kingdom of Peeguu, going thence towards Malaca between the Kingdoms of Racanguy [1] and Anseaom there is a Heathen Kingdom wherein among other great towns there is one exceeding great city which they call Ava [2] inhabited by wealthy merchants where there is much trade in valuable precious stones, rubies and spinels which are found there. Hither gather Moorish, Heathen and Chati merchants from divers lands to purchase them, and also the abundance of musk there is there. And these stones and musk the King takes for himself, and they are sold to foreigners, who come hither to seek for them on his account. From Cambaya they bring here copper, quicksilver, vermilion, saffron, rosewater, opium, coloured Meca velvets, and

----

they call Martavane " ; and allusions are abundant in the eighteenth century. They were also called Pegu Jars, as noted in *Hobson-Jobson* and by Sir R. Temple in Bowrey, p. 193, who quotes a letter of 1678, " If you can meet any Jarres of Pegue buy me some of that sort which usually are for Mangoe Achar."

Numerous instances of the use of the word are given in *Hobson-Jobson, s.v.* Martaban.

[1] See p. 150, n. 2.

[2] Ava was the centre of a Burmese-Shan state at this time, and was distinct from the more purely Burmese Kingdom of Taungū, already alluded to (*supra* p. 148, n. 1). It is evident that little was known of it to the Portuguese of this period, with the exception of the principal articles of export, rubies and musk. It was no doubt from the " Moorish and Chati " merchants, the semi-Arabs and Chettys of Malabar, that Barbosa learnt what he has set down as to the trade, but he knew more about the geography of the country than Tavernier knew a century and a half later, who said that Ava was the port of Pegu. It may be noted that Tavernier (who was an expert in precious stones if not in geography) says that very few fine rubies were to be obtained on account of the King's monopoly (Tavernier, E.T., 1678, Part II, 143-4).

many other things valued among them, in exchange wherefor they take away the aforesaid stones (and musk) which the King causes to be gathered among the mountains and rivers, and to find it they dig very deep pits, the spinels are found on the ground level and the rubies at the bottom, there are always skilful lapidaries in this city who know them right well.   And for the musk,[1] it is found in certain animals as large as gazelles, they have small tusks like those of elephants which produce under their bellies certain growths like boils, and also on their breasts [like unto a *chila* which is found in old men] and after these have come to a head with the matter, they itch so that they scrape themselves on the trees, from which men gather some particles of good and genuine musk.   There are hunters who track them by scent and trap them or catch them in nets and take them alive and convey them to a house kept by the King for that purpose, and there they cut round those swellings through the skin, and let them dry ; what is left is the true musk

---

[1] The stories of the musk-deer and of the methods of obtaining musk circulated for a long period among travellers in the East, and are a mixture of fact and fiction.   The musk-pod is not in reality the result of a boil or similar swelling but a natural formation well known to modern zoologists.   (See Jerdon's *Mammals of India, Moschus moschiferus*, Ed. 1874, p. 266 f.)   On the other hand the adulteration of the musk still continues.   Jerdon says " it is often much adulterated with blood, liver, &c."   The earliest traveller to mention the musk-deer was probably Cosmas Indicopleustes (Cosmas, p. 360).   He says that the musk was " blood collected at the navel."   Marco Polo also attributes it to the same region (Ed. 1871, I, p. 242).   The accounts given by Linschoten (II, 94) and Tavernier (*l.c.*, p. 153) though fantastic approach nearer to the truth ; some of the details in both are perhaps borrowed from Barbosa.   Conti, though he claims to have visited Ava, does not mention the musk-deer.   The Russian traveller Nikitin however (*India in Fifteenth Century*, p. 22), alludes to the supposed deadliness of the fresh musk, but attributes this (if the translation is correct) to its taste and not to its smell.   Our author's version that the smell causes blood to flow from the nose is reproduced by Tavernier (*l.c.*) ; he says " the strength of the perfume would cause the blood to gush out of the nose, so that it must be qualified to render it acceptable, or rather less hurtful to the brain."   This passage gives the clue to the origin of this traveller's tale.   It was evidently an invention of the dealers to excuse their adulteration as a necessity.

pouch, and the most excellent. But very few of them can be got in this way, and they therefore make imitations of them in divers manners. They cut these swellings out of the live animals and apply numbers of leeches to the wounds and let them fill themselves with blood, when full they let them dry in the sun. They apply so many of these that the beast loses all its blood and falls dead, on which they flay it and make counterfeit pouches of its skin which seem like the real pouches. Then having pounded the dry leeches to a powder they make it by hand into grains, and taking a piece of the true musk-pouch and seven or eight of the leeches, they mix the whole together and make it into good musk and so good that if it came thus to our lands they would hold it to be a piece of good fortune, for after this the dealers falsify it yet further, and it is purchased for foreign lands in this city, as the true musk is so strong that if you put it near the tip of your nose it makes you sneeze violently and blood flow from your nostrils.

This King of Ava[1] is a very great Lord owning plenty of jewels and gold. He has great numbers of horses and elephants and fighting-men. The land abounds in food.

---

§ 108. CAPELAM.

AND yet further inland beyond this city and Kingdom there is another Heathen city with its own King, who nevertheless is subject and under the lordship of Ava; which city or Kingdom they call Capelam. Around it are found many rubies[2] which are brought in for sale to

---

[1] Ava fell under the power of the Burmese King of Taungū in 1554, but it did not at once become the capital of the revived Burmese Kingdom, as the conqueror, Bureng Naung, preferred to make the port of Pegu his headquarters (Phayre, 107-8).

[2] The best rubies found in Burma at the present day are those found near Mogok. "The ruby mines are situated in the hills sixty miles east of the Irrawaddy and ninety miles north-west of the City

the Ava market, and are much finer than those of that place.

§ 109. THE KINGDOM OF ANSEAM.

GOING further forward, leaving the Kingdom of Peeguu, along the coast [1] towards Malaca, there is another great Kingdom which they call that of Anseam,[2] belonging to

of Mandalay " (*Burmah Gaz.*, I, 74, Ed. 1908). This corresponds well with the position of Capelam according to Barbosa. Mogok is the modern name of the chief town in the neighbourhood. In Fra Mauro's map, which was based on Conti's information, Capelang appears as the ruby country north of Ava, though it is not mentioned in Conti's narrative (Yule and Cordier, *Cathay*, I, p. 177, n. 1). Yule remarks that "the name was preserved to a much later date, but not now traceable." In the early part of the sixteenth century Capelan, with slight variations in the form of the name, is mentioned by other writers as well as by Barbosa. Quotations will be found in *Hobson-Jobson, s.v.* Capelan. Of these Leonardo di Ca'Masser (1504) gives the form Acaplan. Varthema, 1510, has Capellan, and the Sommario de'Regni in Ramusio Capelangam. Tavernier's mention (*c.* 1660), which is the latest, gives the form Capelan. Linschoten does not mention it. All agree in naming it as a centre of the ruby district. Fitch (*l.c.*, p. 172) says "Caplan is the place where they finde the rubies, saphires and spinelles. It standeth six dayes journey from Ava in the Kingdome of Pegu. There are many great high hills out of which they digge them. None may go to the pits but only those which digge them."

[1] Here the Spanish version inserts " to the south-south-east towards Malaca, eighty-seven leagues from Martaban."

[2] *Anseam.* This form of the name Siam is of occasional occurrence among writers in the early sixteenth century, and this is probably its first appearance. Diego Ribero's map of 1529 has the form Ansian, the Spanish version which he generally follows giving the forms Ansiam and Ansyane. Ramusio, however, has the more usual form Siam. De Barros and Correa do the same, but Cesare Federici as late as 1567 has Asion. (See *Hobson-Jobson, s.v.* Siam.) Yule observes "It is difficult to interpret this *An*seam, but the *An* is probably a Malay prefix of some kind." Dr. J. Anderson (*English Intercourse with Siam*, 1890, p. 17) says that the various forms of the name were " seemingly derived from Siyām, the Malay name of the country, and further modified, for some unknown reason, to Anseam and Asion." It is worth considering whether the same explanation as I have already suggested (p. 150, n. 2) for the first syllable of Aracan may not apply to Anseam also, viz., that it represents an Arabic form

السيام As-Siām, as used by the traders and sailors from whom Europeans learnt so many Eastern names of places.

The most probable explanation of the name Siam is that given in *Hobson-Jobson* (*s.v.* Shan and Siam), which identifies it with the name Shan applied to the tribes often known as Laos, who are widely spread both in Burma and Siam. There seem to be no instances of the use of the name by Europeans earlier than the beginning of the sixteenth

the Heathen. The King thereof is also a Heathen and a very great Lord, he holdeth this coast as far as the other which beyond Malaca turneth towards China, so that he hath seaports on both sides : he is Lord of much folk, both footmen and horsemen, and of many elephants, nor doth he permit the Moors to bear arms in his land. Straightway after leaving the Kingdom of Pegu there is a great city, a sea-haven which they call *Tanaçary*.[1]

---

century. The forms *Hsien* and *Hsien-lo* used by the Chinese travellers evidently have the same origin (W. W. Rockhill, *T'oung Pao*, Vol. XVI, pp. 99, 101).

Spanish version, Ansyan ; Ramusio, Siam.

[1] Tanaçary (Tenassarim), or more probably Mergui at the mouth of the Tenasserim River (on which the old town of Tenasserim stands thirty-seven miles up the river), was the port by which the intercourse of Siam with the Western world was conducted, until the arrival of the Portuguese. A full account of its history and of the various mentions of it by early travellers is given by Dr. J. Anderson in his *English Intercourse with Siam*, pp. 10–42. Conti was the first European to reach this port, and Dr. Anderson shows clearly that he did not reach the town of Tenasserim, but that the port he knew by that name was Mergui at the mouth of the river (*l.c.*, p. 19). It is probable that Barbosa's Tanaçary was the same place, but he seems to have had no personal acquaintance with it and confines himself to an account of its trade. De Barros in his account of Siam gives a list of ports in which occur the names Meguim Tenasarij (not separated by a comma), from this it may be inferred that this name was borne by the port at the mouth of the river. (*Dec. III*, Bk. ii, Ch. 5, f. 37). Fitch also (*l.c.*, 178) speaks of the " Ilands of Tanaseri, Iunsalaon and many others." This can only apply to Mergui, which is on an island, while Tenasserim is not. Iunsalaon (*i.e.*, Junkseylon) is also a large island. It may be conjectured therefore, that a good deal of the trade of the old city of Tenasserim had been transferred to Mergui or at any rate to the mouths of the river. The English merchants were established at Mergui in 1683, and most of the English were massacred there by the Siamese in 1687. The final downfall of Tenasserim came with its conquest and devastation by Alaungpaya, the Burmese conqueror in 1765. It was then lost to Siam, and the whole province has since formed part of Burma. For many centuries the trade route from the West to Ayuthia, the capital of Siam, had crossed the narrow part of the peninsula at this point, but this trade came to an end with the Burmese conquest. Old Tenasserim is now little more than a village though with traces of its former greatness. Mergui is still a port of some importance, owing to its good natural harbour (*Burma Gaz.*, I, 465, 466). T. Bowrey, whose diary is so valuable for many places on the Bay of Bengal, is unfortunately not available for this coast. Sir R. Temple in his edition has noted that the headings Arackan, Pegu and Tanasaree are blank (Bowrey, H.S., p. 234).

The Spanish version inserts " a hundred leagues from the Kingdom of Pegu."

Here are many merchants both Moors and Heathen which deal in goods of every kind, and also possess many ships which sail to Bengala, Malaca and many other places. In the inland country behind this city very good benzoin is found, the resin of a tree which the Moors call Lobam[1] [whereof there are two kinds, one which gives out no sweet smell until it is put on the fire, and the other which is very sweet smelling and good even before] and from it they make the *storax* which is extracted from it in the Levant. Hither come many Moorish ships from divers regions bearing copper, quicksilver, vermilion, cloths dyed in grain, silk, coloured Meca velvets, saffron, white coral threaded, rosewater (which they bring from Meca and Adem in little barrels of tinned copper, selling it by weight with the barrel included), opium great store, and Cambaya cloths; the whole whereof they prize greatly in this Kingdom of Anseam; and the merchants take away hence everything which comes from Peeguu.

And passing this city of Tanaçary there is on the coast towards Malaca another port of this same Kingdom called *Quedaa*[2] where also are many great ships. This is

---

[1] *Lobam.* This is no doubt, as given in Ramusio and the Spanish version, *Lubān-javi* or Java frankincense, now generally known as *benzoin*, and often called *benjamin* by early travellers. See *Hobson-Jobson, s.v.* Benjamin, Benzoin, for quotations, and also a large number of instances of the use of the Portuguese forms *beijoim* and *benjoim* in *Glossario Luso-Asiatico.* Mgr. Dalgado notes that Garcia da Orta in his ninth *Colloquy* was the first European to describe the origin of this incense correctly. It is derived from *Styrax benzoin,* which is found in Sumatra, Siam and Penang. It is, as Barbosa correctly observes, a resin. Orta distinguishes three varieties of *beijoim, amendoado* or filled with white almonds, which was considered very good; *preto* or black, which was less valuable; and the third, *bejoim de boninas* or flowery benzoin, was worth ten times as much as the others.
Spanish version, *lubanjavi*; Ramusio, *lubaniabi.*

[2] *Quedaa* (Quedda or Kedah). This port, which is now included in the Malay States, is mentioned in the *Commentaries,* III, Ch. 17, as a Kingdom bounding Malaca on the north-west and Paam or Pam, *i.e.,* Pahang, is given as the eastern boundary. The author of the *Commentaries* states that until the arrival of the Portuguese, Pahang

a place of wholesale trade, and Moorish ships come hither yearly from divers regions. Here grows abundance of fine pepper which they carry to Malaca and China. And this King of Anseam holdeth also on this coast between Malaca and Tanaçary two or three other havens whereof I know not the names and other great cities and towns and villages as well in the inland country inhabited by Heathen where no Moors may enter or live. If any come there to traffic they do not allow him to bear arms.

In this land of Anseam there is much gold which is found and gathered there chiefly in the Signory of Paam[1] which is beyond Malaca towards China. It ever pertained to this Kingdom but now has risen against it and is subject to the King of Malaca. There is also another Heathen Signory which is under him where much and good tin is found which they take to Malaca where it is used and sold to many countries, which Signory they call *Çaranguor*.[2]

---

was subject to Siam, and it would seem that Kedah was in the same position. When Barbosa wrote it was evidently still subject to Siam, and continued to be so till the present day. T. Bowrey (1669–79) *l.c.*, p. 275, says " The Kinge of Queda is tributary to him of Syam, though the tribute he payeth be but inconsiderable in it Selfe being noe more than annually a gold flower." Schouten, however (*ib.*) in 1663 says that Siamese power did not extend to Perak and Queda, which were subject to Achin. In 1909 the suzerain rights over this and four other small states in the Peninsula lying north of the Federated States were transferred to the British Government.

[1] Pahang (Paam) on the east coast of the Peninsula and Selangor (Çaranguor) on the west coast are included among the Federated States which are under British Protection.

[2] Çaranguor is a correction for Caranguor of the Portuguese text. Lord Stanley has already noted the omission of the cedilla in this as in so many other cases.

Tin continues, as it was in Barbosa's day, to be one of the principal products of these countries, and there is also some gold mining.

Most of the rulers of these states still bear the title of Sultan which before the arrival of the Portuguese was borne by the " Kings " of Malacca and Pahang (as to the latter the author of the *Commentaries* says they were called Coltois, *i.e.*, Çoltões, a plural form of Soltam. (See G. Ferrand, *Malaka*, p. 26.)

A very full account, which is admirably edited by Sir R. Temple, is given of Queda by T. Bowrey (*l.c.*, 259–285). It was noted as producing the best pepper in the Malay Peninsula. The transient

This King of Anseam is a great Lord, a Heathen as I have already said, a worshipper of idols of whose temples he has very many. Their customs differ from those of other Heathen. They go naked save that they clothe themselves below with cotton garments, some of them wear little silk coats. They have food in plenty in the country, great store of rice, flesh meat of their own breeding and also wild, they have plenty of horses and

---

establishment of a trading station by the English company will be found in the notes to Bowrey's narrative.

The name of Queda or Kedah has been supposed by Crawford to be derived from the Malay *Kadah*, " an elephant-trap," while others derive it from Malay *Kwāla*, a port or estuary. It has also been supposed that it is the place called Kalah by the Arab traders (see quotations in *Hobson-Jobson s.v.* Calay) from which the word *ḳalaī* or tin may be derived. There is evidently some connection, but it is not clear that *Ḳalah* refers to Kedah. Mgr. Dalgado (*Gloss. Lus. As., s.v.* Calaim) says that the Ḳalah of the Arabs was probably on the coast of Malaca ; but may refer to Selangor, which was known as a depot for tin, and was called in Malay *Nagri Kālang* or " city of tin."

M. Gabriel Ferrand in his exhaustive investigation into the history of this coast (*Le K'ouen-Louen et les anciennes navigations interocéaniques dans les mers du Sud*, Journ. As., 1919, pp. 246-492 and 5-267), has rejected after a careful examination of all the authorities the identification of Kedah with *Ḳalah*. In his Appendix I, pp. 214-233, he discusses this question, and comes to the conclusions on linguistic grounds (1) that the Arabs never represented the Malay cerebral *d* by *l* ; and that in their allusions to Kedah the early *mu'allims* or pilots kept to the Arabic dental, giving it the names Ḳadah and Kīdā ; (2) that Kalah and its variants probably represent Kra (on the western coast of the isthmus of Kra). This is also called Ḳarā by the Arabs, which represents the Malay Kerah ; (3) that there was also another port called Karā which is the little island of Pulaw Kera, not far from the ancient Kedah, but a little south of it. M. Ferrand does not consider that *Ḳala'ī* "tin" has any connection with the name of Kalah. In face of the fact that the Malay peninsula was from early times the principal source of the supply of tin it does not seem improbable that the Arabic name was derived from some place in that country. It has already been noted in *Hobson-Jobson, s.v.* Calay, that Selāngor between Malacca and Perak was formerly known as *Nagri Kālang* or " the tin country " and that *kalang* is a name of tin in Malay. Selangor, called here Çaranguor by Barbosa, was according to him celebrated for its tin. The tin mines of Johore, Perak, Selangor and Sungei Ujong, are of great importance at the present day (Swettenham, *British Malaya*, p. 228 f.).

Pahang is mentioned under the name of P'eng-fong in the Chinese work *Chan-ju-Kua*, trans. by Hirth and Rockhill as a dependency of Palembang in Sumatra (*Malaka, l.c.*, p. 185).

Kedah is mentioned as dependent on Minankabaw in Sumatra in the coronation document of the Sultans of that country of the eighteenth century (*Malaka*, pp. 99-115). Kedah is included (p. 110) among the regions to which notice of the coronation is to be sent.

nags and many greyhounds and dogs of other kinds for
they are great riders and hunters.   In the interior towards
China there is a Heathen Kingdom subject to Anseam,
wherein when anyone dies his kinsmen and friends eat
him[1] roasted in this manner.   They build a great fire in

---

[1] The custom of devouring dead relatives as a form of funeral
ceremony does not appear to have been observed by any modern
traveller in the regions to the north of Siam towards the Chinese
border.   The mention here is no doubt the earliest in date, and perhaps
the source from which the later writers derived their information.
Barbosa does not, however, give a name to the tribe he describes in
such detail, but it is no doubt identical with the Gueos of De Barros,
Linschoten and Camões.   The passages in which they are mentioned
are the following.
      De Barros, *III*, ii, 5, f. 37 rev.   After alluding to the position of
Camboja between Siam and Choampa he mentions a range of mountains
to the north of them " as rough as the Alps, wherein dwell certain
folk called Gueos who fight on horseback, with whom the King of
Siam is at war perpetually.   They are his neighbours only to the north.
And among them are the Laos who surround all this Kingdom of
Siam as well to the north as to the east along the River Mecon, and
who march with the great region of China, and to the south with the
two Kingdoms of Camboja and Choampa, which are maritime.   And
these Laos who surround the Kingdom of Siam to the north and east
being lords of lands so great that they contain three Kingdoms, are
yet subject to the King of Siam, although ofttimes they rise up against
him.   And if they yield any obedience whatsoever it is because he
protects them against these Gueos, who are so savage and cruel that
they devour human flesh, and to judge from their customs and the
place of their habitation they seem to be the people who Marco Paulo,
in the book which he wrote of his travels, says inhabited a kingdom
which he calls Cangigu.   For these Gueos (whom he does not name as
he does the Kingdom) commonly paint and brand themselves over
their whole bodies as do those of whom he speaks.   We see the Moors
of Barbery to be branded, but in those regions we know no other race
which does so.   And as they dwell in high and rough mountains where
none may enter, they come down from these rugged abodes to the
open lands of the Laos and do great mischief there ; and were it not
for the might of the King of Siam, who wages war against them with
hosts of horsemen and footmen and war-elephants, the Laos had ere
now been destroyed, and even the lands of Siam taken by them."
      The allusion to Marco Polo in this passage is probably to the painted
or tattooed cannibals of the mountain regions of China between
Fohkien and Kian-Si (Yule, *Marco Polo* (1872), II, 179, 181).   But the
custom of their cannibalism (to eat anyone who had not died a natural
death) was quite different from that described by Barbosa ; and the
locality of their country seems to make any identification impossible.
      Linschoten's information is evidently taken from De Barros.   He
says (I, 122) " in the land behind Cambaia (*i.e.*, Camboja) and Siam are
several nations, as Laos which are a great and a mighty people, others
named Avas and Bramas, which dwell by the hills : others that dwell
upon the hills called Gueos, which live like wild men and eat man's
flesh, and marke all their bodies with hote iron, which they esteeme a
freedom."

an open space, they set up three logs of wood in the
fashion of a gallows. In the midst of this they hang an
iron chain with two iron hooks on which they hang the
dead body by the back of the knees, and there his kinsfolk and children roast him making a great lamentation,
and when he is well roasted, with many bowls and cups
of wine they begin to carve and eat the body, drinking
and wailing, and the nearest kinsman makes the first
cut, and there they finish eating the body leaving nought
but the bones which they finish burning and reduce to
ashes ; they say that they do this only to their kinsfolk, for

---

Camões in his stanza (X, 126) quoted by Lord Stanley in his edition,
p. 122, simply says that the Gueos eat human flesh and brand their
own flesh with burning iron. He too evidently drew on De Barros.
  Sir Hugh Clifford in his *Further India*, p. 198, alluding to the weakness
of the Laos after the revolutions of 1528, adds : " The Laos people were
further weakened by protracted wars with the Gueos—hill tribes whose
identity is uncertain—and in a weak moment the aid of Siam was
invoked." The account of De Barros seems to be the foundation for
this statement.
  It may be taken as certain from the locality of their home in the
mountains north of Siam and from their practice of tattooing, that
these Gueos were a branch of the great Tai race to which the Shans
and Laos equally belong. Possibly a survival of the name Gueo
may be found in the *Ngiou* of Carl Bock and the *Ngnio* of H. S. Hallett.
The latter name is applied by Hallett to the Mossi Shans north of
Zimmé (Chieng-Mai), the very neighbourhood where one might expect
to find representatives of the Gueos (*Man : Past and Present*, 2nd
Ed., 1920, p. 192). Possibly the Giao and Giao-Shi mentioned in the
Annals of Champa, in the ninth and tenth centuries, as at war with
that country may be the same race (G. Maspero, *Le Royaume de
Champa*, T'oung Pao, Vol. XII, pp. 57, 240). But there is no evidence
that their custom of eating their relatives has survived, nor cannibalism
in any form such as has been found among the Battas of Sumatra.
  Barbosa's account was derived no doubt from reports circulating
in the seaports of Siam, but there is no reason to doubt its substantial
accuracy. Although no exact parallel can be found to this form of
cannibalism, yet it is in accordance with the ideas prevalent among
many primitive races. The practice of devouring an enemy, for
instance, or a criminal robber or murderer who has been executed, but
not one who has died a natural death (as in Marco Polo's instance
mentioned above), came from the desire to appropriate the courage and
strength of the deceased ; and in a similar way near relations may
have been eaten to keep all their valuable qualities in the family
or tribe.
  Although there is no evidence that this practice survives in Further
India, it is very probable from Barbosa's account that it still existed
in the early sixteenth century among a branch of the Tai race, and
that this branch was identical with the tribe afterwards known by
the name of Gueos.

they can find no better burial place for their own flesh than in their own bodies.   In all the rest of this Kingdom of Siam they burn dead bodies in accordance with the custom of all the Heathen, as I have told above in many places ; this abominable custom is followed only in this inland region.

§ 110.   THE CITY AND REALM OF MALACA.[1]

FROM the aforesaid kingdom of Anseam there stretches forth into the sea a point of land, as it were a Cape,

The first attempt to open up communications with Siam was made by the Portuguese after the conquest of Malacca when Alboquerque sent Antonio de Miranda as ambassador to that country accompanied by Duarte Coelho.   The King of Siam sent back in return a present for the King of Portugal.   Before further orders had been received from Portugal, Duarte Coelho started with Fernão Peres D'Andrade on his unsuccessful voyage to China in August, 1516, which came to grief on the coast of Choampa, i.e., Champa, now Cochin China. Duarte Coelho left him there in a junk and followed the coast to the mouth of the Meinam, where he passed the stormy season, and in 1517 went on to China.   During his stay he went up the river as far as the capital, which De Barros calls Hudia (Ayūthia).   After his return to Malacca a letter and present for the King of Siam having been received from Dom Manoel, King of Portugal, Aleixo de Meneses, the captain of Malacca, chose him on account of his experience to go as ambassador to Siam to make a friendly treaty and arrange for the co-operation of Siam against the Malays.   He started in July, 1518, and arrived in November of the same year.   The historian explains the delay by the fact that the ship in which he travelled was a Siamese ship and put in at several ports on the way.   There he remained till November, 1519, and arranged everything to his satisfaction, the King of Siam even consenting to the erection of a cross in the principal place of the city.   He took a circuitous route in returning to avoid the ships of the King of Bintam, the ex-King of Malacca.   In attempting to cross from the coast of Camboja to the Point of Singapur he was driven ashore on the coast of Pam (Pahang) and fell into the hands of the son-in-law of that monarch, who fortunately was on bad terms with his father-in-law and sent Duarte Coelho safely to Malacca, where he arrived in February, 1520.   These details are derived from De Barros (III, ii, iv, f. 35).   Possibly Barbosa may have obtained his information from Coelho on his return from his first expedition to Siam.

[1] Malaca.   The history of Malacca previous to the arrival of the Portuguese has been dealt with by several well-known authorities, viz., Sir Henry Yule and M. Cordier, Mr. Tiele, Mr. Otto Blagden, M. Pelliot, and Mr. W. W. Rockhill, and the whole subject has been reconsidered in M. Gabriel Ferrand's recent work Malaka, Le Malâyu et Malâyur (in the Journal Asiatique, 1918).   In this work M. Ferrand brings together and reprints all the passages relating to the subject

where the sea turns back towards China ; and on this
point there is a petty Kingdom erstwhile subject to that

from Arab, Chinese, Portuguese and Dutch authorities, a compilation
which is invaluable for purposes of reference. M. Ferrand comes to
the conclusion that the date hitherto accepted for the first foundation
of Malacca by the Malays is much too recent, and that instead of the
early part of the 15th century we should accept the local account as
given by G. Correa in the *Lendas da India* (II, 221), *i.e.*, seven hundred
years before the arrival of the Portuguese (A.D. 1511) or the early
part of the 9th century.   This was derived no doubt from the legends
prevalent among the Malays.   Space does not admit of M. Ferrand's
argument being here set forth in detail, but it is carefully worked out
mainly on the evidence of Chinese writers.   M. Pelliot has brought
together in his *Deux itinéraires* (quoted by M. Ferrand in *Malaka*,
p. 131) certain Chinese passages which show Chinese familiarity with
a port of Malāyu (which from the description of its position can be
identified with no other place than Malacca) in the Mongol period
(from 1281 onwards to 1295).   The Malāyu had then long been
in rebellion against the Siamese, and the Emperor of China intervened in their favour and restrained the King of Siam from
attacking them.   It is clear then that, at whatever date Malacca was
founded, it was an old-established State at the end of the 13th century.
There can be little doubt that it was the *Malaiur* alluded to by Marco
Polo at about the same period (*Malaka*, p. 139).
    In the early part of the 15th century it is certain that Malacca, now a
well-established Muhammadan State, was again in arms against Siam
and that China again intervened on receiving the nominal submission
of the ruler of Malacca.   Chinese evidence is abundant.   The account
from the *Ying yai shêng lan* (A.D. 1439) translated by the late Mr.
W. W. Rockhill (T'oung Pao, Vol. XVI, 1995, p. 114.) is very full.
    The relations between the Malays of the Peninsula and those of
the Island of Sumatra, and especially of the ancient kingdom of Menangkabau, have long been the subject of argument.   It is generally
admitted that the Malays as a whole came from the North, and
spread into the Islands of Indonesia, and it is also probable that
there was a close connection between Menangkabau and Malaca,
and that one was either conquered or colonised by the other.
Marsden in his *History of Sumatra* (Ed. 1783, p. 283 ff.), alludes
to the opinion that Menangkabau was derived from a colony
from the Peninsula which introduced Islam and exterminated
the original inhabitants.   He himself maintained that Menangkabau
was an indigenous kingdom which attained great power in pre-Muham-
madan times, and that although it derived its religion from the conti-
nental Malays it was in no wise destroyed, and this opinion appears
to be well founded.   On the other hand it cannot be doubted that
the kingdom of Menangkabau when at the height of its power had
great influence in the Peninsula, where its suzerainty was widely
admitted, and continued in name even in its decadence.   This is
exemplified by the inauguration of the Chiefs of the Menangkâbos
of Rembau near Malacca by an ambassador from Menangkabau up
to 1832.   These are no doubt the *Monacaboes* of A. Hamilton's *New
Account* (II, 83), who were a " barbarous, savage People," yet " much
whiter than their neighbouring Malayas who inhabit the low-grounds."
Rembau is situated in the hill-country occupied by the savage Malay
and the Jakun tribe (see Skeat and Blagden, *Pagan Races*, Vol. I,
pp. 66–68, and map facing Vol. II, p. 386), but the ruling family was
no doubt Malay, and it can hardly be doubted that the name was

of Anseam, wherein many foreign Moors having established
their trade became so rich thereby that they turned the

---

derived from their ancient subjection to Menangkabau. It may
be noted that the dialect of Malay spoken by some of the Jakuns
resembles that of Menangkabau rather than that of the peninsula
(ib., p. 402).

Godinho de Eredia (1613), Ch. II, alludes to these Monancaboes
of the peninsula " who come down with cargoes of betel from Nany
by the Pancalan River." He also mentions Rombo (Rembau) as the
centre of the Malayas of Johor, " a country also inhabited by Monancaboes " (Malaka, p. 67).

The foundation of Malacca is attributed by Godinho de Eredia
Ch. I (who is a good authority on tradition as he was partly of Malay
descent) to Permiçuri (who chose this place as easily defensible against
the ruler of Pahang, who threatened him), and gave the name of Malaca
from the abundance of Malaca or Myrobalan trees in the neighbourhood.
The name Permiçuri (or Permiçura according to De Barros and the
Commentaries) was evidently Hindu (Sanskrit) in origin, but his successors were Muhammadans. The foundation is attributed by him
to the year A.D. 1411. M. Ferrand (Malaka, p. 61, n. 3) draws attention to the feminine form of the name Permiçuri, which may be a sign
that the ruling monarch was a queen. The other authorities named give
the masculine form.

The derivation of Malacca from the name of the Myrobalan (Phyl-
lanthus emblica) is alluded to in Hobson-Jobson, s.v. Malacca, and
is said there to have been supported by Crawfurd, but I have not been
able to trace the passage. In his Indian Archipelago, Vol. II, p. 374,
he quotes a passage from Marsden's History of Sumatra (Ed. 2, pp.
327-329), giving this explanation in accordance with the local legend,
but does not express his own opinion. None of the other etymologies
which have been proposed seem to have much value. See M. Ferrand's
notes in Malaka, p. 32, n. 2, and p. 61, n. 6. He favours the meaning
Myrobalans.

The history of the Portuguese conquest of Malacca has been very
fully related by all the historians who have dealt with the subject.
The following should be referred to :—

João de Barros. Dec. II, Book vi, Ch. 1 to 6. (The greater
part of Ch. I describing Malacca and relating its previous history
has been translated into French by M. G. Ferrand, Malaka, pp. 45—52.)

Commentaries of A. D'Alboquerque. Hak. Soc. Ed., Vol. III,
Ch. XVII ff. M. Ferrand gives a new translation into French of the
parts of Ch. XVII and XVIII relating to Malacca before the arrival of
the Portuguese in Malaka (pp. 25 to 42). This differs in several
points from Mr. W. De Gray Birch's translation.

F. L. de Castanheda. Historia do Descobrimento e Conquista
da India, Book II, Ch. 110 to 116. Ch. 112, which contains the description and previous history of Malacca, is translated by M. Ferrand
in Malaka, pp. 195·198.

Gaspar Correa. Lendas da India, Vol. III, Ch. 26 to 31. Part
of Ch. 27, pp. 221, 222, is translated by M. Ferrand (ib., p. 52), who
has also translated a passage from Vol. I, p. 69, dealing with Malacca.

Diogo do Couto. Decadas IV, Bk. ii, Part of Ch. I, dealing with
previous history and giving a description of Malacca, is translated
by M. Ferrand (ib. p. 56-60).

Godinho de Eredia. Declaraçam de Malaca e India Meridional
com o Cathay. Ed. Bruxelles, 1882, with a French translation entitled

people of the land into Moors also, and openly declared themselves against the King of Anseam ; and thus all now being Moors, the Kingdom remained independent.[1] And here dwell up to now great wholesale merchants of every kind, both Moors and Heathen, many of them from Charamandel, men of great estates and owning many great ships which they call *juncos*. They trade everywhere in goods of all kinds. Numbers of ships also come hither to take cargoes of sugar, very fine four-masted[2] ships ; they bring great store of silk, very fine raw silk,[3] porcelain in abundance, damasks, brocades,

---

Malaca, l'Inde méridionale et le Cathay. This work which dates from 1613 was first published from a MS. in the Bibliothèque Royale of Brussels in 1882. Considerable extracts are reprinted with notes by M. Ferrand (*l.c.*, pp. 61–67).

The Dutch writer VALENTYN, whose *Oud en Niew Oost Indien* was published at Amsterdam in 1726, deals with the same subjects in his Part V, Book vi, Ch. 2, which has been translated into English by Mr. D. Z. A. Hervey in the Journal of the Straits Branch of the R.A.S., 1884, p. 62 f, and by M. Ferrand (*l.c.*, pp. 68–81).

Many writers of the eighteenth and nineteenth centuries have dealt with this subject and the following may be referred to. (Some of these accounts adopt an extremely censorious tone in dealing with the proceedings of the Portuguese, and do not allow sufficiently for the circumstances and for the ideas and beliefs prevalent at the beginning of the sixteenth century, and to the practices sanctioned in warfare by universal consent in Europe.)

A. HAMILTON.   *A New Account of the East Indies,* 1727, Ch. 39.
W. MARSDEN.   *History of Sumatra,* 1783, p. 322 f.
J. CRAWFURD.   *History of the Indian Archipelago,* 1820, Vol. II, Ch. 8, p. 391 f.
R. S. WHITEWAY.   *Rise of the Portuguese Power in India,* 1890.
K. E. JAYNE.   *Vasco de Gama and his Successors,* 1910, pp. 86–90.
SIR F. SWETTENHAM.   *British Malaya,* 1907, Ch. 4.
SIR H. CLIFFORD.   *Further India,* 1904, Ch. 4.
M. HENRI CORDIER.   *L'arrivée des Portugais en Chine.* T'oung-Pao, Vol. XII, Leiden, 1911.   (Malacca is alluded to in Ch. IV, p. 502.)

M. Cordier quotes the passage in *Ludovico Varthema's Travels* in which he gives an account of Malacca (*circ.* 1503), for which reference may also be made to the Hak. Soc. Ed. by E. Badger, and Ramusio, Vol. I, 1563, f. 166. M. Cordier's extract is from *Les Voyages de Ludovico di Varthema* par Ch. Schefer, pp. 230–232.

[1] Ramusio here reads " having appointed a Moorish King," and the Spanish version the same.

[2] Ramusio and the Spanish version have " two-masted."

[3] Ramusio, *seda in mattasse.*

coloured satins,[1] musk, rhubarb, sewing silk in various colours, [much iron], saltpetre, great store of fine silver, pearls in abundance, sorted seed-pearls,[2] gilded coffers, fans, and many other baubles ; and all this they sell at good prices to the dealers of the country, and in exchange therefor they take away pepper, incense, Cambay cloths dyed in grain, saffron, coral shaped and strung, and ready for shaping, printed and white cotton cloths which come from Bengala, vermilion, quicksilver, opium, and other goods and drugs of Cambaya and one unknown to us which they call *cacho*[3] and another which they call *pucho mangiçam*,[4] that is gall-nuts brought inland from the Levante to Cambaya by way of Meca, which are much prized in China and Jaoa. From the Kingdom of Jaoa also come the great *junco*[5] ships [with four masts] to the city of Malaca, which differ much from the fashion of ours, being built of very thick timber, so that when

---

[1] See Note in Yule and Cordier, *Cathay*, IV, 118.

[2] Ramusio, *avorio assai*.

[3] *Cacho pucho.* See Vol. I, p. 155, n. 1, where I suggested that the term *cachopucho* written as one word represented the Malay *kayu-putih* or *cajeput*. Mgr. Dalgado informs me that he thinks that in the passage annotated the words should be read *cacho, pucho* and that it is not probable that *cajeput* was referred to.   In the present passage the words are certainly separate.   He would also separate *pucho* and *mangiçam* by a comma, and considers that *mangiçam* represents Orta's *majum*, the Arabic *ma'jūn*. The evidence is insufficient to justify any certainty, but I am inclined to think that *cajeput* is not impossible as an explanation of the joint term in the earlier passage. If the words *pucho* and *mangiçam* are to be separated the explanation "gall-nuts brought from the Levante" can refer only to the latter, and in that case we can hardly find the origin in the Arabic *ma'jūn*, an intoxicating confection containing hemp-leaves or opium seeds (to which, incidentally, Bābur was much addicted as he confesses).

[4] Ramusio has "one which they call Puchou and another Cachou, and the other Magican, which are gall-nuts." The Spanish version agrees with Ramusio.

[5] *Juncos.* This description of the method of building junks may be compared with that given by Marco Polo (Ed. 1873, II, 196-7 ; Ed. Yule and Cordier, II, 269) of the ship built at Manzi. Friar Jordanes, Nicolo Conti, and Ibn Baṭūta (see *ib.*, notes) all allude to this construction of ships with two or more skins of planking.

they are old a new planking can be laid over the former [so that there are three or four layers of planks one over the other], and so they remain very strong. The cables and all the shrouds of these ships are made of canes [rattans] which grow in the country. In these ships the Jaos bring hither great store of rice, beef, sheep, swine, deer, " salt meat",[1] fowls, garlic and onions, and also bring for sale many weapons, spears, " daggers," short swords all finely worked and damascened on fine steel [also cubebs and a yellow dye called *cazuba* (Spanish, *cazunba*),[2] and many other small articles [Ramusio : Cubebs of a yellow colour called *cazuba*] and gold which is found in the said Kingdom of Jaoa.

These Jaos who live by sailing the seas take with them their wives and children and homes and families ; they have no other houses of their own nor do they ever go ashore save for their traffic, and there in those ships [they are born and there] they die.

These folk, then, selling their goods, as I have already said, in Malaca at good prices take away in return cloths of Paleacate and Mailapur and others which come from Cambaya, opium, rosewater, vermilion, great store of grains for dyeing, raw silk, saltpetre, iron, *cacho* and *pucho* (which are Cambaya drugs) all of which is much valued in Jaoa. From this city of Malaca ships sail also to the Isles of Maluco (whereof I will treat below) there to take in cargoes of cloves, taking thither for sale much Cambaya cloth, cotton and silk of all kinds, other cloths from Paleacate and Bengala, quicksilver,

---

[1] *Cf.* also p. 191 under Java : *checinar,* " to salt meat."

[2] *Cazunba and Cazuba.* This dye is not mentioned in the Portuguese text.   The name is doubtless the Malay *Kasumba,* a name of Indian origin, and in use in India at the present day in the form *Kusumbhā,* for the safflower dye.   *Cf.* M. Ferrand, *Malaya,* p. 22, 208.

wrought copper, bells and basins, and a Chinese coin[1]
[like a *bagattino* with a hole in the middle], pepper,
porcelain, garlic, onions, and other Cambaya goods
of divers kinds. Thus they sail from this city of Malaca
to all the islands in the whole of this sea, and to Timor
whence they bring the whole of the white sanders-
wood, which is greatly esteemed among the Moors[2]
and is worth much ; and thither they take iron, axes,
knives,[3] cutlasses, swords, cloths from Paleacate [and
Cambaya], copper, quicksilver, vermilion, tin, lead,
great store of Cambaya beads in exchange wherefor
they take away, as well as the sanders-wood, honey,
wax and slaves. These ships also sail from Malaca
to the islands which they call Bandan to get cargoes
of nutmegs and mace, taking thither for sale Cambaya
goods. They also go to the Island of Çamatra, whence
they bring pepper, silk, raw silk, benzoin (great store)
and gold, and to other islands bringing thence camphor
and aloes-wood ; they go to Tanaçary, Peeguu, Bengala,
Paleacate, Charamandel, Malabar and Cambaya, so much
so that this city of Malaca is the richest seaport with
the greatest number of wholesale merchants and
abundance of shipping and trade that can be found in
the whole world. Gold comes thither in such abundance
that the leading merchants dealing in it do not
value their estates nor keep their accounts except in
bahares of gold, which *bahares*[4] are four *quintals* each,

---

[1] This is from Ramusio. The Spanish version has "like *ceutis*
of Portugal pierced in the middle." For the *ceitil* see p. 73, n. 1.
The *bagattino* mentioned by Ramusio was a small bronze coin of Venice,
first struck early in the fifteenth century (Hazlitt, *Coinage of the
European Continent*, 1893, p. 184).

[2] " Indians " in Ramusio and the Spanish version.

[3] Ramusio has *aghi*, " needles."

[4] *Bahares and quintals.*   See Vol. I, p. 157, n. 1.

as I have stated in other chapters. There is a certain merchant there who alone will discharge three or four ships laden with every kind of valuable goods and re-lade them alone from his own stock. " They deal also in victuals of various kinds, and all is well paid for and packed. In this city are many foreigners of various lands, who live there and are born in the country ; these as I say are Moors with their own distinct language and are called *Malaios.*" They are well set-up men and go bare from the waist up but are clad in cotton garments below. They, " the most distinguished among them," wear short coats which come half way down their thighs of silk, cloth—in grain or brocade—and over this they wear girdles ; at their waists they carry daggers in damascene-work which they call *crus.*[1] Their women are " tawny coloured," clad in very fine silk garments and short shirts [decorated with gold and jewels]. " They are very comely, always well-attired, and have very fine hair "[Ramusio : They have long hair, well-dressed with jewels on it, and flowers of some kind among them.]

" These Malaios hold the *Alcoram* of Mafamede' in great veneration," they have their mosques ; they bury their dead ; their sons are their heirs ; they live in large houses outside the city with many orchards, gardens and tanks, where they lead a pleasant life. They have separate houses for their trade within the city ; they possess many slaves with wives and children who live apart and obey all their orders. They are polished and wellbred, fond of music, and given to love.

---

[1] This is an early form of the well-known word *Kris.* Ramusio and the Spanish version have *Querix.* *Cf.* Crawford, *Indian Archipelago* (1820), Vol. I, p. 224 and plate, p. 221. Also Swettenham, *British Malaya,* pp. 146 and 191 and plate. p. 210.

There are here also merchants [*Chetijs*] of Chara-mandel who are very corpulent with big bellies, they go bare above the waist, and wear cotton clothes below.

There are also many *Jaos* living here, who are short stunted men with broad ill-formed chests and wide faces ; they are Moors, they go naked being clad below the waist in cotton garments which they bundle up round them roughly; they wear nothing on their heads and have their hair crisped and standing out on the top [stiff and crisped with care, and some of them shaven]. They are very cunning in every kind of work, skilled in every depth of malice, with very little truth but very stout hearts [and are ready for every kind of wickedness]. They have good weapons and fight without fear. If anyone of these *Jaos* falls sick of any illness he makes a vow to his God that if he restores him his health he will seek out another more honourable death in his service ; and after that he is whole he takes a dagger in his hand with certain wavy edges which they have among them of very good quality, and going forth into the places and streets he slays whomsoever he meets, men, women or children letting none go ; these men they call *Guaniços*,[1] and when

---

[1] *Ganiço or Amouco.* This is probably the first instance of any name being assigned by a European writer to the practice generally known as *Amouco* or *A-muck*, and it is remarkable that in this account that term, which shortly after Barbosa's time was universally employed, is not used. Instead we have the word Guaniço (read Ganiço) which Mgr. Dalgado in his *Glossario Luso-Asiatico* (*s.v. Amouco*, n. 1, on p. 34) states is from the Malay *ganas*, "man-slayer." Here we have an undoubtedly Malay term, while the probabilities seem to be that *Amouco* may be traced to the Skr. *amōkshya*, "which cannot be loosed," and therefore had its origin in India. The whole question has been fully discussed in *Hobson-Jobson* in both editions, *s.v. A-muck*, and more recently by Mgr. Dalgado in the work just quoted, who has noted that in *Hobson-Jobson* the form *Amuco* used in Stanley's translation from the Spanish has been quoted instead of the form *Ganiço*, and has been taken as evidence that the word was used in Malaysia before the arrival of the Portuguese. Ramusio has evidently taken his *Amulo* from the Spanish *Amuco*; the *l* having taken the place of the *c*.

It seems very probable that this word was inserted in the Spanish

M

they see one of them the folk forthwith begin to cry out "*Guanicio*" that men may be on their guard, and with arrows and spears they slay him.

This city of Malaca abounds in fruits and good water ; its chief supply of victuals comes by sea from outside. Its King was a great Lord with great treasures and revenues. [He made the Lord of Paam tributary to him, who had been formerly a lord in the Kingdom of Siam, against which he rose and in this land of Paam there is much gold of low quality.] [1]

The King our Lord sent an order to have this land (of Malaca) explored by Diogo Lopes de Sequeira, a gentleman of his household ; and after he had discovered it the King and the Moors thereof took by treason certain of our men and much merchandize, and slew many of them.   Afonso D'Alboquerque who at that time was

---

version to replace Barbosa's original *Ganiço* after the term *Amouco* had become well known. The first undoubted use of *Amouco* by a Portuguese writer seems to be in the *Peregrina;do* of Fernão Mendez Pinto (see quotations in *Glossario*). The events alluded to are dated 1545 and 1546, and the account was no doubt written after Pinto's arrival at Lisbon, 1558. It is noteworthy therefore that Castanheda writing in 1551 uses another Malay word, *Chaver*, which he says (see quotations *ib.*) "in our language means *dead*, but in India they are generally called *Amoucos.*" Mgr. Dalgado explains *Chaver* by the Malay *shávurra*, "ready to die," and *shávurravan,* "one determined to die fighting."

Now Correa, although he did not finish his work till 1563, is a good witness for events that came under his own notice at earlier dates. His account of the events at Calicut in 1503 (I, p. 364), which occurred a few years before he arrived in India, is no doubt based on the accounts of eye-witnesses, and may be considered as good evidence of the use of the word *amouco* at that time at Calicut. He also gives an instance of its use in Malacca in 1511 (II, 286). There is other good evidence among later writers that the word was in use in Malabar, and on the whole it seems most probable that it found its way to Malacca from India, but did not displace the original Malay terms at once. Whether the Portuguese brought the word with them or whether it had reached Malaysia at an earlier date it is impossible to decide. It is worthy of note that Barbosa attributes the custom to the Javanese and not to the Malays of Malacca. Crawfurd speaks of it as widely spread among all the islands of the Archipelago, especially Celebes (*Indian Archipelago*, 1820, Vol. I, pp. 65-71).

[1] This passage regarding Paam (Pahang) is from Ramusio. The Spanish version has a similar mention. Barbosa mentions it below.

Captain General of India came up against the city with his fleet to demand a reckoning of him for this, and not being willing to discuss terms with him he attacked the city and took it by force of arms, driving the King out from it ; who defended himself with his folk and fought very bravely with abundance of artillery, guns, poisoned arrows and excellent long spears, also with valiant men of Jaoa, and many elephants equipped with wooden castles with fighting men therein after the custom of India. In this assault a great number of Moors were slain and the King fled and with him those who escaped from the fight. The merchants submitted to remain in the city in subjection to the King our Lord, and no injury whatsoever was done unto them.

Forthwith a very fine fortress was built there, which with the city and all the trade thereof and its naviga-tion remained subject to the Portuguese, who took here a rich booty, and obtained great wealth from the inhabi-tants who remained there [and all the trade of the mer-chants was restored to its former condition before the town was taken].

To this city and Kingdom of Malaca is subject the province of Pam[1] which has its own individual King, who was formerly subject to that of Ansiam against whom he rebelled ; and there is much base gold there. The King thereof, perceiving that Malaca had become subject to the King our Lord, sent an embassy and presents to Afonso D'Alboquerque, as he wished to follow the same course.

---

[1] *Pam.* Pam or Pão represents the name Pahang, a state on the East side of the Malay Peninsular which takes its name from the Pahang River. It has since 1888 been included in the Federated Malay States (Swettenham, *British Malaya*, p. 270). Gold-mining is still pursued, but is now exceeded by the production of tin.

The correct reading of the passage in the text is doubtful. Literally translated it would read " This city and Kingdom of Malaca is subject

§ 111.   ARCHIPELAGO OF MALACA.[1]

THROUGH the sea of this city of Malaca there is along the coast a string of many beautiful islands, very rich and fertile of Moors and Heathen (besides other small peoples which dwell there) ; which begins at the Island of Ceylon.

to the province of Pam which has its own independent King," which is in contradiction to the actual fact.   The passage in brackets on p. 178 from Ramusio and the Spanish version on the contrary asserts that the Lord of Paam was tributary to the King of Malaca, and this appears to be the fact.   At the time of the Portuguese conquest he was actually present in Malacca where he had come to make preparations for his marriage with the King of Malacca's daughter (De Barros, *Dec. II*, Bk. **vi**, Ch. 3, f. 139 rev.).   It would seem therefore that the text should be amended as it has been translated above by the insertion of the preposition *a* (to) before the words *Esta cidade e regno de Malaca, etc.*

[1] The Archipelago of Malaca probable includes all the islands in the Southern part of the Bay of Bengal, certainly the Nicobars (the Nacabar of § 112), and perhaps the Andamans as well, and other islands on the Western coast of the Malay Peninsula from Junk Ceylon to Penang, and in the Straits of Malacca.   The Nicobars were well known from an early period as one of the stages or land-marks on the voyage from China to India.   Under the T'ang dynasty Yi-tsing, whose travels have been translated by M. Ed. Chavannes ("Memoire composé à l'époque de la grande dynastie T'ang sur les religieux, etc.," Paris, 1894, quoted in *Malaka*, p. 92), followed the following route: Canton, Palembang in Eastern Sumatra, Maloyu (probably according to M. Ferrand, *ib.*, p. 94, the Jambi River on the North-east coast of Sumatra) Kedah, and " the land of naked men," *i.e.* the Nicobars. Thence the usual route lay straight to Ceylon.   Although the dress of the Nicobarese was very scanty perhaps absolute nudity was more characteristic of the Andamans, but the Nicobars were on the direct route and afforded good anchorages.   Hamilton, *East Indies*, II, pp, 69–72, gives a good description of the islands and people, and found them all able to speak a " little broken Portuguese," so that they were evidently accustomed to visits from the outer world at the end of the seventeenth century.   He describes their attire as follows : " The Men's Clothing is a bit of string round their Middle, and about a Foot and a half of Cloth six inches broad tucked before and behind within that Line.   The Women have a Petticoat from the Navel to the Knee and their Hair close shaved, but the Men have the Hair left on the upper Part of the Head, and below the Crown, but cut so short that it hardly comes to their Ears."   At about the same period (1695) the Nicobars became the resort of a band of pirates, and thence commanded the routes to the Straits of Malacca and to Pegu and Mergui (Anderson, *English relations with Siam*, p. 389 and note 1).   These pirates were of different races but mainly Dutch.   The legend of the Island of Gold appears to have been transferred from the Andamans to the Nicobars, and Careri in his *Giro del Mondo* (quoted by Anderson, *ib.*, pp. 30–31, note 4) gives this as the reason why the Dutch appropriated these islands towards the end of the seventeenth century.   Possibly

§ 112. THE ISLES OF NACABAR.

PASSING the island of Ceylon, and crossing the Gulf before arriving at the [great Island of Sumatra there are five or six] isles which have very good water and anchorages for shipping, inhabited by poor Heathen ; these are called Nacabar.[1] The dwellers therein get much ambergris which is taken to Malaca and other places.

§ 113. THE VERY GREAT ISLAND OF ÇAMATRA.

GOING yet further out and leaving these Isles of Nacabar twenty leagues to the South is the great and beautiful Island of Çamatra,[2] which is seven-hundred leagues in

---

there is some connection between this and the prevalence of Dutch among the pirates.

These islands are shown correctly in Ribero's map of 1529 as *Yaf de Nicobar*.

Thomas Bowrey in the course of his voyages in the Bay of Bengal seems never to have visited the Nicobars, although according to the traveller Dampier he once proposed to make a journey there from Achen, taking Dampier with him, but was forced by bad weather to put back (Dampier's *Voyages*, I, 503 f., quoted in *Countries round the Bay of Bengal*, Ed. Sir R. Temple p. xxxviii).

[1] *Nauacar*, Ramusio ; *Niconber*, the Spanish version.

[2] Barbosa shows a considerable knowledge of the eastern and northern coasts of the great island of Sumatra, the northern part of which became known to the Portuguese from the first days of their expedition to Malacca. Indeed Alboquerque before actually attacking the latter had visited Pedir and Páseh and had had certain dealings with the rulers of those states. Pedir was on the Straits nearly opposite to Malacca, and had long been famous in India as one of the principal entrepôts for pepper. Varthema claimed to have visited it as well as Malacca a few years before, and his account must have been well-known to Alboquerque. Varthema's estimate of the circumference of Sumatra as 4,500 miles is extravagant, and shows the imperfect knowledge prevailing of the real size of the island. Barbosa's 700 leagues is more moderate and closer to the truth. His allusion to the Moors who had " sailed round it on both sides " shows that his information was derived at least in part from the Arab or semi-Arab sailors and merchants who had long been familiar with the Eastern Archipelago. The Portuguese had as yet acquired no knowledge of the Western or rather South-western coast, and their information extended only to the North-eastern coast along which ships passing through the Straits of Malacca must pass. All the ports mentioned in the text are on that coast.

circuit as reckoned by the Moors who have sailed round
it on both sides. [It runs from North-west to South-
east and the Equinoctial line passes through the middle
thereof, and it abounds in victuals of every kind.] It
has many very prosperous seaports, the more part of them
occupied by Moors but some by Heathen,[1] but for the
most part the Heathen dwell inland.   One of the Moorish
ports is called Pedir[2] on the North side towards Malaca

---

[1] *Moors and Heathen.* The statement that the Moors mostly
occupy the seaports while the Heathen, or Aboriginal tribes who have
not adopted Islam, are found in the interior is true even now, and
in the sixteenth century exceptions to the rule were very few.
Marsden who wrote his *History of Sumatra* in 1780 remarked (p. 280)
that Menangcabow was an exception to this rule, its people " are all
Mahometans and in that respect distinguished from the other internal
inhabitants of the island." De Barros also observed that the Heathen
retired from the coast into the inland parts of the island (*Dec. III,
v, 1, f.* 119 and 119 rev.).

[2] *Ports mentioned by Barbosa.* Barbosa commences his list of
ports with Pedir on the North coast, not as might have been expected
with the celebrated town of Acheh or Achin which is situated at the
extreme North-western point of the Island, the reason being probably
that Alboquerque's visit to the coast of Sumatra had dealt with Pedir
and Pāseh only.

Pedir was the capital of a famous Kingdom, but was on its
decline.   De Barros (*III, v, 1, f.* 120) says: " Of all these
Kingdoms that of Pedir was the greatest and most famous in
those regions, and was so before Malacca was inhabited.   In it came
together what went from the west and came from the east by reason
of the emporium and market where goods of all kinds could be found,
and because that city commanded the strait between this island of
Samátra and the mainland.   But after the foundation of Malacca,
and especially at our entry into India, the kingdom of Páçem began
to grow and that of Pedir to decline.   And that of Achem its neighbour
being (then) but of little power is now the greatest of all ; such are the
variations in States of which mankind makes so much account."
The fame and wealth of Pedir were no doubt due, as Barbosa and
other writers have asserted, to its being the principle source of supply
for pepper, a condiment which was so greatly valued by the nations
of the East and West.   The Northern part of the Island of Sumatra,
the Lāmuri of the Arabs, was the country where it was found in the
greater perfection.   This was the ancient country of Sumatra, from
which the name gradually spread to the whole island.   Friar Odoric who
visited the coasts of Sumatra soon after A.D. 1320 names the kingdoms
of Lāmuri and Somoltra, the latter of which he places more to the South.
For a full consideration of the points involved reference should be made
to the notes in Yule and Cordier, *Cathay,* Vol. II, p. 148 f.   The Chinese
knew Lāmuri at least as early as 1349 (which is the date of the *Tao i
chih lio*).   Lāmuri took the forms *Nan-wu-li* and *Nan-po-li,* and
Sumatra *Su-mĕn-ta-la* and *Hsü-wĕn-ta-la.*   Pepper is mentioned as
the chief product of *Su-mĕn-ta-la* in the *Hsing-ch'a shĕng lan* (A.D. 1436),
but neither the earlier Chinese work named nor Friar Odoric seems to

where most excellent pepper grows in abundance and

have mentioned it (W. W. Rockhill, *Notes on the Relations and Trade of China*, Part II, T'oung-Pao, Vol. XVI (1925), pp. 148–157). These Kingdoms of Northern Sumatra had at an earlier date been subject to the great Empire of Menangkabau. (See Marsden, *History of Sumatra*, 1780, pp. 268-270, and G. Ferrand, *Malaka*, 1918, pp. 99–116.)

Pedir in its later stages shows a gradual decline. Linschoten (I, 110) still speaks of it as " a Towne called Pedir which lyeth 20 miles from Acheijn uppon the coast right over against Malacca, from whence commeth much Pepper and Gold." Peter Mundy (1637–38) who gives a full account of Achin does not mention it (*Travels of Peter Mundy*, Ed. Temple, III, pp. 115–145, and 329–338). Thomas Bowrey also whose account of Achin is very full does not name Pedir (*Countries Round the Bay of Bengal*, Ed., Temple, p. 285 f.). Schouten (quoted in *ib.*, p. 285, n. 1) names it in a list of Kingdoms subject to Achin. A. Hamilton (*New Account of the East Indies*, 1727, pp. 126, 127) says: " Twelve Leagues further West (from Pissang) lies Pedier. It has the Benefit of a good River, but being but eight leagues from Atcheen, it has no Trade."

The name *Sumatra* or *Su-mén-ta-la* according to Mr. Rockhill (*l.c.* pp. 152, 159) was often applied to the port of Achin. Sumatra was possibly used in this sense in the letter attributed to " Juan Serano " (which should be Francisco Serrâo), translated by Lord Stanley (pp. 225-229 of his translation of Barbosa). In this letter he speaks both of the island and of the city of Sumatra. He gives a full description of the harbour and city of Pedir which he considers to be " the best of the island," and then proceeds to Samatra city. If his account is correct as regards direction it is difficult to reconcile it with the actual position of Achin. He says " having left Pedir and gone down, the northern coast I drew towards the South and South-east direction, and reached to another country and city which is called Samatra." Following the North coast from Pedir he would have reached Achin at the extreme western point of the island, and after turning South and South-east along the South-west coast he would have arrived at a point beyond that city. Yule in a note on Odoric's Sumoltra (*l.c.*, p. 149) says that the city of Samudra " is believed to have stood between Pasei and Pedir, near the place now called Samarlanga," but this would not explain the existence of the Samatra of the letter of Francisco Serrâo (or of the author of the letter whoever he was, for its attribution is open to doubt). It may be noted that De Barros in his list of places on the coast of Samatra (*III*, v, 1, f. 119) names Dáya and Lambrij as those nearest to Achin on the South-west coast. Dáya is given in Marsden's map as Dyah. De Barros commences his list with Dáya. His words are: " Beginning at the point of the island furthest West and South, and turning round towards the northern side the first is called Dáya, and those which follow along the coast are Lambrij, Achem, Biar, Pedir," &c.

As to Lambri. Yule says in one of his notes in *Cathay* (*l.c.* p. 146, n. 3), " It appears to have lain near the North-west end of the island, and being on that account probably the first port of Sumatra known to the Arabs, naturally gave its name to the whole. I believe the exact position is not now known, but the list of Kingdoms in Murray's *Polo* pt. iii, Ch. xiv, places it South of Daya."

But De Barros, as has been seen, places it north of Daya, and between that place and Achin. Mr. W. P. Groeneveldt in his *Notes on the Malay Archipelago*, 1877, quoted by M. Cordier in *Cathay*, in a note on the above passage, p. 146, comes to the conclusion after considering the

also in some parts of Bengivī[1] [both long and round], but not as fine or strong as that of Malabar.[2]   Much silk is also produced there, but not so fine as that of China.[3]   There is another which they call Pansem [pacem, Ramusio] [from a city which stands in it[4]] [and another called Pacem[5]

Chinese authorities above alluded to in Mr. W. W. Rockhill's work, that "Lambri must have been situated on the North-western corner of the island of Sumatra on or near the spot of the present Achin. We see that it was bounded by the sea on the North and West." Then after alluding to the identification of the Hat Island of the Chinese with the island of Pulo Weh he adds "we venture to think that the position of Marco Polo's Lambri is definitely settled herewith." Yet it is clear that De Barros's infor-mation, no doubt derived from travellers he had consulted, led him to place Lambri between Daya and Achin. It may have been near the latter place, but not so near as to be confounded with it.

It is clear that the Nan-wu-li or Nan-po-li of the Chinese travellers was a country, as well as a town. The *Tao i chih lio* (Rockhill, *l.c.*, p. 148, *l.c.*) says: "This place is the most important trade-centre of Nan-wu-li," and the *Ying yai shêng lan* (*ib.* p. 149) says: "This country borders on the sea. To the East it adjoins Li-tai, to the North-west it adjoins the sea, to the South it is adjacent to high mountains, and South of (these) mountains it borders the sea." From this it seems to have comprised the mountainous cape running West to the South of Achin, with a coast line both North-west and South of the mountains; and the inference is that it was on the South side, and not in the direction of Achin. It was evidently an exposed and dangerous port, "Great mountainlike waves dash against it" says the *Tao i chih lio*, and ships were warned to avoid its dangers. This may account for its decay and the growth of the good haibour of Achin.

The word Sumatra has been the subject of a good deal of discussion and was exhaustively dealt with in *Hobson-Jobson* (*s.v.* Sumatra) and in Yule and Cordier, *Cathay*, II, p. 149, n. 2. The derivation from the Skr. *Samudra*, "the sea," was approved of by Yule, and has been generally admitted. A late Dutch writer, M. Rouffaer, in *Volkenkunde van Nederlandsch Indie*, V, 74, 1918, p. 138, says "That Samudra (of the Nāgarakrètāgama, XIII, stroph. 2), Sumatra, means 'Ocean island' hardly anyone doubts." But M. G. Ferrand who quotes this passage in *K'ouen-Lou n*, p. 44, n. 2, thinks that there is no connection between the two, and discusses the question on philological and other grounds.

[1] *Bengivi*. This place has not been identified. It seems to be intro-duced here not for its position on the coast but as a place noted for pepper. The Spanish version here has Birahem, also unidentified.

[2] *Sic* in the Spanish version but Ramusio has "as strong as that of Malabar."

[3] *Sic* in the Spanish version. Ramusio omits the comparison with China. Çamatra silk is alluded to in *Lembrança*, p. 46.

[4] These words are used by Ramusio of Pedir.

[5] *Pansem or Pacem*. The next port to Pedir on Barbosa's list is Pacem, the modern Pasay. The printed Portuguese text has Panfem, which I have corrected to Pansem; the substitution of *f* for *s* being an evident blunder (the Spanish version has Paser; Ramusio, Pacem).

by reason of a city which has a most excellent port. Great abundance of pepper grows here and ships take in cargoes thereof. Another is called Achem, also on the North coast, situated on a cape of this island on the fifth degree]. Another is called Campar[1] [opposite

---

This port had, like Achin, been prospering at the expense of Pedir and does not seem to have been mentioned by name by any of the earlier Arab or Chinese travellers. It had now become very powerful, so much so that Castanheda (II, p. 178) says " Pacem was the principal matter in Sumatra, and very important for the trade of Malaca by reason of the pepper." Alboquerque visited Pacem after Pedir, and on sailing thence towards Malacca captured a junk on which he found the banished King of Pacem, called by some Geinal and by Castanheda, Çoltàzina, *i.e.*, Sultan Zina, with whom he made a compact to restore him to his Kingdom on condition of his becoming a vassal to the King of Portugal. The succession to the throne of Pacem seems to have been regulated in an extraordinary manner according to De Barros (*III*, v, 1, f. 120). He says " The Kingdom of Pacem had a new custom, of such a nature that no one would desire to become King thereof, for the people gave him no long time to live. And how unfortunate soever was the heir to this succession, which the people gave to whomsoever they pleased, yet it had one advantage not given to all men, which was to know the hour of his death, and if not the hour the day, for however uncertain it did not go beyond the week. For when this madness or fury broke forth among the people all went out into the streets almost as in a concerted song (*em modo de cantiga*), and there were none to go against this cry which offended the ears of none except those of the King and his friends, who as soon as they heard this death-song assembled themselves with him, and sometimes all perished together."

There seems to have been something in this beyond an ordinary popular outbreak, and it is possible we may have here the remnant of an old ceremony by which one King must be killed to make way for his successor. De Barros goes on to say that it was maintained that this custom was of divine ordinance.

Geinal or Zina soon quarrelled with the Portuguese but ultimately recovered his Kingdom, and a rival prince was put on the throne in 1521 by a Portuguese force under Jorge D'Alboquerque with the assistance of an army from Aru. Geinal was killed in the fighting. Pacem afterwards lost its importance and does not figure as a leading port in later times. It is not mentioned either by Linschoten or Hamilton, but in 1780 Marsden writes " Pasay, once the principal seat of Government of this extreme of the island, is situated in a fine bay called Telloo Samoway where cattle, grain and all sorts of provisions are in plenty " (*History of Sumatra*, p. 291).

[1] *Campar.* In Ramusio and the Spanish version as well as in the Portuguese text Campar follows Pacem, although Aru should precede it owing to its position on the coast. In Ribero's map of 1529 the following names can be read to the east of Pacem : Pulaca, no doubt an island, the first part of the name being the Malay *Pulo. Yas de Pescadores. R' : recà darse.* That is the River Recan of Aru, the River Racan which flows through the Aru country. *Baxas de Campara* or Shoals of Campar. No doubt the group of islands in the Straits of Campar. *Ciaca,* the Siac River. *Compar.*

Malaca], another Andragao,[1] another Măcaboo,[2] which
has much gold, found here, which they take to Malaca
in dust. [Manancbo which is the principal source of
the mined gold found in this island.   It is like that found
on the shores of streams and rivers, a wonderful thing.]

The Campar River and the town which stood on it was the seat of
a considerable Kingdom which was one of the first to become known
to the Portuguese, as the King, who was himself a son-in-law of Mu-
hammad Shah the deposed King of Malacca was the first of the neighbouring rulers to offer his submission to the King of Portugal after
Alboquerque's conquest of Malacca, coming himself to Malacca to do so.
(Castanheda, II, p. 218 ; De Barros, *II*, vi, 7, f. 150 rev.)

Campar was one of the regions over which the powerful Kingdom
of Menangkabau had been suzerain, and claimed titular rights long after
they had ceased to exist in reality (*Malaka*, pp. 110, 113).   Campar
seems not to have had much trade in later days.   Linschoten (I, p. 110)
mentions it only as a place whence Menangkabau might be approached,
and Hamilton does not mention it.   Marsden (*History of Sumatra*,
p. 290) writing in 1780 says "Campar, another Kingdon once famous,
is fallen into obscurity."   There is now under the Dutch Administration
a district of Upper Kampar (*Malaka*, p. 113).

[1] *Andragao*, corrected from the Andiago of the printed text(the Spanish
version Andraguide; Ramusio, Andragide) is the Indragiri River which
Ribero's map calls Anderagere, and the map in Marsden's *History of
Sumatra*, Indergeree.   Linschoten does not mention it, but the Dutch
had a factory on this river at a later date.   Hamilton (*New Account
of the East Indies*, II, p. 124) says " The Dutch have also a factory on
the river of Andraghira, called Siack, but of no great moment."   There
seems to be some confusion here, as the River Siac is a long distance
west of the Indraghiri, Campar being between the two.   Hamilton also
states his belief that the Dutch factory of Bankalis opposite Malacca
was on a branch of the Andraghira River.   T. Bowrey (*Countries
round the Bay of Bengal*, Ed. Temple, p. 295) speaks of "Jambee, Andro-
geero and Pryaman " which " pay a much slenderer homage to the
Crowne of Achin than formerly they have done," and in his *Malay
Dictionary* (*ib.*, p. 295, note 3) he alludes to Andragheree as a place which
formerly produced large quantities of pepper.   At a rather earlier period
Mandelslo (under the year 1639) speaks of Dedir (Pedir), Campir and
Andragir as ports famous for pepper (*Travels*, Ed. 1669, p. 112).
Marsden (*History of Sumatra*, p. 290) says of the small Kingdoms on
this part of the coast " They are generally at war with the inland people
who confine them to the sea-coast, and in some parts to the mere rivers.
The principal of these are Indrageree, Siak and Battoo Bara.   The
River Racan, situated between the two latter, and which is considera-
bly the largest in the island, is described to be so rapid, and attended with
so great a swell where it encounters the tide at the mouth, as to be unfit
for navigation.   The country of Aru or Rou often mentioned by the
Portuguese historians borders on its banks."

None of the ports on the central portion of the North-east coast
with the exception of Aru appear to have been mentioned by the Chinese
travellers.

[2] *Macaboo* (Măcaboo), the Spanish version Manancabo ; Ramusio
Menancabo, is the great inland Kingdom of Menangkabau, but it seems
certain that the name also applies to the port by which its communica-

There is another Kingdom of the Heathen called [Zunda from a city[1] of the same name in the degree four and three-thirds, on the South coast].   There also is very fine pepper.   There is also another Kingdom called [two kingdoms one called Andragide and the other]

tions with the North-eastern coast were carried on, *i.e.*, Jambi. As to this port Marsden says (*l.c.*, p. 290) that it "was formerly a port of considerable note, and both the English and Dutch Companies had establishments there. The town is situated about sixty miles from the sea on a large river. The trade consists in gold dust, pepper and canes but it is now esteemed of little importance, the gold being mostly drawn to the western coast across the country."

This port seems to have been known from an early date by the same name as the inland Kingdom. In the seventh century, as appears from the Chinese authorities brought together by M. Pelliot, this country bore the name of Malayu, and the port, undoubtedly Jambi, bore the same name. Malayu of Sumatra as distinished from Malayu of the Peninsula was the early name of Menangkabau. The whole subject with quotations from numerous authorities is dealt with by M. G. Ferrand (*Le Malayu de Sumatra*, in *Malaka*, p. 95 f. and *ib.*, p. 119). It seems equally clear that at a later date the name Menangkabau was used for the same port, and it may be concluded that this is the place designated by Barbosa.

The trade in gold-dust is mentioned by many authorities. The Chinese *Ying-yai-sheng lan* (1425-32) speaking of the Jambi River and Palembang says "if one season they till the soil the third season they gather gold." (See Mr. W. W. Rockhill's interpretation in *Notes on the Relations and Trade of China*, T'oung-Pao, Vol. XVI, 1915, p. 1137, n. 1). Mr, Rockhill quotes Ralph Fitch (see Ed. 1899, p. 181) who says "Jamba is an Island among the Javas also from whence come diamants. And the King hathe a masse of earth which is golde : it groweth in the middle of a river ; and when the King doth lacke golde, they cut part of the earth and melt it, whereof cometh golde."

De Barros (*III*, v, 1, f. 119) speaks of "the great quantity of gold which is found there (speaking of Sumatra generally)." Hamilton speaks of gold-dust obtained by washing in the streams brought into Achin (II, p. 108)and also in the same passage alludes to Andraghiry gold. Marsden says (*l.c.*, p. 135) that gold was found mainly in the central parts of the island, being rarely observed "to the southward of Leemoon, a branch of Jambee River, or to the northward of Nalaboo, from which Acheen is principally supplied." He describes the process of digging and washing the earth in the beds of the rivers.

Palembang an important port in the east of Sumatra famous at a later date, is not mentioned by Barbosa, but will be found in Ribero's map (1529) as Paleban, and is included by De Barros in his list of ports (*Dec. III.* v. 1, f. 119, rev.). An embassy from the King of San-fo-ts'i or Palembang is recorded to have been sent to China in A.D. 1017, the earliest date on which Sumatra is mentioned in Chinese annals. This King is called by a Chinese name which M. Ferrand restores as the Kawi form *Haje Sumutrabhumi* or "King of the land of Sumatra " (*K'iouen-Louen*, p. 43).

[1] *Zunda.* This interpolation (taken from Ramusio) is no doubt another form of the Çunda of the next section, turned into a separate Kingdom in Sumatra.

Ara,[1] belonging to the Heathen, who are eaters of human flesh, " and every foreigner whom they can take they eat without any pity whatsoever." [Principally that of those whom they have slain in war.] Beyond this there are other Heathen Kingdoms away from the coast. In some parts of this island much benzoin is found, also long pepper and another kind as well, camphor, ginger, gold, and silk.[2] [And in all these Kingdoms there

---

[1] *Ara, Aru.* The Spanish version, *Haru*; Ramusio, *Auru*. In Ribero's map it appears as Recandaru, *i.e.*, the River Recan of Aru. Marsden (*l.c.*, 290) speaks of the River of Recan or Arracan, and adds " I suspect that this name is an European corruption of the word Aru," but from the entry in Ribero's map this would seem not to be the case. The country of Aru lay upon the banks of the river Racan, and extended inland to the country of the Battas, as Marsden shows in his map. Hence its connection in the text with the " Heathen who are eaters of human flesh," *i.e.*, the cannibal Batta.

Aru was known to the Chinese of the fourteenth and fifteenth centuries as A-lu (Rockhill, *l.c.*, pp. 141, 142, 143, 144, 146, 152, 156). The country seems to have been known chiefly for its aromatic drugs. The Battak or Batta are alluded to as the " tattooed faced " race of whom the earliest mention is in the *Tao i chih lio* (1349) (*ib.*, p. 146). Nothing is however said about their cannibalism. Among European travellers it has been a commonplace ever since the days of Friar Odoric (Yule and Cordier, *Cathay*, II, pp. 148, 149), who was followed by Conti. Varthema ascribes the custom to Java (which he probably never visited). De Barros (*III.* v, 1, f. 119, rev.) says " The Heathen who dwell in that part of the Island which is over against Malacca, and that tribe thereof which they call Battas, who eat human flesh, the wildest and fiercest people in the whole world."

A. Hamilton (1728) heard of these cannibals at another place on the coast between Aru and Pasay, called Delley or Deli, which no doubt was one of the approaches to the Batta country. He says " The inhabitants on that part of Sumatra are said to be *Canibals*. . . . The inhabitants are uncivilized, murdering all whom they can surprise or master" (II, p. 126). Marsden confirms the statement in the text (from Ramusio) that they devour " prisoners taken in war, and offenders convicted and condemned for capital crimes." Their cannibalism seems to have been of a ceremonial nature, and to have been intended as a punishment and probably also as a means of extorting ransom for prisoners of war (Marsden, p. 301).

For the Arab knowledge of cannibalism of Sumatra see " *Relations de Voyages faits par les Arabes et les Persans*" quoted in Yule and Cordier, *Cathay*, Vol. II, p. 148. An account of the Battas based on the latest anthropological information is given in *Man, Past and Present*, A. H. Keane (Ed. 1920 by A. H. Quiggin and A. C. Haddon, pp. 237–8). They are a well organised and semi-civilized community in spite of their " savage survivals from still more ancient times " than those of the Hindu settlers from whom they seem to have derived some of their culture.

[2] The Spanish version adds " wax." Ramusio has not this passage.

DESCRIPÇÃO DA ILHA
DE IAOA

LEGOAS

ILHA
MA

DV

RA

Crimanlaua

I·BANCA   Chinabato

PAR FE

DA IS HA

DE

SAMATRA

Boqueirão
da
Sunda

ANDRE

GVIR

Vshen

Diego de Adus Fecit

Estreito de Bale

Ilha
de
Bale

Estreito de Balembuam

PANE
RVCA   Panarua
OVALE   Balembuam
Piçharuan

DAIA
Iortam

Apas AGASAI

PANIAM
Surabaia

Sidaio
SODAIO
Tuban
TVBAM
CAIOAM
Choriabana
IAPARA
Pati
IDAMO
Dama
Taggal
Charabon
MARGAM
MATAROM
R·CHIAMO   MATAPON

Dermains

Agiada de
Sucde

Carauam
Xeatara
Zariopate
Tangaram

DATO

Chiquide

Padang

LANTAM

Palanban

Imeda

P
A
R
T
E

I
N
C
O
G
N
I
T
A

&
A
I
M
O
Y

Map of Java. From Lavanha's map in Vol. IV of the *Decadas* of J. de Barros, Madrid, 1615, p. 39.

are many and great cities laid out on the level, with straw houses. Those inland are inhabited by Heathen and those on the sea-coast by Moors.] Hither sail many ships in search of merchandize, bringing Cambaya goods which have a good sale here, also coral, quicksilver, vermilion, rosewater and dried fish[1] " which they bring hither from Maldio." The Moors of this island are very treacherous, and ofttimes murder their own Kings and set up others.[2] [They like the Heathen speak the Malaca language.] Here of late the King our Lord has established a new trading factory.

§ 114. ÇUNDA.

AND beyond this aforesaid Çamatra and facing towards Jaoa, lies Çunda,[3] which is but a small kingdom, wherein is great store of pepper. It has its own King who is willing to submit himself to the King our Lord. Here too there are many slaves, and many ships from China get cargoes.

§ 115. KINGDOM OF JAOA.

YET further on, after leaving the island of Çunda but not the sea thereof on the South-western side are many islands, both great and small, among which is one very great

---

[1] Ramusio adds " cinnabar," and omits the last three items.

[2] See the quotation from De Barros under Pansem. *Supra*, p. 184 n. 5.

[3] *Çunda* or *Sunda*, which gives its name to the Straits of Sunda, between Java and Sumatra, was the name given to an island in the straits, but seems to have been originally applied to the west coast of Java. This country was known to the Chinese in A.D. 1225 under the name of *Sin-to* or Sinda, and is included in a list of regions subject to the Kingdoms of San-fo-ts'i or Palembang (Hirth and Rockhill, *Chao-Ju-kua*, p. 62 and M. Ferrand in *Journal Asiatique*, 1919, p. 166). The forms *Sun-to* and *Sun-la* are also found (W. W. Rockhill, *T'oung-Pao*, Vol. XVI (1915), p. 238). Çunda is shown as an island in Ribero's map of 1529, and the Boqueirão de Sunda in Lavanha's map (facing p. 38 in *Decadas IV* of De Barros (Ed. 1615), which is reproduced

which they call Jaoa,[1] the inhabitants whereof are Heathen
in the inland regions but Moors in the sea-havens, who
possess very great towns and villages, yet all are subject
to the Heathen King, a very great Lord whom they call
Pateudra [2] who dwells in the interior.   Some who rise

in this volume, facing p. 190.   The same map shows Java as
divided into two parts by a narrow strait or channel running across
the island from North to South.   The part west of this channel is
given the name of Sunda.   Linschoten also (I, p. 111) speaks of the Strait
taking its name " from a place so called lying not far from thence
within the Isle of Java."   He adds " the principall haven in the Island
is Sunda Calapa, whereof the Straight beareth the name."
    Sunda is described in *Decadas IV*, i, 12 and 13, p. 38, f., where the
author (probably Lavanha) begins by saying that the Kingdom of Sunda
is one of those of the Island of Java.   He explains that in accordances
with reports of sailors he has divided Java into two islands, although
" the Jaos themselves do not make two islands of Java but one of its
whole extent."   He adds that the whole country was divided from
East to West by a chain of mountains, and that nothing was known
of the South side of the island.   The map shows it as " Parte incognita
da Iaoa."   Ribero's map makes no attempt to show the south coast
at all, but shows only the North side.   It may be added that Lavanha's
map though published in 1615 was by no means up to date, and was
based on much earlier materials.   Yet nothing seems to have been
known about the South side of the island even in Linschoten's time.
The Dutch had founded Batavia in 1611, a few years before Lavanha's
map was published, and it was probably identical with the Sunda Calapa
of Linschoten, the Calapa of the *Decadas*.   On p. 40 of *Decadas IV* there
is a list of the principal towns in Sunda from Chiamo westward.   Chiamo
is placed at the mouth of the imaginary channel which divided Java
into two parts ; no doubt really the estuary of a river which falls into,
the sea some distance east of Batavia.   This is followed by Xacatara
otherwise Caravam (both are given separately on the map), Tangaram,
Cheguide, Pondang and Bantam.   In the middle (on the map between
Tangaram and Cheguide) is Daio, on a river some way from the sea,
which is said to have been the principal town of the island, but to
have much decayed afterwards through war.   Bantam was a thriving
town on the Straits of Sunda, and became one of the principal trading-
centres for the Portuguese, and afterwards for the English and Dutch.
Xacatara or Jacatra was selected by the Dutch as their centre in 1611,
and after they had taken the town in 1619 they founded there their
new capital of Batavia (Crawfurd, *Indian Archipelago*, II, p. 417).

    [1] *Jaoa* is the form used for Java throughout; the older Java Major had
gone out of use and Java Minor, once used for Sumatra, was transferred
to the island of Sumbawa.   It is evident from Barbosa's omission
to mention any of the towns in Java that he had no personal knowledge
of the island, and indeed when he left India the Portuguese had very
little knowledge of it.   With the Jaos or Javanese as a race he was
evidently acquainted, and this knowledge could easily have been
acquired at Malacca.

    [2] *Pateudra*.   This name or title is given in the Spanish version as
Patevdara and in Ramusio as *Pateudora*, which should no doubt be read
Pate Udora.   Pate is evidently a title and Udara or Udora a personal
name.   A similar use of Pate may be noted in Patequatir, a Javanese

up against him he subdues again forthwith.   And some folk bear a great hatred to the Portuguese, while others wish for peace and amity with them.

This island of Jaoa is famed to be the most fruitful island in the world ; therein is abundance of good rice ; flesh meat in great plenty ; sheep, cows, hens, goats, swine of great size both tame and wild, all in great numbers. They have the custom of salting the flesh of deer and kine.   In this island too grow pepper, cinnamon, ginger, *Canna fistula* (*i.e., Cassia fistula*) in abundance, gold also is found.

The inhabitants[1] are stout broad-chested men with

who played a part in Malacca history after Alboquerque's conquest. (His name is transformed into Quatepatir in some passages of Castanheda.) Probably Pate Udora is identical with the Pate Unuz who allied himself with Patequatir against the Portuguese, as is related by De Barros, *II, ix*, 4, f. 207 and Castanheda, II, Ch. 100, p. 334. He is described in the *Decadas* as " the chief Lord of the city of Japára by name Páte Unuz, who afterwards made himself King of Çunda." Castanheda calls him " Lord of Japora in the Island of Jaoa " and " a very powerful nobleman who had been a vassal of the Heathen King of Jaoa against whom he and other Moorish Lords rebelled, who called themselves Kings."   Both historians relate how he encountered the fleet of Fernão Perez D'Andrade and fled to his own country after suffering some losses.   Correa also gives an account of these events under the year 1512 (Vol. II, p. 276, f.).   He gives the name of the Javanese leader as Pateonuz, and calls him simply " a powerful Moor." Raffles (*Hist. of Java*, Ed. 1830. Vol. I, p. xiv) gives the name as Pátch Unrug.   Considerable extracts from De Barros and De Couto as to Portuguese dealings with Java are translated in *ib.*, pp. xv–xxi. See also Crawfurd, *Eastern Archipelago*, II, p. 489.   He gives the name as Pati Unus. Japara is shown on the map in *Decadas IV* on the North coast in the Eastern portion of Java.   It also appears as Jopara in Ribero's map of 1529.

[1] *The Javanese.*   The description of the Jaos or Javanese here given follows to a great extent what has been said above of the same race under Malacca (p. 177).   Barbosa's description is followed very closely by Castanheda in his account of these peoples (*Historia*, Vol. II, pp. 216–218), and it can hardly be doubted that he had Barbosa's account before him when he wrote.   De Barros (*II, ix*, 4, f. 206, 207) says " (Java) is for the most part inhabited by a race of idolaters called *Jaos* from the name of the land, the most civilized people in these parts, who, according to what they themselves say, came from China to settle here : and it would seem that they speak truly, for in their appearance and in the manner of their civilization they follow the Chijns closely, and also have fenced cities, ride horses and deal with governance of the land as they do."

This comparison is undoubtedly based on reality.   Anthropologists

wide faces, the most part of them go bare from the waist up, whereas others wear silk coats which come halfway down their thighs. Their beards are plucked out as a sign of gentility, their hair is shaven in the middle over the top of the head, they wear nothing on their heads, saying that nothing ought to be over the head ; the greatest insult [1] among them is to put the hand on any

are generally agreed that the races of Java, that is the Javanese proper, Sundanese and Madurese as well as the Malays proper, belong to the Oceanic branch of the Southern Mongolian stock, who at some prehistoric period migrated from the Tibeto-Chinese region through Further India by the Valleys of the Irrawaddy, Salwin, Menam and Mekong into the Malay Peninsula and the Sunda Islands. Their descendants are known as Malayan or Proto-Malayan and thus distinguished from the Malays proper, a more specialized branch of the same race. The resemblance to the Chinese is therefore not imaginary, but is due to derivation from the same stock, and not to descent from the Chinese themselves (*Man, Past and Present*, Ed. 1920, p. 220, f. A. C. Haddon, *Races of Man*, 1909, p. 14. *K'ouen-Louen*, G. Ferrand, 1919, p. 227, f.).

M. Ferrand in his K'ouen-Louen has traced the history of the migrations of this stock from Chinese, Annamite and Arab sources and has identified it with the K'ouen-Louen of the Chinese, the Khmer of Further India and the Komr of the Arabs whom he traces through Further India to the islands of the Archipelago, and thence to Madagascar. The connection between Java and China seems to date back to the year A.D. 132 when the King of Java sent an embassy to an Emperor of the Later Han dynasty. In the account of this embassy (Pelliot, *Deux itinéraires*, p. 266) Java is given the name of Ye-tiao (old Javanese *Yawadwīpa* , Skr. *Yavadvīpa*), and the King of Java is called Tiao-pien (old Javanese *Dewawarman* ; Skr. *Devavarman*). These Indian names are evidence that the Indianising process had already made progress in Java (*K'ouen-Louen*, p. 125).

The establishment of the Hindu and the Buddhist religion in Java is well established by abundant evidence and by the magnificent buildings and sculptures still existing. The Heathen Kings and tribes still held their own in many parts when the Portuguese first visited the island, although the conversion to Islam had for some time been in progress.

[1] *An insult to put the hand on any one's head.* The Chinese author of the *Ying yai shêng lan* (1425–32) alludes to this notion of the sanctity of the head. " When in a crowd anyone strikes another's head (*lit.*, ' offends against his head ') or starts a brawl the other strikes him with the dagger he carries in his belt " (W. W. Rockhill, *Notes on the Relations and Trade of China*, T'oung-Pao, Vol. XVI, 1915, p. 240 and Note 1).

A note on p. 40 of *Decadas IV*, i, p. 12 (probably from Do Couto) says " These Jaos are proud, courageous and bold, and so revengeful that for the least offence (and they hold it the greatest of all to lay the hand on the head) they become *amoucos* to obtain satisfaction."

Castanheda, who follows Barbosa very closely in his description of the people of Java, has the following passage :—

" The greatest oath they take is on the head, for they say that

man's head. Nor do they build houses of more than one storey, so that none may walk over the heads of others. They are extremely proud, passionate and treacherous, and above all very cunning. They are very clever at cabinet-making. Other trades which they follow are the making of firelocks and arquebusses, and all other kinds of firearms ; they are everywhere much sought after as gunners. Besides the *junks* which I have already mentioned they have well-built light vessels [1] propelled by oars, and in these some of them go out to plunder, and there are great pirates among them. They are also very cunning locksmiths, and they make weapons [2] of every kind very firm and strong and of good cutting steel. They are also great wizards and necromancers, and make weapons at certain hours and moments saying that he who carries them cannot die at the edge of the sword, and that they kill whensoever they draw blood, and of others they say that their owners cannot be vanquished when carrying them. Sometimes they will spend twelve years in making certain of these weapons, awaiting

---

nothing may be put upon it, and they slay any man who lays his hand thereon ; and that none may walk above the heads of others they build no houses with an upper storey '' (II, p. 216).

[1] *Shipbuilding.* It would seem from the description given by Crawfurd (*Indian Archipelago*, I, p. 193) that the art of shipbuilding had declined since Barbosa's day except in the case of the lighter vessels propelled by oars (prahus). Their larger vessels apparently occupied a high rank in the east, and they must have been able to build good ships of considerable size to carry out their long voyages of an early period. Their four-masted junks have been alluded to above (p. 173). The excellent representation of a large ship in one of the reliefs of Boro-Budūr (a scene from a Buddhist Jātaka) shows great familiarity with the art. It is not necessary to assume that this must have been an Indian vessel as has been done by Mr. H. G. Rawlinson in his *Intercourse between India and the Western World* (1916) and by Mr. Schoff (*Periplus*, p. 245), as the Javanese were experienced navigators and built large ships.

[2] *Weapons.* Crawfurd (*ib.*, p. 191) refers to the skill of the makers of weapons, especially spears and *krises*, of which he says there are fifty-four distinct names in the Javanese language. As to the value placed on special weapons among Malays in general see the remarks on the '' lucky dagger '' in Swettenham's *British Malaya*, p. 146.

N

a favourable day and conjunction for the purpose. These the Kings value greatly and keep in their possession.

Among them also there are many skilful riders and hunters ; they have plenty of good riding-horses and nags and very many and excellent birds of prey ; when they go a-hunting they take their wives with them in horse-waggons which are excellent and fair to see with coaches finely wrought in wood. Their women are exceedingly fair with very graceful bodies ; their countenances are broad and ill-featured. They are great musicians and sempstresses who are very cunning in work of every kind, and are given to love-enchantments.

---

§ 116. JAOA THE LESS.

BEYOND this Island of Greater Jaoa there is another Island which also is very large and fertile and well-furnished with victuals of all kinds. It is peopled with Heathen, and the King also is Heathen. This Island among them is called Cinboaba,[1] but the Moors, Arabs and Persians call it the Lesser Jaoa.

---

[1] Cinboaba (Spanish version, Sumbava ; Ramusio, Ambaba). Oçape (Spanish version, Oçare ; Ramusio, Nucopara). The identity of this island is doubtful. The Spanish version inserts " five leagues to the east," which is not found in Ramusio and probably has no more authority than other similar statements as to distance. Stanley has the following note :—" Java Minor, Ortelius, now Bali, the inhabitants are still pagans ; the island Sumbawa also in Ortelius is not the same as Java Minor but apparently the one here called Oçare as it contains a great volcano."

There can however be little doubt that the island of Cinboaba (corrected from the Cindoaba of the printed text) was really Sumbava. The distance of " five leagues to the East of Java " was certainly not in the original MS., and there is no reason to believe that anything about Bali was known to the Portuguese when Barbosa wrote. If they had heard of it they would have believed it, like Madura, to be in effect part of Java. The fact that it is now known as having preserved a form of Hinduism would not have given it any special claim to notice, as in the early part of the sixteenth century that religion still survived in many parts of Java.

Lord Stanley's note quoted above does not give any good ground for identifying Java Minor with the little volcanic island of Oçape. The

Beyond this is yet another small Island called Oçape[1] in the midst whereof fire is ever burning. Its people are Heathens who travel on horseback and are good riders. "The women wear *Suruces*"[2]; they are great cattle-breeders.

---

§ 117. THE ISLAND OF TIMOR.

GOING yet further after passing these Islands of Jaoa the Greater and the Lesser there are in that sea many other Islands both great and small inhabited by Heathen with some Moors. Among these is one which they call Timor,[3] which has its own independent King and

---

name had for long been applied to Sumatra, but after the name of Sumatra had been recognized as that of the great island, another of the smaller islands beyond Java began to be known as Java Minor. Among others Linschoten (I, p. 114) uses it like our author for Sumbawa. Sumbawa itself is noted for one great volcano, Tambora, noted for its terrible eruption in 1815 when it lost one-third of its height, which is still 9,025 ft. (See *Encyclopædia Britannica, s.v.* Sumbawa, Raffles Hist. of Java, 2nd Ed. I, 29, and Wallace, *Malay Archipelago*, 1869, I, p. 5).

[1] Oçape may with great probability be identified with the little island of Gunong Api near the N.E. coast of Sumbawa, not far from the strait between that island and Flores, which is shown by Wallace in his map of the Volcanoes of the Archipelago as still active (*l.c.*, map facing I, p. 10). Gunong Api is the Malay name for a volcano, and is also applied to a small island in the Banda group (*infra*, p. 197, n.1). The termination *Api*, "fire," shows that its name had some relation to its volcanic character. It may be traced perhaps in the name of the islands called Sappi by A. Hamilton (*East Indies*, II, p. 136 and map facing p. 127). He gives it to a small island in the straits (approximately the island of Komodo), but it may well have applied to the neighbouring Gunong Api. He had not himself been further east than Java.
Ocape in the printed text has been corrected to Oçape.

[2] *Suruces*. This name for a garment has not been traced elsewhere and is not given in the Spanish version or Ramusio. It may very probably be a form of the Malay *Sárong*.

[3] Timor was known to the Chinese for some centuries before the arrival of the Portuguese in the Eastern Archipelago. It is mentioned under the name of *Ti-mĕn* in several works and appears in the list of countries in the *Tao-i-chih lio* (1349) (W.W. Rockhill, *T'aung Pao*, xvi, p. 66).
The Portuguese obtained some knowledge of the island early in the sixteenth century, but there is no early authority for the statement made in later works that they made a settlement at Lifau in 1520. De Barros in his account of Magalhães (III, v, 10 f. 152, 153) says that the Victoria after the death of the leader was guided by a Portuguese traitor João de Lourosa to the island of Banda to obtain mace and to Timor for sandal-wood. The expedition arrived at Timor but

tongue. In this Island there is abundance of white [1] sanders-wood " which the Moors in India and Persia value greatly, where much of it is used. In Malabar, Narsyngua and Cambaya it is much esteemed." The ships " of Malaca and Jaoa " which come hither for it bring in exchange axes, hatchets, knives, swords, Cambaya and Paleacate cloths, porcelain, coloured beads, tin, quicksilver, lead and other wares, and take in cargoes of the aforesaid sanders-wood, honey, wax, slaves and also a certain amount of pepper which grows in that land. [For " pepper " the Spanish version and Ramusio read " silver ".]

§ 118. THE ISLES OF BANDAM.

AND yet further on, after leaving the Island of Timor, are five Isles near one to the other, which form as it were a roadstead in which junks are moored ; which enter

---

sailed along the coast without landing, and made its way through the Straits of Solor into the open sea. Pigafetta however says that it anchored off a port and had communications with the people (Ramusio, I, f. 368 rev.). Castanheda mentions Timor as having been seen by the Castilians, and adds that two of them deserted there, from which it would seem that they must have anchored off the coast (III, p. 21).

The Portuguese made Lifau their capital, but transferred it to Dili in 1618. In the same year the Dutch made a settlement at Koepang in the western part of the island. Ever since then it has continued to be divided between Portugal and Holland, the former holding the eastern and the latter the western part of the island.

[1] Sandal-wood seems to have been the only valuable commodity found in Timor. Garcia da Orta, whose *Colloquies on the Simples and Drugs of India* was published in 1563, says that Timor produces sandal-wood in abundance, but not the red kind. The yellow was the best that could be found, and ambergris also was collected in small quantities. See also Linschoten (I, p. 114 ; II, p. 102) who says "there are 3 sorts of Sanders, that is white, yelow and red : the white and the yelow, which is the best, come most out of the Iland of Tymor, which lyeth by Java."

A. Hamilton gives an account of Timor (*East Indies*, II, pp. 139, 140). He says " the product of the Island is Sandal-wood, the best and largest in the World, which is a great commodity in *China*, also Gold and Bees-wax." Wax and honey were already exported in Barbosa's day, but he says nothing of gold, nor does there seem any authority for the silver which the Spanish version and Ramusio have substituted for Barbosa's pepper.

thereinto on both sides. These Isles they call Bandam.[1] Both Moors and Heathen dwell therein. And in three of them grows abundance of nutmeg and mace on certain trees like unto baytrees, whereof the fruit is the nut ; over it spreads the mace like a flower, and above that again another thick rind. One quintal of mace is worth here as much as seven of nutmeg. The abundance is such that they burn it, and it may be had almost for the asking.

---

[1] *The Banda Isles.* This group of very small isles lying to the South of Ceram attracted the attention of the early Portuguese explorers partly on account of its production of nutmegs and mace and partly on account of its excellent harbour, which is correctly described by Barbosa. The principal islands are " Lontor, a sickle-shaped island which with Neira and Gunong Api forms part of the circle of a crater. In the space between these three there is a good harbour with entrances on either side, which enables vessels to enter on either of the monsoons " (*Encyclopædia Britannica*).

The first expedition which reached Banda was that of D'Abreu in 1512, and it afterwards became a centre of Portuguese trade. D'Abreu's principal object was " to obtain cloves at Maluco and nutmegs at Banda, as De Barros has it (*III*, 5, p. 6.). He did not reach Maluco, but found his way to Banda after leaving Amboyna.

The description given by De Barros is as follows :—

" And even as in this name of Maluco are comprehended the five islands each one whereof has its own name, so in this name of Banda are reckoned five other islands near thereto. It is true that the principal of them is called Banda where all the others meet together at a place called Lutatá, for thither resort all the ships which come for the nutmeg trade ; and the others are called Rosalanguim, Ay, Rom and Neira. . . . Because it was in a region where navigation is easy and it was very safe, and in general junks were accustomed to bring hither the cloves grown in Maluco, they did not trouble themselves to go thither for them. . . . The shape of this sland is like a reaping-hook, about three leagues from point to point (which lie north and south) and one in depth. And in the bay which it makes by its form are situated the villages of the inhabitants and the nutmeg trees. In the island called Gunuápe there are no nutmegs but other trees used for timber and firewood, wherein also is a hole vomiting fire like that of Ternate and the Maluco Islands, and for this reason they give it the name ; for Guno means that fire and Ápe is its proper name."

The names given by De Barros are very close to those now used, viz. :—

Lutatá—Lontor.
Gunuápe—Gunong Api.
Neira—Banda Neira.
Ay—Ai or Wai.
Rom—Run.
Rosolanguim : Probably Susoangi.

De Barros was misinformed as to the meaning of Gunuápe. *Gunung* the ordinary Malay term for " Mountain," while *api* means " fire."

Those who come hither to buy it bring Cambaya cloths, some of cotton and some of silk, and much copper, quicksilver, vermilion, tin, lead, certain hairy caps from the Levant, and large bells,[1] for each of which they g.ve twenty *baares* of mace. And of these Bandam Isles over-against Maluquo[2] which lies to the north there are many more, some inhabited and some desert, in all of which they hold to be rich treasures great bells of metal, ivory, *patolas* (that is to say Cambaya cloths) and fine porcelain.

There is no King[3] in these Islands, and they are subject to none, but sometimes they submit to the King of Maluquo.

Castanheda (VI, v, p. 7) gives it correctly as *serra de fogo*. According to the Portuguese historians the remaining ships of the expedition of Magalhães after leaving the Moluccas visited Banda (De Barros, *III*, v, 10, f. 152 rev. ; Castanheda, III, x, p. 21 ; Correa, II, p. 633) but Pigafetta says distinctly that they did not go there because it was distant from the route they were following (*Ramusio*, I, f. 368).

Banda remained in the possession of the Portuguese till the beginning of the seventeenth century when they were expelled by the Dutch, in whose possessions it is now included. Their chief town is on the island of Neira. An English factory was formed on the island of Wai in 1608, but was not long maintained.

[1] *Large bells.* These seem to be the gongs for which Brunei in Borneo was and still is celebrated (Guillemard, *Life of Magellan*, p. 282). But see *infra*, § 202, n. 1, where Barbosa gives a description of these gongs, and says they came from Java. A description of the Java gongs is given in Crawfurd's *Indian Archipelago* (I, p. 339).

[2] *Malaca* in text.

[3] *The seignory of Maluco.* There was evidently some form of suzerainty exercised over all these southern islands by the Sultan of Ternate. This connection probably depended on the trade relations between these islands, which go far to explain the reason why the Portuguese found Banda to be a good market for the products of the Moluccas. The explanation is given by Castanheda who says that the people of the Moluccas had very good war galleys with a hundred or eighty oars on each side, but adds :

" They have no junks or other ships with high sides, for there are no merchants among them, nor any other commodity to take away save cloves only, and these they do not convey as they have no ships for that purpose. Wherefore the men of Banda went thither in their own junks to fetch them, buying them good cheap in exchange for Indian cloths, which were brought to Banda by Malacca merchants who themselves bought nutmegs, mace and cloves in Banda, and would not go to Maluco, as the voyage there cost them double the time spent in going to Banda and returning to Malacca " (VI, xi, p. 26).

§ 119. AMBAM.

ADVANCING yet further and leaving these Bandam Isles, towards Maluquo, there are many Isles called Ambam,[1] inhabited by Heathen, each of which has its own King. In these are many great rowing barks wherein the Moors make sudden raids from one Island to another, making war, and taking captive or slaying one another.

Cambaya cloths are held in great value here, and every man [2] toils to hold so great a pile of them, that when they are folded and laid on the ground one on the other, they form a pile as high as himself. Whoso possesses this holds himself to be free and alive, for if he be taken captive he cannot be ransomed save for so great a pile of cloths.

---

§ 120. MALUQUO.

AFTER passing these Ambam Islands there are five others, close to one another, which they call Maluquo,[3] wherein

[1] *Ambam.* In the printed text this name is given as Andam, but it is certainly a misreading or misprint of an original Ambam, and has been corrected accordingly. Here, as in Çindoaba for Cimboaba and elsewhere, *d* has been substituted for *b*. The name appears in Ramusio as Ambon, which is still used by the Dutch. The Spanish version has Dandon. The form Amboyna or others like it was also in use at an early period. De Barros has Amboino where, he relates, Antonio D'Abreu touched on his first voyage in 1511, and erected a *padrão* before proceeding to Banda (*Decadas, III*, v, 6, f. 137). Linschoten gives the name as Amboyna. He says that the Portuguese had a small fort there, the island had not much spice, but was useful as a port of call for ships sailing from Malacca to Maluco to take in water. This probably gives the reason for the neglect of this island by the early travellers. After the Portuguese had secured the good harbour and the nutmegs of Banda and the cloves of Ternate they had no special reason to go to Amboyna.

In the seventeenth century the Dutch in pursuit of their monopoly policy after exterminating their rivals attempted to make Amboyna the only source of supply for cloves, and deliberately destroyed the clove plantations elsewhere, wherever they had the power to do so (A. Hamiton, *East Indies*, ed. 1727, II, 141). The Amboyna massacre of 1623 was one incident among many of the extremes to which they were prepared to go to ensure their monopoly.

[2] The practice of collecting a bale of cloth of sufficient quantity to meet the sum demanded by custom for ransom does not appear to be alluded to elsewhere.

[3] Maluquo or Maluco is the name by which the Moluccas or Spice Islands were known to the earliest European travellers. They were

grow all the cloves. They belong both to Heathen and Moors : their Kings are Moors. The first[1] they call Pachel, the second Moteu [the third Machiam], the fourth Tidor and the fifth Tanarte wherein dwells a Moorish King whom they call Soltam Binaracola.   He was formerly

known as the only source from which the supplies of cloves found their way to the west and the Portuguese endeavoured to open up communications with them as soon as possible after the occupation of Malacca.   Before returning to India Alboquerque despatched a flotilla under the command of Antonio D'Abreu with Francisco Serrão as second in command (*sota capitão*) and the flotilla started at the end of December, 1511 (Castanheda, III, lxxv, p. 257 ; De Barros, *II*, vi, 7, f. 151.rev. and *III*, v, 6, f. 136 rev.).   D'Abreu was strictly enjoined to avoid all conflicts and to endeavour solely to make friendly arrangements for trade.   A trading junk under a Malay named Ismail was sent on to prepare the way and to collect cargoes of cloves and nutmegs.   After touching at Agacim in Java on the north coast south of the island of Madura as shown in Lavanha's map of Java which accompanies this volume, D'Abreu sailed as far as Amboino (Amboyna) which was under the suzerainty of the Chiefs of Maluco. The ship of Francisco Serrão proceeding towards the Moluccas was wrecked on the island of Luco-Pino.   He rejoined D'Abreu but was again separated from him in a second storm (apparently intentionally) and eventually reached Ternate, where he was well received by the ruler, and apparently was so comfortable that he remained there, not making any effort to return to Malacca (Castanheda, III, p. 289). According to Castanheda it was he who sent the information regarding these islands to Magalhães which was utilized in organizing the expedition which made the first voyage of circumnavigation. Serrão remained on the Island of Ternate until the expedition of Antonio de Brito sent thither by Lopo Soares D'Albergaria in 1520. D'Abreu returned to Malacca and died on his journey back thence to Portugal.

[1] There can be little doubt that Barbosa's information regarding the more Eastern Islands of the Archipelago was obtained from persons who had taken part in this expedition, as D'Abreu returned some years before he left India.   As to his connection with the Serrão family see Vol. I, Introduction, xlvi.   Possibly some information was sent him by Francisco Serrão.   De Barros (*III*, v, 7, f. 143) has noted as a remarkable fact that Francisco Serrão was killed in Ternate almost at the same time as Magalhães met his death in the Philippines.   Whether João Serrão was related or not to Francisco Serrão is not clear.   De Barros gives his name among a list of captains in the fleet of Magalhães " all Castilians by nation " (*III*, v, 8, f. 148 rev.), but the name is Portuguese rather than Spanish, and his identity with the João Serrão mentioned in Barbosa's letter to Dom Manuel (Introduction, Vol. I, *l.c.*) is at least probable.

The remarkable letter which is appended to the Spanish MS. translated by Lord Stanley, of which he gives a translation on pp. 225–229 of his edition, is stated in its heading to relate to a voyage made by Juan Serano (*i.e.* João Serrão), but from its contents it is evident that it refers to Francisco Serrão and not to João, and that the voyage described is that which he made in D'Abreu's company.   How far it was a genuine communication from Francisco Serrão it is not easy to

King of all five, but now the four have risen against him and are independent. The woods of these Islands are all full of certain trees like unto baytrees and their leaves are like those of the *medronho*[1] (arbutus) ; whereon grow

judge. There is no record that D'Abreu sailed to Pegu before starting on his expedition to the islands of the Eastern Archipelago, but it is possible that Francisco Serrão may have made such a voyage before joining D'Abreu. But it is remarkable that the writer never mentions. D'Abreu, and speaks as if his voyage were an independent venture. He says that he returned to Pedir in Sumatra, and thence went to Achin which is evidently the port intended by his " Samatra." For thi identification reference should be made to Mr. W. W. Rockhill's " Notes on the Relations and Trade of China " published in T'oung-Pao (Vol. XVI, 1915, Leiden), especially to the passage and note on p. 152 in which the letter in question from Francisco Serrão is quoted. The name Samatra it is evident was the *Su-mên-ta-la* of the *Ying yai Shêng lan* (A.D. 1425—1432) and the *Hsü-wên-ta-la* of the *Tao i chih lio* (A.D. 1349), and also that the place referred to was Acheh or Achin. The Chinese had been in communication with Sumatra ever since the time of Kublai Khan in A.D. 1282 (*ib.*, Vol. XV, p. 436). From Acheh the writer says " We stood to the east until we reached the Bandan Islands (which would include Amboina) and then went north-east and east-north-east to Malut " (*i.e.* Maluco), and proceeds to relate how the King of Maluco honoured him and gave him his daughter in marriage. Afterwards he returned by way of Borney (Borneo) and Java. Yet according to all accounts Francisco Serrão died in Ternate just before the arrival of Antonio de Brito, and never returned to Malacca. If the letter is genuine it was evidently sent with the object of persuading his Spanish correspondent (or perhaps Magalhães) that he alone was the discoverer of the Moluccas.

The Molucca group. There is some uncertainty as to the exact names of the islands composing this group. They are given by De Barros (*III*, v, 5, f. 133) as Ternate, Tidore, Moutil, Maquie and Bacham. These correspond with Barbosa's names in reverse order, Tanarte, Tidor, Machiam (in *Ramusio*), Moteu and Pachel. In Ribero's map the names Treanata, Tidor, Macil and Machià can be read while another is indistinct. Linschoten gives only Tarnate and Tidor and adds Maluco and Geloulo to the list. A. Hamilton gives a list very close to that of De Barros, *i.e.* Ternate, Tidore, Moutil, Machain and Batchian, and in modern maps Ternate and Tidor still figure as the principal islands in the north of the group, and Batján (in its Dutch spelling) in the south. But the term Molucca Islands has been extended to include Gilolo and the southern group containing Ceram, Boeroe, Amboyna and the Banda Islands. The earlier writers seem to have understood by the term only the line of islands which lie off the west coast of Gilolo from Ternate to Machiam or Batján. Barbosa uses the term for the northern group only, and speaks of the Bandam Islands (§108) as lying to the south of Maluquo. These were the principal object of contention first between the Spaniards and Portuguese, and afterwards between both and the Dutch. The latter remain in possession to the present day, but the clove monopoly for which they fought has gone, and the world is now supplied with all the cloves it needs by Zanzibar and Pemba. (See Vol. I, p. 28, n. 1.)

[1] *Cloves and Sago.* De Barros and Castanheda compare the clusters of the clove to those of the *Madre silva* or honeysuckle (Castanheda

the cloves in clusters like orange or woodbine flowers
It grows very green and then turns white, but when it is
ripe it is of a fine red colour. Then the natives of the land
gather it by hand and spread it out to dry in the sun,
when it turns black ; and if there is no sun they dry it
in smoke-houses. When it is dry they sprinkle it with
a little salt water that it may not become mouldy and may
preserve its full virtues. And of this they gather so great a
quantity in these five islands that it cannot be conveyed
out of the country, as well as much which they leave
ungathered, or which is lost in the forest. If it is not
gathered for three years the trees run wild, and that which
they yield thereafter is worthless.

Hither every year come ships from Malaca and Jaoa
to take cargoes thereof. In exchange they carry thither
copper, quicksilver, vermilion, Cambaya cloths, *cummin*,
some silver, porcelain, metal bells [1] from Jaoa as large as
great basins (*alguidares*), " which they hang up by the rim ;
in the middle they have a handle, and they strike them

VI, xi, p. 23). Crawfurd compares it to the " laurel, and sometimes
the beech." Crawfurd's description of the growth of the clove may
be compared with that of Barbosa from which it does not differ much.
He says " the fruit, at first of a green colour assumes in time a pale
yellow, and then becomes of a blood red colour, if of the most ordinary
variety." (*Indian Archipelago*, I, p. 495.) No mention is made by Barbosa
of the Sago (*Sagum*) which De Barros describes as one of the most important products of the Moluccas (*III*, v, 5, f. 133). Yet it had
been mentioned by Marco Polo and Friar Odoric (see *Hobson-Jobson*,
s.v. Sago) and was well known in the sixteenth century. The name
Sâgū is Malay. This farinaceous pith was an important article of
food in the Eastern Archipelago, in the region of which the Moluccas
are the centre. (Crawfurd, *l.c.*, I, pp. 385–393, where quotations from the
Herbarium Amboinense of Rumphius are also given.) Pigafetta found
it in Tidore in 1521 (*Ramusio*, I, pp. 366 rev.).

[1] *Bells or gongs*. The word *gong* had not found its way into common
use when Barbosa wrote, but the " bells " he describes are evidently
Javanese gongs which were in demand in the whole Archipelago. He
uses the word *alguidar* or basin, and J. de Barros also calls them basins
(*bacias*). The trade was carried on not only in Maluco but Banda
in the manner described by Barbosa. The Conde de Ficalho (quoted
by Mgr. Dalgado (*Glossario, s.v.* gong) says, " It was said that the trade
of Banda was carried on by barter, great quantities of goods being
given for some object, such as 20 *bahares* of mace for a Javanese *gong*."

with some object to make them sound. The Kings and great men set great value on these and keep them both great and small as a treasure and estate. With these and with basins of metal and tin they make themselves music, also with a copper coin[1] with a hole in the middle brought from China, which is like a *ceitil*. And for these goods they give such and such a quantity of cloves. For a bell or a porcelain bowl if it is large they give twenty and thirty *quintals* and for one bell twenty *baares*, and in the same way for most things, and thus great profit is made between this place and Malaca."

The greatest King here is a Moor, who is almost a Heathen. He has a Moorish wife and three or four hundred Heathen maidservants whom he keeps in his palace. Their sons and daughters are Heathen, only those of the Moorish wife are Moors. He is served by hunchbacked women,[2] whom he keeps for display, whose backbones he has broken in their childhood.

He may have five[3] of these, old and young, who always

For other examples of the early use of the word *gong* see *Glossario*, as above; *Hobson-Jobson*, *s.v.* gong; and *Countries round the Bay of Bengal* (Ed. Temple), pp. 195, 196. In Achin, Peter Mundy says, the " gung " was used not only for announcements and to proclaim the time, but as an instrument of music (*Diary of Peter Mundy*, Ed. Temple, Vol. III, Pt. I, p. 123).

[1] The acquaintance of the Chinese with the Moluccas is shown by an entry in the *Tao i chih lio* (Rockhill, *ib.*, Vol. XVI, p. 259). They are described under the name of *Wên-lao-ku* and cloves are mentioned as one of their products. Mr. Rockhill considered that Ternate was probably the island alluded to. That Chinese trade had continued till Barbosa's time may be inferred from the fact that Chinese coins were in demand, as it appears that they were one of the trade exports .from Malacca to the Moluccas (p. 175, n. 1). De Barros also alludes to the Chinese knowledge of the isles and the circulation of their coins (*III*, v. 5, f. 135).

[2] *Women hunchbacks.* I have not been able to find any other account of this custom of making young women into hunchbacks and keeping them as attendants on the King. On the other hand the custom of head-hunting, and wearing the heads of enemies hung round the neck, which Barbosa does not allude to, is mentioned by Castanheda (VI, xi, p. 25).

[3] Ramusio and Spanish version, eighty to a hundred.

go with him and serve him in everything. Some give him *betel*, another carries his sword on feast days. " This King wishes to serve the King our Lord, to whom he offers himself and his slaves. There are here many red parrots of very fine [hue] and very tame which they call *noires*.[1] These are greatly valued among them. "

§ 121. [THE ISLAND OF CELEBE.]

[HAVING passed the said Isles of Maluco [2] certain other islands are found towards the west,[3] whence come at times certain white folk,[4] bare from the waist up, yet they have garments woven from something like straw,

---

[1] This name is given in the Spanish version as *nure* and in Ramusio as *mire*. The bird referred to is the lory ; the name is taken from the Malay *lūrī* or *nūrī*. Several varieties of the *Loriinæ* are included under the name.

[2] Here the Spanish version adds " to the west of Motil and Machian, at a distance of a hundred and thirty leagues."

[3] *Celebes.* This section is missing in the Portugese MS. and has been here translated from Ramusio with which the Spanish version is in agreement. No mention of Celebes is made by Pigafetta or by the other chroniclers of the Spanish expedition after the death of Magalhães. Celebes was the home of two of the most warlike races of the Eastern Archipelago, the people of Macassar and the Bugis, enterprising navigators and pirates.
Neither De Barros, Castanheda nor Correa gives any information as to the route followed by D'Abreu on his return to Malacca from Banda. He arrived at Malacca in November, 1511, according to Correa (II, p. 267). Possibly he may have visited Celebes and Borneo. Crawfurd (*l.c.*, II, p. 384) says that the Portuguese visited Celebes in 1512, and found some Muhammadans at Macassar, but it is not clear whence he obtained this information. The earliest recorded visit in the sixteenth century histories was that of D. Garcia Henriquez in 1525 who made an expedition to the " Ilhas dos Celebes " to obtain gold, but returned without success (Castanheda, VI, Ch. 127, p. 281 ; De Barros, *III*, x, 5, f. 259 rev.). A fusta was despatched under the Almoxarife of the fort at Ternate, but while ashore was attacked by the natives of the island and got away with difficulty. De Barros says that " the islands of the Selebes were so-called from that being the name of the inhabitants." Celebes was not recognised as being one island, but was believed to be a group of several.

[4] *White folk.* The fairness of the people of Celebes has been noted by various travellers. A. Hamilton (*l.c.* II, p. 144) says, " The Natives are of a light olive colour." Raffles describes the aborigines as having " Tartar features " (*Hist. of Java* (1830), Vol. II, Appendix lxxxvi).

wherewith they cover their private parts. They speak a tongue of their own. Their boats are badly built, and therein they come to take loads of cloves in these islands, also copper, Cambaya cloths and tin, and they take thither for sale very long and broad one-edged swords and other ironwork, and a good quantity of gold. These folk are eaters of human flesh, and if the King of Maluco wishes to put to death any person condemned by law they beg for him to be delivered to them to eat as if they were asking for a pig. These islands, from which these and suchlike people come, are called Celebe.]

§ 122. [THE ISLAND OF BANGAYA.[1]]

[NOT very far off from these islands (to the west-south-west, at thirty leagues away, *Spanish version*) there is another inhabited by Heathen, which has its own Heathen King. The inhabitants thereof have, according to my information, a custom which cannot be believed, that is that while they are yet young they saw off their teeth close to the root, where the gums are, saying that by so doing they make them grow the stronger and closer together. This island is called Tendaya (Spanish, Bangaya). Much iron is found there which is taken to divers countries.]

---

[1] It is probable that this section as well as the preceding one was added to the Spanish MS. of Barbosa's book after the results of Magalhães's voyage had become known. The Spanish form Bangaya seems more likely to be correct than the Tendaya of Ramusio. It is undoubtedly the island of Banggi which lies off the northernmost point of Borneo, which must have been passed by the expedition after the island of Palawan (the Pulacan of Pigafetta) on the way to Brunei. It is not mentioned by Pigafetta, who alludes to the little island of Cagayan more to the east and also to Palawan. These places are shown on Ribero's map also. Bengaya does not appear anywhere. Dr. Guillemard in his *Life of Magellan* speaks of the Trinidad and Victoria " passing between the islands of Balabac and Banguey," but this is no doubt intended simply to indicate the probable course followed. It may be that the two islands mentioned by the so-called Genoese pilot in his *Roteiro* are the islands of Balabac and Banggi. He calls them Bolyna and Bandym (*Collecção de Noticias*, iv, p. 164).

§ 123. SOLOR.

AND passing these Maluquo Islands northwards[1] towards China there is another very large island well furnished with food which they call Solor.[2] Its inhabitants are almost white, Heathen with good figures. This island has its own Heathen king and its own tongue. In it there is much gold " which is found in the surrounding lands " [found by washing the earth, and in grains in the rivers], also great store of seed pearls which the inhabitants collect, and good pearls also " perfect in colour but not in roundness," [fine both in colour and roundness].[3]

---

§ 124. ISLES OF BORNEO.[4]

FURTHER on towards China (to the north, *Spanish version*) from this Island of Solor there is another island also well furnished with victuals, inhabited by Heathen with a

---

[1] Spanish version " seventy five leagues to the north-west."

[2] Solor here evidently refers to the Sulu Archipelago and not to the island of Solor in the Lesser Sunda Islands. The name includes not only the chain of islands between Borneo and Mindanao, but also the north-eastern part of Borneo itself, which still bears the name Sulu. The expression " very large island " can only refer to this tract. The islands were skirted by the Spanish expedition on their way to the Moluccas after leaving Borneo, and are called Zolo by Pigafetta. Colo (*i.e.* Çolo) appears in Ribero's map of 1529.

[3] The Spanish version agrees with the Portuguese text but not with Ramusio in saying that the pearls are of good colour but not round.

[4] Borney in the Spanish version. Ramusio has " Bornei, where the camphor grows." Borneo had for many centuries been known to traders from China, Siam and other countries. M. Pelliot in his *Deux Itinéraires*, p. 287, n. 2 (quoted in M. Ferrand's *K'ouen-Louen*, p. 14), states that in the Chinese work *Man-chou*, which dates from A.D. 860, *P'o-ni* or Borneo appears in a list of countries trading with an unidentified port on the Gulf of Siam. M. Pelliot adds that this is the earliest mention of Borneo under this name.

A later work, the *Hsi yang chao kung tien lu* of 1520, a compilation from earlier works, includes *P'o-ni* in a list of 23 countries tributary to China (Rockhill, *Notes on the Relations and Trade of China*. T'oung-Pao, Vol. XVI, 1915, p. 79).

The first recorded visit of Europeans to the coast of Borneo was that of the Victoria and Trinidad which made their way thither from Sebu after the death of Magalhães. They hit upon the north coast which

Heathen king and a language of its own, where is found
great store of edible Camphor,[1] greatly esteemed by the
Indians and worth its weight in silver.   They carry it

---

they skirted till they arrived at the great town of Brunei, from which
the name of the whole island has been taken.

There seems to have been no Portuguese visit to Borneo before 1530,
when Gonçalo Pereira went there on his way from Malacca to Ternate
with orders from the Governor Nuno da Cunha to make arrangements
for trade.   He visited the capital, Brunei, which Castanheda calls
Borneo, and was well received.   Castanheda mentions five principal
cities on the coast as far as it had been explored, Moduro, Ceravâ,
Lave, Tanjapura and Borneo.   The principal products were camphor
diamonds, eagle-wood and provisions.

Tanjapura is probably the Tanjong Sobar of A. Hamilton's map
(l.c., II, p. 127) which is close to Cape Sabar, the south-western point of
the island, and Lave is Lava in the same map, on the west coast south
of Succodana.   The same towns are named by De Barros in his account
of this visit (Castanheda, VIII, xxi, p. 48 ; De Barros, IV, vi, 19, f. 380).

[1] *Camphor* is alluded to in all the accounts of Borneo as its most
valuable product, especially by both the historians quoted above, and
by Garcia da Orta in his *Colloquy* 12.   The latter says " that of the
Borneos is so highly esteemed that one pound of it is worth as much as
a *quintal* of camphor from China."   Linschoten says " this Isle is full
of trees from which Camfora is taken and is the best in all the East."
(I, p. 120.)

An account of the Malayan as distinct from the Chinese camphor is
given by Crawfurd (l.c. I, p. 516).   It is the product of a large tree, *Dryo-
balanops aromatica*, and not of a shrub (*Cinnamomum camphora*), as is
that of China, Japan and Formosa.   The Malay variety found only in
Borneo and Sumatra is much more valuable than the other.   Yule's
very full notes on the subject in *Marco Polo* (Book III, Ch. xi), Yule and
Cordier (*Cathay*, IV, p. 99), and *Hobson-Jobson*, *s.v.* Camphor, should
be consulted.

In the last-named note he says :

" A curious notion of Ibn Baṭūta's (iv, p. 241) that the camphor of
Sumatra was produced in the inside of a cane, filling the joints between
knot and knot, may be explained by the statement of Barbosa that
the Borneo camphor as exported was packed in tubes of bamboo.   This
camphor is by Barbosa and some other old writers called " eatable
camphor " (*da mangiare*), because used in medicine and with betel.

The phrase in the Portuguese text is *canfor de comer*.   Possibly Ibn
Baṭūta had confused the camphor packed in bamboos with the *tabáshír*,
the secretion formed in the joints of the bamboo, as described by
Garcia da Orta (*Cathay*, Yule and Cordier, IV, p. 98, n. 3).

The belief that Borneo camphor grew in canes was however not
extinct at the end of the sixteenth century, as may be seen from the
following from Hakluyt (*Voyages*, II, i, p. 242, 1599) :

" Camfora being compound commeth all from China, and all that
which groweth in canes commeth from Borneo."

Linschoten (II, p. 118) says," One pound of Borneo Camphora is worth
a hundred pound of Chincheu."

For the export from Sumatra see: *Countries Round the Bay of Bengal*,
Ed. Temple (p. 292, n.2.) ; *Peter Mundy*, Ed. Temple (Vol. III, p. 485)
and A. Hamilton's *East India* (II, pp. 112,113) as regards " Camphira "
obtainable at Lambon and Baros on the west coast of Sumatra.

in powder in cane tubes to Narsyngua, Malabar and
Daquem. This island is called Borneo.[1]

§ 125. CHAMPA.[2]

FURTHER on after leaving this island of Borneo over-
against the Kingdom of Anseam and China there is a
very great island of Heathen which they call Champa[3]

[1] At this point Ramusio makes the note, " Here several lines
are missing." A comparison with the Portuguese text and the Spanish
version however shows that nothing has been omitted.

[2] Ramusio, Campaa, where the aloes-wood grows.

[3] Champa was the name given to an ancient kingdom corresponding
latterly nearly with Cochin-China, which has disappeared from modern
maps. It was known to Arab writers from the ninth century as Ṣanf,
representing the pronunciation Chanf (G. Ferrand, *Relations de Voyage*,
p. viii, p. 12, and Yule and Cordier, *Cathay*, I, pp. 128, 129, notes; I, p. 135,
253). Friar Odoric knew it by the name of Zampa (*ib.*, II, p. 163). M.
Cordier in a note to this passage says that " the Binh-Thuan province
shows more particularly what remains of the Ancient Kingdom."
Champa was conquered by the King of Tong-King in 1471, but the
name survived to a much later period.
    The history of Champa has been fully dealt with by M. G. Maspero
in *Le Royaume de Champa* (T'oung-Pao, Vol. xi and succeeding vols.).
Barbosa's notice is probably the earliest to be found among Portuguese
writers. De Barros calls the country Choampa, and the name lingers
as late as the early eighteenth century. A. Hamilton for instance
(1720) speaks of Chiampo as being subject to Siam (*East Indies*, II,
p. 195), and in his map (p. 160) gives the name of Siampa to the coast
between Cambodia and Cochin-China.
    M. G. Ferrand in his treatise *K'ouen-Louen* (Journal Asiatique, 1919,
Reprint) has summed up the results of modern research by himself,
M. Pelliot, Mr. W. W. Rockhill, M. Maspero and other scholars, into
the evidence of early Chinese dealings with Champa and other countries
surrounding the China Sea. From these it is clear that as early as
A.D. 248 the Chams of Champa attacked Tonkin, then a Chinese province,
and that frequent wars both by land and sea between China and Champa
took place in A.D. 359, 407, 431, 605, 809, 979, and that in 1279 the
fleet of the Mongol Emperor Kubilai Kaan made Champa a starting
point for his fleet on his way to attack Java. Other wars with Annam
and with the Khmers of Cambodia are also recorded. One remarkable
occurrence is recorded under the year 774 when a fleet from some
unnamed country conveying a horde of savage pirates, " eaters of
men," made a raid on the coast of Champa and destroyed a *linga* set
up in honour of S'iwa by a former king Vichitrasagara. This attack
took place in the time of the king S'ri-Satyavarman. According to
M. Maspero this fleet came from Java. This incident shows clearly
what a hold Hindu institutions, illustrated by the worship of S'iwa
and the names of the kings, had obtained in Champa at that period
(*ib.*, pp. 132, 133). This also applied to the neighbouring Khmers
of Cambodia, from which country a Buddhist monk proceeded to China
in the year 506 (*ib.*, p. 130). Hinduism and Buddhism seem to have

which has a Heathen King and its own tongue. Therein are many elephants which they take and convey them to many lands. There also grows abundance of aloes-wood[1] which the Indians call " *Aguila Calambua* "

existed in Champa side by side, for we read that the King Indravarman (in 877) was a fervent Buddhist, yet he restored the ruined *linga* of S'ambubhadrésvara (G. Maspero, *Le Royaume de Champa*, T'oung-Pao, Vol. xii, pp. 56–58). See also *ib.*, pp. 237, 246, 250, 251 (where there is an allusion to the rite of *sati*), 296.

At the tine of the war between Kubilai Kaan and Champa, Marco Polo was in China and gives an account of the country under the name of Chamba, and of the war against it under the year 1278. He was himself in Chamba in 1288 and alludes to the production of lign-aloes and also of Bonüs, *i.e.*, *abnüs* or ebony (*Marco Polo*, Yule, Ed. 1871, pp. 212–14; Ditto, Yule and Cordier, pp. 266–67; G. Maspero, *l.c.* V, xii, p. 474); Cordier, *Ser Marco Polo*, 1920, p. 103).

Friar Odoric also visited Champa which he calls Campe or Zampa in the early part of the fourteenth century. Both he and Marco Polo observe especially the abundance of elephants. He also alludes to the practice of *sati* (H. Cordier, *Les Voyages du Fr. Odoric*, Paris, 1891, p. 187; Yule and Cordier, *Cathay*, II, pp. 163–6; G. Maspero, *l.c.*, Vol. XII, p. 600).

In the first half of the seventeenth century, P. Alexandre de Rhodes spent some time as a missionary in Tonkin, Cochinchina and the province of Cham (then a province of Cochinchina). He says that the people had three religions as in China, but does not describe their nature (*Voyages*, p. 122).

It seems probable that the Kingdom of Champa had its centre in early times much further north than at a later period, and that its capital was situated at Dong-hoi, now called Kwang-binh. (See M. Cordier's note in *Cathay*, II, p. 163.)

[1] *The Aloes-wood of Champa.* The *lenho-aloes* of Barbosa, which Garcia da Orta calls *Aguila brava* (wild Aguila), has been the subject of careful enquiries by many authorities. It will be sufficient here to allude to the following : Yule, *Marco Polo*, Ed. 1871, II, p. 215, n. 3 ; *Ditto* Ed. Yule and Cordier, II, pp. 271–2 ; Hobson-Jobson, *s.v.* Eagle-wood ; Yule and Cordier, *Cathay*, IV, pp. 100, 101, n. ; Dalgado, *Glossario Luso. As.*, *s.v.* Aguila.

The Portuguese undoubtedly took the name *Aguila* from the Malayâlam *Agil*, which is believed to be from the Skr. *agura*. In a former allusion (Vol. I, p. 92 and note) Barbosa used the word *aguila* for the wood which he here calls *lenho-aloes*. Both terms were in use, and the latter has caused great confusion, this aromatic wood being confounded with the true aloes, which is of an entirely different nature. The name aloes according to Yule may (in this connection) be traced to the Arabic *Al-'üd*, " the wood."

The variety of this wood which was found in Champa which Barbosa calls *Aguila Calambua* is derived from " a disease in a leguminous tree, *Aloexylon Agallochum*, while an inferior kind though of the same aromatic properties is derived from a tree of an entirely different order, *Aguilaria Agallocha*, and is found as far north as Sylhet " (*Marco Polo*, Yule and Cordier, pp. 271–2, n.).

P. Alexandre de Rhodes, *Voyages*, 1666, p. 63, says :
" De toutes les terres du monde, il n'y a que la Cochinchine, où

[Aquilam and Calambuco ; and the Calambuco is the finest. This is worth three hundred maravedis the pound in Calicut. *Ramusio*]. [Eagle and Calambuco ; it must be said that the very fine Calambuco and the other eagle-wood is worth at Calicut a thousand maravedis the pound. *Spanish version.*] " The fine quality is much valued among the Indians and Moors and at Calicut it fetches thirty or forty *pardaos* the *arratel*. They require it to mingle with sanders-wood, musk and rose-water to anoint themselves withal."

Among these islands[1] and other Heathen islands on this coast, there is one which is uninhabited, the name whereof I know not, where many diamonds are found which the people gather and sell to foreigners, but they are not so hard as those of Narsyngua [others say that this Campaa is on the mainland. *Ramusio*].

---

vienne cét arbre si célèbre qu'on appelle Calambouc, qui a le bois si odoriferant, et qui sert à tant de médicines. Il y en a de trois sortes ; le plus précieux s'appelle Calamba, l'ôdeur en est admirable, il sert pour fortifier le cœur, & contre toute sorte de venin. En ce país là mesme il se vend au poids d'or, les deux autres sont l'Aquila, & le Calambouc ordinaire, qui sont moindres que le premier : mais ils ne laissent pas d'avoir de très-bons effets."

Linschoten on the other hand says that it is found in Malacca, Sumatra, Camboja, Siam and the countries bordering on the same. He also divides it into three classes, Calamba (" sold by weight against silver and gold "), Palo Daguilla and Aguilla Brava or wild Aquila (II, p. 106).

[1] Which of the islands near the coast of Champa, Cochin China or Annam, is here alluded to it is impossible to say. There was evidently a merchant's story of some uninhabited islands where diamonds were found, but no such island is known. It is most probable that the diamonds were really brought from Borneo, and that some island was used as a depot, that their real place of origin might be concealed. What A. Hamilton says of the Borneo diamonds may be compared with the statement here made. " They have some small diamonds, but their Waters being inclined to be yellow, are not so much in Esteem as those of Golconda " (*East Indies*, II, p. 148). But Raffles considered them of fine quality. (Hist. of Java, I. 265 Ed. 2.) One of the islands of the Pulo Kondor group is the most likely to have been used in this way on account of its convenient position on the trade routes.

§ 126. THE VERY GREAT KINGDOM OF CHINA.

LEAVING these islands which no man can number and the names whereof we know not, some inhabited and some lying waste, I turn to the coast which goes from Malaca towards the Chins [1] [of which I myself know nothing

---

[1] *The first Portuguese communication with China.* It is evident that Duarte Barbosa had left India before any direct communication had been established between the Portuguese and China. He says that his information was derived from Moors or Heathen, no doubt Arab merchants, Malays and Hindus. Had any Portuguese or European expedition been known to him he would undoubtedly have alluded to it. Yet in his account of Ceylon (p. 109, n. 3) he alludes to the creation of a fort by Lopo Soares d'Albergaria, which took place in September, 1518, and the information regarding it must probably, like that of the destruction of Berbera by Saldanha in the same year (see Introduction, Vol. I, p. xlv), have reached him after his return to Portugal. But of the Portugese expedition under Fernão Peres D'Andrade which sailed on its return voyage from China at the end of September 1518, and arrived early in 1519 at Cochin, he evidently had not heard.

But other information from European sources may have come to his knowledge. Mr. Donald Ferguson in his *Letters from Portuguese Captives in Canton*, p. 4, alludes to a passage in a letter from Andrea Corsali to the Duke Giuliano de'Medici to which attention had already been drawn by Yule (Yule and Cordier, *Cathay*, I, p. 180). Corsali gives some information similar to that given by Barbosa but less full and accurate. His letter is dated (see text in *Ramusio*, Vol. I, f. 177 v to 180 v) January 6th, 1515, but this is evidently a mistake, for in this very letter he alludes to the death of Alboquerque, which took place on his arrival from Hurmuz at Goa on December 16th, 1515. The date of the letter should therefore be corrected to January 6th, 1516. Corsali's second letter (*Ramusio*, I, f. 181) gives the date of his own departure from Goa on his return journey as February 8th, 1516.

A letter from Giovanni da Empoli (who afterwards accompanied Fernão Peres d'Andrade to China, where he died in October, 1517), dated from Cochin, November 15th, 1515, is published in *Archivo Storico Italiano*, App. III, pp. 85–87, and translated by D. Ferguson (*l.c.*, p. 5). In this he alludes to China, "where men of ours have been who are staying here." Mr. Ferguson compares the account of China given in this letter unfavourably with "the wonderfully accurate description of China (from hearsay) given by Duarte Barbosa." There are some curious points of resemblance in Giovanni da Empoli's account to that of our author especially the statement that the Chinese dress like the Germans.

There had been an earlier expedition to China regarding which we have little information, viz., that of Jorge Alvares sent out from Malacca in 1514, regarding which we only know from De Barros (*III*, vi, 2, f. 159–160) that he claimed to have arrived in China a year before Rafael Perestrello (who went on a private venture of his own in 1515 and returned to India in August, 1516) and to have erected a *padrão* with the arms of Portugal, and that he was still at Canton when Duarte Coelho arrived on June 21st, 1521, but died a few days after (D. Ferguson, *l.c.*, pp. 3, 4). How far any of these voyages were known to

but have enquired from trustworthy Moors and Heathen who have told me that there were four uninhabited islands ; and through them I have only learned that] after passing by the Kingdom of Ansiam and many others there is the Kingdom of China, which they say is a very great country ruling the main and the sea-coast and inhabited by Heathen. The King thereof is a Heathen and gives great worship to Idols ; he dwells ever in the inland region and holds many great and fair cities. No strangers may enter the inland country, but they may trade in the seaports ; their [chief] trade is in the islands.

Duarte Barbosa it is not easy to say, but if he accompanied the ships he had been ordered by Alboquerque to build and went to the Red Sea, where he was present at the taking of Zeila in 1517 (Introduction, Vol. I, p. xlv) it is probable that he left before Perestrello's return, and before Fernão Peres D'Andrade had started on his last and successful voyage to China.

For the full history of the first Portuguese communications with China reference should be made to Mr. Donald Ferguson's work already quoted and also to an essay by M. Henri Cordier " L'Arrivée des Portugais en Chine," published in Vol. XII of T'oung-Pao (Leiden 1911) which forms the first part of M. Cordier's Histoire Generale des Relations de l'Empire Chinois avec les Puissances occidentales depuis la XVIe siecle jusqu'a nos jours. The introductory portion contains an excellent sketch of the early history of the Portuguese in the East. In this essay (p. 520, n. 2) M. Cordier says that " Mr. Ferguson's work is by far the best there is on this subject."

M. Cordier (p. 512), like Mr. Ferguson, in alluding to the letter of Andrea Corsali mentioned above has not noticed the error in the date. It is evident that we must read 1516 for 1515, and M. Cordier's deduction to the effect that this letter " leaves no doubt as to the year of the arrival of the Portuguese in China, that is to say 1514 " must be modified, the date being 1515.

The letter of Giovanni da Empoli of November 15th, 1515, written from Cochin, must therefore take precedence of that of Andrea Corsali as the first record of Portugese intercourse with China. Giovanni da Empoli had come out in the same fleet as the new Governor and Fernão Peres d'Andrade and accompanied Jorge de Brito, the new Captain of Malacca. Correa tells us (II, p. 473) that " Fernão Peres went to seek for Pacem, where he expected to find a cargo of pepper ready for he had sent with Jorge de Brito a frolentim (Florentine) called Joanes in the ship of Antonio Pacheco, who had collected a good cargo, which was burnt while the ship was loading."

De Barros (III, ii, Ch. 6, f. 42) in his account of this event says " It happened through the sailors' carelessness from a spark of a torch carried below to fetch water that the ship in which Ioannes Impoli went as Captain and feitor was burnt with all the cargo that was below decks."

From these extracts it is evident that Giovanni da Empoli came to India with the special intention of taking part in the Chinese expedition and that he was in a position to obtain all the information available at Cochin.

If any ambassador from another Kingdom comes thither by sea, they first make known to him (*i.e.*, to the King), that they are bringing to him certain embassies and presents, and then he orders the ambassador to go to the place where he is dwelling.

The inhabitants of this land are great merchants ; they are white men, and well built. Both men and women have small eyes, in their beards they have three or four hairs and no more, as a sign of gentility, and the smaller their eyes are the more repute they have as well-bred men. The women are trimly attired in garments of cotton, silk and wool. The manner of dressing among the people of this land is as among the Germans, they eat like us at raised tables with very white cloths thereon, and for as many persons as are to eat at one table they lay a knife, a plate, a napkin and a silver cup : they touch not with the hand anything they eat, but bring the plate near to the mouth, and with certain wooden or silver tongs they convey the food to the mouth in very small pieces because they eat very quickly. They make numerous dishes of flesh, fish and many other things ; they eat good wheaten bread and drink wines of divers kinds and many times at each meal. They eat dogs' flesh and hold it to be very good meat.

They are very truthful men, yet they are not great gentlemen but good merchants dealing in goods of all kinds.

They make here great store of porcelain,[1] which is good merchandize everywhere. This they make from the shells

---

[1] *Porcelain.* This legend of the burial of the materials out of which porcelain is made for some time, which in the Spanish version and Ramusio has been converted into eighty or a hundred years, copied also by Linschoten (I, p.130), has no foundation in fact and Mr. R. L. Hobson, one of our principal authorities on the subject, informs me that it is most improbable and that Chinese authorities mention no such practice. The use of the white of eggs is also imaginary. Sea shells may have been used for lime, but not as one of the ingredients of the paste.

of fish ground fine, from eggshells and the white of eggs and other materials. From these they make a paste which they place under the ground " for a certain time " [for eighty and a hundred years. *Ramusio and the Spanish version*]. This among them is held to be a valuable property and treasure, for the nearer the time approaches for working it the greater is its value [and this paste they leave as a treasure to their sons, and they always have some left to them by their ancient predecessors with records of it, place by place]. And when the time is fulfilled they fashion it in many styles and manners, some coarse, some fine, and after it is shaped they glaze and paint it. [And in the same place where it was buried they place fresh paste, so they always have the old to work on and the new to bury.]

Very good silk is produced here from which they make great store of damask cloths in colours, satins and other cloths without nap, also brocades. There is here also abundance of rhubarb, musk, silver, seed-pearls (although not perfectly round).

In this Kingdom they make many beautiful and gilded ornamental articles such as very rich boxes, wooden dishes, salt-cellars and other cunning things ; and for this there are many very skilful men.

" They wear boots like the people of cold countries."

They sail in *juncos*, which carry sails made of mats " as in Moçambique " [and have two masts fashioned otherwise than ours]. " Their cables and rigging are made of certain canes (*i.e.*, rattans). Some of them are great pirates. They sail [1] to Malaca with all the Chinese

---

[1] *Chinese navigation and trade.* Chinese ships had been accustomed to visit neighbouring countries from an early date. Very full information on this subject from Chinese sources was brought together by the late Mr. W. W. Rockhill in his *Notes on the Relations and Trade of China*, published in T'oung-Pao (Leiden), Vols. XV and XVI. This trade

goods which have a good sale there ; and take cargoes of iron in abundance, saltpetre, raw silk and other small things," such as the Venetians used formerly to bring to us, " also pepper from Çamatra and Malabar which in China is worth fifteen or sixteen cruzados the quintal and upwards according to whither they take it, and in Malaca they buy it at four cruzados more or less. They also take anfiam which we call opium (*opeo*), incense, coral, Cambaya and Paleacate cloths.

These Chins who live by trade and navigation always take their wives and children with them in their ships where they live constantly and have no other houses.

This Kingdom of China marches with *Tartaria* on the northern side.

---

§ 127. LEQUEOS.[1]

FACING this great land of China there are many islands in the Sea, beyond which stretches a very great land

---

reached its greatest extension under the Sung dynasty (eleventh and twelfth centuries), and included all the principal Islands of the Malay Archipelago, as well as India, Arabia and the Persian Gulf. Under the reign of the great Mongol Emperor Kubilai Kaan the trade was vigorously developed, and continued to be active under the Yuan and Ming dynasties (fourteenth and fifteenth centuries). No doubt there was then, as there has been in quite modern times, a great deal of piracy among the maritime population of the islands and inlets of the Chinese coast.

Malacca was a great centre of Chinese trade and there from the time of Alboquerque's conquest the Portuguese got into close relations with the merchants of that country, and often made use of their junks. Alboquerque was especially careful to be conciliatory in his dealings with the Chinese trading class, and was anxious to open up communications with China.

[1] The name Lequeos is taken from the Chinese Lieu-K'ieu or Liu-Kiu formerly commonly called Loo-Choo. This name is now restricted to the group of small islands lying south of Japan (now under Japanese rule and called Riu-Kiu), but up to the sixteenth century it included all the islands facing China from Formosa to Japan, and specially referred to Formosa itself. The Arab writer Ibn Majid (second half of, fifteenth century) and Sulaymān al Mahri (first half of sixteenth century) both speak of the Island of Likyū or Likiwu and identify it with the country of the *Ghūr* (see G. Ferrand, *Malaka*, pp. 174, 175, for quotations).

which [1] they say is the mainland. Hence every year come to Malaca three or four ships like those of the Chins belonging to certain white folk, who they say are great and rich merchants.

They bring a great quantity of gold,[2] silver in bars, silk and rich cloths, a great deal of good wheat, fine porcelains, and many other goods. From Malaca they take the same goods as the Chins take. [These people are called Liquii. *Ramusio.* These islands are called Lequeos. *Spanish version.*] The Malaca people say that they are better men, and richer and more eminent merchants than the Chins. Of these folk we as yet know but little, as they have not yet come to Malaca since it has been under the King our Lord.

De Barros (*II,* iv, 3, f. 89 v.) alludes to the *Lequios* among the races who were accustomed to trade with Malaca. Castanheda also alludes to a great country south-east of Canton called *Lequia* regarding which Fernão Peres D'Andrade obtained information after passing Canton. He describes it as very rich in gold, silver, silk brocades and porcelain, like China (Castanheda, IV, xl, 91).

There are several allusions to the " Gores " in the *Commentaries of Alboquerque* which will be found in M. Ferrand's paper above alluded to. In one place it is stated that " the country of these Gores is called Lequea." Their trade was with Malaca, with Çelate (*i.e.* the strait, Malay *selát. l.c.* p. 178, n. 6) and the point of Singapur on the mainland.

M. Ferrand's essay quoted above, *L'Ile de Ghūr-Lieou-K'ieou= Formose,* is published as Appendix I. to his *Malaka.*

[1] The Spanish version, " a hundred and seventy-five leagues to the east."

[2] The Spanish version and Ramusio, " gold in bars, silver."

ON PRECIOUS STONES.

[The account of precious stones and spices which follows is not
found in the Portuguese text, but is taken from Ramusio.
Lord Stanley's version taken from the Spanish MS. differs
little from Ramusio's. It is not found in the Munich MS.
as he has noted in his p. 207, n. 2.]

MANY kinds of precious stones having been mentioned
in the present work, it is convenient here to add at the
end certain accounts derived from divers merchants,
both Moors and Heathen, skilled in such trade ; and thus
I begin with rubies.

OF RUBIES.

In the first place rubies are produced in the Land of
India and are found chiefly on a river called Pegu.
These are the best and finest, and are called *Numpuclo*[1] by
the Malabares, and when they are clean and without flaw
they fetch a good price. To test their quality the Indians
put them on the tongue ; those which are finest and
hardest are held to be the best. To test their trans-
parency they fix them with wax on a very sharp point
and looking towards the sun they can find any blemish
however slight. They are also found in certain deep
pits in the mountains beyond the said river.

In Pegu they know how to clean but not how to polish
them, and they therefore convey them to other countries,
especially to Paleacate, Narsinga, Calicut and the whole
of Malabar, where there are excellent craftsmen who
cut and mount them.

---

[1] *Pegu Rubies.* The name *Numpuclo* here stated to be used for
the Pegu rubies in Malabar is explained by Mgr. Dalgado in his *Glossario*.
He considers that the initial letter is wrongly given owing to a copyist's mistake, and that the word should be read *chumpuclo*, as in Malayālam the name of the ruby is *chuvappukallu* from *kallu* " stone "
and *chuvappu* " ruby," literally " ruby-stone." For the places where
these rubies are found see §107 and §108.

As to their value it must be observed first that the word *fanam* means a weight greater than two of our *quilates* (carats), eleven fanams make a *Metigal*, and six and a half *Metigals* make an ounce. This word *fanam* also denotes a coin, worth one silver real. This being understood I say :—

	Fanams.
Eight fine rubies weighing 1 *fanam, i.e.*, a little more or less than 2 *quilates*, are worth	10
Four Do. Do.	20
Two Do. Do.	40
One weighing ¾ *fanam*	30
Do. Do. 1 Do.	50
Do. Do. 1¼ Do.	65
Do. Do. 1½ Do.	100
Do. Do. 1¾ Do.	150

(This table continues with similar increments, ending with) :—

One weighing 6 *fanams*, 12 *quilates* ...	1,500

These are the prices commonly given for perfect rubies. Those which are damaged or flawed or of a bad colour are worth much less according as the purchaser may settle it.

Of the Rubies found in the Island of Ceilão.

In the Island of Ceilão, which lies in the second India, are found many rubies which the Indians call Maneca,[1] the more part whereof never attain in colour to the perfection of those treated of above, inasmuch as although red they are pale ; they are notwithstanding very cold and

---

[1] *Ceylon Rubies.* The name *Maneca* is thus explained by Mgr. Dalgado in his *Glossario* :

" Duarte Barbosa tells us that *Maneca* is a ruby, but its original Singalese, *meṇika*, Skr. *maṇika*, means simply a ' precious stone.' "

hard, and the better of them are much esteemed among these peoples. The King of that island keeps them for his own profit, and when the goldsmiths come upon any which is good they place it in fire for a certain number of hours, and if it comes forth whole its colour becomes very bright and of great value. When the King of Narsinga can obtain any such he has them cunningly bored on the lower side, but so that the perforation does not reach beyond the middle, nor does he allow them to be exported from the Kingdom.[1] For the reason mainly that it is known that they have undergone the aforesaid test, they are worth more than those of Pegu even with all their sparkle and transparence.

[The table which follows gives the value of the Ceylon rubies in *fanams*, the weights being given in *quilates*. The *quilate* is stated to be half a *fanam* in weight. Thus a Ceylon ruby of 1 *quilate* (½ *fanam*) is worth 30 *fanams* in money, while two of the Pegu rubies weighing 1 *fanam*, i.e., 1 *quilate*, each are worth 40 *fanams*, i.e., 20 *fanams* each. In the same way a Ceylon ruby of 2 *quilates* or 1 *fanam* is worth 65 *fanams*, while a Pegu ruby of the same weight is only worth 50.]

The table begins thus :—

	Fanams.
One ruby of these weighing 1 *quilate* or *fanam* is worth at Calicut	50
One of 2 *quilates*	65
One of 3 Do.	150
and goes up as far as	
One of 12 *quilates*	2,000
One of 14 Do.	3,000
One of 16 Do.	6,000

[1] This passage is given as follows in the former edition :
"So that the hole reaches to the centre, and they do not pass it, because the stone can no longer leave the Kingdom, and that it may be known

OF SPINEL RUBIES.

There is yet another kind of ruby which we call Spinels
(*Espinellas*) but the Indians call them *Carapuch*,[1] which
are found in the same manner as the fine rubies in the
Kingdom of Pegu ;   they are found in the mountains
on the surface of the ground.   They are not so fine nor of
such good colour, and resemble rather garnets (*granadas*).
Those which are perfect and clear fetch one-half less
than rubies.

OF BALACH RUBIES, WHERE THEY ARE FOUND,
AND THEIR VALUE AT CALICUT.

The Balaches are another kind of ruby, but not so hard.
They are rose-coloured and some nearly white.   They
are found in Balassia [2] (a kingdom of the mainland beyond
Pegu and Bengala), and are brought thence by Moorish

---

that it has been tried in the fire.   And so also these are worth more
than those of Peygu.   Their price are the following if they are perfect
in colour and purity."
  This does not seen to give the correct sense of the original of Ramusio.

  [1] *Spinel Rubies.*   The vernacular term for this word *Carapuch*
here given seems not to be derived from Malayālam ; although Calicut
is the depot alluded to in the text when prices are quoted.   As to
this Mgr. Dalgado says in his *Glossario :*
  " Duarte Barbosa asserts that the Indians give this name to Spinels ;
but the Singalese form of the original *Kareppu* shows that the correct
form should be *carapo* (or *carépu*), pl. *carapos*."
  From the use of a Singalese name it may be deduced that these spinels
came from Ceylon rather than from Pegu.

  [2] *Balach Rubies.*   For quotations as to the rubies known as Balas
or Balash, *i.e.*, the rubies of Balakhshān or Badakhshan, reference
should be made to Yule's notes on the subject first made in *Marco
Polo*, Ed. 1871, I, p. 152, also in *Hobson-Jobson* under " Balass," and to
Dalgado's *Glossario* under " Balais, balax."   The notice by Ibn Batūta
is probably the earliest which correctly explains the meaning of the word.
On Barbosa's notice in the present work Yule remarks (in *Hobson-
Jobson*), " This is very bad geography for Barbosa, who is usually
accurate and judicious, but it is surpassed in much later days."   It
is doubtful however how far Barbosa was responsible for this passage,
which is taken from Ramusio, and does not appear in the Portuguese
text.   Tavernier repeats the blunder ; he speaks of the Balleis-rubies
being found in " the mountains which run along from Pegu to the
kingdom of Camboya " (English trans., Pt. II, p. 144).

traders to all the other countries, that is to say the good
and picked are brought to Calicut to be cut, where
they prepare them and sell them at the same price as
Spinels ; and those which are not good or are bored are
bought by the Moors of Meca and Adem to convey them
into Arabia where they are much used.

OF THE DIAMONDS OF THE OLD MINE.[1]

These diamonds are found in the first India in a Kingdom of the Moors called Decan, and the Moors and Indians
carry them thence to all other countries : there are other
diamonds of poorer quality, yet white enough, which
are entitled " of the New Mine," which is in the Kingdom
of Narsinga.   These are worth one-third less in Calicut
and Malabar, and are prepared in the same kingdom of
Narsinga.   In India also are fabricated false diamonds,.
rubies, topazes and white Sapphires which are good imitations of the true stones and are found only in the Island
of Ceilao.   These stones show no difference from the true
save that they lose their natural colour, and there are
some of which one half has the colour of a ruby and the
other half of a Sapphire or topaz ; some really have these
colours mixed, they bore them in the middle and thread
them on two or three very fine threads, and then call
them cats'-eyes. Of those which come out white they
make many small diamonds which differ not at all from
the true, save by the touch of those practised therein.
They are sold by a weight called *Mangiar*,[2] which is

---

[1] *Diamonds of the Old Mine.*   For diamonds of the " old rock "
see *supra*, Vol. I, p. 226, n. 2.   See also *Tavernier*, Eng. Trans., Pt. II,
p. 144.

[2] *Mangiar* according to the note in *Hobson-Jobson* is a weight used
in South India and Ceylon for weighing precious stones and is the Tamil
manjādi, Telugu *manjāli*.   The later form of the word is *Mangelim*
or *Mangelin*, under which name it is found in Do Couto's *Soldado
Pratico* (Ed. 1790, p. 154) and in Tavernier's *Travels* (English Trans.,
Pt. II, pp. 140–144).   This form is no doubt from the Telugu word, Telugu

equal to two *taras* and two-thirds ; and two *taras* make a *quilate* of good weight, and four *taras* make a *fanão*.

Fanams.

Eight diamonds weighing one *Mangiar*,
(that is to say two-thirds of a *quilate*)
are worth   30

Six	Do.	Do.	..	..	..	40
Four	Do.	Do.	..	..	..	60
Two	Do.	Do.	..	..	..	80
One	Do.	Do.	..	..	..	100

[the list continues up to]

One of 8 *mangiares*   1,400

Thus they go on increasing in value in proportion to their increase in weight.

OF SAPPHIRES.[1]

The best Sapphires come from the Island of Ceilão, they are very hard and fine.[2]   Those which are clear and of a good blue colour fetch the following prices :

Fanams.

One, weighing 1 *quilate*	..	..	..	2
Two Do. 2 *quilates*	..	..	..	6
Do. Do. 3 Do.	..	..	..	10

[continuing showing the increments of price to]

One weighing a *Metigal*, that is 11 fanams
and a quarter or about 23 *quilates*   .. 350

---

being the language spoken in the region of the mines.   See also Mgr. Dalgado's *Glossario, s.v. Mangelim*, where many quotations illustrating its use are given.

[1] *Sapphire.*   The terms here given are explained by Mgr. Dalgado as follows :

Quinigenilao represents the Malayālam *Karin-kallu-nilam* or " dark sapphire stone."   It should be corrected to *Quiniguenilao*, as " intervocalic *k* sounds *g* in Malayālam."   *Carahatonilam* is from Malayālam *Karutta* " black " and *nilam* " sapphire."

" In *cinganoldo* (or *cringanilan*) we have three words, *cin-ga* (for *halla* ' stone ') and *nilam*.   I am not sure about *cin*.   It is probably Malayālam *cherīga* or *cheru* ' small ' in the sense of inferior ; Malayālam *chitta* is ' bad ' and *chera* ' mud.' "

[2] For sapphires and other Ceylon gems s:e *supra*, p. 115, n. 1.

In Ceilão also is found another kind of Sapphire not so large, which they call *Quinigenilão* [*quirin genilam* in the Spanish version]. They are of a dark hue, and how good soever they may be are worth much less, thirteen of them being equal to one of the first named. There is found also in the Kingdom of Narsinga in a Mountain above Bacanor and Mamgalor yet another sort of Sapphire, paler and less fine in colour, which they call *Ciningolão* (in the Spanish version *Cringanilan*); these are somewhat faded, and of little value, so that the most perfect of them weighing 20 *quilates* does not reach the value of a ducat; their colour is slightly yellowish.

Another kind of Sapphire is found on the sea-strands in the Kingdom of Calicut at a place called Capucar; this is by the Indians called *Carahatonilam*; they are very dark and blue and only shine in the air; they are pale and fragile.

The common folk believe that in the sea near Capucar there was in former days a house the windows whereof were of blue glass, and that afterwards, having been covered by the waters, pieces of that glass are daily cast on up the strand; they are very thick and on one side they resemble glass; among the Indians they are little esteemed.

Of Topazes.

Natural topazes are found in the Island of Ceilão, by the Indians they are called *Purceragua*.[1] The stone is very hard and cold and of the same weight as the ruby and Sapphire, all three being of the same species. Its perfect colour is yellow like beaten gold, and when the stone is perfect and clear it is worth at Calicut, be it great or

---

[1] *Topaz.* "*Purceragua* is Malayālam Puṣparāgam, Skr. *puṣparāga*, a topaz" (Dalgado).

small, its weight in fine gold, and this is usually its price. When they are not so perfect they are worth their weight in *fanam* gold, which is a half less ; if white they are worth much less, and with them they counterfeit small diamonds.

OF TURQUOISES.

True turquoises are found at Exeraquirimane[1] (Niexer and Quirimane in the Spanish version), a town of the Xeque Ismael ; the mine where it is found is dry land, that is to say it is found on a black stone which the Moors extract in small pieces and convey to Ormus, whence they are carried to divers countries by land or by sea. The Indians call it *Perose*, it is a soft stone and does not weigh much. To know if it is good or true it should display its turquoise colour by day, but by night in the light it should appear green. Those which are not so perfect do not undergo this change. When these stones are clean and of good colour they should bear adhering to the lower side a black stone in which they are produced, and if some slight vein of this stone is spread over the turquoise it is still better. To be more certain of knowing the true turquoises they plaster them with a little white quicklime moistened with water, like an ointment, and even then

---

[1] *Turquoises.* The town called Exeraquirimane is undoubtedly Karmān, that is Shehr-i-Karmān, the town of Karmān. It was celebrated for the turquoise mines in its neighbourhood which were well-known in Marco Polo's day (Book I, Ch. 17, and Yule's note on it).

One of the latest accounts of these mines is that in Sir P. M. Sykes's *Ten thousand Miles in Persia* (pp. 74, 265). None of them appear to be worked now. The valuable turquoise mines now worked are in Northern Persia, in the neighbourhood of Nishapur (Curzon's *Persia*, 1892, Vol. I, pp. 264–267, where references to other authorities will be found). As Lord Curzon noted there is much trickery in the sale of turquoises, and it is common, as Tavernier said in the passage he quotes (*l.c.*, p. 267) for the purchaser to find his sky-blue turquoises rapidly turning green.

The name *Perose* is the Persian *firūza*, pronounced *firoza* in India.

they should appear coloured. If they have this perfection
their prices are as follows :—

				Fanams.
One weighing 1 *quilate* is worth in Malabar				15
Do.	2	Do.	Do.	.. 40
Do.	4	Do.	Do.	.. 90
[and so on, up to]				
Do.	14	Do.	Do.	.. 550

OF JACINTHS.[1]

Jacinths are found in Ceilão ; they are soft yellow
stones. Those of the deepest colour are the best ; the
more part have bubbles in them which cause them to
lose their beauty. When free from these and perfect in
colour they are, notwithstanding this, worth but little ;
wherefore in Calicut, where they are prepared, they do
not give more than half a *fanam* for those weighing one
fanam, and those weighing 18 *fanams* are barely worth
16. There are other stones such as cats'-eyes.   [There
are also other gems, cats'-eyes, chrysoliths and amethysts
of which no other distinction is made on account of their
being of little value and so also with regard to the jagonzas.]

OF EMERALDS.[2]

Emeralds are found in the Kingdom of Babilonia, which
the Indians call the Sea of Iguan (Mar Deiguan, Maredygua,

---

[1] *Jacinth.* The jacinth or hyacinth here described seems to be a yellow
variety of crystalline stone resembling amethyst in its structure, such
as are sometimes known as citrine. Its softness and small value show
that it could not have been a valuable gem. The hyacinth of ancient
authorities is generally supposed to be the sapphire, and was certainly a
hard stone of blue colour (Middleton, *Ancient Gems*, p. 132 and p.
143).   It was probably one of the transparent stones found in Ceylon
as recorded in the *Periplus*, Sec. 61 (Schoff's *Periplus*, pp. 47, 250).

[2] *Emeralds.* It is not possible to identify the Mardeiguan, or Sea of
Iguan, nor to suggest any place in Babilonia (that is the region of
Baghdad), nor in the adjoining ports of Asia Minor and Persia whence
emeralds may have been brought. They were evidently imported

in the Spanish version), and also in other regions. They are green of a fine colour and beautiful, and besides are light and soft. Many false ones are made, but by looking through them towards the light the counterfeits show little bubbles such as are seen in glass. This is not so in the fine emeralds, the sight of which is pleasing to the eyes. The best give out a ray like the Sun, and when touched by the stone leave a brass-coloured streak. The emerald which does this is the true, and is worth at Calicut as much as the diamond or even more ; not so much by weight as by size, by reason that the diamond weighs more in proportion than the emerald. There is found also another sort of emerald very green but not of so much value, with all the Indians use them to mix with other precious stones. These do not leave the brass colour on the touchstone.

---

into India, and possibly the import may have been from the Persian Gulf, but the country of their origin was almost certainly the African coast of the Red Sea. This had been the case as early as the time of Cosmas Indicopleustes, who says "These people have a great fondness for the emerald stone, and it is worn by their King in his crown. The Ethiopians who obtain this stone from the Blemmyes in Ethiopia, import it into India, and with the price they get are able to invest in wares of the greatest value." McCrindle remarks that "the emeralds were found in the mines of Upper Egypt and were no doubt shipped from Adulê for the Indian markets." (Yule and Cordier, *Cathay*, I, p. 230.) See also note 39, p. 167 in Schoff's *Periplus*, and Bent's *Southern Arabia*, pp. 291-7. Probably Basra may have been the depôt whence the trade was conducted *via* Hurmuz to India in the sixteenth century.

Tavernier's remark is worth quoting. He says "As for Emeralds it is a vulgar error to say they come originally from the East. And therefore when Jewellers and Gold-smiths to prefer a deep-colour'd Emrauld inclining to black, tell ye it is an Oriental Emrauld, they speak that which is not true. I confess I could never discover in what part of our Continent those Stones are found. But sure I am that the Eastern part of the World never produced any of those stones, neither in the Continent nor in the Islands." He then speaks of the importation from America, but had evidently not heard of the Ethiopian mines (*Voyages*, Eng. trans., Part II, p. 144).

THE DIVERS KINDS OF SPICES, WHERE THEY GROW, WHAT THEY ARE WORTH AT CALICUT, AND WHITHER THEY ARE CARRIED.

OF PEPPER.

IN the first place, in the whole of Malabar and in Calicut pepper[1] grows. A *bahar* thereof sells at Calicut at from 200 to 230 *fanans* of which one, as we have already said, is worth a silver real of Spain. Each *bahar* weighs 4 *quintals* (old weight) of Portugal, by which all spices are sold at Lisbon. To the King of Calicut a duty of 12 *fanams* a *bahar* is paid. The merchants have the practice of taking it to Cambaya, Persia, Adem and Meca, and thence to Cairo and Alexandria. At the present day they give it to the King of Portugal at 6,562 *maravedis* the *bahar* (including the duties which are 193½ *fanams*), partly because there is not there such a concourse of merchants to purchase it, and partly on account of the contract made by the King of Portugal with that King, and with the Moors and merchants of the country.

Much pepper grows as well in the Island of Çamatra near Malaca, which is fairer and larger than that of Malabar but not so good or strong as the aforesaid. This is taken to Bengala and China, and some quantity is smuggled into Meca unknown to the Portuguese who do not permit it to be taken thither. It is worth in Çamatra 400 to 600 *maravedis* the *quintal* (new weight) ; and between the new and old there is a difference of 2 ounces to the *arratel*, the old being 14 ounces and the new 16 ounces.

OF CLOVES.[2]

Cloves grow in the islands called Molucos ; they take

---

[1] For the production of pepper in Malabar see *supra*, pp. 88, 92, 97, and for Sumatra, pp. 165, 182-185, 188.

[2] For cloves in the Moluccas see *supra*, pp. 201-202, 201, n. 2.

them to Malaca and thence to Calicut in Malabar. At Calicut a *bahar* is worth from 500 to 600 *fanams*, and if very clean and picked, 700 ; duty is paid at 18 *fanams* the *bahar*. In Moluco where they grow they are sold at one to two ducats the *bahar*, according to the number of purchasers who go there for it, and at Malaca from ten to fourteen, according to the market.

OF CINNAMON.[1]

The good Cinnamon grows in the Island of Ceilão and the bad in Malabar. The good is cheap in Ceilão, but if fresh and well picked it fetches 300 *fanams* the *bahar* at Calicut.

OF BELEDI GINGER.[2]

Beledi Ginger grows around the town of Calicut at from six to nine miles distance. Each *bahar* is worth 40 *fanams*, sometimes 50 ; they bring it in from the mountains to the town for retail sale. The Indian merchants buy it and collect it, and when the ship airives to take cargoes of it they sell it to the Moors at the price of from 90 to 110 *fanams*, for by then it is very heavy.

DELY GINGER.[3]

Dely Ginger grows from Mount Dely up to Cananor. It is small and not so white nor so good. A *bahar* at Cananor is worth 40 *fanams*, and the duty is 6 *fanams* on each *bahar*.

CONSERVE OF GREEN GINGER.

In Bengal also there is much Beledi Ginger of which

---

[1] For fine cinnamon in Ceylon see *supra*, p. 112, n. 1; for the wild cinnamon of Malabar and its growth on Mt. Dely, *supra*, pp. 79, 93.

[2] For Belide or Beledi ginger see *supra*, p. 92, n. 2.

[3] The ginger of Mt. Dely is probably a variety of the Beledi ginger alluded to above. Both cinnamon and ginger seem to have been wild there.

they make abundance of very good Conserve with sugar, and carry it for sale in Martaban jars to Malabar. Each *farazola* (*i.e.*, 22 *arratels* and 6 ounces) fetches 14, 15 or 16 *fanams*. That which is fresh is preserved at Calicut, and is worth 25 *fanams*, sugar being dear there, and this green ginger sold to be preserved is worth ⅔ of a *fanam* the *farazola*.

OF DRUGS[1] AND OF THEIR PRICES AT CALICUT AND IN THE LAND OF MALABAR.

Fanams.

Good Martaban lac, the *farazola*, *i.e.*, 22
    arratels 6¼ ounces new weight of Portugal   18

Country lac   ...   .   the *farazola*   123

Tincal (good), in large pieces ...   Do.   30 and 40
                                             to 50

Coarse camphor in loaves   ...   .   70 to 80

Camphor for anointing idols, a *fanam* and a
    half the *mitigal*, 6¼ of which make an
    ounce.

Camphor for eating and for the eyes, per *mitigal*   3

Aguila (eagle-wood, aloes-wood)   per *farazola* 300 to 400

---

[1] Martaban lac. See Vol. I, p. 56, n. 3 ; Vol. II, p. 158, n 2.
Tincal. See Vol. I, p. 154, n. 7.
Camphor. See Vol. II, p. 207, n. 1.
Eagle-wood ⎫ Vol. I, p. 92, n. 1 ; 209, n. 1. *Glossario, s.v.* Águila.
Aloes-wood ⎭
True Aloes ⎫ See Vol. I, p. 61, n. 1. Dalgado, *Glossario, s.v.* Aloés.
Socotra Aloes ⎭
Musk. See Vol. I, p. 56, n. 4.
Benzoin. See Vol. I, p. 92, n. 3.
Tamarinds. See *Hobson-Jobson, s.v.* Tamarind.
Calamo Aromatico. *The Acorus calamus*, an aromatic astringent.
  See *Glossario, s.v.* Calamo.
Indigo ⎫ Indigo is a term but little used in Portuguese. *Anil* (from
Anil   ⎭ the Arabic *An-nil*) is the usual term. See *Orta*, Col. VII.
Incense. See Vol. I, p. 65, n. 2.
Ambergris. See Vol. II, p. 106, n. 3 ; 108, n. 2.
Myrobalans. See Vol. I, p. 188, n. 3, *Glossario, s.v.* Mirabólano.
Cassia. See Vol. I, p. 188, n. 3.
Sanders-wood. See Vol. II, under Timor, 196, n. 1.

Fanams.

Aloes-wood (true), black, heavy and very fine ... ... per *farazola*	1,000
Musk (good) ... ... the ounce	36
Good beijoim (benzoin) ... the *farazola*	65 to 70
New tamarinds ... ... Do.	4
Calamo aromatico, *i.e.*, *Acorus calamus* Do.	12
Indigo, true and good ... ... Do.	30
Myrrh. ... ... Do.	18 to 20
Good incense in grains ... ... Do.	15
Incense in paste, not so good ... Do.	3
Good ambergris ... ... the *mitigal*	2 to 3
Myrobalan conserve in sugar ... the *farazola*	16 to 25
Fresh and good Cassia [1] ... ... Do.	1½
Red sanders-wood [2] ... ... Do.	5 to 6
Spikenard, fresh and good ... Do.	30 to 40

Spikenard. See Vol. I, p. 154, n. 5.
Nutmegs. See Vol. II, p. 197, n. 1.
Mace. See Vol. II, p. 197, n. 1.
Lombreguera, southern-wood. See Vol. I, p. 154, n. 4, and *Glossario*, *s.v. Erva lombrigueira*.
Turbit. The root and stems of *Ipomœa turpethum*, used as a demulcent and laxative. (Stewart's *Punjab Plants*, p. 150.)
The name is from the Persian *turbud*.
Anil. The *nadador* or "swimming" indigo seems to have received the name from its lightness to distinguish it from the impure kind which would not float.
Zerumba } See Vol. II, p. 92, n. 4.
Zedoary }
Sagapeno. Described by Vieyra as "gum from the fennel giant." The name "serapine" used in the Spanish version is evidently a variant.
Socotra aloes. See Vol. I, p. 61, n. 1.
Cardamoms. The seeds of *Elettaria cardamomum* (ilāchi). See *Glossario*, *s.v.* Cardamomo.
Rhubarb. This is the only mention of Rhubarb growing in Malabar, and it is probable that what was obtained there came from China via Malacca. See Vol. I, p. 93, n. 3.
Tutia. See Vol. I, p. 154, n. 6.
Cubebs. Not mentioned in the text. They are the berry of the *Piper cubeba*, formerly valued in medicine, and are indigenous in Java and Sumatra. See *Glossario*, *s.v.* Cubeba, Watt, *Commercial Products*, p. 890.
Opium. See Vol. I, pp. 55, 122, n. 1, 129, 154, 203. The opium prepared at Cambaya was doubtless the produce of Mālwa.

[1] See Vol. I, p. 188, n. 3, and *supra.*, p. 92, n. 3.
[2] See *supra.*, p. 196, n. 1.

Fanams.

White, and lemon-coloured sanders-wood,
    which grows in an Island called Timor Do.   40 to 60
Nutmegs from the Island of Bandão (where
    the *bahar* is worth 8 to 10 *fanams*) are
    worth at Calicut ...   ... per *farazola* 10 to 12
Mace, from Bandão where the *bahar* is worth
    50 *fanams*, sells at Calicut at per *farazola* 25 to 30
Lombreguera, good herb (given only in the
    Spanish version) ...   ... per *farazola*   15
Turbit   ...   .   Do.   13
Anil nadador, very good   ...   Do.   30
Anil, heavy, mixed with sand (see also
    Indigo)   ...   . per *farazola* 18 to 20
Zerumba ...   .   Do.   2
Zedoary ...   . ·   ...·   Do.   1
Sagapeno (serapine gum in Spanish ver-
    sion) ...   .   per *farazola*   20
Socotra aloes   ...   .   Do.   8
Cardamoms in grains   ...   ...   Do.   20
Rhubarb, which grows in abundance in Mala-
    bar, and which comes to Malacca from
    China   ...   . per *farazola* 40 to 50
Myrobalans, Emblic   ...   ...   Do.   2
Do., Belleric   ...   .   Do.   1½
Do., Chebulos and Citrine, all being of the
    same species   ...   ... per *farazola*   2
Do., Indian, which grow on the same tree as
    the Citrine ...   . per *farazola*   3
Tutia (tutenàg) ...   .   Do.   30
Cubebs, which grow in Java, are sold here at
    a low price, and by sight.
Opium from Aden, where it is prepared, is sold
    at Calicut ...   . per *farazola* 280 to 320
Opium which is prepared at Cambaya   Do.   200 to 250

WEIGHTS OF PORTUGAL AND OF INDIA, AND THE CORRESPONDENCE BETWEEN THESE AND THOSE OF PORTUGAL.[1]

The *arratel*, old weight, contains 14 ounces.

Do., new weight, contains 16 ounces.

Eight old *quintals* make 7 new, and each new *quintal* contains 128 *arratels* of 16 ounces.

Each old *quintal* is 3½ quarters of the new *quintal*, and is of 128 *arratels* of 14 ounces.

A *farazola* contains 22 *arratels* of 16 ounces, and 6½ ounces over.

Twenty *farazolas* make a *bahar*.

A *bahar* is 4 old *quintals* of Portugal.

All the Drugs and Spices and everything else which comes from India is sold in Portugal by the old weight, while other goods are sold by the new weight.

---

[1] See Vol. I. p. 157, n. 1.

FURTHER NOTES AND EMENDATIONS TO VOL. I.

Page xli, lines 29 to 32. Mgr. Dalgado informs me that the abbreviation *Mem* stands for *Mendo*, the ancient form of *Mendes*, the first form being used as the personal name and the second as a surname. Also that *Frēz* is an abbreviation of Fernandez.

Page 7, n. 1. In a review of this volume in the *J.R.A.S.* Sir Richard Temple suggests that such variations of name as are here found may be due to the inflection of the root in the indigenous premutative languages taking place at the commencement of their words, and that accordingly it is in the last syllables thereof that the true sense or form is to be sought.

Page 24, n. 2. The earlier history of the colonization of Madagascar from the islands of the Eastern Archipelago has formed the subject of much recent investigation, in which M. Gabriel Ferrand has taken a leading part. The results are summed up in his essay *K'ouen-Louen* (*Journal Asiatique*, 1919) (see pp. 220–226), and he comes to the conclusion that the settlers were a branch of the Khmer race (from which Ḳomr, the name they gave to Madagascar, is derived), that they had occupied some of the western islands of the Archipelago, and there were subject to a strong Indian influence, and that about the commencement of the Christian era they colonized Madagascar.

Page 28, n. 1. The early history of Zanzibar has recently been investigated by Major F. B. Pearce (*Zanzibar, the Island Metropolis of Eastern Africa*, 1920). He examined and cleared the ruins of ancient towns both in Zanzibar and Pemba ; these he thinks were flourishing in the twelfth and thirteenth centuries, but had probably decayed by the fifteenth. Had there been any important towns on these islands it seems probable that they would have been mentioned by Barbosa and other Portuguese writers. The present town of Zanzibar appears to be of more recent origin.

Page 63, n. 3. Mgr. Dalgado also reads this word *Carabolim* as *Cambolim*, and quotes this passage in his *Glossario, s.v.* Cambolim. He gives numerous other instances of its use, the earliest, of 1514, from Alboquerque's letters.

Page 82, n. 1. Uzun Ḥasan should have been described as prince of the Ak Kuyunlu or White Sheep, and not of the Karā Kuyunlu or Black Sheep. Ismáil is usually alluded to as Shah Ismáil and not as Ismáil Shah. I have used both forms in speaking of him, but the former is preferable. Both forms are however used on his coins.

Page 90, lines 1 and 2. I have not succeeded in tracing any allusion to these strange fish, nor any explanation of the story.

Page 92, line 8. The words here translated " saffron, indigo " are " açafram, indyo " in the Portuguese text. Mgr. Dalgado informs me that in his opinion they should be read without the comma, and translated as " Indian saffron." He adds that the word " indigo " was not used by the Portuguese, the only word being *anil*. Indigo as well as *anil* is however given in the table of drugs at the end of the book (p. 230), but as this is taken from Ramusio it cannot be considered as an instance of the use of the word by the Portuguese.   I therefore adopt the reading "Indian saffron." This is no doubt the "Açafram da terra" or Country Saffron of Orta (*Coll*. 18, p. 163 of Markham's translation). It is no doubt the turmeric, *Curcuma longa.*   See *Hobson-Jobson, s.v.* Saffron, and *Glossario, s.v.* Açafrão da India.

Page 126, n. 1.   Mr. H. Beveridge points out that the port of Balāwal was in Akbar's time a favourite place of embarkation for Mecca pilgrims, and that Akbar's foster-brother Mirza Koka, the Khān Āzam, sailed thence in his thirty-eighth year, returning in 1595.   Balāwal is evidently another form of Verāwal.   Although the Mirāt-i-Ahmadi says it was held by the Europeans it does not appear to have been ever actually annexed by the Portuguese.

Page 129, *Gingelly.*   This word has long been commonly used in India to denote the *Sesamum Indicum* and the oil extracted from it, and all the modern forms in European and Indian languages can be traced to the Portuguese *gergelim*, of which the use by Barbosa in this and other passages in his book (as on pp. 13, 89 and 154), is probably the earliest example.   The word, as Mgr. Dalgado shows in his *Glossario*, already existed in Portuguese and was derived from the Arabic *juljulān*, as to which Dozy and Engelmann's glossary quoted in *Hobson-Jobson* should be consulted.   Possibly Arabic itself borrowed the word from Persian, for its form suggests a Persian origin.   The first syllable has the appearance of the Persian *gul*, a flower, and the original form may well have been one of the numerous names of plants and flowers commencing with that word.   The Hindustani form jinjali is derived either direct from the Portuguese or from the English word ; the real vernacular term is *til.*   The earliest English use given in *Hobson-Jobson* is that of A. Hamilton, " gingerly oil." *New Account of the East Indies* (1727), I, p. 128.

Page 134, n. 2.   The part of this note suggesting an identification with the roads of Couali mentioned by Tavernier requires correction. The true name is restored by inserting the cedilla which is not given in the English edition of Tavernier, and reading Çouali, *i.e.* the roads of Suwally near Surat.

Page 138, n. 1.   Mgr. Dalgado points out that the French *mascaret* comes from the Portuguese *macareo* through the form *macreo*, and adds " Jaucigny writes *maqueric* (bore) in 1854 (*Indo Chine*, p. 295).   See also note *s.v.* Macareu in *Gonçalo de Viana*, p. 156, and in *Glossario.*

Page 139, n. 1.   The mistake about the Indus running unto the sea at Cambay was very persistent.   A. Hamilton repeats it in his *New Account of the East Indies* (1727), I, p. 129.

Page 152, n. 1.   The note in *Cathay*, Yule and Cordier, III, p. 76, n. 3, should however be referred to.   The identification of the Sibor of Cosmas with the Subāra of Mas'udi however seems improbable.   Chaul seems more suitable when the ancient forms of the name are considered (see *infra*, p. 159, n. 1), and this view is supported by Prof. H. Cordier in another note in *Cathay* (I, p. 227, n. 6).   Nor does the identification of Subāra with Suali seem probable.

Page, 155, n. 1.   *Cachopucho.*   Mgr. Dalgado informs me that he thinks it more probable that this should be read cacho, pucho, and that the two words are distinct as given under Malacca (Vol. II, p. 173, n. 3). Nevertheless I think that the explanation here given is not an improbable one, and that *Cachopucho* may represent the Malay *Kaya-putih.*

Page 161, n. 2.   *Corja.*   The derivation of this word requires reconsideration.   In the first place in Dalgado's *Glossario* the origin from the Malayālam *Korchchu*, a bundle or threaded string (like a string of pearls), is advocated. Mgr. Dalgado points out that the *ch* of Malayālam is commonly represented by *j* in Portugese as in *jágara* for *chákkara, jaca* for *chakka*, etc. He considers that this term having been adopted by the Portugese was influenced by the widely-spread use of the Indo-Aryan forms *kŏḍī* and *kŏṛi* in the sense of a score, and passed into general commercial use. In modern Portuguese he says the word has taken another meaning, that of a crowd or rough assembly in a depreciatory sense. As the Portuguese obtained their first acquaintance with Indian terms in Malabar this origin is probable. Nevertheless the meaning of " a score " was in full use in Barbosa's time, and Varthema found a similar if not identical term (*curia*), although it may be noted that in the text of Varthema given by Ramusio the word does not occur. *Kŏṛī* or *Kŏḍī* is clearly the origin of the present meaning of the word, but Sir George Grierson informs me that the derivation of this word from the Skr. *Kŏṭī* is very doubtful, as the change of meaning from 10 millions to 20 is too extreme. He considers it possible that it may be a borrowing from the Munḍā languages where it also occurs, as these languages count by twenties.

A Dravidian origin for *Corge* had already been put forward in *Hobson-Jobson*, and the subject was dealt with by Mr. Crooke in the 2nd Edition of that work. As to this Sir George Grierson says " I cannot venture to say that Yule and Burnell (the latter a Dravidian scholar) are wrong in saying that Kanarese *Korji* is a corruption of *Kori*, but I must confess that until it is explained, it seems to me to be a violent etymology." He adds that it is not to be found in Kittel's *Kanarese Dictionary*. He considers still that it is most likely that *Kŏṛī* a score is Munḍā in origin, and that Gujarāti and Marāthī could have received it from the Bhils or Kŏrkīs.

For the Dravidian origin of *Corge* the difficulty seems to be the great transition in meaning from a "bundle or indefinite collection of objects " to a "score," and the fact that it was already established as a trade-word in the latter sense as early as Barbosa's day. If the Dravidian origin is admitted as possible the Malayālam form mentioned by Mgr. Dalgado seems more probable than the rather doubtful Kanarese, especially as trade-words are most likely to have come into use on the Malabar coast.

Page 169, n. 2. On these names Mgr. Dalgado has favoured me with the following note :

" *Arapatam* must be the Malayālam *aḍapayaṛu*, the bean of the *aḍo*, a kind of fried cake. Marāthī *harbharā, Pisum sativum*, " ervilha da India," *greengram*. Properly *cheṛupayaṛu*, " pequena ervilha " or *pulse, Muruary*, Malayālam *Muḷayari*, bamboo-seed, which is eaten in various parts of India."

Brandis' in his *Forest Flora of N.W. India* (p. 566) remarks under *Bambusa arundinacea*, that "the seed of this and other species of Bamboo has often saved the lives of thousands in times of scarcity, 1812 in Orissa, 1864 in Camara, and 1866 (probably B. Tulda) in Malda." F. Buchanan in his *Journey* (1807) also alludes to the use of bamboo seed as food by the Chensu of Mysore (I, p. 169) and by the Malasir of Malabar (II, 341).

Buchanan also gives the following names :

I, p. 103. Avary = Dolichos Lablab.
            Tovary = Cytisus Cagan.
I, p. 108. Hervary of the Deccany Musalmans = Cicer Arietinum.

On the whole I am inclined to think that this word, *i.e.* the Marāthī *harbharā* is the origin of Muruary, and that we should read *Huruary* for *Muruary*.

Page 170, n. 2. With regard to early mentions of Goa, Sir George Grierson informs me that the Sanskrit name for Goa is Gômanta, and that the Kônkani language spoken there is still called Gômântaki. Mgr. Dalgado writes as follows : " There are other copper-plates earlier than the fourteenth century which mention Goa. That of 1054 gives it the name of Gopâcpur. The original was lost in the Lisbon earthquake, but it exists in a badly done Portuguese translation (Sahyâdri Ghanda by Dr. Gomantâchala, edited by G. da Cunha)."

It would seem that the identity of Gowâpura and Gopâcpur with Gômanta is a question which deserves further investigation.

Page 177. The three classes of vessels, *atalayas, fustas* and *xambucos*, have been alluded to several times in the course of this work. For *atalaya* see pp. 132, n. 1, and 133, n. 1 ; for *fusta* (or " foist ") p. 159, n. 1, and for *xambuco* pp. 167, 169, 185, 189. In this passage they seem to be mentioned in order of size ; the *atalayas* were shore boats often used for patrolling; the *fustas* made longer voyages, and were employed in the attack from Gujarât on Lourenço D'Almeida's ships at Chaul. The *xambucos* were larger sea-going craft like the Arab *dhows*, and were much used in trade.

Page 180, n. 2. With regard to these *laudes* or quilted coats Mgr. Dalgado informs me that this word was a Portuguese word known before their arrival in India (sing. *laudel*, pl. *laudeas*). It is derived by Portuguese lexicographers from the Latin *lodix*.

Page 182, n. 2. On the question of the identification of *Danseam Rayen* with a Marâthâ principality, Mr. S. Krishnaswâmi Aiyengar, who is engaged on a work on Vijayanagar history, writes that he considers this " is perhaps the best way to look at it in the circumstances."

Castanheda (Bk. II, Ch. 16) also gives a list of the five provinces of Narsinga :

(1) Talinate, extending along the sea from Cintacora on the border of Daquem for about 50 leagues.
(2) Teârragei, which lies in the interior and is conterminous with Daquem. This is evidently the Danseam Rayen of Barbosa, and corresponds with it in position.
(3) Canarâ, also in the interior.
(4) Choramandel, which extends along the sea from the end of the kingdom of Coulâo as far as the Mount Udigirmela which divides Narsinga from the kingdom of Uriâ.
    This gives far too great a northward extension to Choramandel, and makes it take in the coast up to Orissa, which properly belonged to Telingâna.
(5) This is in the interior and is called Telengue. Except that the last-named has been robbed of its coast the classification agrees well with Barbosa's.

Page 190, n. 2. Mgr. Dalgado in his *Glossario, s.v.* Berido, quotes a passage from Castanheda bearing on duels in Vijayanagar. I give a translation of the passage in full.

Castanheda, Bk. II, Ch. 16 (p. 53). There are many duels on account of love of women wherein many men lose their lives. Those who fight ask the King for a field, which he gives them and also seconds(*padrinhos*, " stepfathers "), and if they are men of position he goes to see the duel. They fight on foot in a place surrounded with steps, whereinto they enter naked and wearing turbans. They are armed with swords and shields and are girt with daggers. They have seconds and judges who give judgment as to the fight, and duels are so usual among them and the King takes so great delight therein that any man whom he knows to be a valiant knight he orders to wear a golden chain on his right arm to show that he is the bravest of all, and this he must defend in arms against any who come to demand it, if he would not lose it.   And he who wishes to fight tells the king he has insulted him by giving the chain to one who is not so good a knight as he . . . . and these duels also take place among the officials as to which of them knows his duties best, and also among any skilled in matters known to men, for he who knows best wears the same chain, which is called *berid.*"

In this note in Vol. I a mistake was made in attributing to Yule a remark as to this passage as it appears in Ramusio.   But a further reference makes it clear that Yule referred to a possible interpolation in Ramusio's text of Marco Polo, and not his text of Barbosa.

Page 220, n. 1.   The following account of the practice in modern times, as given by Sir George Grierson, may be read with interest :

" In the seventies I tried a number of people for hook-swinging in Rangpur (Bengal).   I saw the so-called " victim " the day after the affair and he did not seem a bit the worse for it.   He was a strong hefty fellow with a grin on his face.   The hooks were inserted on each side of his back below the shoulder-blades, and went under the muscles there.   These supported his weight.   The wounds were quite small, and gave him apparently little or no inconvenience when I saw him. The defence was that the swinging did not hurt the victim, who certainly was quite voluntary.   He was low-caste, and I daresay, like other men of his kind, did not easily feel pain.

Page 233, n. 2.   Mgr. Dalgado informs me that the Chronicle of the King of Portugal alluded to by Ruano in Orta's *Colloquy* is the *Chronica do Principe D. João* of Resende where the words quoted occur in the Miscellanea, an Appendix to the Chronicle.

Page 235, n. 1.   Sir George Grierson writes, referring to the word *pázan*, that according to Horn (Grundriss der Neupersischen Etymologie, p. 272), it is derived from the Pehlevi *páchan*.   The same form, *páchan*, survives in the western dialect of Balochi.

ERRATA, VOL. I.

Page xxv, line 4. *For* Balâão *read* Bulhão
Page lxvii, line 22. *For* Patemxy *read* Patenexy
Page 47. The name at the head of § 30 Meca, should be within square brackets ; and the commencement of the following line also.
Page 56, lines 3 and 5 from bottom. *For* de Orta *read* da Orta
Page 58, line 8 from bottom. *For* (Cor ?) *read* (Çor)
Page 65, line 2 from bottom. *For* shirh *read* shihr
Page 72, note 3. *For* Profame *read* Profam
Page 73, line 12 from bottom. *For* straits of *read* straits to
Page 78, line 28. *For* Maynard *read* Meynard
Page 80, last line. *For* Imâm *read* 'Omân
Page 93, line 36 (14 from bottom). *For* of *read* or
Page 94, lines 23 from top and 15 from bottom. *For* Garciâ de Orta *read* Garcia da Orta
Page 96, note 1. *For* Castelha *read* Castella
Page 108, note 1. *For* Basay *read* Baxay
Page 108, n. 3, line 4 from bottom. *For* fâshtra *read* râshtra
Page 108, n. 3, line 3 from bottom. *For* rxtent *read* extent
Page 108, n. 3, line 2 from bottom. *For* erom *read* from
Page 124, n. 2. *For* falcoes *read* falcões
Page 126, n. 1, line 8 from bottom. *For* Batâwal *read* Balâwal
Page 138, n. 1, line 11. *For* Sc fi's *read* Schoff's
Page 147, n. 1. *For* Appendix B *read* Appendix
Page 151, n. 1. *For* de Orta *read* da Orta
Page 155, n. 1, lines 24 to 27, first words of each line. *For* as *read* A : *for* Aarly *read* early ; *for* esee *read* (see ; *for* (last *read* last
Page 156, line 33. Omit comma at end of line.
Page 158, line 7 from bottom. After p. 162, n. 1, insert)
Page 162, n. 1, line 4. *For* note 1 *read* (p. 159, n. 1)
Page 195, n. 2, line 7 from bottom. *For* (avegação *read* (Navegação)
Page 216, n. 1. *For* Canti *read* Conti
Page 226, n. 2. *For* de Orta *read* da Orta
Page 233, n. 2. *For* de Orta *read* da Orta

APPENDIX I.

EXTRACTS FROM THE "DECADAS" OF JOÃO DE BARROS.

I.—*Decadas I*, Book ix, Ch. 3, f. 180 b.

According to what we have obtained of their writings from certain books interpreted for us, at the time when we entered India it was 612 years past that in the land which they call *Malabar* there was a King named Sarama Pereimal whose state was all the land along the coast for eighty leagues (as we have said above). Which King was so powerful that in memory of his name they used to make a reckoning of the period of his reign (which they abandoned at our arrival) making it the starting point of their era.

The principal establishment of this King was at Coulam where the leading merchants in spices assembled for many hundreds of years ; and in his time the Arabs, now converted to the sect of Mahamed, began to trade with India ; not indeed as altogether new to it, for they and the Persians had long been masters of those two narrow seas by which eastern goods came to these regions of Europe, but as people who began now to propagate the creed they had adopted . . . . and in order to make it more acceptable they took their daughters as wives, a matter which these Heathen hold to be an honour ; until, when they were well settled in the country, this King Sarama Pereimal became a Moor, and showed them great favour and assigned them a place of habitation. It was at Calecut, for there is the flower of the pepper and ginger trade. Then they persuaded him that for his salvation he ought to end his life at the house of Mecha. He agreed . . . . and determined to make a partition of his state among his nearest kindred.

To the highest of these he gave the Kingdom of Coulão where was situated the see of the Brammane religion. To the next he gave Cananor, with the title of King and to others lands and titles of honours in accordance with their custom. . . . The last of these was the city of Calecut, where the Moors already had their own settlement, as one who delivered himself entirely into the hands of that race who had shown him the way of salvation, ... and as Calecut was the last property he held in his own hands to divide, he held that with the help of these Moors, the Lord of that place should be suzerain over the others. This place although but small, he wished to give to a nephew who was his favourite, and as a new name of power over the rest he called him Çamorij, as it might be Emperor among us. He left him two pieces which he was accustomed to use : a *lamp* which is used before great persons ; like a torch among us, wherefore our people give it this name . . . . and the other was a *sword* which signified the royal power. He was to have the secular power, and the King of Coulam the religious, as the Head of the Bramanes, to whom he left the name of Cobritem[1] as he was their pontiff ; and in temporal matters this King of Coulam and the King of Cananor might (not ?) strike money, as the Çamorij was their superior, and the other Lords might not roof their houses with tiles. Regarding dignities to be held by each of them nothing is written as far as we have discovered up till now . . . . For the husbandman is distinct from the fisher and the weaver from the carpenter, etc. . . . . and the Naire is the noblest in blood among this folk, and the Jews in their time did not perform so many purifications when they touched a Samaritan as they perform should they by mischance touch anyone of the people. Thus they treat them as if they themselves were a glorified body and the others foul beasts.

(Then he goes on to state that there are the following castes : (1) the Chingalas, whom we call Chatijs who come from the Choromandel coast, the mercantile caste ; (2) Moors of two kinds, *i.e.* the natives or Naiteas, half Arab by descent, and the foreigners, Arabs, Persians, or Guzarates and others ; (3) Jews, and (4) Heathen of various classes.)

The Naires are the most warlike of all, and though held to be the most noble yet they may be called sons of the common people, for they know not with certainty who are their fathers, the Naire women being common to all of their rank. For this caste does not restrict itself as to the most noble, except

---

[1] Cf. Cobertorim in text, p. 4 and note.

among their own people ; and is so free that when a woman of this Naire blood is ten years of age, when she is held to be ready for marriage following certain ceremonies, she may receive in her house as many Naires as she will, and Bramenes, who are their clergy, are also privileged to be received, for whom, being of another race, they are very eager, even for adulteresses. And they, both men and women, are so free from the matrimonial bond that if one dislikes the other it is enough for them to separate in a manner of repudiation, yet as long as they are in accord the man must support the woman. And if any outside Naire is with her no one may go in or know what she is doing when he finds the sword and shield of the other at the door, nor is there any jealousy nor cause of offence in this. Hence none of them considers a child borne by the woman as his own, nor is bound to maintain him, and their true heirs are their nephews, sons of their (sisters ?) brothers. They say that this is a very ancient law among them, and that it springs from the wish of a certain prince to relieve the men of the burden of maintaining sons and leave them free and ready for warlike service to which they are bound whensoever the King calls upon them. They have great privileges and liberties so much so that when one of them goes any whither he continues to shout out his " ou elle po, po," that is " Take care," " Take care," and (save only other Naires) everyone leaves the street or road out of respect for his person, as it is a religious matter not to touch anyone outside his own honour. If this happens he must purify himself from the contagion with certain ceremonies. No one may call himself a Naire until he has been knighted . . . . When he reaches the age of seven years he must go to the fencing school, the master of which (whom they call Panical) he holds to be in the place of a father on account of the teaching he receives from him, and, next to the King or Lord whom they serve, they hold him in reverence. (Then follows a description of the training, the arms carried, the ceremony of the knighthood, etc.)

II.—Extracts from the Geographical Chapter, *Decadas I.*
Bk. ix., Ch. 1, f. 176, Rev.

And from this cape (Segógora), which our folk call Palmeiras,

Q

where we come to the end of the kingdom of Orixa (at one and twenty degrees) to the other boundary of the Kingdom of Bengala which is the city of Chatigão at two and twenty good degrees it may be one hundred leagues as we have said. Halting however at this distance of a hundred leagues on turning Cape Segógora there is an inlet of the kingdom of Orixa where discharges itself the River called Ganga of which we spoke above which traverses the greater part of this Kingdom and passes by the city of Ramana the metropolis thereof, and flows into the River Ganges, where it as well falls into the sea. And whereas this whole distance from Cape Segógora to Chatigão can be better depicted than described in writing by reason that all that land is cut into islands and shallows, which form at the mouths of the Ganges through the abundance of its water we name not the cities and towns on these islands, yet those curious as to their position may see it in the plates in our Geography. [These were never published, but Lavanha's map in *Decada IV* here reproduced takes their place as far as Bengal is concerned.] Wherefore continuing along our under finger to the sixth part of the general division which we have made, that which begins at Chatigão and ends at the Cape of Singapura, which is but one degree to the north of the equinoctial line and forty [leagues] east of our city of Malaca, the whole may be 380 leagues, which we divide as follows : From the Cape of Negraes at the 17th degree where beginneth the Kingdom of Pegu, 100 leagues : in which are these towns, Chocoriá, Bacalâ, Arracão (the capital city of the Realm of that name), Chubode, Sedoe and Xarā (which is on the point of Negraes). Hence passing by the city of Tâvay at 13 degrees (the last of the Realm of Pegu) there is then a great gulf with many islands and shoals formed like those of the Ganges by another mighty river which divides the land of Pegu ; which river flows from the Lake of Chimay, 200 leagues to the north in the inner part of the country, whence flow six rivers ; three of which join others and form the great river which flows through Siam [the Menam], and the others fall into the Bay of Bengala. One traverses the country of Caor whence it takes its name and through Camotáy and Cirote (where are made all the eunuchs of that part of the East),

and comes forth above Chatigão into that remarkable arm of
the Ganges in front of the Isle of Sornagão. [This river Caor
flowing into the Meghna opposite Sunargãon is probably the
Brahmaputra.] The other, that of Pegu, passes through the
kingdom of Avà which is in the interior [the Irrawaddy] and
the third [the Salween] comes forth in Martabâo between Tâvay
and Pegu (at 15 degrees). And the towns outside this gulf of
islands of Pegu and going along the coast thereof are Vagaru,
Martabâo, a city known for its great trade, and yet further
Rey Tagala and Tâvay, at which city of Tâvay a short time
before we entered India began the Kingdom of Sião and it
ended on the other sea of the East in the Kingdom of Camboja;
and into it projected the Kingdom of Malaca which we
conquered from a Moorish usurper (*tyranno*) who had risen
against the King of Sião, as will be told in its proper place.
On this coast, still following the index finger which we have
drawn, up to the point thereof, to wit the Cape of Singapura,
and thence turning upwards to its junction with the middle
finger (where may be placed the Kingdom of Camboja), there
will be 500 leagues of coast more or less, all pertaining to this
Heathen prince. He has lost the greater part thereof in the
changes of time, more especially after that we had taken
Malaca, for the Malay Moors after they had been cast out
thence sought for new settlements along that coast, and, that
race being the fiercest of all in those regions, they took possession of all the best ports for trade and navigation, which the
natives of the land used not, and made themselves Lords
thereof, and some of them took the title of Kings. Thus with
the changes of time and more which we have related above,
when Affonso de Alboquerque took Malaca this coast was left
without division of states. And the towns from Tâvay to
Malaca are these : Tenassarij a celebrated city, Lûngur, Torrâo,
Quedâ (the flower of the pepper of all that coast), Pedâo,
Perâ, Solungor and our city of Malaca the capital of the Kingdom so called, which lies at two degrees and a half north.
Following forward for 40 leagues there is the Cape of Çingapura,
whence begins along the index finger the seventh division
which is from that point to the River of Sião, of which (as
we have said) the greater part of the waters flow from the

Q 2

Lake of Chimay. This river by reason of the great abundance of its waters the Siames call Menão (Menam) that is to say "the mother of waters." It falls into the sea at the latitude of 13 degrees. On this coast the towns of note are these : Pam, the capital of the Kingdom of that name, Ponticão, Calantão, Patane, Lugor, Cuy, Perperij and Bamplacot which is at the mouth of the Rio Menão.

EXTRACTS FROM THE DESCRIPTION OF THE KINGDOM OF BENGAL.

Decada IV, Bk. ix, Ch. 1, of J. de Barros (compiled and edited from his notes by Lavanha).

In the general description which we made above of the Indian Coast in our first *Decada* (Bk. ix, Ch. 1) we gave no further information regarding Bengal than of the dimensions of its Gulf, and of the entry into it of the River Ganges (called by the natives Ganga). It has therefore seemed to us fit that we should here deal with what happened to our people in that Kingdom and with the customs of the races who dwell therein. The Kingdom of Bengal then is situated in that region where the River Ganges discharges its waters by two principal branches into the Eastern Ocean, and where the land drawing further back from its waters forms the great Gulf which geographers term Gangetic and which we now name from Bengal. Into the mouths of these two branches two notable rivers discharge themselves, one from the east, the other from the west, both being boundaries of the Kingdom. One of these our people call the River of Chatigam, as it enters the eastern mouth of the Ganges at a city of this name, the most celebrated and richest of that Kingdom by reason of its port whither all the merchandize of the east runs together. The other river enters the western arm of the Ganges below another city called Satigam, also a great and noble place, but less resorted to than Chatigam as the port is not so convenient for the entry and departure of ships. The Chatigam river rises in the mountains of the kingdoms of Avà and of Vagarù, and flowing from N.E. to S.W. divides the Kingdom of Bengala from the lands of Codavascam (Khuda Bakhsh Khān), and along the course of this river lie the Kingdoms of Tipora and of Brema Limma which surround Bengala in the east [*i.e.*, this river is the Karnaphulli and not a branch of the Ganges]. Bending round to the east these mountains separate the Bengalas from the Patane peoples, and, lower down towards the south, from the Kingdom of Orixa, the level lands of Bengala lying between the mountains and the stream of the Ganges. The other river which enters the Ganges below Satigam runs through the kingdom of Orixa and its source is on the slopes of the mountains called Gate (Ghāts) by the Indians in those parts which are near Chaul. And as this river is a great one and flows through many lands, the natives, in imitation of the Ganges into which it discharges its waters, give it also the name of Ganga, and hold its waters to be as holy as those of the Ganges itself. In this manner lies the Kingdom of Bengala on its sea-coast which faces southwards between these two rivers, this of Satigam to the west and that of Chatigam to the east, and the two branches of the Ganges into which they flow form the figure of the Greek letter Delta, as do all great rivers which enter the sea by several mouths.

Page 557. *Islands from the Eastern Mouth* :
Tranquetiâ, Sundivà, Ingudià, Mularangue, Guacalà, Tipurià, Bulnei, Sornagam, Angarà, Merculij, Noldij, Cupitavaz, Pacuculij, Agrapara.

The Estate of Codovascam, a Moorish prince and a great Lord, is between Bengalla and Arcacam.

The Bengallas reckon it to be within the bounds of their Kingdom, and that of Tipora as well, but these lands being very mountainous the Bengallas say that certain powerful Lords therein have risen against the King of Bengalla, and whereas there was ever hatred and rivalry between the Bengallas and the Tiporitas, as there is wont to be between neighbour Kingdoms, when one claims to be greater than the other, the Tiporitas allied themselves with those of the kingdom of Cou, also unfriendly to the Bengallas.

(He then explains how these two mountain Kingdoms although strong in warriors and horses were overcome by Bengal through the military discipline and artillery introduced by the Moors.)

Page 558. The saying is quoted regarding the great King-doms of India, that

Bengalla was famous for its numerous infantry.
Orixà for elephants.
Bisnagà for soldiers skilled in sword and shield work.
Delij for its cities and villages.
Cou for its horses.

Hence they were known as :—

Espatij, i.e., Aśvapati—Cou=Kūch Bihar.
Gaspatij, i.e., Gajapati—Orissa.
Noropatij, i.e., Narapati—Bengal.
Buapatij, i.e., Bhumipati—Delhi.
Coapatij, i.e., Sarvapati ? Vijayanagar.
(Çoapatij ?).

[That is to say :—

Aśvapati = Lord of horses.
Gajapati = Lord of elephants.
Narapati = Lord of men.
Bhumipati = Lord of lands.
Sarvapati = Lord of all (?).]

Page 559. The principal city of this Realm is called Gouro, on the Ganges, said to be three of our leagues in length, with 200,000 inhabitants. On one side the river defends it . . . Its trade and that of all Bengalla was such before the Patanes took it that Soltham Badur [Sultān Bahādur Shāh of Gujarāt] would say that he was one, the King of Narsinga two and the King of Bengalla three, that is that the King of Bengalla alone held as much as he and the King of Narsinga held jointly.

FIRST EXPEDITION TO BENGAL AS RELATED BY DE BARROS
(ABSTRACT), III, ii, 6, f. 41, 42.

Fernam Perez D'Andrade having been sent out by Lopo Soares D'Albergaria to go first to China and afterwards to Bengala and Pegu went first to Pacem in Sumatra where his ship was accidentally burnt. Thus he lost the proper season (mouçam) for the voyage to China and determined to go to

Bengalla, sending on before him one Joam Coelho in the ship of a Moor called Gromálle (Ghulam Ali) a relative of the Governor of Chatigam. He was not allowed by Jorge de Brito, Captain of Malaca, to carry out this plan, but was ordered to go to China. The reason was that Rafael Perestrello had been sent there in a junk by Jorge D'Alboquerque, and had not yet returned. F. Perez D'Andrade therefore sailed on 12 Aug. 1516, passing Cochin China in the middle of Sept., but the *mouçam* having come to an end he was caught in a storm and had to take refuge on the coast of Choampá, with all his ships except a junk in which was Duarte Coelho who took refuge in the Menam River After many adventures he got away at the end of Sept. following the coast between Malaca and Siam to the port of Patane, which he took, and after making peace returned to Malaca. Rafael Perestrello had now returned from China and had made great profits. Then F. Perez decided to go to China and not to Bengal. He went first to Pacem to get a cargo of pepper and stayed there till May, 1517. He went back to Malaca, but was again delayed, Jorge de Brito having died and a dispute as to the succession to the captaincy having arisen ; he at last started in June, 1517, and arrived at the Island of Tamão (Beniaga) on Aug. 15, 1917.

Decada II, ii, 3. EXPEDITION TO THE MALDIVES AND BENGAL (ABSTRACT).

J. da Silveira sent by L. Soares to the *Maldives*. Took a ship on which was Gromálle ; on returning he was sent to Bengal via Ceylon. Arrived at the Arracam River. where the people wished to accompany him as they were at war with Bengal. He did not agree. Arrived at Chatigam, where he was regarded as a pirate. Joam Coelho sent by Fernam Perez had the day before arrived there with a message from the King of Portugal. There was a difference between them, J. da Silveira being jealous of Coelho, whom he detained in his ship. This made the Governor still more suspicious, he thought F. Perez was the true messenger and Silveira a pirate. He could not obtain supplies and was perpetually attacked and owing to the monsoon he could not leave the river. At last the

· Governor made peace with him fearing that ships coming to the port would be taken by him when the monsoon was over.

Correa gives no information on these points but see II, p. 530, where he simply says that Fernão Peres had been appointed by the King to go to Bengal, but Dom Alexio would not agree to this and made him return to India (apparently after he had come back from China), on the ground that the Governor had given the Bengal expedition to his brother-in-law D. Joam da Silveira.

APPENDIX II (a).

[The following is an account of the *Ariyiṭṭu vāzhcha* (coronation of the Zamorin) adapted from an account written in Malayālam by the late Zamorin of the ceremony that took place in October, 1909. The Zamorin then installed was the author's immediate predecessor. The author was installed as Erālpād at the same time. He himself became Zamorin in December, 1912, at the age of sixty-seven, and died in July 1915. His full name and titles were as follows :—Padnichāne Kovilagath Mānavikraman (Ettan) Rāja Mānavikrama Rāja, Zamorin of Calicut. His portrait, from a photograph sent by Mr. J. A. Thorne, appears as a frontispiece to this volume. He appears in the costume worn during the *diksha* period, that is during the mourning for his predecessor. The inset bust represents the Rāja of Cochin, with whom the Zamorin brought about a reconciliation after the dynasties had been at enmity for centuries.]

The *piṇḍam* ceremony of the late Zamorin and the *ariyiṭṭu vāzhcha* of the present Zamorin and of the Erālpād and Mūnnārpād took place on Tulam 2nd, at the Kizhakke Kovilagam, Kottakkal, with great éclat. By the previous evening most of the principal Nambutirippads, Nambudiris, and chieftains of Malabar had arrived at the Kovilagam.

The first ceremony is a giving of presents called " *Ekōdrishtam* " to all Brahmanas. About a thousand *panams* are so distributed. This is to ensure the bliss of the deceased Zamorin in the next world. Next comes the " *Pulakuli* " (*i.e.*, bathing to remove the death pollution). A feature of this with the Zamorins is as follows :—

As the Zamorin stands in the water of the tank, the Valia Raja of Punnathur (on this occasion a minor under the Court of Wards), comes to the place and with his right hand takes the left hand of the Zamorin. Both of them then plunge under the water. As soon as they are under the water the Nambidi (*i.e.*, the Pannathur Raja) lets go the Zamorin's hand, dives through the water and goes out of the tank by another flight of steps, carefully averting his gaze from the Zamorin. The Pannathur Raja has the right of dining with the Zamorin on this day.

Next comes the " *Punyāham* " (purification).

Then comes the *Visit to the temple* to worship the family diety, the Bhagavati of Srivalayanād.

When a Zamorin dies, the *Vīra sankhalas* (*i.e.*, heavy bracelets) worn by him on arms and legs are placed below the image of Bhagavati, the significance of which is that they revert to the deity on his death. The first duty of the new Zamorin is to take them from the priest of Bhagavati when he goes to the shrine and put them on.

The next ceremony is the " *Vayarāttam.*" The nature of this ceremony is a secret, known only to the Zamorin and to the Vayara Panikkars who perform it. It has been practised for very many centuries.

Then comes the " *Vāl Pūja* " (worship of the sword). This is the sword given to the original Zamorin by Cheramān Perumāl with the injunction " Strike and slay and conquer." It is still preserved in a copper sheath, and is daily worshipped by the Zamorin. As soon as a Zamorin dies it is laid at the feet of Bhagavati, where worship is offered to it by the priest. It is first worshipped by the new Zamorin on this day (*i.e.*, the day of his installation).

Then comes the *Interview with the Āzhuvāncheri Tambrākkal.* The Tambrākkal has to stop at a place two miles from the Kovilagam ; he is not allowed to stay nearer the Kovilagam. From there at about 11 a.m., he proceeds in state and with musical honours to a temple not far from the Kovilagam. At the same time the Zamorin proceeds to the temple from the Kovilagam in equal state. They meet at the temple and the Tambrākkal then whispers some secret counsel in the Zamorin's ear. It is said that one of the instructions so given is "Do thou protect the cow and the Brahman and thou shalt reign as Lord of the hills and waves " (*Kunnala-kōnātiri*). When this is finished purānas are read for some time.

Then follows the *Grihasānti.* Silver censers are filled with water in which is placed a decoction made of the four milky trees (*i.e.*, Ficus Racemosa, Ficus Venosa, Ficus Religiosa and Ficus Indica) and other herbs. These are blessed by the Chēnnāss Nambūtirippad (the *tāntri* and instructor in *mantrams* to the Zamorin's family) and placed by them in front of the various Sthānis (*i.e.*, the five Rajas). Then each Sthāni in order, beginning with the Zamorin, comes forward to the place where his censer is placed, and does obeisance to it. The Nambūtirippad, as each comes forward, pours the decoction over him precisely as Abhisēkham is done to deities. The Sthānis then bathe and put on fresh clothes. (Up to that time each has been clad only in a single garment, tucked up before and behind in an unusual manner.) Then another visit is paid to the Bhagavati shrine, and many presents are distributed there. The Chēnnāss Nambūtirippad then instructs each Sthāni in the mantrams proper to his Sthānam.

Then comes the *Visit to the Kalari* (school of arms) and *Taking of the Sword*. All Zamorins of old were trained in arms ; on the death of a Zamorin, until this day (the day of the installation) no weapon would be touched by the new Sthānis, and in that period no warfare could be carried on. The ceremony now referred to would give the new Zamorin the right to resume his arms.

(A story in this connection is related of a feudatory chieftain of the Zamorin called the Tōṇiyil Nāyar. On the death of a certain Zamorin the Nayar thought the laying down of arms a good opportunity of showing his independence. He marched to the Kovilagam with a large force of men and took up his stand at the Vayaru-taḷam. The Mangāt Achan and other chieftains went against him and overcame him and ignominiously threw him out by the scruff of the neck. From that day it has been customary for the Nāyar to come to the Kovilagam, where the manner of his discomfiture is exhibited in play. During the *Tiruvantali* period, *i.e.*, after the *Sanchayanam* and before the installation he appears with his men and mounts the Vayaru-taḷam, and the Mangāt Achan takes him by the neck and ejects him. The Nayar has then to return home, his men with arms reversed. On this occasion this ceremony was dispensed with, the sole surviving member of the Nāyar's family being an invalid.)

The instructor in arms to the Zamorin's family is a chieftain called the Dharmōth Panikkar. (These Panikkars were formerly the hereditary Commanders-in-Chief of the Zamorin's army; the other principal chieftains of the Zamorin being the Mangāt Achan, the Tenayanchēri Eḷayad and the Rayiranallur Pāra Nambi).

On the Karali the Dharmōth Panikkar places 27 lotus flowers denoting 27 deities, after the deities have been invoked and worshipped by a Nambūtiri priest. The Zamorin goes to each in turn and does obeisance, followed by the other Sthānis in order. The Zamorin then receives the sword from the Panikkar, who girds it upon him. The Zamorin gives a present of two bundles, each containing 101 panams, to the Panikkar.

Preparations are then made for the *Ariyittu vāzcha* (installation by pouring of rice). This takes place for the Zamorin on the Vayaru-taḷam (a raised platform) ; for the other Sthānis, elsewhere.

First comes the *Adorning.* The Sthānis are adorned from head to foot in ornaments containing the nine jewels. A personage called the " Nandāvanathu Nambi " has the office of adorning the Zamorin : the Punnassēri Nambi does the same office for the Erālpād ; and Nambūtiri priests for the other Sthānis. In the procession to the Vayaru-taḷam each Sthāni goes holding the hand of the person who has adorned him. The Zamorin proceeds to the Vayaru-taḷam, which is handsomely decorated and crowded with the chief Nambūtiris and lords of his country. He takes his seat on the white cloth (Vella) and dark woollen cloth (karimpadam) which are customarily spread for great men, facing the east, and in front of an image of his family deity Bhagavati. The place resounds with the squealing of pipes, thunder of drums, and explosion of guns. A diadem is then placed on the Zamorin's head, and the *Pouring of the rice* then takes place. This is done by the three chief Nambūtirippads (ādhyans) of three grāmams, *viz.,* Pūmuḷḷi, Varikāssēri and Kirāngāt Nambūtirippads.

After the death of a Zamorin his successor, before the rice-pouring ceremony is performed, cannot sign any document of state. The signing in the interval is done on his behalf by the Chittūr Nambutirippad, and all the necessary correspondence is seen to by the Mangāt Achan in the name of the family priest, the Talappaṇṇa Nambūtiri. So the first present at the installation is given to the Chittūr Nambūtirippad. Presents are then given to the other people assembled, including the Ālūr Kanisan (the astrologer).

Immediately after the rice-pouring comes the *Signing of the documents.* The Zamorin signs four documents. The significance of the proceeding is this : On the death of the Zamorin it was formerly the custom to stop all activity in the country until the installation ceremony. This was called the stopping of " fight, toll, shipping and trade." The four documents signed by the Zamorin would authorise the resumption of these four activities.

Then follow the rice-pouring ceremonies of the other four Sthānis. No diadem is placed on their heads but in other respects the ceremony is somewhat on the same lines as for the Zamorin. Each in turn falls at the Zamorin's feet and does homage and receives his blessing. Then each sits on Veḷḷa and Karimpaḍam in his appointed place, with an image of Bhagavati before him. Rice is poured on them only by two persons, *viz.*, the Varikkāssēri Nambūtirippad and the Zamorin himself.

This over, there follows the *Writing of the Charters.* Each Sthāni signs such a document in memory of the time when each was ruler of a part of the Zamorin's dominions and swore to fealty in this fashion before going to his Division.

Then all visit the temple in great state preceded by elephants and accompanied by all the chieftains and thousands of Nāyar followers. With the procession is carried one of the insignia of the Zamorin—a door-panel (known as paḷḷi mārādi) draped with a silk cloth and carried on a pole. The story is that when the Srivalayanad Bhagavati first appeared to the Zamorin and became his family deity, she stood behind a door, and that the Zamorin in accordance with the Bhagavati's command preserved the door for use in processions in the goddess's honour.

Before the Zamorin go seven beautiful girls sprinkling

water from silver dishes. In the same way five girls go before the Erālpād and three before the Mūnnārpād. Each Sthāni is carried in a litter inlaid with ivory. On the back of one of the elephants is placed the sword of Bhagavāti.

On return from the temple to the Kovilagam each Sthāni takes his seat in the porch on Veḷḷa and Karimpaḍam. The girls aforesaid then come each carrying lighted wicks in a silver saucer, and go thrice round the Sthānis, keeping them on their right (pradakshinam). As they go they turn and throw rice and other things over their shoulders. This ceremony is intended to avert the evil eye ; and with this the investiture of the Sthānis is complete. It only remains to give presents of rice and money to the chieftains and their followers. The money presents vary from two annas to one rupee per man of the followers. Of the Brahmans each Pattar receives four annas, each Embrāntiri six annas and each Nambūtiri eight annas ; this present is called *pratigraham*.

The next day the Zamorin and the other Sthānis go in solemn state to say farewell to the Āzhuvāncheri Tambrākkal. The Zamorin gives him a handsome present before they part, so do the other Sthānis and all receive his blessing.

NOTE ON THE ABOVE ACCOUNT BY MR. THORNE.

The author concludes his account with a thankful mention of the fact that the ceremony was not marred by any birth or death pollution. Two Tamburāttis were confined on that day—a lady of the Padinhare Kovilagam at Calicut, and a lady of the Kizhake Kovilagam at Kottakkal (where the ceremony took place). But the news of the former was brought only in the evening, and the latter event happened after the ceremony was over. Considering that the family contains some hundreds of members the author might well congratulate himself.

This particular ceremony took place at the Kizhakke Kovilagam at Kottakkel, since the Zamorin then installed was of that Kovilagam. Present-day Zamorins for the most part live in the Kovilagams to which they themselves belong. Of these the Padinhare (western) Kovilagam is at Mānkāvu just outside Calicut, the Puthiya (New) Kovilagam at

Tiruvannur a few miles outside Calicut, and the Kizhakke eastern) Kovilagam at Kottakkal in Ernad about 85 miles from Calicut.

The Zamorin of this account is an instance of the truth of Barbosa's remark that " the Kings of Malabar are always old." He was born in August, 1844; he became Valia Tamburān (*i.e.*, head) of his Kovilagam in March, 1900; Neduthrāppād (5th Raja) in December, 1901; Edatrāppād (4th Raja) in April, 1903; Mūnnārpād (3rd Raja) in May, 1903; Erālpād (2nd Raja) in April, 1904; and Zamorin in October, 1909, at the age of 65.

The previous Zamorin died on Kanni 19th 1085 M.F. (*i.e.*, October 5th, 1909). The installation of his successor took place on Tulam 2nd (*i.e.*, October 19th). Thus Barbosa's " thirteen days " for the period of general mourning is correct ; and the account confirms the statement that in this interval the new Zamorin could not take up his duties. I presume however that this quiescence is a sign of mourning, rather than of "waiting lest there should be someone to oppose him." The " cahimal " who acts as Regent meanwhile appears to be the Mangāt Achan. This personage has no longer any but a formal connection with the Zamorin ; he receives a yearly token of 200 panams (Rs. 57-2-4) from the Zamorin.

Buchanan (ii, p. 394) gives the Zamorin's ministers as Mangutachan (Mangāt Achan), Tenancheri Elliadi (Tenayancheri Elayad), Bermamuta Panycary (Dharmōth Panikkar), and Para Nambi (Rayiranallur Pāra Nambi).

APPENDIX II (b).

Note on the Funeral Ceremonies of the Zamorin.

The rites are somewhat the same as those observed by Nayars which are described on pp. 185-187 of the *Malabar Gazetteer*.

Among Nāyars when a man is about to die it is imperative to remove him to the floor from his bed before he breathes his last. But the Zamorin's body is left on the bed until his successor or near relations arrive. When he is at the point of death water from the Ganges or from Rameswaram is sprinkled on him, and presents (dānam) given to Brahmans. As soon as the death takes place, it is announced by the firing of sixteen mortars (*Kathina*). A number of coconuts cut in two, with lighted wicks of cotton inside them, are placed in lines from the place where the dead body lies up to the gate of the Kovilagam. Then begins afresh the giving of presents (*dakshina*) to Brahmans—ordinarily eight annas to a Nambūdiri, six annas to an Embrāntiri and four annas to a Pattar, or more if the Zamorin's successor can afford it.

Information of the death is at once sent, not only to the Tamburāns of the three Kovilagams, but also to the Maharaja of Travancore, and many other chieftains of the West Coast ; and to the collector of Malabar.

The body is removed from the bed on the arrival of the Zamorin's successor. It is covered with silk or a new cloth. Lines of cow-dung ashes, paddy, and rice are drawn on the ground around the corpse : and the Zamorin's successor, the nearest relations, and the attendants (known as Kurikkār Kuṭṭikaḷ) sit around it till the arrangements for the cremation are complete.

There is a special family (Edavalath), a member of which serves as priest for the funeral rites. They belong to the Attikurissi caste—a low Nāyar caste employed by Nāyars for removing death pollution. When all is ready the Zamorin's successor, the near relations, and the attendants (who are

Nedungadi, Eradi, or Vallodi by caste, and thus Samāntans
like the Zamorin) plunge into the tank. After bathing they
take the corpse, dip it in the tank, and place it on a frame-work
of fresh bamboos covered with new silk or cloth. They then
carry it to the cremation ground in the premises of the Kovilagam. The pyre has already been built there, lying north and
south. The body is carried three times round the pyre,
and placed on the pyre with the head to the south. The Tamburāns then place billets of wood upon the body. The fuel
used should be sandal-wood ; if that is found impossible,
mango-wood and cakes of cow-dung will serve. Before the
pyre is fired offerings (*bali*) of raw rice, gingelly-seed, etc.,
are made to the dead Zamorin, under the direction of the
priest above mentioned. The pyre is then set alight. A
special family of oil-monger Nāyars (Kārinkara Nāyars) have
the duty of drumming at the cremation, and the drumming
must continue incessantly till the *Sanchayanam* ceremony.
A lamp must also burn night and day till the *Sanchayanam*.

After the cremation begins the *udaka-kriya*, *i.e.*, offering
of *bali* and other ceremonies in honour of the deceased ; and
this continues until the *Sanchayanam*.

The Sanchayanam, *i.e.*, gathering of the bones—is generally
on the 7th, 9th, or 11th day after death. An auspicious
day has to be carefully chosen by an astrologer (Kanisan),
with reference to the day of the week and the star under
which the Zamorin's successor was born.

After the corpse is taken from the Kovilagam to the pyre
on the cremation day a woman of the Pullāre house (Menon
by caste) after bathing collects the ashes, paddy and rice
which were traced around the corpse, and the cloth with which
the corpse was covered, and keeps them on a plank at that
place. She stays there, with a lamp burning day and night,
till the *Sanchayanam* day, when she takes the articles to the
cremation ground and leaves them there. (NOTE.—Among
Nāyars the duty is performed by a younger sister or niece
of the deceased.)

The *Sanchayanam* is performed with much pomp. All
the chieftains connected with the Zamorin are invited. Before
the Zamorin's successor, the other Tamburāns and the

Kurikkár Kuikal proceed to the ceremony they have to bathe and put on the clothes brought for the occasion by a Mannáthi (Mannán -woman). The procession, headed by elephants and accompanied by drummers and musicians, goes to the cremation ground from the Kovilagam. Before the ceremony begins, various rites—the chief of which is *bali*—are performed. Then the Zamorin's successor seats himself facing east at the southern end of the pyre, and the others take their places according to seniority. Each is provided with a small pouch of green areca leaf (*pala*), and a pair of tweezers, which should be of gold or silver, but may be formed of the branches of a particular plant (*nyezhuku*). The bones are picked up with the tweezers and placed in the pouches. The ashes are taken to the nearest river or sea and scattered therein. The place of cremation is thoroughly cleaned, and all kinds of grain are sown there, and a coconut planted in the middle. (NOTE.— In the case of Náyars a plantain is so planted.) The bones are washed well in pure water, and then in milk, and placed in a new earthern pot : this is well covered and placed under a jack or coconut tree in the compound of the Kovilagam. A few of the bones are kept apart, and subsequently taken to a holy river or to the sea and thrown therein.

After the *Sanchayanam* the party returns to the courtyard of the Kovilagam, where various ceremonies are performed. One of these is curious. The priest above mentioned holds a knife, spade or axe parallel to the ground and the Tamburáns, facing east, have to stoop and pass under it. This is called " Bending under the branch." They must then bathe, and perform the daily *bali*, which is continued till the 15th day. After the *Sanchayanam* and before the 14th day the Tóniyil Náyar pays a visit which is conducted in the manner described in the account of the Ariyittu vázcha.

On the 14th night or rather very early on the 15th morning about 3 or 4 a.m. there is a ceremony called *Pula pindam* (*pula* means pollution, and *pindam* means the offering of rice-balls to the deceased). This takes place at the spot where the dead body lay till it was removed to the cremation ground, *i.e.*, in the *vadakkini* or northern wing of the Kovilagam. The Attikurissi priest presides at this ceremony, and only the

Zamorin's successor and two junior Tamburāns take part. At the close of it the priest purifies them by sprinkling a mixture of oil and milk on their feet in the courtyard of the Kovilagam the Tamburans standing with their faces to the east on a piece of cloth spread on the ground. All that then remains to remove the death pollution is the *pula kuli* (described in the account of Ariyiṭṭu vāzcha), which takes place early on the 15th morning.

The Zamorin has to continue his daily *bali* for a year, until the *Tirumāsam* brings to a close his period of *Dīksha*.

NOTE.—In the foregoing account the Indian calculation of time is adopted. Barbosa speaks of thirteen days of mourning, with the installation on the 14th. The Indian reckons in the day of death also, and thus speaks of a 14 days' pollution period, and installation on the 15th day.

APPENDIX II (c).

ROYAL TITLES IN MALABAR. BY MR. J. A. THORNE.

Çamidre or Zomodri is a fairly close transliteration of the Malayālam Sāmūtiri abbreviated to Sāmūri (corrupted also into Tāmūri), hence by the addition of the nasal (*cf.* Comorim and Cochim) by the Portuguese, Samorim or Zamorim, the modern Zamorin. The accepted derivation is that given by Gundert, Sāmūdri from Sanskrit *Samudra* "sea," thus " lord of the sea." This however cannot stand, for the following reasons :

(1) The Zamorin was *not* lord of the sea. It is true that by his alliance with the Muḥammadan settlers he found useful sea-robbers who served his turn. It is unlikely that he would derive his principal name from the assistance given to him by them, but it may be much more ancient. He was lord of the land long before he became powerful on the sea.

(2) There is no parallel in Malabar nomenclature for a " fancy title " of this sort. It is true that the Muḥammadan Sultan of Cananore is called among other things Azhi Raja, and that Azhi means sea, but it is a mere conjecture, and in my opinion an unlikely one, that his title is " sea-king." He is more commonly called Adi Raja or Ali Raja, which might mean anything. And in any case we cannot deduce from the title of a Muḥammadan Chief any parallel with that of a (more ancient) Hindu sovereign.

The true etymology of " Sāmūtiri " was suggested to me by an Indian gentleman and has, so far as I know, never appeared in print. The word is a compound of two Sanskrit words, *Svāmi* and *S'rī*. *Svāmi* becomes *sāmi* or *sāmu* commonly in proper names. S'ri becomes *tiri* by ordinary *tadbhavam* rules as in countless other words. So we get *Sāmitiri* or *Sāmūtiri*. The second syllable becomes lengthened so often before the termination -*tiri* (*e.g.*, Nambūtiri) and we get Sāmūtiri. It is surprising that this derivation should have been overlooked so long. The termination -*tiri*, which is almost universal in the designations of Malabar dynasties and is common in the names of high castes, *e.g.*, Nambūtiri, Embzantiri, Bhattatiri, Akkitiri, Sornattiri, should have given the clue.

A popular derivation still more far-fetched than "lord of the sea " supposes the name a compound of *Samudra* and *giri, i.e.*, " lord of the sea and hills " or " lord of the land between the sea and hills."

According to the derivation I have suggested Sāmūtiri is merely a grandiloquent term for " lord "—and that is quite in keeping with South Indian royal titles generally. It is noticeable that Barbosa is on the right scent in speaking of the title as " a point of honour above the others."

As for the Ali Raja, even if he is Azhi Raja and that means " lord of the sea," that proves nothing. He *was* " lord of the sea," ruling the Laccadives and possessing his own fleet. But I doubt the soundness of the derivation. The Ali Raja has personally disclaimed to me the title Azhi Raja. He says it is not so in the records of his dynasty. He is called Adi Raja (which might mean " first king "), or Ali Raja (deriving I suppose from the Arabic proper name " Ali "). I have no doubt that Azhi Raja is a Hindu invention like Kunnalakkon with the purpose of turning a title into Malayālam. The Keralolpatti appears to be the source of it.

Maly Conadary, Cunelavadyri. Maly Conadary of the Portuguese text would be Mala Konattiri ; *mala* being a synonym for *kunnu*, "hill." The *Cunelavadyri* of the Spanish text may be Kunnalattiri, "lord of the hills and waves." The Keralolpatti gives as titles of the Zamorin, Kunnalakon (*i.e.*, " king of the hills and waves ") and Kōnninu Kunātiri, " king of the hills." These forms may be taken to give support to the meaning of Sāmūtiri, a "lord of the hills and sea," which I have rejected. But it is easy to see how the title arose. Some Malabar pandit deciding that Sāmūtiri came from *Samudra* and *giri*, proceeded to show his ingenuity by turning it into honest Dravidian : he was no doubt rewarded for his pains and the name stuck. Similarly a Sanskrit variant has also been invented, *viz.*, *Śailābdhīśvara* (śaila, abdhi, iśvara). These etymological extravagances are common among Indian scholars.

Mala Kōnāttiri is not open to any objection on the ground of its being a fancy title. The meaning of "king of the Hill Country" was applicable to the Zamorin especially, as the country was generally known as Mala or Malayālam. Barbosa does not, I think, make the blunder that this was the personal name of the Zamorin then reigning. It is, of course, his title, not his name. Every Zamorin, whatever his personal name, drops it when he becomes Zamorin, and takes the name of Mānavikraman. Among males of the Zamorin's family there are only three names, viz., Mānavikraman, Mānavedan and Virarāyam. The Zamorin always becomes Mānavikraman but that name may always be taken as a personal name by his juniors. There are two devices to avoid confusion :

(a) The prefixes S'ri and Piru are used, that gives three variations for each name.

(b) Nicknames or pet names are commonly used ; these are mostly of the form "little Brother," "Uncle," "Boy," etc.

Benatediry, i.e., Vēṇāṭṭ-tiri, still a title of the Travancore Raja. It means "lord of the Vēṇād, "which is the Travancore Country. No satisfactory derivation has been suggested for Vēṇād.

NOTE.—Mr. Thorne's explanation of these titles, and especially of Zamorin, is novel and appears to me to be satisfactory, far more so than any derivations previously suggested. Whether such a formation as Svāmi-S'ri is admissible in Dravidian languages is for experts to decide ; but if there is no philological objection I think that the origin of the title Zamorin must be considered as solved. The explanation as "lord of the sea" has never seemed to me to be convincing. That -tiri as a termination is S'ri seems undeniable.

M. L. D.

INDEX.

Reimas, I. 190, 190 n.[1]
Reinel's Maps, 1516 and 1517,
I. 73 n.[1], 76 n.[1]
Rennell, J., Map of India, 1782 ;
Memoir on the Map of Hindostan,
1793, I. 105 n.[2], 196 n.[1].
II. 103 n.[2], 132 n.[2]
Resbutos (Rájputs), I. 108 n.[4],
109, 109 n.[1], 118, 118 n.[1]
Revadanda, I. 159 n.[1], 162 n.[2],
163 n.[1]
Revoleens (Eravallar caste), II.
67, 67 n.[1]
Reynel (Randēr), I. 108 n.[1],
145-148, 145 n.[1], 146 n.[2],
147 n.[1]; Appendix, Vol. I.
237-8
Rhinoceros, see Ganda
Rhodes (Knights of St. John of),
I. 133 n.[1]
Rhodes, Père Alexandre de
(Voyages), II. 208 n.[3], 209 n.[1]
Rhubarb (of Babilonia), I. 93,
93 n.[3]. II. (Of China), 214,
231 ; (of Malabar), 229 n.[1],
231
Ribeiro, João (Fatalidade Historica da Illa de Ceilão), II.
113 n.[1]
Ribero, Diego, 2nd Borgian Map,
I. liii-lviii,[1] 30 n.[3], 32 n.[1],
38 n.[1], 52 n.[1], 58 n.[3], 69 n.[1],
70 n.[1], 74 n.[1], 75 n.[3],[4], 76 n.[1],
78 n.[1], 79 n.[1], 90 n.[1]. II.
180 n.[1], 186 n.[2], 188 n.[1], 189
n.[3], 206 n.[2], 205 n.[1]
Rice, I. 21, 27, 56, 123 ; (black),
185, 186, 195, 195 n.[1], 197;
(white), 188 ; cultivation and
names of varieties, 192, 192
n.[2],[3], 194. II. (Imported into
Ceylon), 111, 111 n.[3]; (in
Pegu), 153 ; (in Siam), 165
Rishahr, I. 79 n.[1]
Risley, Sir H., People of India,
I. lxix. II. 45 (note)
Roçaque (in 'Omān), I. 72,
72 n.[1]
Rockhill, W..W. (Relations and
Trade of China), II. 85 n.[3],
97 n.[1], 108 n.[2], 109 n.[1], 125 n.[2],
145 n.[3], 161 n.[1], 162 n.[2], 169
n.[1], 182 n.[2], 186 n.[2], 188 n.[1],
189 n.[3], 192 n.[3], 195 n.[3], 203
n.[1], 206 n.[4], 208 n.[3], 214 n.[1]
Rosalgate, Cape of (Rāsa'l-Hadd)
I. 58 n.[3], 66 n.[3], 68 ,68 n.[1]
Rose, Mr. H. A., I. lxix

Roteiro (Route-book) (of Vasco
da Gama), I. lx, 4 n.[1], 13 n.[2],
15 n.[2], 19 n.[3], 29 n.[2], 31 n.[1],
193 n.[1]. II. 86 n.[1], 88 n.[2] (Of
De Castro), I. 51 n.[1], 61 n.[1],
62 n.[1]
Rubão (for Ar. rubbān, a pilot),
I. 51 n.[2]
Rubies, II. (Ceylon), 115, 116,
118 n.[1]; (Burma), 159, 161,
161 n.[1]; (general), 217-219 ;
(spinel rubies), 220, 220 n.[1]
Russell, R. V., Castes and Tribes
of Central Provinces, I. lxix,
110 n.[2], 117 n.[1], 144 n.[2], 217 n.[2]

Sabaio, title of, I. 86 n.[1], 172,
172 n.[1], 181, 181 n.[2]
Sadashēogarh, I. 170 n.[2]   .
Saddles, I. 119, 119 n.[1], 180,
180 n.[1]
Sago, II. 201 n.[1]
Saifu'd-dīn (of Ormus), I. 97
n.[2], 102 n.[1]
Sa'īd, Sultān or Sayyid, of
Zanzibar, I. 19 n.[1], 21 n.[1],
28 n.[1], 31 n.[1]
St. Bartholemew (Abyssinia),
I. 41
St. Catherine, Convent on Mt.
Sinai, I. 45, 45 n.[1]
St. Thomas, (Abyssinia), I.
40, 40 n.[2]. II. (India), 88 n.[3],
89, 93, 98, 98 n.[1], 99-101, 126,
126 n.[2], 127-129, 129 n.[1]
Saimūr, I. Arabic form of
Chaul, 159 n.[1]
Sakti-pūja in Malabar, II. 22
n.[1]
Saldanha, Antonio de, I. xlv,
lxxxiv, 19, 19 n.[1], 34, 34 n.[2]
II. xxiv, 211 n.[1]
Salsette, I. of, I. 152 n.[1]
Sam Lourenço, see Madagascar
Sāmantan (title of non-Ksha-
triya members of the ruling
caste in Malabar), II. 7 n.[1],[2],
13 n.[2],[3]
Samtiago (Santiago), the phrase
" to give Santiago," I. 103,
103 n.[1]
São Martim, Andres de, astrologer on the expedition of Magalhães, I. xlvii, lxxiii
São Sabastião, Cape of, I. 3,
3 n.[1]
Sandal-wood, Sanders-wood, II.
196, 196 n.[1]

𝕿𝖍𝖊 𝕳𝖆𝖐𝖑𝖚𝖞𝖙 𝕾𝖔𝖈𝖎𝖊𝖙𝖞, established in 1846, has for its object the printing of rare and valuable Voyages, Travels, Naval Expeditions, and other geographical records. Books of this class are of the highest interest to students of history, geography, navigation, and ethnology ; and many of them, especially the original narratives and translations of the Elizabethan and Stuart periods, are admirable examples of English prose at the stage of its most robust development.

The Society has not confined its selection to the books of English travellers, to a particular age, or to particular regions. Where the original is foreign, the work is given in English, fresh translations being made, except where it is possible to utilise the spirited renderings of the sixteenth or seventeenth century. The works selected for reproduction are printed (with rare exceptions) at full length. Each volume is placed in the charge of an editor especially competent—in many cases from personal acquaintance with the countries described—to give the reader such assistance as he needs for the elucidation of the text. As these editorial services are rendered gratuitously, *the whole of the amount received from subscribers is expended in the preparation of the Society's publications.*

One hundred volumes (forming Series I., see pages iv. to xiv.) were issued from 1846 to 1898 ; fifty volumes of Series II. (see pages xv. to xx.) have been issued in the twenty-three years ending 1921. A brief index to these is given on pages xxi. to xxvii., and a list of works in preparation on page xx.

THE Annual Subscription of ONE GUINEA—entitling the member to the year's publications—is due on January 1, and may be paid to

Messrs. BARCLAY and Co., 1, Pall Mall East, London, S.W.1 ;
The GUARANTY TRUST Co., 140, Broadway, New York.

Members have the sole privilege of purchasing back or current issues of the Society ; these tend to rise in value, and those which are out of print are now only to be obtained at high prices.

The present scale of charges is as follows :—

FIRST SERIES.

Sets, **omitting** Nos. 1 to 14, 16, 17, 18, 19, 22, 24, 25, 26, 32, 36, 37, 39, 42, 52 and 99 (71 vols.) . . . £70 0s. 0d.

Single Copies.—Nos. 29, 31, 34, 46, 47, 51, 53, 55, 56, 58, 60 to 73, 77, 79, 80, 82 to 87, 90 to 94, 96, 97, 98, at . 20s. 0d.

Nos. 28, 30, 41, 45, 48, 49, 50, 57, 74, 76, 78, 81, 88, 89, 95, 100, at . . . . . 30s. 0d.

Nos. 20, 21, 23, 27, 33, 35, 38, 40, 43, 44, 54, 59, 75, at . . . . . . 40s. 0d.

SECOND SERIES.

Nos. 1-10 *are out of print.*

Nos. 11 to 22, 28, 29, 31, 35, 39, 45, 46, 47, 48, 50, at . . . . 20s. 0d.

Nos. 23, 24, 25, 26, 27, 30, 32, 37, 38, 40, 42, at . 25s. 0d.

Nos. 33, 34, 36, 41, 43, 44, 49, at . . 30s. 0d.

Ladies or Gentlemen desiring to be enrolled as members should send their names to the Hon. Secretary, with the form of Banker's Order enclosed in this Prospectus. Applications for back volumes should be addressed to the Society's Agent, Messrs. B. QUARITCH, LTD., 11, Grafton Street, New Bond Street, London, W.1.

WORKS ALREADY ISSUED.

FIRST SERIES.

1847-1898.

1—The Observations of Sir Richard Hawkins, Knt.,

In his Voyage into the South Sea in 1593. Reprinted from the edition of 1622, and edited by ADMIRAL CHARLES RAMSAY DRINKWATER BETHUNE, C.B. pp. xvi. 246. Index.
(First Edition out of print. See No. 57.) Issued for 1847.

2—Select Letters of Christopher Columbus,

With Original Documents relating to the Discovery of the New World. Translated and Edited by RICHARD HENRY MAJOR, F.S.A., Keeper of Maps, British Museum, Sec. R.G.S. pp. xc. 240. Index.
(First Edition out of print. See No. 43. Two copies only were printed on vellum, one of which is in the British Museum, C. 29. k. 14.)
Issued for 1847.

3—The Discovery of the Large, Rich, & Beautiful Empire of Guiana,

With a relation of the great and golden City of Manoa (which the Spaniards call El Dorado), &c., performed in the year 1595 by SIR WALTER RALEGH, Knt. . . . Reprinted from the edition of 1596. With some unpublished Documents relative to that country. Edited with copious explanatory Notes and a biographical Memoir by SIR ROBERT HERMANN SCHOMBURGK, Ph.D. pp. lxxv. xv. 1 Map. Index.
(Out of print. Second Edition in preparation.) Issued for 1848.

4—Sir Francis Drake his Voyage, 1595,

By THOMAS MAYNARDE, together with the Spanish Account of Drake's attack on Puerto Rico. Edited from the original MSS. by WILLIAM DESBOROUGH COOLEY. pp. viii. 65. *(Out of print.) Issued for 1848.*

5—Narratives of Voyages towards the North-West,

In search of a Passage to Cathay & India, 1496 to 1631. With selections from the early Records of . . . the East India Company and from MSS. in the British Museum. Edited by THOMAS RUNDALL. pp. xx. 259. 2 Maps.
(Out of print.) Issued for 1849.

6—The Historie of Travaile into Virginia Britannia,

Expressing the Cosmographie and Commodities of the Country, together with the manners and customs of the people, gathered and observed as well by those who went first thither as collected by WILLIAM STRACHEY, Gent., the first Secretary of the Colony. Now first edited from the original MS. in the British Museum by RICHARD HENRY MAJOR, F.S.A., Keeper of Maps, British Museum, Sec. R.G.S. pp. xxxvi. 203. 1 Map. 6 Illus. Glossary. Index.
(Out of print.) Issued for 1849.

7—Divers Voyages touching the Discovery of America

And the Islands adjacent, collected and published by RICHARD HAKLUYT, Prebendary of Bristol, in the year 1582. Edited, with notes & an introduction by JOHN WINTER JONES, Principal Librarian of the British Museum. pp. xci. 171. 6. 2 Maps. 1 Illus. Index. *(Out of print.) Issued for 1850.*

8—Memorials of the Empire of Japon

In the Sixteenth and Seventeenth Centuries. (The Kingdome of Japonia. Harl. MSS. 6249.—The Letters of Wm. Adams, 1611 to 1617.) With a Commentary by THOMAS RUNDALL. pp. xxxviii. 186. 1 Map. 5 Illus.
(Out of print.) Issued for 1850.

9—The Discovery and Conquest of Terra Florida,

By Don Ferdinando de Soto, & six hundred Spaniards his followers. Written by a Gentleman of Elvas, employed in all the action, and translated out of Portuguese by RICHARD HAKLUYT. Reprinted from the edition of 1611. Edited with Notes & an Introduction, & a Translation of a Narrative of the Expedition by LUIS HERNANDEZ DE BIEDMA, Factor to the same, by WILLIAM BRENCHLEY RYE, Keeper of Printed Books, British Museum. pp. lxvii. 200. v. 1 Map. Index. *(Out of print.) Issued for* 1851.

10—Notes upon Russia,

Being a Translation from the Earliest Account of that Country, entitled Rerum Muscoviticarum Commentarii, by the BARON SIGISMUND VON HERBERSTEIN, Ambassador from the Court of Germany to the Grand Prince Vasiley Ivanovich, in the years 1517 and 1526. Translated and Edited with Notes & an Introduction, by RICHARD HENRY MAJOR, F.S.A., Keeper of Maps, British Museum, Sec. R.G.S. Vol. 1. pp. clxii. 116. 2 Illus.
(Vol. 2 = No. 12.) *(Out of print.) Issued for* 1851.

11—The Geography of Hudson's Bay,

Being the Remarks of Captain W. COATS, in many Voyages to that locality, between the years 1727 and 1751. With an Appendix containing Extracts from the Log of Captain MIDDLETON on his Voyage for the Discovery of the North-west Passage, in H.M.S. "Furnace," in 1741-3. Edited by JOHN BARROW, F.R.S., F.S.A. pp. x. 147. Index.
(Out of print.) Issued for 1852.

12—Notes upon Russia.

(Vol. I. = No. 10.) Vol. 2. pp. iv. 266. 2 Maps. 1 Illus. Index.
(Out of print.) Issued for 1852.

13—A True Description of Three Voyages by the North-East,

Towards Cathay and China, undertaken by the Dutch in the years 1594, 1595 and 1596, with their Discovery of Spitzbergen, their residence of ten months in Novaya Zemlya, and their safe return in two open boats. By GERRIT DE VEER. Published at Amsterdam in 1598, & in 1609 translated into English by WILLIAM PHILIP. Edited by CHARLES TILSTONE BEKE, Ph.D., F.S.A. pp. cxlii. 291. 4 Maps. 12 Illus. Index.
(Out of print. See also No. 54.) Issued for 1853.

14-15—The History of the Great and Mighty Kingdom of China and the Situation Thereof.

Compiled by the Padre JUAN GONZALEZ DE MENDOZA, & now reprinted from the Early Translation of R. Parke. Edited by SIR GEORGE THOMAS STAUNTON, Bart., M.P., F.R.S. With an Introduction by RICHARD HENRY MAJOR, F.S.A., Keeper of Maps, British Museum, Sec. R.G.S., 2 vols. Index. *(Vol. 14 out of print.) Issued for* 1854.

16—The World Encompassed by Sir Francis Drake.

Being his next Voyage to that to Nombre de Dios. [By SIR FRANCIS DRAKE, the Younger.] Collated with an unpublished Manuscript of Francis Fletcher, Chaplain to the Expedition. With Appendices illustrative of the same Voyage, and Introduction, by WILLIAM SANDYS WRIGHT VAUX, F.R.S., Keeper of Coins, British Museum. pp. xl. 295. 1 Map. Index. *(Out of print.) Issued for* 1855.

25—Early Voyages to Terra Australis,

Now called Australia. A Collection of documents, and extracts from early MS. Maps, illustrative of the history of discovery on the coasts of that vast Island, from the beginning of the Sixteenth Century to the time of Captain Cook. Edited with an Introduction by RICHARD HENRY MAJOR, F.S.A., Keeper of Maps, British Museum, Sec. R.G.S. pp. cxix. 200. 13. 5 Maps. Index. (*Out of print.*) *Issued for* 1859.

26—Narrative of the Embassy of Ruy Gonzalez de Clavijo to the Court of Timour, at Samarcand, A.D., 1403-6.

Translated for the first time with Notes, a Preface, & an introductory Life of Timour Beg, by SIR CLEMENTS R. MARKHAM, K.C B., F.R.S., ex-Pres. R.G.S. pp. lvi. 200. 1 Map. (*Out of print*). *Issued for* 1860.

27—Henry Hudson the Navigator, 1607-13.

The Original Documents in which his career is recorded. Collected, partly Translated, & annotated with an Introduction by GEORGE MICHAEL ASHER, LL.D. pp. ccxviii. 292. 2 Maps. Bibliography. Index.
Issued for 1860.

28—The Expedition of Pedro de Ursua and Lope de Aguirre,

In search of El Dorado and Omagua, in 1560-61. Translated from Fray PEDRO SIMON'S "Sixth Historical Notice of the Conquest of Tierra Firme," 1627, by WILLIAM BOLLAERT, F.R.G.S. With an Introduction by SIR CLEMENTS R. MARKHAM, K.C.B., F.R.S., ex-Pres. R.G.S. pp. lii 237. 1 Map. *Issued for* 1861.

29—The Life and Acts of Don Alonzo Enriquez de Guzman,

A Knight of Seville, of the Order of Santiago, A.D. 1518 to 1543. Translated from an original & inedited MS. in the National Library at Madrid. With Notes and an Introduction by SIR CLEMENTS R. MARKHAM, K.C.B., F.R.S., ex-Pres. R.G.S. pp. xxxv. 168. 1 Illus. *Issued for* 1862.

30—The Discoveries of the World

From their first original unto the year of our Lord 1555. By ANTONIO GALVANO, Governor of Ternate. [Edited by F. DE SOUSA TAVARES.] Corrected, quoted, & published in England by RICHARD HAKLUYT, 1601. Now reprinted, with the original Portuguese text (1563), and edited by ADMIRAL CHARLES RAMSAY DRINKWATER BETHUNE, C.B. pp. iv. viiii. 242.
Issued for 1862.

31—Mirabilia Descripta. The Wonders of the East.

By FRIAR JORDANUS, of the Order of Preachers & Bishop of Columbum in India the Greater, *circa* 1330. Translated from the Latin Original, as published at Paris in 1839, in the *Recueil de Voyages et de Mémoires*, of the Societé de Géographie. With the addition of a Commentary, by COL. SIR HENRY YULE, K.C.S.I., R.E., C.B. pp. iv. xviii. 68. Index. *Issued for* 1863.

32—The Travels of Ludovico di Varthema

In Egypt, Syria, Arabia, Persia, India, & Ethiopia, A.D. 1503 to 1508. Translated from the original Italian edition of 1510, with a Preface, by JOHN WINTER JONES, F.S.A., Principal Librarian of the British Museum, & Edited, with Notes & an Introduction, by the REV. GEORGE PERCY BADGER. pp. cxxi. 321. 1 Map. Index. (*Out of print.*) *Issued for* 1863.

33—The Travels of Pedro de Cieza de Leon, A.D. 1532-50,
From the Gulf of Darien to the City of La Plata, contained in the first part of his Chronicle of Peru (Antwerp, 1554). Translated & Edited, with Notes & an Introduction, by SIR CLEMENTS R. MARKHAM, K.C.B., F.R.S., ex-Pres. R.G.S. pp. xvi. lvii. 438. Index.
(Vol. 2 = No. 68.) *Issued for* 1864.

34—Narrative of the Proceedings of Pedrarias Davila
In the Provinces of Tierra Firme or Castilla del Oro, & of the discovery of the South Sea and the Coasts of Peru and Nicaragua. Written by the Adelantado Pascual de Andagoya. Translated and Edited, with Notes & an Introduction, by SIR CLEMENTS R. MARKHAM, K.C.B., F.R.S., ex-Pres. R.G.S. pp. xxix. 88. 1 Map. Index. *Issued for* 1865.

35—A Description of the Coasts of East Africa and Malabar
In the beginning of the Sixteenth Century, by DUARTE BARBOSA, a Portuguese. Translated from an early Spanish manuscript in the Barcelona Library, with Notes & a Preface, by LORD STANLEY OF ALDERLEY. pp. xi. 336. 2 Illus. Index. *Issued for* 1865.

36-37—Cathay and the Way Thither.
Being a Collection of mediæval notices of China, previous to the Sixteenth Century. Translated and Edited by COLONEL SIR HENRY YULE, K.C.S.I., R.E., C.B. With a preliminary Essay on the intercourse between China & the Western Nations previous to the discovery of the Cape Route. 2 vols. 3 Maps. 2 Illus. Bibliography. Index.
(*Out of print ; see also Ser. II., Vol. 33.*) *Issued for* 1866.

38—The Three Voyages of Sir Martin Frobisher,
In search of a Passage to Cathaia & India by the North-West, A.D. 1576-8. By GEORGE BEST. Reprinted from the First Edition of HAKLUYT's Voyages. With Selections from MS. Documents in the British Museum & State Paper Office. Edited by ADMIRAL SIR RICHARD COLLINSON, K.C.B. pp. xxvi. 376. 2 Maps. 1 Illus. Index. *Issued for* 1867.

39—The Philippine Islands,
Moluccas, Siam, Cambodia, Japan, and China, at the close of the 16th Century. By ANTONIO DE MORGA, 1609. Translated from the Spanish, with Notes & a Preface, and a Letter from Luis Vaez de Torres, describing his Voyage through the Torres Straits, by LORD STANLEY OF ALDERLEY. pp. xxiv. 431. 2 Illus. Index. (*Out of print.*) *Issued for* 1868.

40—The Fifth Letter of Hernan Cortes
To the Emperor Charles V., containing an Account of his Expedition to Honduras in 1525-26. Translated from the original Spanish by DON PASCUAL DE GAYANGOS. pp. xvi. 156. Index. *Issued for* 1868.

41—The Royal Commentaries of the Yncas.
By the YNCA GARCILASSO DE LA VEGA. Translated and Edited, with Notes & an Introduction, by SIR CLEMENTS R. MARKHAM, K.C.B., F.R.S., ex-Pres. R.G.S. Vol. 1. (Books I.-IV.) pp. xi. 359. 1 Map. Index.
(Vol. 2. = No. 45.) *Issued for* 1869.

42—The Three Voyages of Vasco da Gama.
And his Viceroyalty, from the Lendas da India of GASPAR CORREA ; accompanied by original documents. Translated from the Portuguese, with Notes & an Introduction, by LORD STANLEY OF ALDERLEY. pp. lxxvii. 430. xxxv. 3 Illus. Index. (*Out of print.*) *Issued for* 1869.

43—Select Letters of Christopher Columbus,

With other Original Documents relating to his Four Voyages to the New World. Translated and Edited by RICHARD HENRY MAJOR, F.S.A., Keeper of Maps, British Museum, Sec. R.G.S. Second Edition. pp. iv. 142. 3 Maps. 1 Illus. Index.
(First Edition = No. 2.) *Issued for* 1870.

44—History of the Imâms and Seyyids of 'Omân,

By SALÎL-IBN-RAZÎK, from A.D. 661-1856. Translated from the original Arabic, and Edited, with a continuation of the History down to 1870, by the REV. GEORGE PERCY BADGER, F.R.G.S. pp. cxxviii. 435. 1 Map. Bibliography. Index. *Issued for* 1870.

45—The Royal Commentaries of the Yncas.

By the YNCA GARCILASSO DE LA VEGA. Translated & Edited with Notes, an Introduction, & an Analytical Index, by SIR CLEMENTS R. MARKHAM, K.C.B., F.R.S., ex-Pres. R.G.S. Vol. II. (Books V.-IX.) pp. 553.
(Vol. 1. = No. 41.) *Issued for* 1871.

46—The Canarian,

Or Book of the Conquest and Conversion of the Canarians in the year 1402, by Messire JEAN DE BÉTHENCOURT, Kt. Composed by Pierre Bontier and Jean le Verrier. Translated and Edited by RICHARD HENRY MAJOR, F.S.A., Keeper of Maps, British Museum, Sec. R.G.S. pp. lv. 229. 1 Map. 2 Illus. Index. *Issued for* 1871.

47—Reports on the Discovery of Peru.

I. Report of FRANCISCO DE XERES, Secretary to Francisco Pizarro. II. Report of MIGUEL DE ASTETE on the Expedition to Pachacamac. III. Letter of HERNANDO PIZARRO to the Royal Audience of Santo Domingo. IV. Report of PEDRO SANCHO on the Partition of the Ransom of Atahuallpa. Translated and Edited, with Notes & an Introduction, by SIR CLEMENTS R. MARKHAM, K.C.B., F.R.S., ex-Pres. R.G.S. pp. xxii. 143. 1 Map. *Issued for* 1872.

48—Narratives of the Rites and Laws of the Yncas.

Translated from the original Spanish MSS., & Edited, with Notes and an Introduction, by SIR CLEMENTS R. MARKHAM, K.C.B., F.R.S., ex-Pres. R.G.S. pp. xx. 220. Index. *Issued for* 1872.

49—Travels to Tana and Persia,

By JOSAFA BARBARO and AMBROGIO CONTARINI. Translated from the Italian by WILLIAM THOMAS, Clerk of the Council to Edward VI., and by E. A. ROY, and Edited, with an Introduction, by LORD STANLEY OF ALDERLEY. pp. xi. 175. Index. A Narrative of Italian Travels in Persia, in the Fifteenth and Sixteenth centuries. Translated and Edited by CHARLES GREY. pp. xvii. 231. Index. *Issued for* 1873.

50—The Voyages of the Venetian Brothers, Nicolo & Antonio Zeno,

To the Northern Seas in the Fourteenth century. Comprising the latest known accounts of the Lost Colony of Greenland, & of the Northmen in America before Columbus. Translated & Edited, with Notes and Introduction, by RICHARD HENRY MAJOR, F.S.A., Keeper of Maps, British Museum, Sec. R.G.S. pp. ciii. 64. 2 Maps. Index. *Issued for* 1873.

51—The Captivity of Hans Stade of Hesse in 1547-55,

Among the Wild Tribes of Eastern Brazil. Translated by ALBERT TOOTAL, of Rio de Janiero, and annotated by SIR RICHARD FRANCIS BURTON, K.C M.G. pp. xcvi. 169. Bibliography. *Issued for* 1874.

WORKS ALREADY ISSUED.

SECOND SERIES, 1899, etc.

1-2—The Embassy of Sir Thomas Roe to the Court of the Great Mogul, 1615-19.
Edited from Contemporary Records by WILLIAM FOSTER, B.A., of the India Office. 2 vols. Portrait, 2 Maps, & 6 Illus. Index.
(Out of print.) *Issued for* 1899.

3—The Voyage of Sir Robert Dudley to the West Indies and Guiana in 1594.
Edited by GEORGE FREDERIC WARNER, Litt.D., F.S.A., Keeper of Manuscripts, British Museum. pp. lxvi. 104. Portrait, Map, & 1 Illus. Index.
(Out of print.) *Issued for* 1899.

4—The Journeys of William of Rubruck and John of Pian de Carpine
To Tartary in the 13th century. Translated and Edited by H. E. the Hon. WM. WOODVILLE ROCKHILL. pp. lvi. 304. Bibliography. Index.
(Out of print.) *Issued for* 1900.

5—The Voyage of Captain John Saris to Japan in 1613.
Edited by H. E. SIR ERNEST MASON SATOW, G.C.M.G. pp. lxxxvii. 242. Map, & 5 Illus. Index.
(Out of print.) *Issued for* 1900.

6—The Strange Adventures of Andrew Battell of Leigh in Essex.
Edited by ERNEST GEORGE RAVENSTEIN, F.R.G.S. pp. xx. 210. 2 Maps. Bibliography. Index.
(Out of print.) *Issued for* 1900.

7-8—The Voyage of Mendana to the Solomon Islands in 1568.
Edited by the LORD AMHERST OF HACKNEY and BASIL THOMSON. 2 vols. 5 Maps, & 33 Illus. Index.
(Out of print.) *Issued for* 1901.

9—The Journey of Pedro Teixeira from India to Italy by land, 1604-05;
With his Chronicle of the Kings of Ormus. Translated and Edited by WILLIAM FREDERIC SINCLAIR, late Bombay C. S., with additional Notes, &c., by DONALD WILLIAM FERGUSON. pp. cvii. 292. Index.
(Out of print.) *Issued for* 1901.

10—The Portuguese Expedition to Abyssinia in 1541, as narrated by
CASTANHOSO and BERMUDEZ. Edited by RICHARD STEPHEN WHITEWAY, late I.C.S. With a Bibliography, by BASIL H. SOULSBY, F.S.A., Superintendent of the Map Department, British Museum. pp. cxxxii. 296. Map, & 2 Illus. Bibliography. Index.
(Out of print.) *Issued for* 1902.

11—Early Dutch and English Voyages to Spitzbergen in the Seventeenth Century,
Including HESSEL GERRITSZ. "Histoire du Pays nommé Spitsberghe," 1613, translated into English, for the first time, by BASIL H. SOULSBY, F.S.A., of the British Museum : and JACOB SEGERSZ. van der Brugge, "Journael of Dagh Register," Amsterdam, 1634, translated into English, for the first time, by J. A. J. DE VILLIERS, of the British Museum. Edited, with introductions and notes by SIR MARTIN CONWAY. pp. xvi. 191. 3 Maps, & 3 Illus. Bibliography. Index.
Issued for 1902.

22—History of the Incas.

By PEDRO SARMIENTO DE GAMBOA. 1572. From the MS. sent to King Philip II. of Spain, and now in the Göttingen University Library. And The Execution of the Inca Tupac Amaru. 1571. By Captain BALTASAR DE OCAMPO. 1610. (British Museum Add. MSS. 17, 585.) Translated and Edited, with Notes and an Introduction, by SIR CLEMENTS MARKHAM, K.C.B. 2 Maps and 10 Illus. Index. pp. xxii. 395.

———— Supplement. A Narrative of the Vice-Regal Embassy to Vilcabambal 1571, and of the Execution of the Inca Tupac Amaru, Dec. 1571. By FRIAR GABRIEL DE OVIEDO, of Cuzco, 1573. Translated by SIR CLEMENTS MARKHAM, K.C.B. Index. pp. 397-412. *Issued for* 1907.

23, 24, 25—Conquest of New Spain.

The True History of the Conquest of New Spain. By BERNAL DÍAZ DEL CASTILLO, one of its Conquerors. From the only exact copy made of the Original Manuscript. Edited and published in Mexico, by GENARO GARCÍA, 1904. Translated into English, with Introduction and Notes, by ALFRED PERCIVAL MAUDSLAY, M.A., Hon. Professor of Archæology, National Museum, Mexico. Vols. I.-III. (Vol. I) pp. lxv. 396. 3 Maps. 15 Illus. ; (Vol. II) pp. xvi. 343. Map and 13 Panoramas and Illus. ; (Vol. III) pp. 38. 8 Maps and Plans in 12 sheets. *Issued for* 1908 *and* 1910. (Vol. IV and V = Nos. 30 and 40.)

26, 27—Storm van 's Gravesande.

The Rise of British Guiana, compiled from his despatches, by C. A. HARRIS, C.B., C.M.G., Chief Clerk, Colonial Office, and J. A. J. DE VILLIERS, of the British Museum. 2 vols. 703 pp. 3 Maps. 5 Illus. *Issued for* 1911.

28—Magellan's Strait.

Early Spanish Voyages, edited, with Notes and Introduction, by Sir CLEMENT R. MARKHAM, K.C.B. pp. viii. 288. 3 Maps. 9 Illus. *Issued for* 1911.

29—Book of the Knowledge.

Book of the Knowledge of all the Kingdoms, Lands and Lordships that are in the World. . . . Written by a Spanish Franciscan in the Middle of the XIV Century ; published for the first time, with Notes, by MARCOS JIMENEZ DE LA ESPADA. Translated and Edited by SIR CLEMENTS MARKHAM, K.C.B. With 20 Coloured Plates. pp. xiii. 85. *Issued for* 1912.

30—Conquest of New Spain.

The True History of the Conquest of New Spain. By BERNAL DIAZ DEL CASTILLO. . . . Edited by GENARO GARCÍA. Translated, with Notes, by ALFRED P. MAUDSLAY, M.A., Hon. Professor of Archæology. Vol. IV. pp. xiv. 395. 3 Maps and Plan. 3 Illus. *Issued for* 1912. (Vols. I-III, V = Nos. 23-25, 40.)

31—The War of Quito.

The War of Quito, by CIEZA DE LEON. Translated and Edited by SIR CLEMENTS MARKHAM, K.C.B. pp. xii. 212. *Issued for* 1913.

82—The Quest and Occupation of Tahiti.

The Quest and Occupation of Tahiti by Emissaries of Spain during the years 1772-1776. Compiled, with Notes and an Introduction, by B. GLANVILL CORNEY, I.S.O. Vol. I. pp. lxxxviii. 363. 3 Charts, 8 Plans and Illus. (Vol. II, III = No. 36, 43.) *Issued for* 1913.

B

33—Cathay and the Way Thither.

Cathay and the Way Thither. Being a Collection of Mediæval Notices of China. Translated and Edited by Colonel Sir Henry Yule, K.C.S.I., R.E., C.B. New Edition, revised throughout by Professor Henri Cordier, de l'Institut de France. Vol. II. pp. xii. 367. Map & 6 Illus. *Issued for* 1913.
(Vols. I, III-IV = Nos. 38, 37 and 41.)

34—New Light on Drake.

New Light on Drake. Spanish and Portuguese Documents relating to the Circumnavigation Voyage. Discovered, translated, and annotated by Mrs. Zelia Nuttall. pp. lvi. 443. 3 Maps and 14 Illus. *Issued for* 1914.

35—The Travels of Peter Mundy.

The Travels of Peter Mundy in Europe and Asia, 1608-1667. Edited by Sir Richard Carnac Temple, Bart., C.I.E. Vol. II. pp. lxxix. 437. 2 Maps and 29 Illus. *Issued for* 1914.
(Vol. I, III = No. 17, 45, 46.)

36—The Quest and Occupation of Tahiti.

The Quest and Occupation of Tahiti. Edited by B. Glanvill Corney, I.S.O. Vol. II. pp. xlvii. 521. 8 Plans and Illus. *Issued for* 1915.
(Vol. I, III = No. 32, 43.)

37—Cathay and the Way Thither.

Cathay and the Way Thither. Being a Collection of Mediæval Notices of China previous to the XVIth century. Translated and edited by Colonel Sir Henry Yule, K.C.S.I., R.E., C.B. A new edition by Professor Henri Cordier, de l'Institut de France. Vol. III. pp. xv. 270. Map and Portrait. *Issued for* 1914.
(Vols. I, II and IV = Nos. 38, 33 and 41.)

38—Cathay and the Way Thither.

Cathay and the Way Thither. Being a Collection of Mediæval Notices of China previous to the XVIth century. Translated and edited by Colonel Sir Henry Yule, K.C.S.I., R.E., C.B. A new edition by Professor Henri Cordier, de l'Institut de France. Vol. I. pp. xxiii. 318. Map and Portrait. *Issued for* 1915.
(Vols. II, III and IV = Nos. 33, 37 and 41.)

39—A New Account of East India and Persia.

A New Account of East India and Persia. In eight Letters, being Nine Years' Travels, begun 1672, and finished 1681. By John Fryer, M.D. Edited, with Notes and an Introduction, by William Crooke, B.A., Bengal Civil Service (retired). Vol. III and last. pp. viii. 271. *Issued for* 1915.
(Vols. I-II = Nos. 19, 20.)

40—Conquest of New Spain.

The True History of the Conquest of New Spain. By Bernal Diaz del Castillo. Translated, with Notes, by A. P. Maudslay. Vol. V and last. pp. xiv. 463. 3 Maps and 2 Plates. *Issued for* 1916.
(Vols. I-IV = Nos. 23-25, 30.)

41—Cathay and the Way Thither.

Cathay and the Way Thither. New edition. Vol. IV and last. pp. xii. 359. Map and Plate.
(Vols. I-III = Nos. 33, 37, 38.) *Issued for* 1916.

42—The War of Chupas.

The War of Chupas. By CIEZA DE LEON. Translated and edited by
SIR CLEMENTS MARKHAM, K.C.B. pp. xlvii. 386. 2 Maps and 2 Plates.
Issued for 1917.

43—The Quest and Occupation of Tahiti.

The Quest and Occupation of Tahiti. Edited by B. GLANVILL CORNEY,
I.S.O. Vol. III and last. pp. xlix. 270. 1 Map and 7 Plates.
(Vol. I, II = Nos. 32, 36.)   *Issued for* 1918.

44—The Book of Duarte Barbosa.

The Book of Duarte Barbosa. An Account of the Countries bordering on the
Indian Ocean . . 1518 A.D. A new translation by MR. LONGWORTH DAMES.
Vol. I. pp. lxxxv. 238. 2 Maps.   *Issued for* 1918.
(VOL. II = No. 49.)

45, 46—The Travels of Peter Mundy.

The Travels of Peter Mundy in Europe and Asia 1608-1667. Edited by
SIR RICHARD CARNAC TEMPLE, Bart., C.B., C.I.E. Vol. III, Parts i and ii.
pp. l. 316. 6 Maps and 36 Illustrations.
(Vols. I-II = Nos. 17, 35.)   *Issued for* 1919.

47—The Chronicle of Muntaner.

The Chronicle of Muntaner. Translated and edited by LADY GOODENOUGH.
Vol. I, pp. xc. 370. 2 Maps.   *Issued for* 1920.
(VOL. II = NO. 50.)

48—Memorias Antiguas Historiales del Peru.

Memorias Antiguas Historiales del Peru by LIC. FERNANDO MONTESINOS.
Translated and edited by PHILIP AINSWORTH MEANS, M.A. pp. xlvii. 130.
10 Plates.   *Issued for* 1920.

EXTRA SERIES.

1-12—The Principal Navigations, Voyages, Traffiques, & Discoveries of the English Nation,

Made by Sea or Over-land to the remote and farthest distant quarters of the
earth at any time within the compasse of these 1600 yeeres. By RICHARD
HAKLUYT, Preacher, and sometime Student of Christ Church in Oxford.
With an Essay on the English Voyages of the Sixteenth Century, by
WALTER RALEIGH, Professor of the English Language in the University of
Oxford. Index by Madame MARIE MICHON and Miss ELIZABETH CARMONT.
12 vols. James MacLehose & Sons : Glasgow, 1903-5.   (*Out of print.*)

13—The Texts & Versions of John de Plano Carpini and William de Rubruquis.

As printed for the first time by HAKLUYT in 1598, together with some shorter
pieces. Edited by CHARLES RAYMOND BEAZLEY, M.A., F.R.G.S.
pp. xx. 345. Index. University Press: Cambridge, 1903. (*Out of print.*)

14-33—Hakluytus Posthumus or Purchas His Pilgrimes.

Contayning a History of the World in Sea Voyages and Lande Travells by
Englishmen and others. By SAMUEL PURCHAS, B.D. 20 vols. Maps &
Illus. With an Index by Madame MARIE MICHON. James MacLehose and
Sons : Glasgow, 1905-7.

THE ISSUES FOR 1921 ARE:

49. The Book of Duarte Barbosa. An Account of the Countries bordering on the Indian Ocean, 1518 A.D. A new translation by MR. LONGWORTH DAMES. Vol. II. [See above, No. 44.]

50. The Chronicle of Muntaner. Translated and edited by LADY GOODENOUGH. Vol. II. [See above, No. 47.]
    One of the rarest and, at the same time, one of the most interesting chronicles of the Middle Ages, written between 1325 and 1330, midway between Joinville and Froissart.

OTHER VOLUMES IN ACTIVE PREPARATION ARE:

Diary of the Journey of Father Samuel Fritz, Missionary of the Crown of Castile in the Rio Marañon, from S. Joaquin de Omaguas to the City of Gran Pará in the year 1689. Translated from the Evora MS., and edited, with an Introduction and Notes, by the REV. DR. GEORGE EDMUNDSON.

William Lockerby's Journal in Fiji, 1808. Edited by SIR EVERARD F. IM THURN, K.C.M.G., K.B.E., C.B., and L. C. WHARTON, B.A.

The Autobiography of Jón Ólafsson Indíafari. Translated by MISS BERTHA PHILLPOTTS, O.B.E., LL.D. Edited by SIR R. C. TEMPLE, Bart., C.B., C.I.E.
    The memoirs of an Icelandic farmer's son, who took service under Christian IV of Denmark. After voyages to the White Sea and to Spitzbergen he volunteered for service in India, and in 1423-1424 made a stay at the Danish fortress Dansborg on the Coromandel coast.

La Guerra das Salinas. One of the civil wars of Peru in the sixteenth century. By CIEZA DE LEON. Translated and edited by SIR CLEMENTS MARKHAM, K.C.B.

Anales del Peru, by LIC. FERNANDO MONTESINOS. Translated and edited by PHILIP AINSWORTH MEANS, M.A.

Itinerario de las Missions Orientales, by FRAY SEBASTIAN MANRIQUE. Translated and edited by COL. CHARLES ECKFORD LUARD, M.A., D.S.O.
    One of the most authoritative and valuable of the works by early travellers in Asia.

The Travels of Peter Mundy in Europe and Asia, 1608-1667. Edited by SIR R. CARNAC TEMPLE, Bart., C.B., C.I.E. Vol. IV.

INDEX

TO THE FIRST AND SECOND SERIES OF THE SOCIETY'S
PUBLICATIONS, 1874-1920.

LAWS OF THE HAKLUYT SOCIETY.

I. The object of this Society shall be to print, for distribution among the members, rare and valuable Voyages, Travels, Naval Expeditions, and other geographical records.

II. The Annual Subscription shall be One Guinea (for America, five dollars, U.S. currency), payable in advance on the 1st January.

III. Each member of the Society, having paid his Subscription, shall be entitled to a copy of every work produced by the Society, and to vote at the general meetings within the period subscribed for ; and if he do not signify, before the close of the year, his wish to resign, he shall be considered as a member for the succeeding year.

IV. The management of the Society's affairs shall be vested in a Council consisting of twenty-two members, viz., a President, three Vice-Presidents, a Treasurer, a Secretary, and sixteen ordinary members, to be elected annually; but vacancies occurring between the general meetings shall be filled up by the Council.

V. A General Meeting of the Subscribers shall be held annually. The Secretary's Report on the condition and proceedings of the Society shall be then read, and the meeting shall proceed to elect the Council for the ensuing year.

VI. At each Annual Election, three of the old Council shall retire.

VII. The Council shall meet when necessary for the dispatch of business, three forming a quorum, including the Secretary ; the Chairman having a casting vote.

VIII. Gentlemen preparing and editing works for the Society shall receive twenty-five copies of such works respectively.

LIST OF MEMBERS.—1921.*

Members are requested to inform the Hon. Secretary of any errors or alterations in this List.

A.

1920 Abbot, Lieut-Col. Fred W., 16, Rue de la Pépiniére, Paris (viii°).
1899 Aberdare, The Right Hon. Lord, 83, Eaton Square, S.W.1
1847 Aberdeen University Library, Aberdeen.
1913 Abraham, Lieut. H. C., Topographical Survey Office, Taiping, Perak, Fed. Malay States.
1895 Adelaide Public Library, North Terrace, Adelaide, South Australia.
1847 Admiralty, The, Whitehall, S.W.1. [2 COPIES.]
1847 Advocates' Library, 11, Parliament Square, Edinburgh.
1847 All Souls College, Oxford.
1919 Allen, William Henry, Esq., Bromham House, Bromham, near Bedford.
1847 American Geographical Society, Broadway at 156th Street, New York, U.S.A.
1901 Andrews, Capt. F., R.N., H.M. Dockyard, Malta.
1906 Andrews, Michael C., Esq., 17, University Square, Belfast.
1919 Anstey, Miss L. M., 23, Cautley Avenue, Clapham Common, S.W.4.
1847 Antiquaries, The Society of, Burlington House, Piccadilly, W.1.
1909 Armstrong, Col. B. H. O., C.M.G., R.E., 24, Montague Road, Richmond.
1847 Army and Navy Club, 36, Pall Mall, S.W.1.
1919 Arnold, Arthur, Esq., Wickham, Hants.
1847 Athenæum Club, Pall Mall, S.W.1.
1912 Aylward, R. M., Esq., 7a, Avenida Sur, No. 87, Guatemala.

B.

1920 Baker, G. H. Massy, Esq., Kerema, Gulf Division, Papua.
1909 Baldwin, Stanley, Esq., M.P., Astley Hall, nr. Stourport.
1918 Bannerman, David A., Esq., M.B.S., B.A., 6, Palace Gardens Terrace, Kensington, W.8.
1893 Barclay, Hugh Gurney, Esq., M.V.O., Colney Hall, Norwich.
1920 Barclay, W. S., Esq., 39, Bark Place, Bayswater, W.2.
1919 Barrett, V. W., Esq., 1, Raymond Buildings, Gray's Inn, W.C.1.
1919 Barry, Eugene S., Esq., Ayer, Mass., U.S.A.
1899 Bassett, M. René, Doyen de la Faculté des Lettres d'Alger, Villa Louise, rue Denfert Rochereau, Algiers.
1921 Bateman, Frederick W., Esq., Westergate, Ealing, W.
1920 Beasley, Harry T., Esq., Haddon Lodge, Shooter's Hill, S.E.18.
1913 Beaumont, Major, H., Rhoscolyn, Holyhead, N. Wales.
1920 Bedford-Jones, H., Esq., 601, E. Seaside Blvd., Long Beach, California, U.S.A.

* *Sent to press, June, 1921.*

1899 Belfast Library and Society for Promoting Knowledge, Donegall Square North, Belfast.
1913 Bennett, Ira E., Esq., Editor *Washington Post*, Washington, D.C., U.S.A.
1920 Benstead, W., Esq., Bedo Station, Par Andriba, Magunya, Madagascar.
1914 Bernice Pauahi Bishop Museum, Honolulu, Hawaii Island.
1920 Bethell, Frank, Esq., c/o Messrs. The Straits Trading Co., Ltd., Singapore, Straits Settlements.
1913 Bewsher, F. W., Esq., St. Paul's School, Kensington.
1921 Bickerton, F. H., Esq., Castle Malwood, Lyndhurst, Hants.
1911 Bingham, Professor Hiram, Yale University, New Haven, Connecticut.
1847 Birmingham Old Library, The, Margaret Street, Birmingham.
1875 Birmingham Public Libraries (Reference Dept.), Ratcliff Place, Birmingham.
1910 Birmingham University Library.
1920 Black, G. J., Esq., Box 134 P.O., Gisborne, New Zealand.
1899 Board of Education, The Keeper, Science Library, Science Museum, South Kensington, S.W.7.
1847 Bodleian Library, Oxford.
1917 Bombay University Library, Bombay.
1920 Bone, H. Peters, Esq., 5, Hamilton Mansions, King's Gardens, Hove.
1847 Boston Athenæum Library, 10½, Beacon Street, Boston, Mass., U.S.A.
1847 Boston Public Library, Copley Square, Boston, Mass., U.S.A.
1912 Bourke, Hubert, Esq., Feltimores, Harlow, Essex.
1899 Bowdoin College, Brunswick, Maine, U.S.A.
1894 Bower, Major-General Sir Hamilton, K.C.B., c/o Messrs. Cox and Co., 16, Charing Cross, S.W.1.
1912 Boyd-Richardson, Commander, S. B., R.N., Highfield Paddock, Niton-Undercliff, Isle of Wight.
1920 Brewster, A. B., Esq., Eelengrove, Chelston, Torquay.
1919 Brickwood, Sir John, Portsmouth.
1893 Brighton Public Library, Royal Pavilion, Church Street, Brighton.
1890 British Guiana Royal Agricultural and Commercial Society, Georgetown, Demerara.
1847 British Museum, Department of British and Mediæval Antiquities.
1847 British Museum, Department of Printed Books.
1896 Brook, Henry G., Esq., 1612, Walnut Street, Philadelphia, Pa., U.S.A.
1920 Brook-Fox, Evelyn, Esq., Tokerwadi, P.O., Poona District, India.
1899 Brookline Public Library, Boston, Mass., U.S.A.
1899 Brooklyn Mercantile Library, 197, Montague Street, Brooklyn, N.Y., U.S.A.
1899 Brown, Arthur William Whateley, Esq., Sharvells, Milford-on-Sea, Hants.
1920 Brown, Dr. C. J. Macmillan, Holmbank, Cashmere Hills, Christchurch, N.Z.
1916 Browne, Prof. Edward G., M.A., M.B., Firwood, Trumpington Road, Cambridge.
1920 Browne, Lieut.-Comdr. R. R. Gore, British Naval Mission to Poland, Warsaw, c/o Admiralty, S.W.1, I.D. Room 41.
1921 Bryant, George Clarke, Esq., Ansonia, Conn., U.S.A.
1920 Busby, Alex., Esq., Martins Heron, Bracknell, Berks.
1920 Butler, G. Grey, Esq., Ewart Park, Wooler, Northumberland.
1921 Byatt, Sir Horace A., K.C.M.G., Government House, Dar-es-Salaam, E. Africa.
1914 Byers, Gerald, Esq., c/o Messrs. Butterfield and Swire, Shanghai.

C.

1904 Croydon Public Libraries, Central Library, Town Hall, Croydon.
1893 Curzon of Kedleston, The Right Hon. the Marquess, K.G., G.C.S.I., G.C.I.E., F.R.S., 1, Carlton House Terrace, S.W.1.

D.

1913 Dalgliesh, Percy, Esq., Guatemala, C.A.
1847 Dalton, Rev. Canon John Neale,· C.V.O., C.M.G., 4, The Cloisters, Windsor.
1917 Damer-Powell, Lieut. J. W., R.N.R.
1913 Dames, Mansel Longworth, Esq., Crichmere, Edgeborough Road, Guildford.
1899 Dampier, Gerald Robert, Esq., I.C.S., Dehra Dun, N.W.P., India.
1847 Danish Royal Navy Library (Marinens Bibliothek), Grönningen, Copenhagen, K.
1912 Dartmouth College Library, Hanover, N.H., U.S.A.
1908 Darwin, Major Leonard, late R.E., 12, Egerton Place, S.W.3.
1920 Dawson, Rev. J. C., M.A., Asterby Rectory, Louth, Lincs.
1920 Dealy, T. K., Esq., 19, rue Voltaire, au 2me, Grenoble, Isère, France.
1920 Dearing, F. Morris, Esq., American International Corpn., 120, Broadway, New York, U.S.A.
1894 De Bertodano, Baldemero Hyacinth, Esq., Cowbridge House, Malmesbury, Wilts.
1911 Delbanco, D., Esq., 9, Mincing Lane, E.C.3.
1919 Derby, Rt. Hon. The Earl of, c/o Major M. H. Milner, Knowsley, Prescot.
1899 Detroit Public Library, Michigan, U.S.A.
1919 Digby, Bassett, Esq., c/o S. Johnson, Esq., National Provincial Bank House, Gorleston-on-Sea, Suffolk.
1893 Dijon University Library, Rue Monge, Dijon, Côte d'Or, France.
1918 Dominion Museum, The, Wellington, New Zealand.
1919 Douglas, Capt. H. P., C.M.G., R.N., Hydrographic Department, Admiralty, S.W.1.
1920 Douglas, W. Bruce, Esq., Messrs. W. H. & F. J. Horniman & Co., Ltd., 27 to 33, Wormwood Street, E.C.2.
1919 Dracopoli, J. H., Esq., Oak Hall, Bishops Stortford, Herts.
1919 Dracopoli, Mrs. K. H., Oak Hall, Bishops Stortford, Herts.
1902 Dublin, Trinity College Library.
1921 Dunn, William, Esq., " Holmleigh," Stoneygate Road, Leicester.
1920 Dunlop, Capt. A. C., Netherland Legation, 42, Seymour Street, W.1.
1917 Durban Municipal Library, Natal (Mr. George Reyburn, Librarian).

E.

1913 École des Langues Orientales Vivantes, Paris.
1905 Edge-Partington, J., Esq., Wyngates, Burke's Rd., Beaconsfield.
1919 Edgell, Commander I. A., R.N., Hydrographic Department, Admiralty, S.W.1.
1892 Edinburgh Public Library, George IV. Bridge, Edinburgh.
1847 Edinburgh University Library, Edinburgh.
1920 Edwardes, H. S. W., Esq., Godshill, Fordingbridge, Hants.
1847 Edwards, Francis, Esq., 83, High Street, Marylebone, W.1.
1920 Elger, L. C., Esq., c/o Queen's House, Kingsway, W.C.2.
1913 Eliot, Sir Charles, K.C.M.G., C.B., The University, Hong Kong.
1919 English, Ernest E., Esq., c/o The Eastern Telegraph Co., Gibraltar.
1906 Enoch Pratt Free Library, Baltimore, Md., U.S.A.
1917 Essex Institute, The, Salem, Massachusetts, U.S.A.
1917 Evans, J. Fred, Esq., 65, I Street, Salt Lake City, Utah, U.S.A.

F.

1910 Fairbrother, Colonel W. T., C.B., Indian Army, Bareilly, N.P., India.
1899 Fellowes Athenæum, 46, Millmont Street, Boston, Mass., U.S.A.
1920 Fenton, A. H., Esq., The United Serdang Rubber Plantations, Ltd., c/o Harrisons & Crosfield, Ltd., Medan, Sumatra.
1920 Ferguson, Henry G., Esq., 2330, California Street, Washington, D.C.
1919 Fisher, Gordon, Esq., Queen Anne's Mansions, St. James's Park, S.W.1.
1896 Fitzgerald, Major Edward Arthur, 5th Dragoon Guards.
1914 FitzGibbon, F. J., Esq., c/o The Anglo-South American Bank, Old Broad Street, E.C.2.
1920 Fleming, Dr. G. W. T. H., Boddam S.O., Aberdeen.
1893 Forrest, Sir George William, C.I.E., Rose Bank, Iffley, Oxford.
1902 Foster, Francis Apthorp, Esq., Edgartown, Mass., U.S.A.
1893 Foster, William, Esq., C.I.E., India Office, S.W.1.
1919 Frazer, Sir James G., c/o Mr. James Bain, 14, King William Street, Strand, W.C.2.
1920 Frere, Major A. G., c/o Messrs. Thos. Cook & Son, Bombay.
1920 Freshfield, Douglas W., Esq., D.C.L., 11, Hans Place, S.W.1.

G.

1913 Gardner, Harry G., Esq., Hongkong and Shanghai Bank, Hankow, China.
1919 Gardner, Stephen, Esq., 662, West 12th Street, Chicago, Ill., U.S.A.
1920 Gauntlett, R. M., Esq., 55, Penerley Road, Catford, S.E.6.
1847 George, Charles William, Esq., 51, Hampton Road, Bristol.
1920 Gibraltar Garrison Library.
1920 Gibson, Sir Herbert, K.B.E., Compton Hurst, Eastbourne.
1920 Gilbert, W. L., Esq., 267, Calle 25 de Mayo, Buenos Aires.
1901 Gill, William Harrison, Esq., Marunouchi, Tokyo.
1847 Glasgow University Library, Glasgow.
1913 Glyn, The Hon. Mrs. Maurice, Albury Hall, Much Hadham.
1920 Goddard, Miss Isobel G., The Ashes, Icklesham, Sussex.
1919 Goss, Lieut. C. Richard, 2, Colherne Court, Earl's Court, S.W.5.
1920 Goss, Mrs. George A., 30, Church Street, Waterbury, Conn., U.S.A
1919 Gosse, Philip, Esq., 25, Argylle Street, Kensington, W.8.
1920 Gostling, A. E. A., Esq., c/o Messrs. Scott & Hume, Maipu 73, Buenos Aires.
1847 Göttingen University Library, Göttingen, Germany.
1877 Gray, Sir Albert, K.C.B., K.C. (President), Catherine Lodge, Trafalgar Square, Chelsea, S.W.3.
1903 Greenlee, William B., Esq., 855, Buena Av., Chicago, Ill. U.S.A.
1920 Grievé, T., Esq., Kuala Lumpur, Federated Malay States.
1899 Grosvenor Library, Buffalo, N.Y., U.S A.
1847 Guildhall Library, E.C.2.
1887 Guillemard, Francis Henry Hill, Esq., M.A., M.D., The Old Mill House, Trumpington, Cambridge.
1920 Gwyther, Capt. H. J., Secretariat, Accra, Gold Coast, West Africa.
1919 Gwyther, J. Howard, Esq., 13, Lancaster Gate, W.2.

H.

1910 Hackley Public Library, Muskegon, Mich, U.S.A.
1919 Haigh, Ernest V., Esq., C.B.E., Royal Thames Yacht Club, 80, Piccadilly, London, W.1.

1847 Hamburg Commerz-Bibliothek, Hamburg, Germany.
1901 Hammersmith Public Libraries, Carnegie (Central) Library, Hammersmith, W.6.
1898 Hannen, The Hon. Henry Arthur, The Hall, West Farleigh, Kent.
1920 Hardwicke, Charles, Esq., Director, Serbian Relief Fund, Nish, Serbia.
1916 Harrington, S. T., Esq., M.A., Methodist College, St. John's, Newfoundland.
1906 Harrison, Carter H., Esq., 311, The Rookery, Chicago.
1919 Harrison, T. St. C., Esq., Central Secretariat, Lagos, Nigeria.
1905 Harrison, William P., Esq., 2837, Sunnet Place, Los Angeles, Cal., U.S.A.
1920 Hart-Synnot, Brig.-Gen. A. H. S., D.S.O., Ballymoyer, White Cross, co. Armagh.
1847 Harvard University, Cambridge, Mass., U.S.A.
1920 Hawkes, W. Blackburne, Esq., c/o W. E. White, Esq., Pendarves Road, Camborne, Cornwall.
1913 Hay, E. Alan, Esq., Bengeo House, Hertford.
1919 Hay, G. Goldthorp, Esq., 18, Stonebridge Park, Willesden, N.W.10.
1919 Heape, Bernard, Esq., Hartley, High Lane, via Stockport.
1887 Heawood, Edward, Esq., M.A., Church Hill, Merstham, Surrey (*Treasurer*).
1920 Hedley, Theodore F., Esq., 26, Beechwood Avenue, Darlington.
1921 Hemingway, Mrs. B. M., 26, Elgin Park, Bristol.
1904 Henderson, George, Esq., 13, Palace Court, W.2.
1915 Henderson, Capt. R. Ronald, Little Compton Manor, Moreton-in-Marsh.
1920 Hill, H. Brian C., Esq., c/o Messrs. King. Hamilton & Co., Calcutta.
1917 Hinks, Arthur Robert, Esq., C.B.E., F.R.S., Sec. R.G.S., 1, Percy Villas, Campden Hill, W.8.
1874 Hippisley, Alfred Edward, Esq., 8, Herbert Crescent, Hans Place, S.W.1.
1921 Hirst, Maurice H., Esq., Elmdon Road, Marston Green, Warwickshire.
1920 Hobden, Ernest, Esq., c/o The Eastern Extension Australasia and China Telegraph Co., Ltd., Singapore, Straits Settlements.
1913 Hong Kong University, c/o Messrs. Longmans & Co., 38, Paternoster Row, E.C.4.
1899 Hoover, Herbert Clark, Esq., 1, London Wall Buildings, E.C.2.
1921 Hopkins, Major R. B., Eldama Ravine, Kenya Colony.
1887 Horner, Sir John Francis Fortescue, K.C.V.O., Mells Park, Frome, Somerset.
1911 Hoskins, G. H., Esq., c/o G. & C. Hoskins, Wattle Street, Ultimo, Sydney, N.S.W.
1915 Howland, S. S., Esq.
1890 Hoyt Public Library, East Saginaw, Mich., U.S.A.
1899 Hügel, Baron Anatole A. A. von, Curator, Museum of Archæology and Ethnology, Cambridge.
1894 Hull Public Libraries, Baker Street, Hull.
1913 Humphreys, John, Esq., 69, Harborne Road, Edgbaston.
1920 Hutton, J. H., Esq., Kohima, Naga Hills, Assam.
1915 Hyde, Charles, Esq., 2 Woodbourne Road, Edgbaston.
1920 Hyderabad, The Nizam's Government State Library.

I.

1912 Illinois, University of, Urbana, Ill., U.S.A.
1899 Im Thurn, Sir Everard, K.C.M.G., K.B.E., C.B., Cookenzie House, Preston Pans, East Lothian.

1847 India Office, St. James's Park, S.W.1. [8 COPIES.]
1899 Ingle, William Bruncker, Esq., 10 Pond Road, Blackheath, S.E.3.
1919 Inman, Arthur C., Esq., Garrison Hall, Garrison Street, Boston, Mass., U.S.A.
1919 Inman, Miss Helen M., 12, Sloane Terrace Mansions, S.W.1.
1892 Inner Temple, Hon. Society of the, Temple, E.C.4.
1916 Ireland, National Library of, Dublin.

J.

1920 Jackson, Richard H., Esq., Wellington Lodge, Oldham.
1899 Jackson, Stewart Douglas, Esq., 61, St. Vincent Street, Glasgow.
1898 James, Arthur Curtiss, Esq., 39, East 69th Street, New York City, U.S.A.
1920 Jeffery, Charles T., Esq., 3314, Sheridan Road, Chicago, Ill., U.S.A.
1907 Johannesburg Public Library, Johannesburg, South Africa.
1847 John Carter Brown Library, 357, Benefit Street, Providence, Rhode Island, U.S.A.
1920 John, Reginald, Esq., 31, Kensington Court, W.8.
1847 John Rylands Library, Deansgate, Manchester.
1847 John Hopkins University, Baltimore, Md., U.S.A.
1910 Jones, L. C., Esq., M.D., Falmouth, Mass., U.S.A.
1914 Jones, Livingston E., Esq., Germantown, Pa., U.S.A.
1919 Jourdain, Lieut.-Col. H. F. N., C. M.G., Fyfield Lodge, Fyfield Road, Oxford.
1913 Jowett, The Rev. Hardy, Ping Kiang, Hunan, China.
1919 Joyce, Capt. T. Athol, British Museum, W.C.1.

K.

1903 Kansas University Library, Lawrence, Kans., U.S.A.
1917 Kay, Richard, Esq.
1887 Keltie, Sir John Scott, LLD., 3, Rosecroft Avenue, Hampstead, N.W.3. (Vice-President).
1919 Kempthorne, Major H. N., R.E., c/o Director of Trig. Survey, Military Siding, Nairobi, E.A. Protectorate.
1909 Kesteven, Sir Charles H., 17 Park Lane, W.1.
1898 Kinder, Claude William, Esq., C.M.G., " Bracken," Churt, near Farnham, Surrey.
1890 King's Inns, The Hon. Society of the, Henrietta Street, Dublin.
1920 Kirkpatrick, Lieut.-Colonel A. R. Y., C.M.G., D.S.O., Kilternan Lodge, Kilternan, Co. Dublin.
1899 Kitching, John, Esq., Oaklands,Queen's Road, Kingston Hill, S.W.15.
1912 Koebel, W. H., Esq., Author's Club, 2, Whitehall Court, S.W.1.
1913 Koloniaal Instituut, Amsterdam.
1910 Koninklijk Instituut voor de Taal Land en Volkenkunde van Neder-landsch Indie. The Hague.

L.

1899 Langton, J. J. P., Esq., 802, Spruce Street, St. Louis, Mo., U.S.A.
1899 Larchmont Yacht Club, Larchmont, N.Y., U.S.A.
1913 Laufer, Berthold, Esq., Field Museum of Natural History, Chicago.
1920 Laycock, Major T. S., M.C., 88, Dunvegan Road, S.E.9.
1919 Leeds Central Public Library, Leeds.
1899 Leeds Library, 18, Commercial Street, Leeds.
1899 Lehigh University, South Bethlehem, Pa., U.S.A.
1918 Le Hunte, Sir George R., G.C.M.G., Coombe Meadows, Ascot, Berkshire.

1893 Leipzig, Library of the University of Leipzig.
1912 Leland Stanford Junior University, Library of, Stanford University, Cal., U.S.A.
1918 Lethbridge, Alan B., Esq., Wellington Club, Grosvenor Place, S.W.1.
1912 Lind, Walter, Esq., Finca Helvetia, Retalhuleu, Guatemala, C.A.
1847 Liverpool Free Public Library, William Brown Street, Liverpool.
1899 Liverpool, University of Liverpool.
1911 Loder, Gerald W. E., Esq., F.S.A., Wakehurst Place, Ardingly, Sussex.
1920 Logie, W. J., Esq., 90, Graham's Road, Falkirk.
1847 London Library, 14, St. James's Square, S.W.1.
1899 London University, South Kensington, S.W.7.
1920 Long, Arthur Tilney, Esq., C.B.E., Office of the Union Agent, Laurenço Marques, S. Africa.
1895 Long Island Historical Society, Pierrepont Street, Brooklyn, N.Y., U.S.A.
1899 Los Angeles Public Library, Los Angeles, Cal., U.S.A.
1899 Lowrey, Sir Joseph, K.B.E., The Hermitage, Loughton, Essex.
1912 Luard, Colonel Charles Eckford, M.A., D.S.O., 12, Elm Tree Road, N.W.8.
1880 Lucas, Sir Charles Prestwood, K.C.B., K.C.M.G., 65, St. George's Square, S.W.1.
1895 Lucas, Frederic Wm., Esq., 21, Surrey Street, Strand, W.C.2.
1912 Luke, H. C., Esq., M.A., St. James's Club, Piccadilly, W.1.
1898 Lydenberg, H. M., Esq., New York Public Library, Fifth Avenue and Forty-second Street, New York City, U.S.A.
1880 Lyons University Library, Lyon, France.
1920 Lytton Library, The, M.A.O. College, Aligarh, India.

M.

1920 McDonald, Allan M., Esq., 87, Calle Maipu, Buenos Aires.
1908 Maggs Brothers, Messrs., 34, Conduit Street, W.1.
1920 Makins, Capt. A. D., 143, Richmond Road, Twickenham, S.W.
1847 Manchester Public Free Libraries, King Street, Manchester.
1916 Manchester University.
1899 Manierre, George, Esq., Room 416, 112, Adams Street, Chicago, Ill., U.S.A.
1919 Mardon, Ernest G., Esq., Eastwood Manor, East Harptree, near Bristol.
1892 Marquand, Henry, Esq., Whitegates Farm, Bedford, New York, U.S.A.
1919 Marsden, W., Esq., 7, Heathfield Place, Halifax, Yorks.
1919 Marsh-Edwards, J. C., Esq., Church Hatch, Ringwood, Hants.
1847 Massachusetts Historical Society, 1154, Boylston Street, Boston, Mass., U.S.A.
1905 Maudslay, Alfred Percival, Esq., D.Sc., Morney Cross, Hereford.
1919 Maxwell, Lieut.-Commander, P. S. F R.N., c/o Hydrographic Department, Admiralty, S.W.1
1919 Mayers, Sidney F., Esq., British and Chinese Corporation, Peking, N. China.
1914 Means, Philip Ainsworth, Esq., 64, Vera Cruz, Lima, Peru.
1913 Mensing, A. W. M., Esq. (Frederik Muller and Co.), Amsterdam.
1901 Merriman, J. A., Esq., c/o Standard Bank, Cape Town, S. Africa.
1920 Merriman, Lieut. Reginald D., R.I.M., Port Office, Basra.
1911 Messer, Allan E., Esq., 2, Wyndham House, Sloane Gardens, S.W.1.
1913 Meyendorff, Baron de, Ambassade de Russie, Madrid.

1893 Michigan, University of, Ann Arbor, Mich., U.S.A.
1899 Middletown, Conn., Wesleyan University Library, U.S.A.
1920 Milford Haven, Admiral The Marquess of, P.C., G.C.B., G.C.V.O., K.C.M.G., Fishponds, Netley Abbey, Hants.
1920 Miller, H. Eric, Esq., 1–4, Great Tower Street, London, E.C.4.
1847 Mills, Colonel Dudley Acland, R.E., Drokes, Beaulieu, Hants.
1912 Milward, Graham, Esq., 77, Colmore Row, Birmingham.
1896 Milwaukee Public Library, Milwaukee, Wisconsin, U.S.A.
1895 Minneapolis Athenæum, Minneapolis, Minn., U.S.A.
1899 Minnesota Historical Society, St. Paul, Minnesota, U.S.A.
1899 Mitchell Library, 21, Miller Street, Glasgow.
1899 Mitchell, Wm., Esq., 14, Forbesfield Road, Aberdeen.
1902 Mombasa Club Library, Mombasa, c/o Messrs. Richardson & Co. 26, King Street, St. James', S.W.1.
1899 Monson, The Right Hon. Lord, C.V.O., Burton Hall, Lincoln.
1919 Montagnier, Henry F., Esq., 6, Promenade Anglaise, Berne.
1918 Moore-Bennett, Arthur J., Esq., Peking, China.
1918 Moreland, W. Harrison, Esq., C.S.I., C.I.E., Bengeo Old Vicarage, Hertford.
1919 Morrell, G. F., Esq., Avenue House, Holly Park, Crouch Hill, N.
1920 Morris, D. Llewellyn, Esq., c/o E. K. Green & Co., Ltd., P.O. Box 1192, Cape Town.
1893 Morris, Henry Cecil Low, Esq., M.D., The Steyne, Bognor, Sussex.
1899 Morrison, George Ernest, Esq., M.D., H.B.M. Legation, Peking.
1899 Morrisson, James W., Esq., 200-206, Randolph Street, Chicago, Ill., U.S.A.
1919 Morse, Hosea Ballou, Esq., Arden, Camberley, Surrey.
1895 Moxon, Alfred Edward, Esq., 2, Spring Gardens, Teignmouth, S. Devon.
1899 Mukhopadhyay, Hon. Sir Asutosh, Kt., C.S.I., D.Sc., LL.D., 77, Russa Road North, Bhowanipur, Calcutta.
1920 Muller, W. J., Esq., Kuantan, Pahang, Federated Malay States.
1920 Munns, John Willoughby, Esq., Kent End House, 59, London Road, Forest Hill, S.E.23.

N.

1913 Natal Society's Library, Pietermaritzburg, S. Africa.
1899 Nathan, Lt.-Col. Sir Matthew, G.C.M.G., R.E., Government House, Brisbane, Queensland.
1920 National Geographic Society, Washington, D.C., U.S.A.
1894 Naval and Military Club, 94, Piccadilly, W.1.
1920 Navy League, The Wellington Branch of The, Ballance Street, Wellington, New Zealand.
1909 Nebraska University Library, Lincoln, Nebraska, U.S.A.
1913 Needham, J. E., Esq., Bombay Club, Bombay.
1880 Netherlands, Royal Geographical Society of the (Koninklijk Nederlandsch Aardrijkskundig Genootschap), Saxen-Weimarlaan 28, Amsterdam.
1899 Netherlands, Royal Library of the, The Hague.
1847 Newberry Library, The, Chicago, Ill., U.S.A.
1847 Newcastle-upon-Tyne Literary and Philosophical Society, Westgate Road, Newcastle-on-Tyne.
1899 Newcastle-upon-Tyne Public Library, New Bridge Street, Newcastle-on-Tyne.
1920 Newport Public Libraries, Dock Street, Newport, Mon.
1899 New South Wales, Public Library of, Sydney, N.S.W.
1899 New York Athletic Club, Central Park, South, New York City, U.S.A.

1895 New York Public Library, 40, Lafayette Place, New York City, U.S.A.
1847 New York State Library, Albany, New York, U.S.A.
1894 New York Yacht Club, 37 West 44 Street, New York City, U.S.A.
1897 New Zealand, The High Commissioner for, 13, Victoria Street, S.W.1.
1917 Nicoll, Lieut. C. L. J., Royal Indian Marine, c/o Director R.I.M. Bombay.
1911 Nijhoff, Martinus, The Hague, Holland.
1920 Noll, Maurice G., Esq., c/o Mina da Panasqueira, Cazegas, Beira Baixa, Portugal.
1896 North Adams Public Library, Massachusetts, U.S.A.
1893 Northcliffe, The Right Hon. Lord, Elmwood, St. Peter's, Thanet.
1917 Northwestern University Library, Evanston, Illinois, U.S.A.
1899 Nottingham Public Library, Sherwood Street, Nottingham.

O.

1919 Olsen, O. Grolle, Esq., Post Box 225, Bergen, Norway.
1890 Oriental Club, 18, Hanover Square, W.1.
1919 Oriental Studies, School of, 11, Finsbury Circus, E.C.2.
1919 Oury, Libert, Esq., 3, Thames House, Queen Street Place, E.C.4.
1899 Oxford and Cambridge Club, 71, Pall Mall, S.W.1.
1847 Oxford Union Society, Oxford.

P.

1911 Pan-American Union, Washington, D.C., U.S.A.
1847 Paris, Bibliothèque Nationale, Rue de Richelieu, Paris.
1847 Paris, Institut de France, Quai de Conti 23, Paris.
1880 Peabody Institute, Baltimore, Md., U.S.A.
1893 Peek, Sir Wilfred, Bart., c/o Mr. Grover, Rousdon, Lyme Regis.
1904 Peirce, Harold, Esq., 222, Drexel Building, Philadelphia, Pa., U.S.A.
1920 Pennington, The Venerable Archdeacon G. E., The Vicarage, Greytown, Natal, S. Africa.
1920 Pennsylvania University Library, Philadelphia, Pa., U.S.A.
1911 Penrose, R. A. F., Esq., Bullitt Buildings, Philadelphia, U.S.A.
1919 Penzer, N. M., Esq., 12, Clifton Hill, St. John's Wood, N.W.8.
1899 Pequot Library, Southport, Conn., U.S.A.
1920 Perry, F. Arthur, Esq., c/o British American Tobacco Co. (China), Ltd., Hankow, China.
1920 Peters, Sir Byron, K.B.E., Windlesham Moor, Windlesham, Surrey.
1913 Petersen, V., Esq., Chinese Telegraph Administration, Peking, China.
1895 Philadelphia Free Library, 13th and Locust Street, Philadelphia, Pa., U.S.A.
1899 Philadelphia, Library Company of, N.W. corner Juniper & Locust Streets, Philadelphia, Pa., U.S.A.
1899 Philadelphia, Union League Club, 8, Broad Street, Philadelphia, Pa., U.S.A.
1918 Philipps, Capt. J. E., Kigezi, Uganda.
1919 Pitt, Colonel William, C.M.G., Fairseat House, Wrotham, Kent.
1920 Plummer, G. S., Esq., Klang, Selangor, Federated Malay States.
1921 Plymouth Command Naval Officers' Library, R.N. Port Library, Devonport.
1899 Plymouth Proprietary and Cottonian Library, Cornwall Street, Plymouth.
1920 Plymouth Public Library, Plymouth.
1920 Poliakoff, V., Esq., 49, Queen's Gate Gardens, Kensington, S.W.7.
1920 Poole, Major F. G., 12, Palace Street, W.

1899 Portico Library, 57, Mosley Street, Manchester.
1919 Potter, J. Wilson, Esq., Enton Mill, nr. Godalming, Surrey.
1916 Princeton University Library, Princeton (N.J.), U.S.A.
1912 Provincial Library of British Columbia, Victoria, British Columbia.

Q.

1894 Quaritch, Bernard, Esq., 11, Grafton Street, New Bond Street, W.1.
     (12 COPIES).
1913 Queen's University, The, Kingston, Ontario, Canada.
1920 Quigley, Richard, Esq., c/o Borax Consolidated, Ltd., Casilla 12 y 13,
     Antofagasta, Chile.
1913 Quincey, Edmund de Q., Esq., Oakwood, Chislehurst.

R.

1890 Raffles Museum and Library, Singapore.
1920 Rand Club, Johannesburg, South Africa.
1920 Rawnsley, Mrs. Walter, Well Vale, Alford, Lincs.
1914 Rawson, Lieut. G., Royal Indian Marine, Bombay.
1847 Reform Club, 104, Pall Mall, S.W.1.
1920 Rhodes, Miss Alice G., The Elms, Lytham, Lancs.
1920 Richards, F. J., Esq., I.C.S., c/o Messrs. Binny & Co., Madras,
     S. India.
1907 Ricketts, D. P., Esq., Imperial Chinese Railways, Tientsin, China.
1915 Riggs, E. Francis, Esq., 1617, Eye Street, Washington, D.C., U.S.A.
1911 Rio de Janeiro, Archivo Publico Nacional, Sa da Republica, No. 26.
1919 Rio de Janeiro, Bibliotheca Nacional do, Rio de Janeiro.
1917 Robertson, Wheatley B., Esq., Gledswood, East Liss, Hants.
1920 Robieson, W. D., Esq., 93, Millbrae Road, Langside, Glasgow.
1917 Rodger, A., Esq., F.L.S., Rossendale, Maymyo, Burma.
1920 Rose, H. A., Esq., Milton House, La Haule, Jersey, Channel Islands.
1906 Rotterdamsch Leeskabinet, Rotterdam.
1917 Rouse, W. H. D., Esq., Litt.D., Perse School House, Glebe Road,
     Cambridge.
1917 Routledge, W. S., Esq., 9 Cadogan Mansions, Sloane Square, S.W.1.
1911 Royal Anthropological Institute, 50, Great Russell Street, W.C.1.
1921 Royal Asiatic Society, 74, Grosvenor Street, London, W.1.
1847 Royal Colonial Institute, Northumberland Avenue, W.C.2.
1896 Royal Cruising Club, 1, New Square, Lincoln's Inn, W.C.1.
1847 Royal Engineers' Institute, Chatham.
1847 Royal Geographical Society, Kensington Gore, S.W.7.
1890 Royal Scottish Geographical Society, Synod Hall, Castle Terrace,
     Edinburgh.
1897 Royal Societies Club, 63, St. James's Street, S.W.1.
1847 Royal United Service Institution, Whitehall, S.W.1.
1899 Runciman, The Right Hon. Walter, M.P., Doxford, Chathill, North-
     umberland.
1900 Ryley, John Horton, Esq., 8, Rue d'Auteuil, Paris.

S.

1899 St. Andrews University, St. Andrews.
1899 St. Deiniol's Library, Hawarden, Flintshire, N. Wales.
1890 St. Louis Mercantile Library, St. Louis, Mo., U.S.A.
1899 St. Martin-in-the-Fields Free Public Library, 115, St. Martin's Lane,
     W.C.2.

1911 Saise, Walter, Esq., D.Sc., M.Inst.C.E., Stapleton, Bristol.
1913 Salby, George, Esq., 65, Great Russell Street, W.C.1. [3 COPIES.]
1915 San Antonio, Scientific Society of, 1 and 3, Stevens Buildings, San Antonio, Texas, U.S.A.
1920 Sanders, Bernard H., Esq., Itabira de Matto Dentro, Minas Geraes, Brazil.
1899 San Francisco Public Library, Civic Centre, San Francisco, Cal., U.S.A.
1920 Scholefield, Dr. Guy Hardy, O.B.E., c/o Mrs. Bree, Kirk Street, Otaki, New Zealand.
1919 Schwabe, A. J., Esq., 11, Place Royale, Pau, B.-P., France.
1899 Sclater, Dr. William Lutley, 10, Sloane Court, S.W.1.
1920 Seager, Richard B., Esq., c/o Baring Bros. & Co., 8, Bishopsgate, London, E.C.2.
1899 Seattle Public Library, Seattle, Washington, U.S.A.
1906 Seligman, C. G., Esq., School of Economics, Clare Market, W.C.2.
1919 Selinger, Oscar, Esq., Ivy Lodge, Lordship Park, N.16.
1921 Sewell, Fane, Esq., c/o The Canadian Bank of Commerce, Spadina and College Branch, Toronto, Ontario, Canada.
1894 Seymour, Admiral of the Fleet the Right Hon. Sir Edward Hobart, G.C.B., O.M., G.C.V.O., LL.D., Hedsor View, Maidenhead. (Vice-President.)
1920 Sharman, J. D., Esq., Public Works Dept., Victoriaborg, Accra, Gold Coast.
1898 Sheffield Free Public Libraries, Surrey Street, Sheffield.
1914 Sheppard, S. T., Esq., Byculla Club, Bombay, No. 8.
1920 Sheppard, T. Clive, Esq., Correo Casilla 84A, La Paz, Bolivia.
1847 Signet Library, 11, Parliament Square, Edinburgh.
1890 Sinclair, Mrs. William Frederic, 102, Cheyne Walk, Chelsea, S.W.10.
1913 Skinner, Major R. M., R.A.M. Corps, c/o Messrs. Holt and Co., 3, Whitehall Place, S.W.1.
1921 Smith, Gordon P., Esq., Pasaje de Aguirre, Guatemala, C. America.
1906 Smith, J. de Berniere, Esq., 4, Gloucester Terrace, Regent's Park, N.W.1.
1913 Smith, The Right Hon. James Parker, 41, Drumsheugh Gardens, Edinburgh.
1904 Smith, John Langford, Esq., H. B. M. Consular Service, China, c/o E. Greenwood, Esq., Frith Knowl, Elstree.
1918 Smith, Capt. R. Parker, Clarendon Road, Brooklands Avenue, Cambridge.
1920 Snow, G. H. A., Esq., Yokohama, Japan.
1899 Società Geografica Italiana, Via del Plebiscito 102, Rome.
1847 Société de Géographie, Boulevard St. Germain, 184, Paris.
1920 Solomon, Lieut.-Colonel Harold J., Cavalry Club, 127, Piccadilly, W.1.
1899 South African Public Library, Queen Victoria Street, Cape Town, South Africa.
1916 Soutter, Commander James J., Fairfield, Edenbridge, Kent.
1904 Stanton, John, Esq., High Street, Chorley, Lancashire.
1919 Steers, J. A., Esq., "Wycombe House," 2, Goldington Avenue, Bedford.
1916 Stein, Sir Aurel, K.C.I.E., D.Sc., D.Litt., 23, Merton Street, Oxford.
1918 Stephen, A. G., Esq., Hongkong & Shanghai Bank, Shanghai.
1920 Stephens, Robert, Esq., Jehol, Chihli, N. China.
1847 Stevens, Son, and Stiles, Messrs. Henry, 39, Great Russell Street, W.C.1.
1919 Stevenson, J. A. D., Esq., c/o Messrs. R. and H. Green and Silley Weir, Ltd., Royal Albert Dock, E.16.

1847 Stockholm, Royal Library of (Kungl, Biblioteket), Sweden.
1920 Stradbroke, Colonel The Earl of, Henham, Wangford, Suffolk.
1919 Stuart, E. A., Esq., Alor Star, Kedah, Malay Peninsula.
1904 Suarez, Colonel Don Pedro (Bolivian Legation), Santa Cruz, 74, Compayne Gardens, N.W.6.
1920 Superintendent Hamidya Library, Bhopal State, Central India.
1919 Sutton, Morris A., Esq., Thorney, Howick, Natal, S. Africa.
1909 Swan, J. D. C., Dr., 9, Castle Street, Barnstaple.
1920 Sweet, Henry N., Esq., 60, Congress Street, Boston, Mass., U.S.A.
1908 Sydney, University of, New South Wales.
1899 Sykes, Brigadier-General Sir Percy Molesworth, K.C.I.E., C.B., C.M.G.
1919 Symons, C. T., Esq., Government Analysts' Office, Colombo, Ceylon.

T.

1914 Taylor, Frederic W., Esq., 3939, West Seventh Street, Los Angeles, California.
1917 Taylour, Charles, Esq., Belmont Road, Sharples, Lancs.
1899 Temple, Lieut.-Col. Sir Richard Carnac, Bart., C.B., C.I.E., India Office, S.W.1.
1920 Theomin, D. E., Esq., c/o Messrs. Glendermid, Ltd., 18, Dowling Street, Dunedin, New Zealand.
1894 Thomson, Sir Basil Home, K.C.B., 81, Victoria Road, Kensington, W.8.
1906 Thomson, Colonel Charles FitzGerald, late 7th Hussars, Kilkenny House, Sion Hill, Bath.
1915 Thorne, J. A., Esq., I.C.S., Quay House, Kingsbridge, S. Devon.
1920 Tilley, G. S. Esq., 11, Gymkhana Chambers, Bombay, India.
1904 Todd, Captain George James, R.N., The Manse, Kingsbarns, Fife.
1920 Torkildsen, Vilhelm, Esq., Postbox 38, Bergen, Norway.
1914 Toronto Legislative Library, Toronto, Ont., Canada.
1896 Toronto Public Library, Toronto, Ont., Canada.
1890 Toronto University, Toronto, Ont., Canada.
1911 Tower, Sir Reginald, K.C.M.G., C.V.O., Travellers' Club, Pall Mall, S.W.1.
1847 Travellers' Club, 106, Pall Mall, S.W.1.
1899 Trinder, Arnold, Esq., River House, Walton-on-Thames.
1913 Trinder, W. H., Esq., Northerwood Park, Lyndhurst, Hants.
1847 Trinity College, Cambridge.
1847 Trinity House, The Hon. Corporation of, Tower Hill, E.C.3.
1920 Tucker, H. Scott, Esq., 2, Laurence Pountney Hill, E.C.
1911 Tuckerman, Paul, Esq., 59, Wall Street, New York, U.S.A.
1918 Turnbull Library, The, Bowen Street, Wellington, New Zealand.
1902 Tweedy, Arthur H., Esq., Widmore Lodge, Widmore, Bromley, Kent.

U.

1847 United States Congress, Library of, Washington, D.C., U.S.A.
1899 United States National Museum (Library of), Washington, D.C., U.S.A.
1847 United States Naval Academy Library, Annapolis, Md., U.S.A.
1916 University Club Library, Fifth Avenue and 54th Street, New York, U.S.A.
1920 University College Library, Cathays Park, Cardiff.
1847 Upsala University Library, Upsala, Sweden.
1920 Usher, Harry, Esq., Calle Florida 783, Buenos Aires.

V,

1920 Van den Bergh, Henry, Esq., 8, Kensington Palace Gardens, W.8.
1919 Vaughan, Paymaster-Lieut. H. R. H., R.N. Mediterranean Club, Gibraltar.
1899 Vernon, Roland Venables, Esq., c/o Ministry of Munitions, Whitehall Gardens, S.W.1.
1899 Victoria, Public Library, Museums, and National Gallery of, Melbourne, Australia.
1887 Vignaud, Henry, Esq., LL.D., 2, Rue de la Mairie, Bagneux (Seine), France.
1909 Villiers, J. A. J. de, Esq., British Museum (*Hon. Secretary*) (2).

W.

1920 Wakefield, Major T. M., Royal Artillery Mess, Kowloon, Hong Kong.
1919 Wales, National Library of, Aberystwyth, Wales.
1920 Walker, Capt. J. B., R.A.F., 11, Broom Water, Teddington, S.W.
1902 War Office, Mobilisation and Intelligence Library, Whitehall, S.W.1.
1847 Washington, Department of State, D.C., U.S.A.
1847 Washington, Library of Navy Department, Washington, D.C., U.S.A.
1918 Watanabe, Count Akira, 7, Takanawa Minamicho, Shibaku, Tokyo, Japan.
1899 Watkinson Library, Hartford, Connecticut, U.S.A.
1921 Weir, John, Esq., " Dunbritton," The Drive, South Woodford.
1920 Weissert, Charles A., Esq., Hastings, Michigan, U.S.A.
1899 Weld, Rev. George Francis, Weldwold, Santa Barbara, California.
1899 Westaway, Engineer Rear-Admiral Albert Ernest Luscombe, Meadowcroft, 15, Longlands Road, Sidcup, Kent.
1913 Western Reserve Historical Society, Cleveland, U.S.A.
1898 Westminster School, Dean's Yard, S.W.1.
1914 White, John G., Williamson Building, Cleveland, Ohio, U.S.A.
1893 Whiteway, Richard Stephen, Esq., Grayswood, Haslemere.
1921 Widdowson, W. P., Esq., Christ Church, Oxford.
1899 Williams, O. W., Esq., Fort Stockton, Texas, U.S.A.
1914 Williams, Sidney Herbert, Esq., 32, Warrior Square, St. Leonards-on-Sea.
1920 Williamson, H., Esq., Flat B., Valley Court, Valley Drive, Harrogate.
1920 Wilson, G. L., Esq., Holland House, Bury Street, London, E.C.3.
1895 Wisconsin, State Historical Society of, Madison, Wisc., U.S.A.
1918 Wood, A. E., Esq., Secretariat for Chinese Affairs, Hongkong.
1913 Wood, Henry A. Wise, Esq., 25, Madison Avenue, New York.
1900 Woodford, Charles Morris, Esq., C.M.G., The Grinstead, Partridge Green, Sussex.
1899 Worcester, Massachusetts, Free Library, Worcester, Mass., U.S.A.
1910 Worcester College Library, Oxford.
1920 Wright, Rev. Frederick George, B.D., Kingscote, King Street, Chester.
1913 Wright, R., Esq., The Poplars, Worsley Road, Swinton, Lancs.

Y.

1847 Yale University, New Haven, Conn., U.S.A.
1919 Young, L. W. H., Esq., Shepherd Buildings, 120, Frere Road, Bombay.

Z.

1847 Zürich, Stadtbibliothek, Zürich, Switzerland.